A Million Truths
A Decade in China

A Million Truths
A Decade in China

Linda Jakobson

M. Evans and Company, Inc.
New York

M. Evans and Company, Inc.
216 East 49th Street
New York, New York 10017

Originally published in Finland by Kirjayhtyma, Helsinki

Library of Congress Cataloging-in-Publication Data

Jakobson, Linda.
[Miljoona Totuutta. English]
A million truths : a decade in China / Linda Jakobson.
p. cm.
Includes bibliographical references and index.
ISBN 0-87131-873-3
1. China—Social conditions—1976- 2. China—Description and travel. I. Title.
HC427.92.J34 1998
951.05'9—dc21 98-20765

BOOK DESIGN AND TYPESETTING BY RIK LAIN SCHELL
CHINESE CHARACTERS BY ARTIST J.G.²

Printed in the United States of America

9 8 7 6 5 4 3 2 1

For my parents, Marilyn and Max

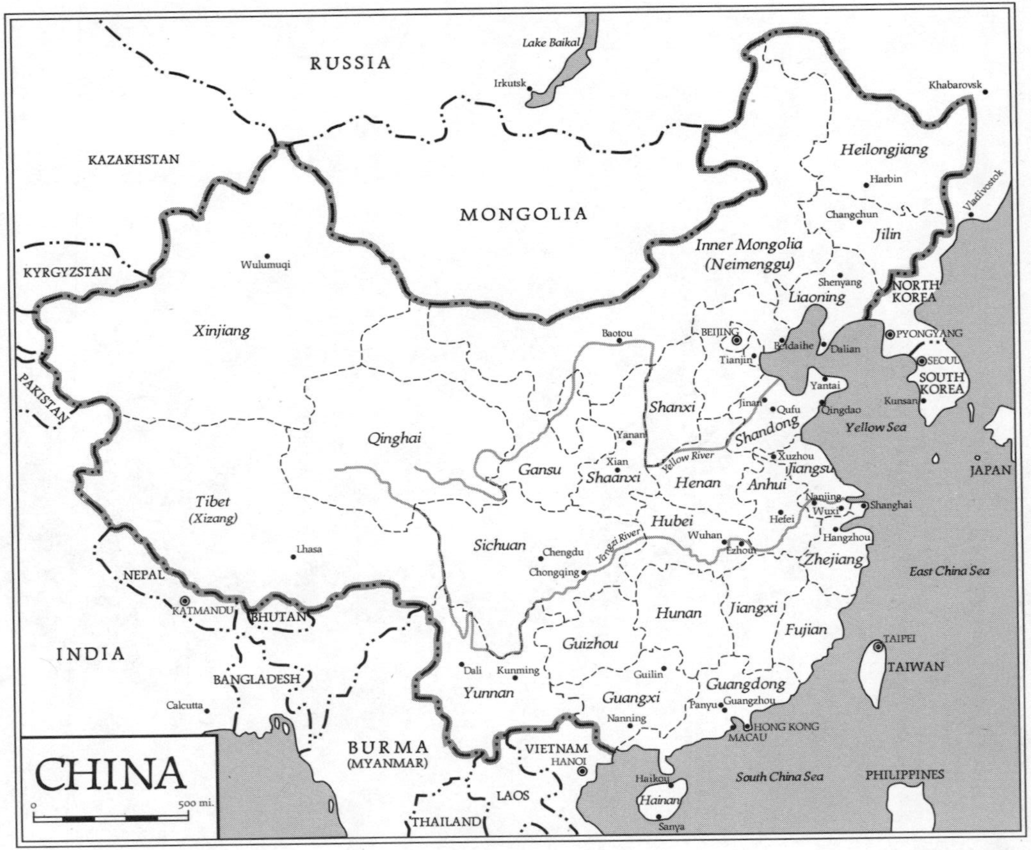
CHINA
0
500 mi.
RUSSIA
KAZAKHSTAN
MONGOLIA
KYRGYZSTAN
PAKISTAN
INDIA
NEPAL
BHUTAN
BANGLADESH
BURMA
(MYANMAR)
VIETNAM
LAOS
THAILAND
NORTH KOREA
SOUTH KOREA
JAPAN
TAIWAN
PHILIPPINES
Lake Baikal
Irkutsk
Khabarovsk
Vladivostok
Wulumuqi
Xinjiang
Qinghai
Tibet
(Xizang)
Lhasa
KATMANDU
Calcutta
Heilongjiang
Harbin
Changchun
Jilin
Inner Mongolia
(Neimenggu)
Shenyang
Liaoning
Baotou
BEIJING
Tianjin
Beidaihe
Dalian
PYONGYANG
SEOUL
Kunsan
Yantai
Qingdao
Jinan
Qufu
Shanxi
Shandong
Yellow Sea
Yanan
Xian
Gansu
Shaanxi
Yellow River
Xuzhou
Jiangsu
Henan
Anhui
Nanjing
Wuxi
Shanghai
Hefei
Hubei
Wuhan
Ezhou
Hangzhou
Sichuan
Chengdu
Chongqing
Yangzi River
Zhejiang
East China Sea
Hunan
Jiangxi
Fujian
Guizhou
TAIPEI
Dali
Kunming
Yunnan
Guilin
Guangxi
Guangdong
Panyu
Guangzhou
Nanning
HONG KONG
MACAU
HANOI
Haikou
Hainan
Sanya
South China Sea

Contents

To Begin With

Before embarking on this book, I leafed through my first book about China, published in 1988—*Mureneva muuri: Vuosi kiinalaisena* (The Crumbling Wall: One Year as a Chinese). It brought back fond memories of the wonderful year I spent studying Chinese in Beijing and then teaching English in Jinan. But I was also aghast. Where had I found the courage—or chutzpah—to write a book based on a single year? Now, after ten years in China, I am far more humble. The more I know about China, the more complexity I discover in this vast country of nearly 1.3 billion people. There is no one truth about any country. In China there are at least a million truths.

This book does not pretend to sum up all of China, or even all of my experiences there. A single volume cannot possibly encompass the research and observations of a decade. Many important topics, such as environmental problems or the fate of the country's minorities, are mentioned only in passing. Several proposed chapters, such as "Honking the Horn for a Thousand Miles," which my colleague John Lee and I talked through on a long car trip to Northeastern China, did not end up in the final version.

After my first year in China (1987–1988), I returned to Beijing for two more years (1989–91) to continue Chinese-language studies and research. In December 1992 the leading Finnish newsmagazine, *Suomen Kuvalehti*, sent me to Beijing as their Far East correspondent. For the next four and a half years, I learned to view China through a new prism. A foreign journalist's life is very different from that of a teacher or researcher, for reasons I explain in the introduction.

The Finnish version of this book was written in 1997 while I was still living in China. I had long hoped to rewrite the book in English, but would never have dared to take the plunge without the encouragement and support of my friend, Jim McEnteer. Ever since we were fellow

Fellows at the Shorenstein Center on Press, Politics, and Public Policy at Harvard University in 1990, Jim—a writer, world-traveler, and occasional university professor—has offered to help me with an English-language version of my next China book. Though I have spoken English with my mother, Marilyn, since childhood, and attended school from age six to thirteen in Pelham, New York, this English edition would not have been possible without help. I am deeply grateful to Jim, who worked tirelessly with me on the English manuscript, despite his other preoccupations. His wife, Tina, gave birth to their first child a few weeks before my manuscript's deadline. Jim and Tina and I will never forget the drama of our late-night drive through the rainy Pennsylvania countryside on March 3, 1998, when little Nicolas decided to arrive in the midst of our editorial labors.

I am also very indebted to my other stoic English-language polisher, Nancy Hearst, who pruned my manuscript with a red pen and the meticulous eye for which she is famous. Nancy, the Librarian at the Fairbank Center on East Asian Research at Harvard University, first took me under her wing in 1996, when I spent a month in the library doing research for the Finnish version of the book.

Many others helped me make it to the end of this dual-language book project in one piece—to all of whom I offer my warm-hearted thanks: My father, Max, and Marja "Magi" Sarvimäki, my friend of over twenty years, each read several drafts of the original book and offered invaluable comments; Susan Lawrence, friend and colleague, has been a source of enormous support throughout my years as correspondent. I also want to pay tribute to my friend, the late Topi Honkavaara, who unwaveringly encouraged me to adapt a historical perspective in order to probe more deeply into all facets of Chinese society.

Edie Holway and Crystal Leslie each provided me with homes in Boston, as did Matthew Watkins in Hong Kong, various research and editing visits. John Lee graciously gave me some of his best photograghs, taken during our many trips across China together, as a farewell present. My former Beijing colleagues, Kathy Chen, Peter Hannam, Steve Hucheon, and Mia Turner, patiently answered my frantic e-mail queries regarding misplaced statistics or names. The Nordic Institute of Asian Studies (NIAS) in Copenhagen awarded me a guest fellowship to rewrite the last chapter of this English edition. And Jan Wong put me in touch with my agent, Michael Cohn, who introduced me to my publisher, George de Kay, President of M. Evans and Company. I am very grateful to all of them, including everyone at M. Evans for admirably managing this transatlantic publishing project!

To Begin With

My most profound thanks go to my Chinese friends to whom I will be forever indebted. It is they who have made these past ten years so memorable. However, despite liberalization and the loosening of official controls at the grass-roots level, friendship with a foreign journalist is still not risk-free for a citizen of the People's Republic. Consequently, nearly all of my friends asked to be identified by pseudonyms. But China is changing even in this respect—a few friends insisted that I use their real names. Naturally, an individual's own status in society has a bearing on the extent of the dangers of knowing a foreign journalist.

A Million Truths: Ten Years in China is dedicated to my parents, Marilyn and Max, with love and gratitude for their wholehearted support during the long process of fulfilling my dream to write a book about China in English.

Linda Jakobson
Helsinki, July 1, 1998

My brother David and my goddaughter Tongtong taking a break at the Beijing Amusement Park in the summer of 1995. (Photo: Yaoyao's father)

介绍

Ten Chinese Years

It's Not Easy Being a Godmother and Journalist

I had spent an exhausting day with my goddaughter Tongtong and her cousin Yaoyao at Beijing's new amusement park.* It was time to think about dinner. "We're going to McDonald's, aren't we?" five-year-old Tongtong chirped.

"No, we're not," I cut her off. "Chinese food is ten times tastier. And healthier."

Eleven-year-old Yaoyao also had his heart set on hamburgers. "Haven't you seen the advertisement on television?" he said, with a puzzled look. "McDonald's promises every child a gift. It's part of a series you can collect."

"And I have only two parts, and *Gege* already has three," Tongtong explained.

I should have guessed. Whether I am in Helsinki with my nieces or in Beijing with these two, it is the same story.

Tongtong calls her cousin *Gege*, which means elder brother. The children live in the same apartment. Tongtong, Yaoyao, and their parents share three rooms and a kitchen. The children's fathers are brothers.

At McDonald's, I told Tongtong that there was not a single place like this in China when she was born in the autumn of 1991; that was five years earlier. She looked at me in disbelief until Yaoyao saved the day by recalling that he had heard about Beijing's first McDonald's from a classmate. He had just started school that year (1992).

"And now there are already twenty McDonald's in Beijing, and soon there will be thirty," Yaoyao mimicked the ad on television.

The children went into fits of giggles when I listed the other things that did not exist five years ago. The amusement park, which even my spoiled

*Throughout this book I use the *pinyin* transliteration system for Chinese names, places, terms, and so on—Peking is now Beijing, Canton is now Guangzhou, and Mao Tse-tung is now Mao Zedong.

Western nieces loved when they visited me in China, had not yet been built, nor any of the huge shopping complexes which have sprung up all over the capital. Television advertising was still a novelty at that time, and Yaoyao was content to play in a nearby park on weekends.

"And there weren't any *miandi*-cabs. Your father took your mother to the hospital on a tricycle-wagon when you were about to be born," I told my goddaughter.

"Are you sure?" the little girl questioned. I could tell by her astonished look that this was definitely something she was going to have to ask her mother about.

Miandi-cabs are small vans, which charge 10 yuan ($1.20) * for 10 kilometers (6.2 miles). They appeared on the streets of Beijing in 1993, when the city was bidding to host the Olympic Games for the year 2000, and have since become a popular means of transport. Before *miandi*-cabs, there were only "fine taxis," used by foreigners and wealthy Chinese. I did not tell the children that I had been furious with Tongtong's father for not taking a taxi that night when Tongtong was born. You are only allowed one child in China, and the family could certainly have afforded a 20-yuan taxi ride.

"Why waste money when there was plenty of time to pedal?" said the happy father, Xiao Ping, at the time. He laughed away my irritation as he described the ride to the hospital amidst the thousands of other bicyclists on the road that evening. That had been his attitude in 1991. Now, the family jumps into a *miandi* whenever they come to visit me or go on an outing.

It is difficult to explain to children that ten years ago their parents did not have the money to spend 60 yuan ($16) on an entrance ticket to an amusement park or to buy toys on the spur of the moment. Yaoyao's parents both still worked for a state-owned work unit, a *danwei.* They earned about 130 yuan ($35) a month. My godchild's mother was not even part of the family yet. She and Tongtong's father, Xiao Ping, were university students and had just started to go out together. The government gave Xiao Ping a measly stipend of 49 yuan ($13) every month because both his parents had passed away. The family did not go hungry, but everyone did their utmost to avoid any unnecessary spending. Thanks to their economizing they were able to buy a television and later, other household appliances.

---

* The exchange rate of Chinese currency (RMB, or yuan) has fluctuated a great deal during the past ten years. When I first moved to China in 1987, one U.S. dollar was about 3.70 yuan (according to the official exchange rate). Since the monetary reform that took effect in 1994, one dollar has been about 8.15 to 8.50 yuan. The references to yuan in this book have been converted according to the official rate at the time being discussed.

My goddaughter Tongtong and her cousin Yaoyao in 1992. (Photo: Yaoyao's father)

Even children much older than Tongtong and Yaoyao cannot fathom how much Beijing, and the whole of China, has changed so quickly. Whenever I think of the circumstances in which Tongtong's and Yaoyao's parents, who are approximately my age, were brought up, not to mention their grandparents, the Chinese ability to adapt amazes me. "If Olympic medals were awarded for adapting and enduring, the Chinese surely would have two golds every time," Yaoyao's father, whom I also call *Gege* (elder brother), once mused.

Forms of address in Chinese are an endless labyrinth. Family members seldom use the given name when addressing each other, but rely on the word that expresses one's relationship to the other person, for instance "elder sister" (*Jiejie*), "elder brother" (*Gege*) or "elder sister-in-law" (*Saozi*). This applies especially when speaking to an older member of the family. For this reason, I have never heard Tongtong's father, Xiao Ping, call his elder brother anything other than *Gege,* though his brother addresses Xiao Ping either as *Didi* (younger brother) or by his given name. For years I did not even know his elder brother's or his sister-in-law's real names because no one ever used them. Since I got to know the family through Xiao Ping and because his brother and sister-in-law are both a year or two older than I am, I too call them *Gege* and *Saozi*.

Being part of the family in my godchild's home has taught me the most about the Chinese way of thinking and everyday urban life. I got to know Xiao Ping in 1987, my first year in China, when he was a university student. We became good friends. In the beginning, the other family members were timid in my presence, but over the years, I have developed a close relationship with each and every one. I think of them as an average Beijing family because, when I met them, they were all rank-and-file members in their work units. None of them had any previous contact with foreigners. Except for Xiao Ping, no one speaks English. Tongtong's parents, both university graduates, are by Chinese definition intellectuals, while *Gege* is a worker and his wife, *Saozi,* is an office staff member.

I can talk to them about any subject I wish. Once, as we drank tea after supper in 1997, we discussed the changes that had taken place in China in the years we have known one another. In a matter of moments nearly every aspect of society was mentioned, from the dramatic increase of private sector employment to the much higher costs of education. Ten years earlier, rural residents were not permitted to move about freely to look for employment, and the hordes of peasants had not yet invaded the big cities. We all agreed that corruption, prostitution, and crime were much greater problems than a decade earlier. "Now you have to watch out for cheats, whatever you do," *Gege* said.

But when I asked what had not changed in the last ten years, I was met with a long silence. This is quite common in China. Change is talked about so much that it numbs the senses. No one could think of a single thing. "Even our leaders have changed," *Saozi* retorted. "For the worse."

Only after I mentioned that family members still communicate with one another as they always have and that opposition to the one-child policy in the countryside is as strong as ever, did my friends admit that some things were as they had been before. "Ten years ago I dreamed my son would one day get into university, and I still hope so," *Gege* agreed.

Everyone found it hilarious when I mentioned that even the most modern-minded young women, when they give birth, still behave exactly like their mothers and grandmothers and their great-grandmothers before them. "Even without a traditionally strict mother-in-law in this family, you still adhered to ancient tradition and stayed in bed for a month after Tongtong was born," I pointed out to my godchild's mother.

"That's right. Because elder-sister-in-law scared me with all her tales of how I would get sick and suffer if I didn't," she responded indignantly. Everyone burst out laughing.

Not only does a Chinese woman rest for thirty days after giving birth, but to rest her eyes, she is not supposed to read or watch television. Nor is she allowed to wash her hair, in order to avoid coming into contact with "wind and cold." The Chinese notion of "cold" does not correspond to the Western one. For example, fruit is considered cold and must be avoided after birth. New mothers are supposed to eat one hundred eggs and other body-strengthening foods such as chicken and corn porridge. And, of course, she cannot go outside!

"I was stubborn and didn't listen to my mother. That's why I started suffering from rheumatism at the age of thirty. I caught cold," *Saozi* said. I could tell that she was dead serious. Her son was born in August, when the average temperature in Beijing is over 86 degrees Fahrenheit.

In every Chinese family I know, the mother has stayed in bed for a month after giving birth and followed a long list of traditional do's and don'ts (mostly don'ts). Admittedly, small allowances seem to be made these days regarding nutrition. Besides the eggs and chicken broth, new mothers may also eat previously taboo vegetables and meat. But, it has been pointless for me to explain that Westerners think fresh air and a little exercise is healthy. Even an ultra-modern woman I interviewed, Xue Ruixia, who works for a Western fashion company and travels all over the world, conceded to having been "a victim of tradition" after her son was born. "I cheated a bit and read in secret," she confided.

In the home of my godchild I have been able to put my feet up and just be myself, a tremendous privilege. A foreigner living in China is always an alien, not only because we look different, but because the Chinese make a sharp distinction between us and them. Chinese rarely think it is possible to communicate with a foreigner on an equal footing, so the atmosphere is seldom totally relaxed. Either the foreigner is nearly suffocated with excessive friendly attention and made to feel like a prized piece of breakable crystal, or else he or she is met with a glued-on grin and stock phrases exalting the friendship between foreigners and Chinese, without ever getting a real sense of what the other person feels deep down. And, of course, there are always those who flatter you and seem ready to stand on their heads for you in the hope of striking up a business deal or arranging a trip abroad or in some way reaping a benefit from the relationship. Only in the company of close friends and some older-generation intellectuals do I really feel that the extra "foreigner" tag is nonexistent.

Even tourists in China readily become familiar with the word *waiguoren*, which literally means "outside-country person." In the cities, kids shout it out spontaneously whenever they see a non-Chinese face. In the countryside, everyone turns to stare at the foreigner. Throughout China, people make comments about the *waiguoren*, or even more colloquially the *laowai* ("old outsider"). In the big cities now, people are used to foreigners, but there are always visitors from more remote places who have never seen a "big nose," as we Westerners were called in the old days.

The complex range of conflicting emotions that Chinese have toward foreigners can best be understood in terms of the immense pride their long history evokes. Somewhere in the subconscious the image of the Middle Kingdom (*Zhongguo*; that is, China) still looms—China was once the center of the world. Beyond the borders of the empire lived inferior vassals and barbarous peoples. But, at the same time, they are haunted by the demise of their great civilization. As the revered American historian John K. Fairbank wrote in his last book, "China's history when surveyed over the last two thousand years contains a great paradox that bothers all Chinese patriots today."[1] If China was more advanced than Europe in the year 1200, why and how did it fall so far behind? In the eighteenth century, the standard of living in Europe and China were still comparable. Why did China miss the train to modernization? As Fairbank points out, there is no single answer to such a large question. Because the Chinese believed they already possessed everything anyone could wish for, they turned inward and chose isolation. That aloof seclusion, among many other factors, kept changes at bay.[2]

Though educated Chinese today readily admit that the imperialist aspirations of the West and Japan were not alone to blame for two centuries of misery, foreigners are still a dominant part of the equation when Chinese assess the decline of the Chinese Empire. Under the surface linger feelings of humiliation that outsiders inflicted upon the Chinese, starting from the middle of the eighteenth century when the British systematically began to sell the Chinese opium, followed by the decades after the Opium Wars (1840–1842 and 1858–1860) when Chinese were treated as second-class citizens in areas controlled by foreigners.[3] When Mao Zedong founded the People's Republic in 1949, China's economy was ravaged after years of fighting the Japanese and civil war. The Communists promised to restore China to its rightful place of respect among the peoples of the world, appealing to deep feelings of national pride and xenophobia.

I have never tired of listening to elderly people talk about their lives before and during the first years of the People's Republic. Although educated people later suffered terribly in Mao's political campaigns, and businessmen saw their property and fortunes confiscated by the government, the Communist take-over meant a general improvement in living standards. But regardless of family background, when older Chinese reminisce about the past they inevitably remember their hope that China would rise up from its state of destitution. Over and over again, I have heard the same feelings expressed about the mood in the 1950s: "We truly believed in Mao's ability to build a New China." "We were excited. We trusted Mao and sincerely wanted to be a part of the rebuilding of the country." Even those who harbored doubts in their hearts about the ideology of the new rulers said they felt the Communists offered the best possible alternative. China needed a leader like Mao. People were exhausted after years of war.

Of course, the Communists' actions did not please everybody. Approximately one million landlords lost their lives during the land reform.[4] In addition, large numbers of "running dogs of imperialism" and "Guomindang reactionaries and their accomplices" were killed.* But, recalling the early years of the People's Republic, people emphasize the general feeling of hopefulness. A better tomorrow lay ahead.

I have met a number of Chinese who could have gone abroad before the Communist takeover. They chose to stay—in many cases, despite pressure by family members to leave—because they wanted to take part in the building of a New China. For the same reason, some Chinese residing abroad returned to their homeland. The scientist Bao, who was thirty-two when Mao came to power in 1949, was one of the stubborn ones. Today, Bao's modestly furnished apartment of less than 350 square feet could be the home of any typical elderly intellectual in Beijing. The floor is concrete, the toilet is equipped with a makeshift shower comprised of a water heater, hose, and sprinkler. His brother is a professor who lives in the States. His sister is a medical doctor in England.

"I didn't listen, though they begged me to join them when they fled with our parents to Hong Kong at the end of 1948. My father was a banker and I would have had the financial means to pursue any career I wished," Bao sighed, when I asked him about his youth. "It's so easy to be wise in retrospect, but times were different in those days. I had a degree from Harvard and I wanted to serve my country. So did many of my friends. We plunged enthusiastically into our work and were greatly inspired by the

* The civil war was fought between the armies of the Nationalist government, led by the Guomindang Party, or Kuomintang, and the Communists.

cause. Okay, you might describe the atmosphere as euphoric, but I still say that in the beginning the Communists were on the right track."

In 1957, Bao was singled out for discipline during the Anti-Rightist movement* because of suggestions he had made regarding the restructuring of engineering education. He was sent to do physical labor in the Northeast. All told, he has spent seventeen years of his life in the countryside.

"I grieve the most because of my children," Bao said quietly. "My brother's and sister's children are all university-educated and live comfortable middle-class lives in the West. My children were barred from studying because their father had the wrong political background. My son always reminds me of my ill-fated choice."

Each time Mao launched a new political campaign, Bao, like many others who had relatives abroad, suffered because of his foreign connections. Once, when we sat looking at the family album, I spotted a photo of an elegantly dressed Bao at his sister's wedding in Shanghai in 1947. Bao's middle-aged son remarked: "When I was growing up I was taught that all capitalist countries are the dens of devils. America was our biggest enemy. Afterward I felt so ashamed—actually, it's absurd—that I cursed our relatives abroad and called them the ox devils and snake demons just because they had chosen to live in a rotten enemy country." He paused a moment and added: "It's the irony of history that my own children are now infatuated with anything and everything American. It's gone a bit overboard really."

When I visited China for the first time in 1985, a mere six years had passed since the Communist Party had officially declared modernization a priority, and the emphasis on ideological work had started to wane. In 1979, China embraced what has come to be known as Deng Xiaoping's "reform and open-door policy."[5] The four modernizations program, aiming to improve agriculture, industry, defense, and science and technology, was the doctrine of the day. Everywhere I went I saw huge billboards proclaim, "welcome to our foreign friends." The significance of those words dawned on me two years later, when I moved to Beijing and came face-to-

* The Anti-Rightist movement was one of Mao's many campaigns, officially to root out "impure thought" among the population, but, in reality, to silence critics of the Party. The label "rightist" was given to hundreds of thousands of people, mostly intellectuals. This followed the Hundred Flowers campaign (1956–1957) when intellectuals had been encouraged to speak out about Party shortcomings, until the leaders decided that unchecked criticism was weakening Party control.

face with another kind of reality. As in the days of Imperial China, the authorities were still fearful of foreigners polluting Chinese minds. Although there was an acute need for foreign technology, and foreign money and know-how were wholeheartedly welcome, there were a host of rules and regulations designed to keep foreigners and Chinese apart.

In 1987, few friends dared visit me in my dormitory because guests had to register at the university gate—which meant taking the risk that contact with a foreigner would be reported back to their work unit. For the same reason, others never invited me to visit them in their homes. There were exceptions, of course, especially among university students who said they "couldn't care less," but most adults, who remembered earlier days of persecution, wanted to avoid registering. "You never know if contact with a foreigner might one day get you in trouble," a girlfriend, Wu Hua, said when I was studying in Beijing. Not everybody was as blatantly straightforward.

By Chinese definition, Wu Hua is a cadre.* She works as a secretary at the Railway Bureau, where political discipline is tighter than in a department store or in a hospital. Her generation lived through the Cultural Revolution period* when mere possession of a foreign book was reason enough to be branded a "capitalist roader." She stressed that there would be no immediate reprisals if her work unit were to find out about our friendship. The open-door policy, after all, encouraged Chinese to study foreign languages. She would be reprimanded much more discreetly than in Mao's time. Our friendship might be used against her if she were to fall out of favor with one of her superiors or colleagues. "Or maybe it would hurt my chances when the section chief chooses the lucky few who will be permitted to continue their studies or be promoted. You can never be too careful," she said.

I felt the same way. Especially in the company of younger friends, I was more cautious than they were on their own behalf. I knew that a Chinese citizen could haphazardly and irrationally be accused of "leaking state secrets" to a foreigner. Wu Hua had shown me a list of subjects deemed state secrets. Even the addresses of important government buildings could be considered state secrets. The long list was a sober reminder that in times of political uncertainty just about any conversation with a foreign-

---

* A cadre is a civil servant, but not necessarily a member of the Communist Party. Of China's almost 1.3 billion people today, only about 60 million are Party members.

* During the Cultural Revolution, Mao's most ferocious campaign, ideology was pushed to the extreme. Though the first years were the most turbulent, an entire decade—1966 to 1976—is referred to as the Cultural Revolution period. (See chapter 3.)

er could be used as evidence of illegal activity. The last item on the list was: "Anything intended to be kept secret."

Today, only ten years later, the situation is far more complex. As the authorities' grip on people's personal lives erodes, as it has in numerous ways, contact with foreigners has become much easier. This is especially true in the big cities where the number of foreigners has also increased tremendously. Surveillance has become lax because not everybody depends on the state as before. A person may have his own company or his own apartment, with no obligation to register at either. Also, lower levels of authority have a more easygoing attitude toward foreigners. On various occasions during the 1990s, I spent nights with friends in apartments which belonged to their state-run work units. But no one ever bothered to fill out any sort of registration form because of my visits.

Dealings between Chinese and foreigners are still not entirely problem-free. It all depends on who the Chinese is just as much as who the "big nose" is, and when and where in China they strike up a friendship.

During my years as a student, teacher, and researcher, my life was more casual and I had the opportunity to get to know ordinary Chinese people more easily than if I had, from the start, worked as a journalist. That is why I wanted to spend some years in China getting to know the country at the grass-roots level before pursuing a job as a correspondent. The life of a foreign correspondent was—and to a certain extent still is—circumscribed by numerous regulations, though the ways the rules are implemented varies from place to place.

My Chinese friends and I discussed my intention to apply for a job as a correspondent many times. From the point of view of a Chinese citizen, contact with a foreign journalist is ten times riskier, and much more difficult to explain, than contact with a teacher or researcher. I did not want any of my friends to get into trouble just because they spent some of their free time in my company.

Before 1989, my friends resolutely shrugged off my fears. "Don't be so silly. No need to worry," many friends assured me. "China has changed. Those days are long gone when we might get into trouble because of you." Each of them reminded me that we had become friends when I was just a "normal person," a student and a teacher, and that made our relationship safe. When I spoke of my plans in the home of scientist Bao, his son first cracked a joke about how the Chinese government lumps diplomats and foreign journalists together, and considers them all spies. But he was quite adamant that I should keep in touch with the family. "Don't get stressed out," he told me. "This family is quite used to being accused of having contact with spies. My father has always had that cloud hanging over him because of our relatives abroad. But you won't be a problem as long as we do not start gathering information for you. And none of us has that kind of position in society."

The massacre perpetrated by the Chinese army on June 4, 1989, sent shock waves throughout the country. Political discipline was tightened in workplaces and people became more cautious. During the latter part of 1989, I concentrated on the research report I was working on and maintained contact with only a few people. I waited until after dark to venture down the alley I know so well to visit my godchild's family. It was a depressing time. I will always remember the tension which hung over the city when I made my way back from a farewell dinner at their home at the end of 1989. The city still buzzed with rumors of vengeful incidents involving angry citizens attacking soldiers on patrol.

Suddenly, as I bicycled down a narrow lane, two soldiers leaped from the shadows, and grabbed my handle bars. They asked to see my passport. I shuddered to think that I had just barely succeeded in persuading Tongtong's father, Xiao Ping, not to escort me home. Knowing a foreigner was not a crime, but a report of this nightly encounter would probably have been sent to his work unit. In those days it was safer to remain invisible. One year later when I returned to China, Beijing was slowly returning to normal. During that year (1991) Tongtong was born, and my dropping by their apartment in broad daylight was not a problem.

To my relief, the atmosphere had improved decisively when I finally moved to Beijing as the correspondent for Finland's main news weekly in December 1992. Earlier that year, Deng Xiaoping had been on his famous southern tour, urging his countrymen to pursue economic reforms more boldly and more rapidly. There was no doubt that the patriarch wanted China to rid itself of the gloom that had followed in the wake of the Tiananmen Square events. Conservatives who had demanded a return to ideological indoctrination were forced to ease their grip. Fresh new winds swept over the country. But the tragic ending of the Tiananmen demonstrations in 1989 was stark proof of how quickly the barometer can fluctuate in China. Authoritarian rulers will not hesitate to use brutal force when they think their power is being threatened.

I became even more determined to shield my friends from the dangers of my occupation. I kept them at bay even when I knew they would have enjoyed meeting my associates or joining me at some of the interesting events I have attended as a journalist. In the 1980s, I divided Chinese into two categories: the very few who had dealings with "big noses," and the vast majority of the population who had none at all. Though this division still holds, many new categories have arisen in the 1990s. Because of my profession, the distinction between "official" and "unofficial" China has been all the more important.

Especially after the mid-1990s, some of my younger friends ridiculed my caution, but I preferred to endure their scorn than to risk their safety, and suffer a guilty conscience for the rest of my life. My godchild's family and older Chinese have always, in their own discreet ways, made it clear that they have approved of my prudence.

Though the political atmosphere in China appears more relaxed than ever before, foreign journalists have only to recall Lena Sun's experiences in 1992 to remind themselves that appearances may be deceiving. Lena Sun of the *Washington Post* was caught with "secret documents" in her possession. In the aftermath of the incident, two of her Chinese friends, a couple—parents of a young daughter—were sentenced to prison for ten and six years.[6]

Admittedly, my nationality has been a great advantage while working as a correspondent. Finland and China have "very friendly relations" and the Information Department of the Chinese Foreign Ministry has had little reason to be interested in a Finnish journalist. To a large extent, my unorthodox housing arrangement has been possible for this reason.

I leaped at the opportunity when my former student offered to rent me his apartment when he and his wife moved to Canada. He had earned a small fortune in the late 1980s as a private businessman and had purchased a two-room apartment in one of Beijing's first privately owned apartment buildings in 1991. There was already a foreign teacher living in the building and no system of registering at the entrance. In fact, I was a familiar face in the building from the times I had visited my former student. On these occasions, he had always politely introduced his "Lin Teacher" to the elevator ladies, who oohed and aahed because they had never met a foreigner who could speak Chinese.* In retrospect, these little chats in the elevator proved very useful. When I moved in, they immedi-

* My Chinese name is Lin Da, meaning "to reach out to the forest." Because the first character of a name in Chinese is always the surname, which is put before a person's title, people who know me from the days when I was a teacher usually call me *Lin laoshi,* literally "Lin Teacher."

Western dress is predominant in the cities, though elderly men still often wear "Mao suits." This photo was taken outside the apartment building where I have lived as a correspondent since December 1992 (seen in background, right). (Photo: John Lee)

ately remembered me and welcomed "Lin Teacher" back to Beijing. And I have been "Lin Teacher" to them ever since.

Though these elevator ladies are not in the same position as street committee members,* and therefore are not obligated by the authorities to keep an eye on people, they are notorious gossips and busybodies. They have nothing else to do all day than to listen to tenants complain of quarrelsome neighbors or to watch enviously as the nouveau riche acquire a new sofa or the latest video recorder model. Once, when I was suffering a severe bout of the flu, one of the elevator ladies said to a friend of mine who was coming to visit: "You really should tell Lin Teacher not to drink soda when she has a bad cold. It's not good for her." (Soda is considered "cold" even when not refrigerated and thus should be avoided when one is ill.) Earlier in the day, my transparent shopping bag holding several bottles of soda had disclosed my "crime."

Before my former student moved to Canada, he told the elderly lady who manages the affairs of the building that his former teacher was going to look after the apartment for him. He did not do anything illegal, and in any case, I knew he was planning to become a Canadian citizen, so I did not have to worry about him getting in trouble with the Chinese authorities. Actually, many of the apartments in our "privately owned building" are occupied by relatives of owners residing abroad. The elderly lady's main task is to collect electricity and water fees from the tenants. From her point of view, the most important thing was that I could speak Chinese. "It would be so inconvenient otherwise," she had said to my former student.

In principle, every foreign correspondent is supposed to acquire his or her apartment through the Diplomatic Service Bureau. In the eastern part of Beijing, three apartment building areas with walls around them and guards at the gates, are "officially designated places of residence" for diplomats and foreign correspondents. These "foreign ghettos" were so crowded in the late 1980s that new correspondents were obliged either to live in hotels or in one of the new commercial residential blocks for foreigners, built by hotels or real estate companies. Rents in these newer buildings for foreigners, which are also fenced-off and guarded, were (and still are) astronomical.

I wanted to avoid living in a foreigners' building. To begin with, I could not afford to pay $3,000 monthly rent for a one-bedroom apartment.

---

* The street committee is a grass-roots-level unit of surveillance in urban China. Each block or street has its own street committee which, besides keeping an eye on the comings and goings of the residents, is responsible for overseeing birth control, sanitation, traffic, etc. Sometimes street committee members also supervise nursery groups.

Second, few of my Chinese friends would ever have dropped by, not because Chinese are not allowed to visit the "foreign ghettos," but because the foreign host must pick up his or her Chinese guests at the gate and escort them in to avoid their having to register with the authorities. Only Chinese who are either privileged citizens or part of the younger generation of "happy-go-lucky bohemians" have the knack of skillfully floating in and out of the foreigners' world of Beijing.

My housing arrangements may sound complicated to someone unfamiliar with China, but Chinese accept them as a matter of course. Keeping parts of one's life secret is quite normal in a society where even average citizens want to avoid surveillance by the state. Ever since it became possible to earn extra money outside one's regular place of employment, just about every Chinese I know has some kind of second job, which he or she wants to keep secret from their main employer. My friends never batted an eye when I told them that I have not let my occupation be known within my apartment building.

"You arranged your life in Chinese fashion," my godchild's father said with a grin when the whole family visited me for the first time in my apartment. From their point of view the situation has been ideal. They come and go as they please without ever having to answer any questions about who they are. "We would never have visited you if you had lived among the diplomats. Meeting us at the gate would not have made the least bit of difference," his brother *Gege* added. "I simply wouldn't have summoned enough courage to go past the guard. We're just normal people. We don't have any reason to visit the home of a foreign journalist."

I have invited only trustworthy friends to my apartment and I have dealt with matters related to my work at a nearby club, situated in a commercial residential area for foreigners. As a club member I have used the club address for all work-related correspondence. It has been a perfect arrangement. In many ways, my life in China exemplifies the complexity of Chinese society today. At the club, my work as a foreign correspondent has been public knowledge. After all, mail addressed to my magazine has been delivered to this address for the last four-and-a-half years and I have made full use of the club's post office, bank, business center, and lounge facilities. Yet, just down the road I have lived in a Chinese apartment building, known only as "Lin Teacher."

Many other foreigners have since moved into our apartment building. There is nothing illegal about it, since all the apartments are privately owned. In my case, my occupation has been a breach of law. However, since the mid-1990s, I have heard of other foreign correspondents who

The rich and poor live side by side in Beijing. This pie and dumpling soup stall, run by a family from faraway Anhui province, is situated behind my apartment building. In the daytime the stall is their place of work, at night it becomes their makeshift home. (Photo: Linda Jakobson)

also have arranged their accommodations "unofficially." The ridiculously high rents in the commercial apartment buildings for foreigners have forced people to be imaginative. Renting an apartment on the free market has also become popular among well-to-do Chinese.

I doubt whether I would have enjoyed my life in China so much had I been confined to a foreign ghetto. My godchild, Tongtong, could not have come over to play nor could my out-of-town friends from my teaching days have stayed with me. Whenever I walk down the *hutong* (little lane) behind my apartment building, I am reminded that this is China in a microcosm: rural peasants building a huge commercial center across from our building, shopkeepers complaining about competition getting tougher with each new day, city folk haggling with country folk over prices, state-run work unit employees standing side by side with the nouveau riche buying vegetables at the market place though, to judge by their shopping bags, the wealthy purchase most of their goods at a downtown supermarket. Every evening, young women in attire almost too skimpy to be called miniskirts appear outside the obscure nightclub beside the neighboring movie theatre. Twenty yards further down the lane, my favorite pie seller and his family struggle in a makeshift shack which serves as their private pie-and-noodle stand by day and their lodgings by night.

The pie seller, from faraway Anhui province, brings a new member of the family to Beijing after each Chinese New Year.* When a baby-faced teenage girl appeared by the coal stove in the spring of 1997, I could not help but ask him: "Shouldn't she still be in school?" The man smiled broadly, disclosing his two missing front teeth. "What would be the point?" he retorted. "It's much better that she earns some money while there's money to be earned. I've promised to build her a fine solid house when the time comes to look for a husband." The girl blushed and continued flipping pies in the sizzling oil. On the other hand, the old lady who runs the nearby sweets and ice cream stall tells me she is saving every penny so her granddaughter can go to university. This old Beijinger still remembers some of the French she was taught by the Jesuits at age eight. "My granddaughter's such a bright child," she always says when I stop to chat.

Going about my everyday chores has taught me much about everyday life in China. I am constantly reminded how tradition still dominates people's attitudes and behavior. But sometimes I shake my head in disbelief at how quickly some people seem to adapt to new ideas. I have become friendly with a few neighbors and we have burned many a candle together during prolonged blackouts. Electricity cuts were especially frequent in our building in 1993 because we consumed more than our allotted amount of electricity. Only after one of the tenants managed to find "a friend of a friend" in the Electricity Bureau was our building granted permission to install a bigger generator. As always in China, money and the right "connections" solved the problem. Also during that first year, the fuses in my apartment blew out just about every other day and I became a professional at changing Chinese fuses. Unlike in the West, where the fuse is in a capsule or in a plug, you have to replace the fuse wire yourself each time. My girlfriend Marja, visiting from Finland, was horrified the first time she saw me balancing on a chair, screwdriver and fuse wire in hand.

I cannot claim that living in a Chinese apartment has not been a bit inconvenient at times, especially when the fuse blows just before a deadline. But my work as a journalist, fascinating as it has been in a constantly changing society, would not have kept me in China for so many years had I been in a foreign ghetto, segregated from my Chinese friends. We have shared both good times and bad. Their friendship has been the most precious treasure of this past decade.

---

* The date of the Chinese New Year, "Spring Festival" in Chinese, depends on the lunar calender. Usually it falls at the end of January, or the beginning of February.

I could hardly recognize my old hometown, Jinan, when I returned to visit for a month in the autumn of 1996. A Chinese fast food restaurant, with waitresses gliding to and fro on roller skates, would have been unimaginable ten years earlier. (Photo: Linda Jakobson)

Returning to My Chinese Roots

Society Works through the "Back Door"

I boarded the train for Jinan on a bright, warm September day, as leaves danced in the wind.[1] Nine years earlier, almost to the day, I had also taken a train to Jinan. Then, I was on my way to teach English at the local college of economics. Now, I was returning for a month to revisit my "Chinese roots." It was in Jinan that I had first tasted Chinese urban life and met my closest Chinese friends. There was no better place to begin my new book.

Jinan is situated south of the Yellow River in Shandong province, about 300 miles from Beijing, in an area considered the cradle of Chinese civilization. The great sage of Chinese philosophy, Kong Qiu, better known as Confucius, was born there in 551 B.C. Today, Shandong has a reputation for being conservative. There is a saying that the leaders of Shandong will not embark upon a new reform policy before it has proved its worth elsewhere.

Jinan is a typically dismal Chinese industrial city of 2.5 million people. When I first heard about the teaching job, I checked the *Lonely Planet* guidebook to see what it had to say. The opening lines were not encouraging: "Go no further than the railway station. I am dead serious. The further you go, the worse it gets." Now, even that famous, German-built railway station with its distinctly foreign-looking tower has been demolished. In its place stands one of the many thousands of nondescript modern buildings that litter the landscape of modern China. But to me, Jinan, for all its outward ugliness, is still one of the dearest dots on the map of China.

Chinese always ask each other about their *laojia*, which literally means "old" or "ancient home," and refers to one's ancestral home, one's roots. Despite the industrialization of recent years, agrarian values, which identify a person with his home village, still influence the way people think. When strangers strike up a conversation they talk about their *laojia*. And one does not merely say "My family comes from Minnesota." One's *laojia* is the name of a village in a certain district in a certain county. That exchange of information often evolves into a comparison of the characteristics and traits of people from different provinces. For instance, in addition to being considered conservative, natives of Shandong are known to be honest, modest, and courageous.

Talk inevitably turns to the most common topic of all—food. It is sometimes highly amusing to sit and listen to fellow passengers on trains discussing food for hours on end. Such talk is also traditional. Classical narrative literature is full of elaborate descriptions of meals, written in the most sensual and imaginative style. Every area has its own cuisine, and eating habits vary greatly. Men, especially, pride themselves on their cooking talents. A true Chinese gentleman is also an accomplished chef.

On my latest journey we started "talking food" before the train had left Beijing Station. The man sitting opposite me rushed out of the car at the last moment and returned carrying a large red box. "I'm going back to my *laojia* and I want the children to taste some traditional Beijing pastries," he explained, as he stowed the box carefully into his bag. His rural home was in the eastern part of Anhui province. He made his living touring the country to buy toys, stuffed animals, and Christmas decorations, which he then sent for resale to his older brother in Moscow.

When he learned that I was a Finn, he asked if I was familiar with all the different pastries on sale in a Russian bakery. He then proceeded to describe them in detail to the other passengers in our compartment. He had spent a month in Moscow. "Most of my family is living there now—my elder brother, my younger brother, my elder sister-in-law, her younger sister," he said. He looked about thirty-five and was neatly dressed in pale cloth trousers and a blue-and-white striped collar shirt.

"I could never survive a whole month without real rice," the woman sitting beside me declared. She was in her forties and lived in Wuhan, an industrial center along the Yangzi River. She traveled about the country too, selling spare computer parts for the small subcontracting company she had started with her husband.

"I know what you mean," the man answered. "That's why I took two huge sacks of rice with me when I visited Moscow last year." The other passengers smiled in the way that people do when they want to convey sympathy. Except for young people, most Chinese do not think much of Western food. "You can't even eat yourself full on it," is a common remark, which conveys the major role of rice or wheat in a Chinese meal. In the South, rice is the main staple, but in the North, people also consume a variety of different kinds of noodles and pies, and something called *mantou* that resembles a steamed bun. (To me *mantou* tastes like an unleavened, raw lump of dough.)

And then it was time for their all-too-familiar question to me: "Are you used to Chinese food?" It is no exaggeration to say that I have heard those words a thousand times. And when I said that I was and added that I loved Chinese food, the woman from Wuhan nodded approvingly: "Well, then. That explains why you like living in China." I did not want to spoil her day by pointing out that I knew many foreigners who think Chinese food is delicious, but still hate living in China.

The importance of food is summed up by the colloquial way of greeting someone, *chi fan le ma?* which literally means "Have you eaten rice?" One always answers, "Yes, I've eaten rice," as one responds in English, "Fine, thank you," when asked "How are you?" Not many decades ago, one's entire well-being was directly linked to whether or not one had eaten one's portion of rice.

Another expression, "his rice bowl was broken," has also become common since the virtually bankrupt state-run factories started laying off workers in recent years. And it is worth remembering that even today not all Chinese have enough rice to eat, though more than 200 million people have been lifted above poverty level over the last twenty years. In remote villages and in vast mountainous areas, 58 million Chinese live below the official poverty line. That is the Chinese government's estimate. According to the World Bank, the figure might be five times larger, depending on how one defines poverty.[2] Every day in China, a population at least as large as that of France struggles against starvation.

A long train journey is always a memorable experience in China. It not only reminds the traveler of the country's huge size, but chatting with one's fellow passengers and watching them interact also dramatizes the numerous contradictions that exist among the various social classes. By Chinese standards, Jinan is just a stone's throw from Beijing, only seven hours by train. After my stay in Jinan, I went to visit a girlfriend's mother in a nearby small city, and from there I continued on another train ride, this one lasting forty-five hours, to Guangzhou (formerly Canton). Enough time to hear many a life story.

Passengers tend to be very sociable and talkative on Chinese trains, even with strangers. When my fellow travelers recover from their initial surprise that a foreigner can speak Chinese, they usually start to fire off a hundred and one questions about the West. The compartment becomes more and more congested with curious people from other seats crowding around to hear what the "big nose" is saying. In this respect, nothing has changed in ten years; there are always people who want to know everything under the sun about the outside world.

One change is evident though. Politics is discussed much more openly in public places than it was a decade ago. In the spring of 1996, I was sitting on a train when the midday news started blaring from loudspeakers: Party Secretary Jiang Zemin had lashed out at the United States for meddling in Taiwan's affairs. The American carrier, "USS Independence," was approaching the Taiwan Straits. All around me, people began excitedly to discuss the Taiwan issue and the possibility of war. In 1987, this kind of discourse would never have taken place in a crowded train, especially in the presence of a foreigner. An elderly engineer sitting opposite me must have read my thoughts. He shook his head in amazement.

"Times have really changed," he said. "Here we are discussing sensitive political issues. Ten years ago, when someone wanted to voice an opinion about the Party Secretary's speech, he would have leaned over and confided it in a hushed voice to a trusted friend. And he would have constantly been looking over his shoulder to make sure no one else was listening." The man sitting beside him exclaimed: "And twenty years ago no one would have dared to utter an opinion about anything, even to his own wife. In those days there was only one view on any given issue, and that was Mao's view." Everyone burst into laughter.

Now, on my September train ride to Jinan, politics intruded again. Beside the man with the brother in Moscow sat two female university students, on their way to Hefei, the capital of Anhui province, to visit friends. The young women studied law in Beijing. When I asked them about their plans for the future, one of them said she wanted to specialize in business law and find a job in a big company, while the other one said she hoped to practice law. Listening to these carefree, self-assured young women, I realized they represented the future of China.

Suddenly, the older woman from Wuhan blurted out: "How I admire, but also envy the two of you!" She spoke from the heart, making no effort to conceal her bitterness, as she continued in an agitated voice: "I belong to the generation who lost out every time the political winds changed. First, we were deprived of the right to study. Then, as we were approaching middle age, the iron rice bowl was taken away from us. And now, as we grow old, no one will take care of us." What a mouthful, I thought to myself—all the complaints of her generation in a nutshell. The embarrassed university students were at a loss for words. Undeniably, their future looks radically different than it did for the older woman at their age.

Because of the Cultural Revolution (1966–1976), an entire generation received almost no education. For a time, schools were closed and when they reopened, children were taught only the virtues of Mao Zedong Thought. When the "ten years of madness" ended and this so-called "lost generation" had come of age, China embraced the reform policy, which in turn threatened their dull, but secure lives in a work unit. The demand for profitability meant fewer workers. Middle-aged employees have been the hardest hit by the layoffs. Considering themselves too old to learn a new occupation, they find it difficult to compete with the younger generation for jobs either in the service sector or in private industry.

"We country people have never had those worries because we never had an iron rice bowl," the man who had been to Moscow remarked to the woman. "My father always says that communism has been of no use to our family since the land reforms (in the early 1950s). We have always had to rely on our own hard work and even then, the state has taken an exorbitant part of our grain."

His statement was a bit of an exaggeration because one of the biggest achievements of the Mao era was the improvement in basic education and health care in the countryside. Besides, the man had already told us that his older brother had been a physics major, initially sent to Moscow by the state to finish his doctoral degree. Here was one boy from a peasant family who had certainly reaped the benefits of better access to education under Mao! But the claim, which one often hears in the West, that the Communists took upon themselves the social welfare of the whole population, is truly an illusion. The communes were responsible for education and health care, but the services varied greatly in both quality and accessibility from region to region. Nonetheless, the way the toy merchant responded to the woman from Wuhan reveals the difference in attitudes between urban and rural Chinese. A wide gulf separates them.

After the founding of the People's Republic, city dwellers started to rely on what was called "the iron rice bowl"; that is, a secure job and social welfare provided by the state. The work unit, *danwei*, cared for its members from the moment they were born to the moment they were buried. Even today, larger work units tend to be self-contained worlds, with their own day-care centers, schools, movie theaters, sports facilities, and health care centers. A worker's salary is often intended to cover only the cost of food, purchased at subsidized prices at the work unit's own shops. When I lived on the university campus in Jinan, my colleagues were constantly reminding me to go and pick up a box of apples or a heap of cabbages to which I was entitled as a member of the work unit. I soon realized there were few occasions when it was necessary to venture outside the gates of the university. Many of my colleagues seldom did.

I asked the woman from Wuhan where she had worked previously.

"In the office of a huge iron works which loses money. Officially, I have not been fired. I just haven't been paid a salary for four years now."

Money-losing state factories are one of China's biggest headaches. According to Western economists, two-thirds of them are in the red. Though the growing private sector is widely talked about in China and the West, 70 percent of urban residents are still employed by the state sector; half of them work in money-losing factories.[3] The government pumps money into these faltering state enterprises to try to retain its influence in major industrial areas and because it fears that mass unemployment will lead to urban unrest.

"I am still reimbursed for my medical expenses, but it's only a matter of time before I will lose that benefit as well," the woman from Wuhan continued. "I really shouldn't complain. I'm better off than many other laid-off workers. The small computer parts company my husband started is somewhat profitable, and I have enough work, as long as I have the stamina to travel around the country selling parts. But we only earn enough to live on day to day. Who will take care of us when we are old and sick?"

Her words sparked a lively conversation about the cost of health care. In adjoining compartments, I heard people muttering about the price of medicine and doctors' fees. "And you can't even see a doctor, unless you have a 'back door' or find some other way to slip him a gift," grumbled a stylishly dressed elderly man from across the aisle.

Before my godchild Tongtong was born, I had naively thought that free health care was a citizen's privilege in a Communist country. Then, when she was just a few weeks old, Tongtong began to run a fever that the doctors suspected might indicate a serious blood disease. The family had to pay 1,500 yuan ($278) before the baby could be admitted into hospital. Though the first diagnosis proved to be incorrect, and Tongtong returned home a healthy baby, three months of consulting with doctors and taking tests cost about 2,000 yuan ($371). Because the child's father, Xiao Ping, was working for a state-run unit, he was reimbursed for most of the "official" medical expenses. But he still paid out about 200 yuan ($37) to buy presents and to treat people to meals at restaurants so that he could find Tongtong a "back door" to treatment. In those days, his monthly salary was 195 yuan ($36). The baby's illness just about ruined the family.

China works through the "back door," as the expression goes. You open the back door with connections, *guanxi*. Without *guanxi*, it is impossible to deal with any major problem. You have to have connections to get your child into a good school or to change jobs or to buy a train ticket to a popular destination during the high season. You can do anything in China with the right connections. *Guanxi* is more important than the law, a situation that average citizens complain about openly and bitterly.

The man who had been to Moscow taught me a pun, which I had heard in slightly revised form from an acquaintance in Beijing: "Before, justice was obtained with power (*i.e., guanxi*), now you can get justice with cash."

As early as the late 1980s, money could buy things which previously required good connections. The importance of money has grown in the 1990s, partly because of the explosive increase in consumer items. Almost anything you can find for sale at Macy's is now also available at the huge department stores scattered around Beijing. You no longer have to rely on *guanxi* to acquire luxury goods. You just need a fat wallet. But in the business world, and when dealing with practical matters of everyday life, *guanxi* is still essential. "You need money, and you also need good connections," said a businessman in 1997 when I asked which was the more significant.

"*Guanxi* is still the crucial factor, but you can buy connections with money, whereas before, doing the other party a favor was more important," he explained. His colleague added: "To keep up good *guanxi* you need a lot of money."

"In other words, money is now the decisive factor?" I asked.

"Yes, as long as you are skillful enough to use your money to acquire the right connections," he shot back. I had to be content with an ambiguous answer. That is often the case in China.

Though the service industry has grown rapidly in recent years and the availability of goods has also improved immensely, people instinctively rely on their *guanxi*. It is a way of life. "If you don't use *guanxi*, you can never be sure of the quality of what you are buying and, in any case, you can never trust the reliability of service after you have made a purchase, regardless of what it says on the warranty certificate," my downstairs neighbor advised me when I was contemplating different brands of air-conditioners.

"You just listen to me," he said determinedly and phoned his brother-in-law, whose younger brother sold air conditioners. The brand was the same as one I had seen in a department store and the price was slightly cheaper. But besides the actual cost, I also ended up paying for dinner at a nearby restaurant on three consecutive evenings. First, I took the salesman out to dinner, the next evening I dined with the men who actually installed the machine in my apartment, and finally, when the air conditioner was humming away and working without a hitch, I treated my downstairs neighbor and his brother-in-law to a meal. Any attempt to convey gratitude starts off with a meal in China.

But I cannot complain. Every summer, when the air conditioner has needed cleaning and service after the long winter's idleness, all I have had to do was phone my neighbor's brother-in-law. Within hours someone would show up at my door. And I have never paid a penny for the service. "No need," says the repairman, who always declines my offer. "We're all friends, aren't we?"

On top of everything else, my downstairs neighbor was pleased because he had rid himself of a "debt" to me. He had used my fax machine a few times during the previous winter when his was being fixed.

I learned a lot more about connections and their importance for medical treatment during the coming weeks in Jinan. I stayed with a friend who was doing her best to care for two elderly relatives. Her mother-in-law had suffered a stroke a few months earlier and was bedridden in the hospital. Her own father, who had terminal cancer, was being cared for at home. I hardly caught a glimpse of my girlfriend during the month I stayed in Jinan because she divided her time between the hospital and her parents' home, where she often stayed the night.

"That was my boss, who wanted to know how I'm coping," *Jiejie* said on the first morning after getting off the phone. "He said that his cousin's daughter is a nurse, and she can get us morphine quickly when the time comes for Father. Sweet of him to remember me like that," *Jiejie* sighed, visibly touched by her superior's thoughtfulness. *Jiejie* is a wonderfully warm and vivacious person, and I admired the way she kept her positive frame of mind despite the difficult circumstances in which she was living. I call her "elder sister" (*Jiejie*), because when I was living in Jinan I first got to know her younger brother, Yang, and he always spoke about his *Jiejie*. When I visited his family for the first time and asked his sister's name, his mother said: "She's a year older than you are, so call her *Jiejie*."

Jiejie said that she and her brothers were already prepared for the day when their father would have to be taken to a hospital, and they had managed to secure a hospital bed for him. "When I am not taking care of Father or Mother-in-law, I tear around the city trying to use our *guanxi* to arrange medicine or doctors for them," she said with a grimace. "But it's no use complaining about the system. If you don't have *guanxi*, you are utterly helpless in a situation like this." (Her father's condition deteriorated six weeks later and he was taken to hospital where he passed away.)

We went to visit Auntie Gu, as I call *Jiejie*'s mother-in-law, whom I had known from my teaching days. In 1987, she was still active as a traditional Chinese *jingju*-singer, quite famous on the provincial level. She used to sing for us in the tiny one-room home where she lived with her husband. It is difficult for a Westerner to envision how we all physically fit into this room of about 86 square feet. In addition to *Jiejie*, her brother Yang, and me, there was the husband, a neighbor, and, of course, the singer herself. In these dwellings, built around a courtyard, food is customarily prepared in the shared courtyard under a makeshift roof. All the residents who live in similar cramped courtyard dwellings have to make do with the one and only public outhouse at the end of the lane.

The courtyard houses, like the one where Auntie Gu once lived, have been torn down. In their place stand a block of modern high-rise apartment buildings and a commercial center. Hundreds of thousands of courtyard houses in cities all over China have met similar fates. As compensation, Auntie Gu was given an apartment far from the center of town where she lived with her son and daughter-in-law (*Jiejie*), and their small child, until *Jiejie* was granted a better-located, more spacious apartment by her own work unit. It was most confusing to listen to *Jiejie* discuss the family's living arrangements. One evening I wrote in my diary:

> *I really cannot make heads or tails of the housing situation in Jinan. It seems that* guanxi *is more important than money in a city like this as opposed to Beijing because as far as I know,* Jiejie's *mother-in-law has no money other than her pension, but she has managed to get herself yet another apartment. Also, it seems that the lack of housing is not as acute here as in the capital, as I noticed back in 1987. Auntie Gu has her present apartment way out in the suburbs, as compensation for that tiny room in the courtyard house down the alley. When* Jiejie's *husband disappears and says he is going to their other home, I presume he means this far-off apartment.*
>
> *Then* Jiejie *was given this apartment where I am staying by her work unit and now she tells me that her mother-in-law will get a brand-new apartment right opposite this one, in one of the new buildings which are being constructed. It was granted to her mother-in-law by a decree signed by the city mayor himself. I know that her mother-in-law was something of a celebrity back in the 1980s and she was a member of the Cultural Affairs Council of Jinan, but still, when I asked how on earth she had managed to pull it off,* Jiejie *shrugged and replied: "I really don't understand it either. All I know is that some people know how to wangle themselves apartments, like Mother-in-law, who has been to see the mayor and has pestered him about this at least a hundred times."*

Jiejie's mother-in-law had been in the hospital since her stroke in June. All things considered, I thought she was in amazingly good shape. The partially paralyzed side of her body had started to show signs of recovery and she gingerly exercised her wrist and fingers during our visit.

"Mother-in-law has the will to live," *Jiejie* agreed, when I said how lovely it was to see Auntie Gu in such a positive mood. The hospital surroundings were enough to dampen even a healthy person's spirits. When we climbed the stairs to the second floor, we were met by the smell of urine, and the corridor was as untidy as that in any work-unit dormitory. Boxes and baskets were stacked up against the walls and patients' laundry hung from a line that stretched from one end of the corridor to the other. There was even a bicycle parked beside the door to Auntie Gu's room, which she shared with two other patients.

Jiejie had hired a girl from the countryside to shop and prepare meals for her mother-in-law. This did not surprise me because, when my godchild's grandmother was in the hospital, various family members took turns bringing her food in tin boxes with secure lids three times a day. According to my friends, hospital food in China is of such inferior quality that a patient would never recover from any illness if he or she had to eat it. "I pay the girl 100 yuan ($12) a month," *Jiejie* said. "That is only a fraction of the sum that the hospital would charge us for their inedible food. This way Mother-in-law is fed fresh vegetables and meat from the market every day."

Employing a maid has become common in the China of the 1990s. Ten years ago only the privileged could afford hired help, but as the restrictions on moving from place to place have been lifted and the growing middle class has become more affluent, many tens of millions of people from the countryside have converged on the cities. They are prepared to do any kind of work, and are given the jobs that city people find demeaning. Mao Zedong's catch phrase "to serve others is capitalistic heaven" has not only been forgotten, but buried. Mao wanted to destroy the old way of thinking in China, but, in reality, all he did was sweep it under the carpet for thirty-odd years. Older people say that today's China, with its clear-cut class divisions, reminds them more and more of the China of the 1930s.

Already in 1987, the tendency to divide people into classes struck me as odd. I remember writing in my first book: "Nowhere have I been more aware of the divisions between classes than in Communist China."[4] Party members looked down on nonmembers, university graduates—by Chinese definition intellectuals—were snobbish toward workers, and city people were arrogant toward their country cousins. The situation has become more complex in the 1990s. Young people often say that there is only one way to classify people and that is on the basis of money, but that is a bit of an exaggeration. It is true though that money is now a factor when assessing a person's social status. A person can enjoy a high standard of living without being a Party member and can be a respected member of the community without a formal education. But the class boundaries of the past, which have their roots in Imperial China, still affect attitudes simmering under the surface.

The people from the countryside work on construction sites in the cities, or they renovate apartments, slave away in private workshops, and work as garbage collectors, waiters, and waitresses. You can spot them everywhere. They do not waste their money on new clothes and they do not dine in restaurants because they send every extra penny to the folks back home. Even though their labor is needed, the city people look down on them and blame them for the rise in crime and the feelings of insecurity that are now becoming prevalent in larger urban areas. The women who operate the elevators in our apartment building turn up their noses in disgust each time a group of men from the countryside arrives to renovate an apartment. "There are too many of those outsiders," they sneer. City people regard themselves as superior human beings to these country bumpkins, regardless of their own education or social status.

Once, when I arrived at the home of scientist Bao, his daughter-in-law was in an uproar. The family's maid had gone out to do her daily round of shopping and had not returned. "This just goes to show that peasants are good-for-nothing scoundrels," she fumed. "Not a word of warning; I tell you they're all unreliable cheats." The downstairs neighbor had also lost her maid. Everyone assumed that the two peasant girls had found better employment in a private restaurant. "I'll just have to go to Chongwenmen tomorrow to find a new one, not that there is much hope that the next one will be any better," Bao's daughter-in-law ranted. A civilized gentleman, like Bao, would never speak like this, but I have heard many city people vent feelings similar to those of his daughter-in-law.

Everyone knows Chongwenmen. It used to be just one of the many busy intersections near the railway station, but these days Chongwenmen, and a certain small bridge area to the north of Beijing, are known as "maid markets." Every morning, dozens and dozens of girls from country villages gather there in the hope of finding employment as maids in private homes or as waitresses in one of the thousands of small private restaurants. In Beijing, a maid's salary varies from 200 to 400 yuan ($24 to $48);

The gap between social classes has widened during the 1990s—waiting on others is no longer frowned upon as it was in Mao's days. Photo from Chongqing in Sichuan province, 1996. (Photo: John Lee)

in Jinan it is only half that. Room and board are provided for free. When the girls make their annual trek home each winter to celebrate Chinese New Year, they have usually saved far more money than their parents have been able to accumulate from work in the fields.

To my surprise, a maid showed up one day even in the home of my godchild. The family's standard of living took a decisive turn for the better after Xiao Ping's sister-in-law, *Saozi*, left her job in a state work unit and went to work for a private travel agency. Her salary shot up from 400 yuan ($48) to 2,000 yuan ($241) a month. When I said something about the young peasant girl busy at work in the kitchen, *Saozi* looked at me as if it was the most natural thing in the world: "Oh, her. She's from my mother's *laojia*, the daughter of our relative's neighbor." Though the girl was treated in a matter-of-fact manner and probably better than in many other families, her own behavior could not but transform the atmosphere in their home. Overnight a class division had arisen. No one bothered introducing the girl to me.

Some families even have two maids. Many of my neighbors employ a slightly more experienced peasant woman as their main maid and a young girl to work as her helper. Watching the ladies of the house, clad in fur coats and fashion-designer attire, sail out of the elevator with their entourage in tow has been quite an eye-opener. But these members of the "new rich" class are in a completely different economic position than my godchild's family and many other families like theirs, in which one spouse has found work in a private company and the other has stayed in the state sector to hang on to the apartment and medical benefits, provided by the work unit. These families, which I classify as middle-class, have the money to employ a maid and to indulge in some consumer goods, but it would be a utopian dream for them even to contemplate buying their own home. Some of them, however, do rent out their work unit's apartment (for which they pay nominal rent) on the free market and earn quite a tidy sum on the side, while the family moves in with the wife's or husband's parents. The authorities started to crack down on this practice in 1996. Legally, the money earned by renting out an apartment should be going to its rightful landlord, the work unit, and not into the pockets of the tenant.

People like my neighbors, who have purchased private apartments, undoubtedly belong to the "new rich" class. My former student bought the one-bedroom apartment in 1991 for 120,000 yuan ($22,260), *i.e.*, a sum sixty times the monthly salary of *Saozi* in my godchild's family and nearly 600 times the salary of her husband, who is still working for the state. In 1996 a similar apartment was sold in our building for the astronomical sum of 600,000 yuan ($72,300). Our elevator is full of well-dressed people who conspicuously fiddle with their cellular phones or twirl their car keys. The front of our building becomes more congested each year as more and more new cars compete for the limited parking spots. Car owners are the new yuppies of Beijing, except that theoretically a yuppie is "a well-off, *educated*, young urbanite." My neighbors are not necessarily educated. "They've been smart enough to take advantage of the new reform policies in business. And they probably had good *guanxi* to begin with," my friends always remind me when we discuss my neighbors.

I thought of my neighbors as I listened to the radio during Chinese New Year in 1996. The phone-in talk show, "Tell us of your problems," was being bombarded by yuppie housewives, annoyed with their maids for going off to spend the most important holiday of the year with their families in the countryside. The poor ladies were having a terrible time coping with the housework. And then it was time for the news. Some government minister had made a speech: China was marching boldly forward on the road to socialism.

The new rich in Jinan make up a by far smaller proportion of the population than in Beijing. When I visited Jinan in the autumn of 1996, my friends reckoned that perhaps about 2 percent of the population—50,000 people—could be considered wealthy. Private apartment buildings were still a novelty, and the real-estate market was sluggish. On the other hand, it was obvious that a middle class had arisen, with money to spend on consumer goods and entertainment. The whole city center had been rebuilt and the most popular shopping streets were lined with shops offering the latest camera and computer models, flashy hairdressers, and clothing stores. The Hong Kong–based Bossini and Giordani shops were chock full of brand-name conscious customers. The department stores stocked everything a person could wish to buy.

My first wander among the crowds in the city center was mind-boggling. Though I had visited Jinan at regular intervals during the past ten years, I had always spent the limited time available to me at the homes of friends. Especially the past few years, the weekend visits had zipped by as I attended their weddings or entertained their young children. In 1996 there was little left to remind me of the primitive backwater where I had lived in 1987. The new city center boasted a dozen skyscraper hotels and commercial centers, with another dozen being built. A colorful crush of vehicles filled the streets, most prominently the fleets of *miandi*-cabs and scooters, driven by chic-looking women in helmets and flapping skirt hems.

When I lived in Jinan, taxis were still unheard of. The small number of tourists or business travelers were obliged to book a chauffered car at one of the few hotels. The only four-wheeled vehicles on the streets in those days were buses, horse-pulled wagons, and the odd official car. Now there were a variety of passenger cars, though I was told that, unlike in Beijing, a private person could not yet own his own car. Officially, a car had to be registered either by a state work unit or private company. In 1987, the only three-star hotel was the Qilu, of which I have—literally—warm memories. My apartment at the college was so cold that I used to escape to the Qilu and sit in the lobby bar as I sipped pots of tea and corrected homework. Now there were six or seven three- and four-star hotels.

Even Kentucky Fried Chicken has found its way to Jinan. A young couple waiting in line for an order of Colonel Sanders told me that the opening festivities in January of that year had been quite an event. "Jinan has really developed," the young man exclaimed in a loud voice in English, and he looked puzzled when I answered: "It certainly has, though I really don't think American fast food is a sign of development." The couple said that they usually popped in for an "American-style lunch" a few times a week; they did not bat an eye at the bill of about 40 yuan ($4.80). The man was a bank clerk and the woman worked as an accountant in a joint venture company. Less than a decade earlier, their jobs would have barely earned them as much each week as the sum they now spent on chicken legs.

"Quite a change, eh?" my engineer friend Song chuckled, when I collapsed in an armchair in his home after my long wander through the city. "But we still have a long way to go before we catch up to Beijing." He was right. For all the consumer goods and blinking neon lights, there was still a parochial small-town feeling about Jinan, and there probably always will be.

Jinan's economy took off in early 1993. As in the rest of China, Deng Xiaoping's famous tour of the South in the beginning of 1992 ignited an unprecedented construction boom. Loans were doled out readily and local leaders gave their blessings to a number of infrastructure projects. All of a sudden, previously unheard of opportunities arose for private businessmen. Shandong's economy was one of the fastest growing of all the provinces in 1993 and 1994.

Shandong in particular has benefited from the establishment of diplomatic ties between China and South Korea in August 1992. I remember engineer Song arriving in Beijing in January of 1993 to help me install a new water heater for my shower and telling me that "the Koreans have invaded." "It seems that there's a new Chinese-Korean joint venture company on every other street corner of Jinan," he said. Industrious South

Korean businessmen, who had been kept away from the Chinese market for political reasons, were swarming into Shandong province. The coastal cities of Yantai and Qingdao were the main beneficiaries of this "Korean invasion" (it's only 270 miles from Yantai to the South Korean port of Kunsan), but Jinan was not doing badly either. By the end of 1996, the South Koreans had become the largest foreign investors in Shandong.[5]

"I've heard that there are more than two thousand foreign joint venture companies in Jinan now. They are starting to have a psychological impact," Song said as we recalled the days when I was one of the city's few foreign teachers and he was studying for his master's degree. "Young people working in joint venture companies are the envy of their friends. Partly because of their higher salaries, of course, but also because of the foreign ideas and habits they are picking up." This was no news to me; foreign joint venture companies have had this effect in Beijing, Shanghai, and numerous cities in the South for the past fifteen years. But it was interesting to hear Song speak like this because he had always claimed that conservative Jinan would be the last place in China to modernize. He is no stranger to Western life. He spent a year as a graduate student in Great Britain.

"Wait until you meet my wife's younger brother," Song said. "I'm sure you remember that shy boy who had quite evidently spent a sheltered life in the company of his old-fashioned parents. He's become an outgoing, independent-minded salesman. And though he has not yet been abroad, his outlook on life has changed because of his contacts with foreign colleagues and superiors." Song had already told me over the phone some months earlier that he had helped his wife's brother secure a job with a multinational company. "He doesn't have any formal business training, but he's a bright young man and I'm sure he'll get on well with the customers. At least, he is trustworthy," Song had justified his decision to recommend his brother-in-law to a British friend who was in need of a salesman in Jinan.

I had met this younger brother, Little Yan, at Song's wedding and during my last visit to Jinan, when we had spent National Day* at the home of Song's in-laws. He had struck me as a sympathetic young man, though he seemed a bit insecure and uneasy in the company of strangers. Like his parents, Little Yan had studied engineering and, upon graduation, he had been assigned a job in the same factory where his parents worked. He still lived with them as well as he did not have the slightest chance of being allocated his own apartment before he married. Marriage is the minimum requirement for an apartment in a Chinese work unit and, even then,

* The founding day of the People's Republic of China, October 1, 1949, is a national holiday.

young couples sometimes have to wait for years before they are assigned a place of their own.

My hairdresser in Beijing told me that his younger brother and wife have shared one room of about 190 square feet with his parents for four years. "What right do I have to complain about how crowded my own home is? At least I live in a room about the same size as my brother's, but with only my wife and child," he once remarked. Because housing facilities vary greatly from work unit to work unit, the amount of one's salary is not really a true indicator of one's standard of living. My hairdresser reckons he and his family will never be eligible for anything bigger than their current tiny room. His work unit simply does not have the money to build new apartment buildings.

When Little Yan arrived for dinner, it did not take me long to see Song's point. This twenty-six-year-old, looking very smart in gray slacks and a dark blue blazer, behaved like a perfect gentleman and seemed quite at ease discussing any number of topics. I recalled the words of an acquaintance who heads a Finnish-Chinese joint venture company: "It's heartening to watch our younger Chinese staff members. They're bright and well-educated people in their twenties, optimistic about the future and very proud of their country."

"That new job has done him a world of good. You've given him a wonderful start in life," I said to Song after Little Yan had left.

"It's up to him whether he succeeds or not. I just made the introduction," Song shrugged off my praise. There is nothing more natural to a Chinese than helping a family member. It is something one does automatically, whether it is a small favor, like taking your cousin's child to the dentist, or something major, like arranging an apartment or a job for a brother-in-law.

The family has been the foundation of Chinese society throughout history and has always been considered more important than the individual. Besides the traditional function of bearing offspring, the family has had numerous political, economic, and social responsibilities. Family members have had to rely on each other, not only to survive, but also because in the old days there was a responsibility system in which the whole family could be punished for the crimes of one family member. When the Communists took over and branded the son of a landlord "the offspring of a bad element," they were actually just continuing, in revised form, a centuries-old custom whereby a son could be held responsible for his father's wrongdoings.

"The family" does not refer to the nuclear family in the Western sense, but rather it is an ambiguous term which may encompass all of one's relatives. In the former agrarian society, only the relatives on one's father's side mattered. Today, urban residents keep in contact with both their mother's and their father's relatives. "My wife's family is just as important as my own," Song explained when I asked him about his relationship with his in-laws. "Last week I was given a big box of apples by my work unit. Instinctively, I divided it into three parts, one for my parents, one for my parents-in-law, and one for us."

One of the pioneering works on Chinese sociology is *From the Soil: The Foundations of Chinese Society*, written by the eminent sociologist Fei Xiaotong. Though the book was first published in 1947, the values and social networks it describes still comprise the key to understanding the Chinese way of thinking. Chinese society consists not of organizations arranged systematically, but, to quote Fei, of "webs woven out of countless personal relationships."[6] Fei explains the bonds of Chinese society by

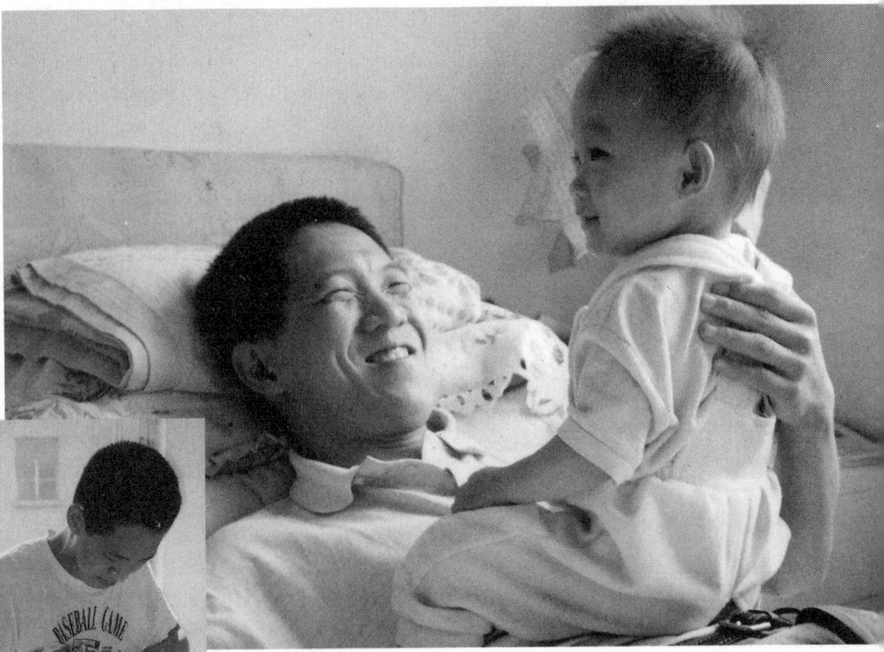

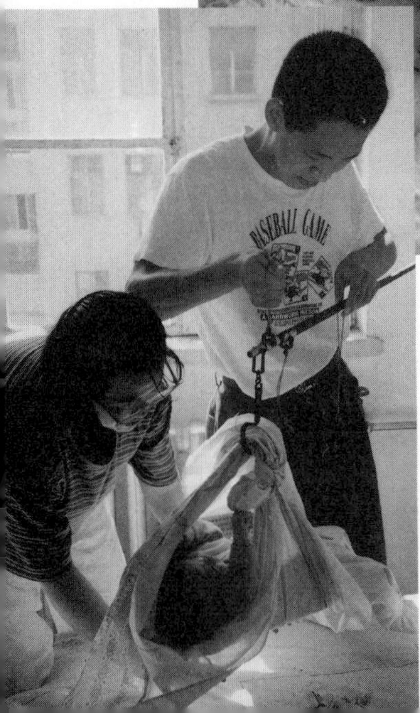

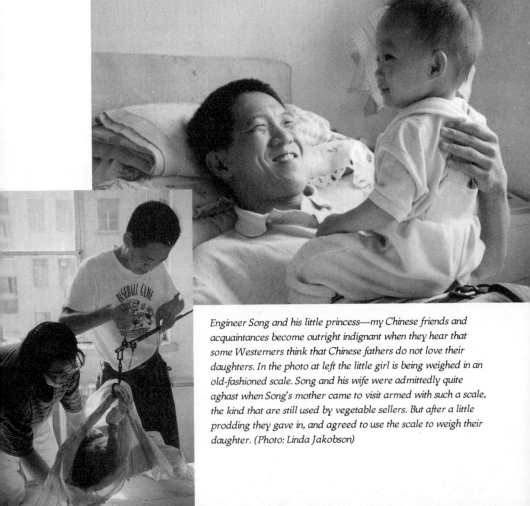

Engineer Song and his little princess—my Chinese friends and acquaintances become outright indignant when they hear that some Westerners think that Chinese fathers do not love their daughters. In the photo at left the little girl is being weighed in an old-fashioned scale. Song and his wife were admittedly quite aghast when Song's mother came to visit armed with such a scale, the kind that are still used by vegetable sellers. But after a little prodding they gave in, and agreed to use the scale to weigh their daughter. (Photo: Linda Jakobson)

likening them to the concentric circles that appear on the surface of a lake after a stone is thrown in. The innermost circle is the family. Each larger circle represents a new network toward which an individual has responsibilities, but on which he can also rely for support. The further away the circle is from the center, the weaker the bond.

As I follow the lives of my Chinese friends, I often recall these circles that gracefully expand on the surface of a lake. There is no limit to the amount of effort that goes into assisting family members—they often help each other out financially as well. On countless occasions, I have seen a friend use the equivalent of half a month's salary to bail out a sibling in need. One acquaintance, who is an accountant, offered to tutor his cousin's daughter in math in preparation for her high school entrance examinations. It took him a good hour to bicycle to his cousin's home, to which he faithfully went twice a week for over a year.

Of course, taking family support for granted has its drawbacks. I have heard hair-raising stories of Chinese who, after becoming successful in the West, have had to put up with a never-ending stream of visiting (and demanding) relatives.

Nevertheless, the way in which my former colleague at the economics college in Jinan, Teacher Yuan, cares for her family is not at all unusual. She has done well for herself, not so well that she can be considered rich, but she has a well-paying job as the marketing manager of a plywood factory on Hainan Island. "I'm the only one in our family who had a chance to study at university. Now, it's my responsibilty to see to it that the next generation does at least as well as I have. I want my niece and nephew to get on in life, and they must have a proper education," she explained her philosophy. Each month, out of her salary of 2,000 yuan ($240), she sends home 350 yuan ($42). Part of this goes to support her elderly mother and the rest pays for tutors for her niece and nephew. In addition, the entire family has spent a month on holiday visiting her in Hainan, all at her expense.

One is also loyal toward the so-called second circle, comprised of close friends, former classmates, and, in some cases, neighbors. One's colleagues and more distant neighbors form the third circle. These three circles represent connecting networks of *guanxi* in varying degrees of intensity. Without them, it is impossible to survive in Chinese society.

Most employees of state-run units live in apartments provided by their work unit. Although still nominal, rents in state-owned apartments are rising, and the whole urban housing system is being revamped. But the provision of housing is still the main reason that people are reluctant to leave their jobs in the state sector. This apartment block belongs to Shandong Polytechnic University in Jinan. (Photo: Linda Jakobson)

二

The Closed World of a Work Unit

Changes Have Been Mostly Materialistic

I stepped into a totally different world when I went to visit my former work unit, the economics college in Jinan. I had not been there since my contract as an English teacher expired in 1988, and I did not really know what to expect. The only person in the work unit with whom I have kept in touch was a girlfriend, Teacher Yuan, and she moved to Hainan Island the year after I left.

At first glance, the campus had undergone enormous changes. The bumpy muddy road which had led to the university was now a six-lane highway. The familiar donkey and mule carts were still going strong, but at least they seemed to keep to the side of the road these days. When I arrived in 1987, the university had just moved to this far-flung suburban campus, and I remembered it as bleak and half-finished. Now it appeared to be a much friendlier place, with lots of bushes and trees growing among the apartment buildings and colorful flowers lining the asphalt paths. No more leaping over the mud puddles on your way to work every morning, I thought, taking note of the scooters parked side by side the bicycles outside my former apartment building. There were no such vehicles in my time. The campus had acquired an impressive-looking science center, a new library, and an array of new sports facilities. But appearances can be misleading, and during the following weeks I realized that most of the changes were mainly materialistic. The narrow-mindedness and cautiousness which had dominated the atmosphere back in 1987 were still intact. Attitudes change slowly in the closed world of a state-run work unit.

It was for this reason that Teacher Yuan had decided to resign. "I can't stand the thought of spending the rest of my life in this bastion of conservatism, where everyone meddles in others' affairs and the leaders don't do anything except make their own lives more comfortable," Teacher Yuan had written to me about her plans to move. "The rest of China is changing rapidly, but this university is going to stay the same as long as the present leaders are still alive. And who knows if it will change even after that? I have no chance to develop myself if I stay here."

Back in 1989, it took courage to leave the security of a university teaching post and move to a new economic zone (Hainan). Only in 1992, after Deng publicly prodded his countrymen to pursue economic growth more boldly and imaginatively, did it become popular among cadres to give up their secure state jobs. Ministries, provincial government offices, and local bureaus—even universities—promptly set up commercial companies, sometimes openly and sometimes under intricately camouflaged webs of subsidiary companies. Many civil servants jumped at the chance to escape the dull, disciplined environment of their work units and "leapt into the sea," as one says in Chinese. Suddenly, leaping into the sea was everywhere, referring to tens of thousands of cadres who were leaving their posts and going into business. In one province alone (Liaoning), 39,000 civil servants reportedly resigned during 1992.[1] But not all actually went to the private sector and gave up the rights and social security benefits of cadres, as Teacher Yuan had. Many went to work for state-run or state-sponsored enterprises. As former civil servants they had excellent connections with government officials, and many of them made full use of these good *guanxi.* The consequences are not difficult to envision. Corruption, already widespread, grew like voracious weeds in a poorly kept garden.

As I strolled about the campus, I wondered how many of my former students, most of whom had graduated the year before with Bachelor of Arts degrees, had followed Teacher Yuan's example and "leapt into the sea." Nine years ago, many of them had expressed their disdain at having been assigned a teaching position upon graduation. The main reason was the poor pay. In 1987, Teacher Yuan's monthly salary was 98 yuan ($26.50), while a factory worker earned 1.3 times that amount (about 130 yuan, or $35.10). The other reason was the tendency of school leaders to be even more old-fashioned than others. Educational reforms intended to clarify the division of responsibilities between school administrators and Party Secretaries had been half-hearted. In industry, the reform policy had been more effective and the managing director of an enterprise usually had the final say, whereas in schools and universities it was still often the Party Secretary, not the dean, who was the most influential. The situation has not essentially changed during the 1990s. In fact, the Party Secretary's power increased as a result of the Tiananmen events in 1989. And in

April 1996, the Xinhua New China news agency reported that the Party Secretary was the number-one ranking member in all units associated with education.[2]

The first thing I did was to look up my former boss, Mr. Jiang, who had been head of the "foreign affairs department." It would be a lie to claim that I had ever missed him since leaving the university in Jinan. I had nicknamed him "Mr. Sphinx," a typical middle-aged cadre, always very polite and restrained in his manner, but never letting on what he was truly thinking. I was always left wondering if there might be some hidden meaning behind his words. He and I were often at odds with each other because his job compelled him to monitor my contact with the students and my free-time activities. I learned the hard way what every Chinese living in a work unit knows instinctively: It is absolutely fruitless to ask "why?" or "with what right?" You simply have to accept, or at least outwardly appear to submit to, authority and handed-down orders, and then do your best to slink about in a manner which arouses the least possible attention.

Mr. Jiang had been assigned a new job. In 1993, he had finally persuaded his superiors to let him return to teaching. He was now a faculty member in the foreign trade department.

"You must have been happy to wash your hands of all the grievances of the foreign teachers," I chided him, as we sat sipping our tea in the teachers' room. From his initial greeting, I had noticed a previously undisplayed trace of casualness in his manner. Though he clearly understood my hint, he merely replied: "I was ecstatic because the old job was so boring. I had to sit in the office of the foreign affairs department from nine to five every day, even though I had nothing to do. Now I am much freer. I teach six hours a week and apart from that I can stay at home."

A university teaching post might mean a monotonous life in a sheltered environment, but at least the work load is one of the world's lightest. (To be honest, this is true of many posts in China.) I remember how taken aback I was when I realized how little was required of my teaching colleagues nine years ago. One of them had to teach a total of ten hours a week, and she never stopped complaining about her miserable lot in life. Most of the younger teachers, like my former students, had not yet been given any teaching assignment at all. They would probably be required to teach two to four classes during the next school year. I had been employed to help them improve their English conversation skills.

"Nothing much has changed," said Teacher Wang with a giggle the next day, when I managed to track down a group of my former students and invite them out to dinner. These were people in the prime of their lives and they taught only four hours a week! They had no other responsibilities. In an overpopulated nation, there is no limit to how many human resources are wasted. An automobile-engineer friend, who graduated with flying colors from Qinghua, the equivalent of MIT (the prestigious Massachusetts Institute of Technology) in China, has, on countless occasions, related what it felt like to twiddle his thumbs for four years in a government research institute. He later emigrated to the United States.

"I have not been assigned any teaching at all. I can spend all my time at home, except for political study once a week," said the burly, six-foot-tall Teacher Qin. He had brought his nine-year-old daughter along. "I could not be happier. I can help my daughter with her schoolwork when she comes home and do my own research work in the mornings. Last year I managed to write eight academic articles. They will be counted as merits when our department chooses a new assistant professor." The others all promptly pointed out that few people were as conscientious as Teacher Qin. The vast majority of teachers idled away the day at trivial activities.

I told them about the courtesy call I had paid the day before on the university president, Dean Hu, with the prompting of Mr. Jiang. As I stepped into the dean's office, I was impressed to see the dean hard at work at his computer. I could see that he was using a Windows program. In 1987, the university had just acquired its first computers, but no one knew how to use them. In Chinese work-unit style, the computers had been kept locked up and were only put on display for visitors. Dean Hu was, however, clearly not yet totally computer literate because he still relied on his little chequered notebook when he wanted to give me a statistical run-through of the work unit: The number of students enrolled at the university had risen from 1,600 to 3,600 since 1987. The number of teachers had correspondingly increased from 160 to 360, but the university had been "very cautious about employing other staff members." Despite this, there were more people who had nothing to do with education on the unit's payroll than actual teachers. There were altogether 440 "other staff members" who worked either as office personnel or in the university's day care center, transportation department, canteen, health center, custodial division, and so on.

"In a state-run factory, the disproportion between people who actually work in production and people who do something unrelated to production is even larger," Teacher Li remarked. "Because our university is a newly founded one, we don't yet have retirees to support. Just think of how much money a middle-sized factory, which was started back in the 1950s, doles out each month in pensions. No wonder so many of them are unprofitable."

Reunion in Jinan: Meeting my former students at a hot pot restaurant in the autumn of 1996. From left, Teachers Lu, Yu, Li, Qin, Qin's daughter, and Teacher Wang. (Photo: Linda Jakobson)

Teacher Li had not changed a bit, except around the waist. He must have put on twenty pounds since I last saw him. The female teachers present, Teachers Wang and Lu, were still as petite as they had been nine years ago, though they were now mothers of school-age children. Teacher Li was still the most outgoing of the group, the only one who was willing to take the initiative. Rank-and-file members in a Chinese work unit tend to be hesitant in any sort of situation which requires even the most insignificant decision. But Li was a lively soul and he had been one of my favorite students, though his English language skills, and especially his pronunciation, had been among the worst in the class. Everyone's English was very rusty from lack of practice. I could not coax any of them into even trying to speak English with me, except, of course, Teacher Li, who every now and again blurted out an English phrase or two. All of them had matured. I remember how, as their teacher, I'd had trouble getting used to their childish manners and innocent pranks. They had seemed more like teenagers than twenty-three- and twenty-four-year-old adults.

I asked why Dean Hu had said that the university was constantly on the lookout for new teachers. "We have too few people who can teach computer technology," Teacher Li replied. "The students need a whole array of computer skills, but computer specialists can easily find jobs elsewhere. They have no incentive to become university teachers and be paid 550 or 650 yuan a month ($66 or $78)."

The fact that an individual now has the freedom to look for a job is a revolutionary state of affairs. When I moved to China in 1987, the work place, the family, and politics were all intertwined. More so, according to *The Economist*, than in any other country, including totalitarian North Korea and Albania.[3] An urban resident was assigned a job by the state and, in principle, had to stick with that job for the rest of his life. Already ten years ago, a person had been given the right to leave his or her work unit, but there were very few alternatives except in the largest cities, like Beijing or Shanghai. Even there, the choices were few and far between. Also, it was much more difficult then to find an apartment to rent than it is today. In most urban families, one's place of work and the apartment assigned by the work unit went hand-in-hand from one generation to the next. That did not mean that a plumber's daughter necessarily became a plumber, but the plumber's work unit was responsible for arranging employment for the daughter.

In the 1980s, university graduates were still assigned jobs where their services were needed, with almost no regard for one's own personal wishes or for one's spouse's place of work. To a Westerner, it is utterly incomprehensible that couples were forced to live hundreds of miles apart from each other just because some higher authority deemed it in the interest of the state. Changing one's work unit was next to impossible without very good connections. People complained about this bitterly during my first years in China. When the students started to stage demonstrations in 1989, one of their demands was that university graduates be given a say about their own job assignments. This demand was actually fulfilled, in spite of the bloody crackdown on the protest movement.

The entire system of employment has undergone a major renovation in the 1990s. Though the rules and their enforcement vary from place to place, individuals now have a more genuine chance to influence, at least to a much greater extent than before, decisions concerning what subject they would like to major in and what sort of job they will take. Of course, this new freedom has resulted in reduced job security, as it did for the lady from Wuhan with whom I had spoken on the train. Employers can now lay off workers indiscriminately and force them to find new employment on their own. The new system favors the educated and the more industrious and enterprising. Though changing from one state-run unit to another still requires a fair amount of effort and in many cases *guanxi* (as does anything of importance in China), young adults now have a vastly greater range of opportunities than people ten years their senior. If the job assigned by the state does not appeal to you, you can negotiate on your own with another state-run unit or turn to the private sector, which is becoming an increasingly important employer. One other option is simply to start your own business.

Zhang, who serviced my fax machine periodically, is a good example of a young man who turned to the option of self-employment. Having failed the university entrance examinations, he studied at a technical institute for two years, after which he was assigned a job as an electrician in one of Beijing's middle-sized electricity companies. "My salary was 430 yuan ($74) per month, and the housing situation of our work unit was hopeless. I knew that I would have to wait at least ten years before I would be given a one-room apartment. I decided that this was not the life for me, so I tried to figure out an appropriate line of business. I decided fax machines were the appliances of the future and I borrowed money from my parents to buy one," the twenty-four-year-old recalled, during his first visit to my apartment in 1994.

I liked him from the moment he walked in. He is a sympathetic, polite young man and, most important, trustworthy. "I wrote to the manufacturer in Hong Kong and asked them for some repair manuals. Then, I took the whole machine apart and spent all my free time studying each part, one by one," he said, smiling shyly. He had just recently quit his job as an electrician and had become one of the growing number of private entrepreneurs. From the pathetically modest business card he gave me I could tell that he did not have a penny to waste. I had found him because he had been smart enough to leave his contact number at all the major stores selling fax machines in Beijing. From the very first day he had more work than he could handle. There is so much dust in Beijing that every machine needs to be serviced at regular intervals. He charged 100 yuan ($12) for a home visit and he had enough time to service about six machines a day. I calculated that his monthly income must be over 10,000 yuan ($1,205). Not bad compared to the 430 yuan he had earned as an electrician. When I last saw him, he had just bought himself a brand-new car. Until then he had used the public bus, or, in urgent cases, a *miandi*-cab.

Zhang, like just about every private enterpreneur I know, pays a nominal fee in taxes. Before the mid-1990s, taxes were almost unheard of. Recently, the government has stepped up its efforts to collect taxes, but most small-time businessmen and their employees still manage to evade them. Though Beijing residents should, according to the law, pay taxes on all monthly income over 850 yuan ($100), the only people I know who actually do so are the ones working in foreign joint venture companies, and they pay only because their employers force them to. Everyone else comes up with the most ingenious ways to bend the rules and avoid taxation.

The teachers I had invited out to dinner, all of whom were my former students, had decided to remain in their original job assignments. Of the seventeen teachers in my class, eight were still employed by the university. One was working for a Ph.D. in Beijing and was not expected to return. Eight others had found jobs elsewhere. When I asked how many had "leapt into the sea" everyone burst into laughter.

"I suppose it's inevitable that one learns that expression in Beijing," Teacher Wang chaffed. "In Jinan there haven't been as many opportunities." Of the eight who had left the work unit, one was still teaching, but at another university. Two had become businessmen in state-run enterprises in Jinan. One (Teacher Yuan's husband) had tried his hand at an array of jobs before ending up in a state-run import-export company on Hainan Island. Two had gone abroad and had not been heard of since, and two had found commercial work in the private sector.

"And all of them earn much, much more than we do," Teacher Yu remarked.

"On the other hand, I presume that all of you have already been given an apartment by the university, and none of you can complain about being overworked," I pointed out, and they all nodded.

"And we don't have to fret about being laid off like workers or even cadres in factories," Teacher Wang added.

I was happy to note that, with the exception of Teacher Yu, all of them seemed quite content with their lives. I had been prepared for the kind of moaning and groaning that was common among teachers nine years ago. Younger faculty members had constantly grumbled about their rotten luck: "Who wants to be a teacher?" Admittedly, when we were speaking about job assignments and career choices, Teacher Lu did utter the all-too-familiar phrase "*mei you banfa*" which roughly means "there's nothing one can do about it," a saying that even non-Chinese-speaking foreigners learn while living in China. This expression of resignation is used for any situation in which one wants to convey a sense of helplessness (or unwillingness) to deal with a matter or to solve a problem. But Teacher Lu did not say it with malice, merely as a simple statement of fact.

I was delighted to hear that all of my former students had continued their studies during the 1990s and had completed at least master's degrees. Teachers Li and Yu had been to study in Beijing, Qin at another university in Jinan, Wang in Shanghai, and Lu in Nanjing. "It was the hardest on me because I'm so old," Teacher Lu sighed. She had just turned thirty-nine the previous week and had taken her last examination on her birthday. Considering herself old at age thirty-nine is quite normal in China, where one's youth is deemed over at age thirty.

Later, when I told my friend, engineer Song, about the dinner, he belittled my former students' accomplishments and said that the main incentive for them to continue their studies was to obtain an apartment. Universities favored people with master's degrees when new and more spacious apartments were allocated. I did not think this reward made their achievement any the less admirable.

"At any rate, a cadre is paid the same salary whether he is officially working or continuing his studies," Song continued.

"Well, these people are paid the same salary if they sit at home doing absolutely nothing. That is what working, in their case, mostly entails," I responded. I asked why it was less commendable to finish a master's degree after one had already started to work rather than straightaway after graduating from college (as he had done). "I have not forgotten that you had to survive on a tiny 49 yuan ($13) stipend. On the other hand, the value of money has changed too. But, whichever way you look at this, the same mental effort was demanded of all of you."

Song raised his hands as a sign of surrender. "I'm only trying to make you look at things realistically," he said while poking fun at me for getting emotional. We have been friends for many years, and he knows I get worked up when anything and everything is evaluated in China nowadays solely on the basis of money or material benefit.

My former students were visibly pleased to see me. I suddenly felt guilty about not having kept in touch with them. But the endless rows with Mr. Jiang and the suspicion with which foreign teachers were looked upon by the leaders of the university had left me frustrated and kept me away. When I told them this, they all nodded and said that they understood.

"We remember how annoyed you were when Mr. Jiang always told you that he was only trying to look after of your safety. We could not say anything at the time, but surely you knew that your safety was not the real issue at stake," one of them said. I certainly did. The university leaders not only wanted to keep an eye on their own countrymen, they also wanted to make sure that a foreigner did not peek too closely at Chinese society. During my stroll through the campus, I had noticed a new three-story building which was solely for foreign teachers. I had no doubt that segregating the "big noses" was still the aim of the leadership. As a teacher, I had lived in an apartment building with Chinese neighbors. Though all sorts of people tried to keep tabs on me, it was a lot easier then for visitors to pop into an apartment building than into the new foreign teachers' residence which had its own doorman.

During the following weeks, I met with my former students on many occasions. Because I presumed that it would be inconvenient to invite such a big crowd to anyone's home, I nostalgically suggested a picnic to Thousand Buddha Mountain or an excursion to Baotu Hot Springs Park. That is how I had often spent my free time as a teacher. In those days, there were no other alternatives. And that was still the case for teachers struggling to survive on small salaries. Not that Jinan did not have more to offer these days, but dining in a restaurant or spending the evening in a karaoke bar was far too expensive, and everyone said they were too old to learn how to bowl. That was their courteous way of declining my offer to treat them to an afternoon in a bowling alley. Bowling alleys have

In 1987, most people in Jinan spent their spare time in parks or on outings to Thousand Buddha Mountain. Even today, teachers trying to survive on small fixed salaries cannot afford to do much else. The photo shows some musicians taking a break in Baotuquan Park in central Jinan in the autumn of 1996. (Photo: Linda Jakobson)

Bowling has become very popular among the nouveau riche, and there are bowling alleys in all major cities. In 1997, my godchild's family, whom I consider to be middle-class, decided they wanted to find out what it is all about. Though they enjoyed thamselves, they decided that it is still beyond their means. My godchild's cousin Yaoyao, trying for a strike. (Photo: Yaoyao's father)

become immensely popular with people of all ages, including many much older than my former students.

In 1987, I had hiked in the nearby mountains nearly every weekend. In those days, I was not accompanied by my own students, but by some of the young people actually studying at our university or by friends from other work units in Jinan. I had presumed that my own students had been told not to spend their free time in my company, and now they confirmed my earlier suspicions. I am not quite sure whether the eagerness with which they met me now was a natural consequence of the more relaxed general atmosphere or due to their own changed status as seasoned teachers with ten years' experience. In any case, keeping in contact with one's teachers is a tradition in China. It is quite usual for students to visit their former teachers and to present them with small gifts or some fruit before the New Year—quite a touching gesture.

I would have loved to take my students out to dinner a second time but I did not want to put them in an awkward position. As we clambered into two *miandi*-cabs on our first evening out and I wondered out loud about a suitable place to go, I realized that none of them could recommend a single restaurant. Somewhat haphazardly, on the advice of the taxi driver, we ended up in a Mongolian hot pot restaurant. As we dipped paper-thin slices of lamb into the steaming pot, which is placed, Swiss fondue-style, in the middle of a round table, Teacher Wang told me that she had never tasted Mongolian hot pot before in her life. "You don't eat out on a 600 yuan ($72) monthly salary," she said. Teacher Li added: "And even if a friend can treat you and charge the bill on an expense account, you feel too embarrassed to accept such an offer more than once when you know you cannot possibly return the invitation." The Mongolian hot pot place was certainly no expensive upscale venue, just an average restaurant which was packed to the last seat. Dinner and beer for seven cost 209 yuan ($25).

Only after I had asked my engineer friend, Song, to write down all the normal monthly expenses of his four-person household did I truly understand my former students' standard of living. "Better ask my wife," Song answered with a grin. "She is in charge of the family economy." That is the case in many families I know, though a Chinese wife does not control the purse strings quite as tightly as in Japan, where a husband literally hands over his salary at the end of each month and then receives pocket money from his wife. Song's wife, who is a middle-school teacher, calculated that the family usually spent about 1,200 yuan ($145) per month. But, she reminded me, that sum does not include a single extra item, like a new winter jacket for the child or a Sunday outing to the zoo. The family spent 570 yuan ($69) on food alone; the phone, water, and heating bills amounted to 140 yuan ($17), rent was 47 yuan ($5.70), and the maid's salary was 230 yuan ($28).

"If both of us were still working in the state sector, we would have to lower our standard of living quite considerably, because our joint income would be just barely 1,300 yuan ($156) a month. I earn 560 yuan ($67) and he, as an engineer, would probably get 150 or 200 yuan ($18 or $24) more," Song's wife explained. "And remember, every now and again we have to dole out money for the most ridiculous reasons. Just yesterday I had to buy two month's salaries worth of bonds (1,120 yuan, or $134). Officially, it's voluntary, but everyone knows that you're asking for trouble if you don't heed the work unit's so-called requests. In principle, we are repaid this money with interest in five years time, but, in any case, the money is tied up for that period." Many work units accumulate money for new investments by selling such bonds. I have the impression that at least once a year, one of the adults in my godchild's family has had to draw money from their savings account to buy the work unit's "voluntary" shares.

Song works in a private company and his basic monthly salary is 3,200 yuan ($385). He also receives a minimum of one month's salary as a bonus at the end of the year. They do not live luxuriously by Western standards. Their apartment, which belongs to his wife's work unit, is located in the same kind of scruffy run-down building you see everywhere in Chinese cities. But the family has room to maneuver financially in a way unknown to people like my former students. None of the spouses of the teachers I know at the economics college have left their jobs in the state sector, so whole families have to manage on about 1,200 yuan ($145) per month.[4] Song and his wife have a live-in nanny who doubles as a maid. They go out to dinner occasionally, and they do not have to think twice about buying good-quality meat or taking a taxi.

My former students do, however, have one thing going for them. Their apartments are nicer than any I have ever seen in any state-run work unit. I was genuinely astonished when Teacher Yu invited us all over to his place on my second-to-last evening in Jinan.

"Do you know that not even a sixty-year-old professor in Beijing has such a modern and spacious home?" I asked Yu as he showed me around. He and his wife live in a three-room apartment, with a reasonably sized bathroom and well-equipped kitchen. The plastered walls are painted white, with tiling on the floor. Most important, the bathroom is covered with white ceramic tiles from ceiling to floor. It is totally different in appearance from what I am used to in China. Song's and my other friends' apartments are all pretty much the standard Chinese work unit apartment—the floor is concrete, as are the unpainted walls. The washing facilities are very primitive.

The university had acquired new land over the years and recently built four new apartment buildings, where most of my former students now lived. Apparently the leaders of the school lived in even better conditions. As I walked toward Teacher Yu's home I could not help noticing that one of the new buildings was of conspicuously higher quality and finer design than the others. "That's where our leaders live," my former students confirmed. It did not strike me as anything out-of-the-ordinary. After all, the school leaders had not only invested in new facilities for themselves but had seen to the needs of their personnel as well. But the next morning, while visiting another university campus, I saw a huge, ostentatious office building which had clearly cost hundreds of thousands of yuan to construct. It is typical of small-minded unit leaders to waste money on status symbols rather than to improve the living conditions of their staff. I could not help noticing, right beside the monstrosity of an office building, the row of wretched one-story buildings where that university's teachers were obliged to live.

Teacher Yu, at age thirty-two, was the youngest of our group. He still had a boyish look and a roguish twinkle in his eye. He repeatedly excused himself for not having tidied up. "My wife's in Beijing studying English, and I have not been very good about cleaning in her absence," he smiled and bustled about like any Western man in similar circumstances. He had recently "finally married" and he was eager to show me the couple's extravagant-looking leather wedding album. They had photographed themselves in four different outfits at a wedding studio. Page after page showed them posing in borrowed attire, ranging from a Western black tie and a glamorous evening gown to traditional Mandarin-style costumes. The props were part of the studio's package deal, which also included three poster-sized prints of the couple. I did not have the heart to tell Teacher Yu what I thought about this craze of photographing oneself in Western wedding attire. My thirty-eight-year-old friend, *Jiejie*, who had married in the early 1980s before this fad had become widespread, had still just the other week dragged her husband to such a studio.

"Initially, I thought it was absolutely frivolous to spend 530 yuan ($64), nearly a whole month's salary, on these photographs, but my wife insisted," Teacher Yu said. "Our actual wedding was all the more modest because of it. We had dinner at my parents' place. But now, I have to admit that I enjoy looking at these pictures." He waved his hand at the photo on the living room wall, in which he looked like Clark Gable in a scene from *Gone With The Wind*. "I'll never in my life have another chance to put on a tuxedo, or afford to wear a genuine Rolex watch. Actually, it was fun to live in a world of fantasy for half a day."

Teacher Wang teased him for being the eternal dreamer.

"You're right. I dream of flying right out of this place and exploring new horizons," Teacher Yu grinned. He imitated a bird flapping his arms in the air. Then he said soberly, "But, in all honesty, I wish I could find a way to teach in Beijing. I really enjoyed the atmosphere at the People's University when I was continuing my studies. It was so different from Jinan."

"That says quite a lot," I interrupted him. "The People's University is reputed to be one of the more conservative schools in Beijing."

"Really?" Yu looked at me in disbelief. Then he turned toward the others. "Did you hear that? The People's University is considered conservative among Beijingers, but to me, the atmosphere was markedly relaxed. I thought it was great."

Teacher Li told me he had tried to transfer to Beijing College of Economics, where he had done his master's degree. "I would have loved to stay there, and they even had a suitable vacancy," Li said and grimaced as people do when they have to concede failure. "The transfer of my residence permit would have cost 10,000 yuan ($1,205) and I was prepared to borrow the money from relatives to be able to pay it. But my wife and child could have moved with me only if I had paid an additional 100,000 yuan ($12,050). And that was an impossible sum."

Though moving from one place to another is still not totally permitted in China, more than one hundred million people from the countryside have found work on their own in cities all over the country. And millions of businessmen live in places other than the one in which they have an official residence permit. Officially, they are all just temporarily working in another location.

Every Chinese has a *hukou*, a residence permit, which, in principle, decrees where a person is supposed to live. In 1987, a person still needed this permit. Without it, he could not acquire grain coupons or arrange for his child to attend school. With the transition now taking place in Chinese society, the whole system is beginning to unravel. In some social classes, the *hukou* has become an insignificant piece of paper, as grain coupons are no longer distributed and children may attend private schools, if their parents have enough money. The authorities, who understandably want to restrict the overcrowded big cities from becoming even more congested, have dealt with the situation by raising the price of a residence permit in popular urban areas. But this practice has only widened the rift between the new rich and average Chinese citizens.

I once asked my neighbor in Beijing where he was officially supposed to reside. He laughed and answered, "I really don't know. I suppose my *hukou* is in Nanjing, where my parents live. I rely on money in any situation that requires showing my residence permit." Another neighbor said he paid 120,000 yuan ($14,460) to purchase Beijing residence permits for himself and his wife. "The two permits actually cost a total of 100,000 yuan, but an additional 20,000 yuan was needed to pay off my *guanxi*," he explained.

A residence permit is still a necessity for anyone employed by the state. That much I knew, but I still did not quite grasp Teacher Li's complex dilemma. "You see, if a resident of another city finishes a master's degree at a Beijing university, he is given an 80 percent reduction if he or she wishes to purchase a Beijing *hukou*. So, instead of 50,000 yuan ($6,025), I would only have had to pay 10,000 yuan ($1,204). But my wife, who is a worker, and my child would have been charged the full price," he explained as he sat swinging his two-year-old daughter to and fro on his lap. "It is because of this little girl that I am still here."

At times, it is impossible to fathom the intricate labyrinth of rules, which is largely a result of the rapid social changes. The most ingenious (and the wealthy) often find loopholes. I am forever at a loss in trying to understand why, in some instances, rules are followed haphazardly and then again, in other cases, they are strictly enforced.

We spent a leisurely evening at Teacher Yu's home. We sipped tea and ate watermelon, as we had nine years earlier, when colleagues and students spent many an evening at my apartment. But conversations did not stray into controversial topics. They never do at any gathering that includes several members of the same work unit. Probably the fact that my former students knew that I was preparing to write a book about China also had a bearing on the atmosphere. I am sure I could have had a fruitful conversation with any one of them about a number of sensitive subjects, but it would have had to have been private or only in the company of close family members. In the terms of the sociologist Fei Xiaotong, my former students belonged to one another's outermost circle of connections. They worked in different departments and did not know each other very well. None of them had ever been to Teacher Yu's home before.

I was careful not to pry. I had already heard a bitter rundown of the goings-on at the school from another teacher at our university, a friend of Teacher Yuan. "Nothing has changed," she assured me when I invited her out to dinner at one of the new Korean restaurants in downtown Jinan. "When the provincial scholarships to study abroad were announced last spring, whom do you think won them? The offspring of the leaders' friends, of course. Plus two older Party members. And when the term began two weeks ago and the annual promotions were announced, yet again those who had bought enough presents for the leaders were awarded. Teacher Yuan was truly wise to move to Hainan. If only I had persuaded my own husband. Now it's too late. Our child is already in school." Her description of the intrigues at the university were very similar to ones I had witnessed as a teacher in 1987.

The top leadership of China may indeed want to introduce genuine change when, for example, it decides that scholarships should henceforth be awarded solely on the basis of merit. But, at numerous decision-making levels below them, the leaders have no incentives to change their

The peasants are no longer bound to the land as they were during the Mao era. Tens of millions of Chinese have left their homes in the countryside to find employment in the big cities. Officially, they are classified as "temporary residents," and their residence permits still decree that they are rural residents. Photo from central Xuzhou in Jiangsu province in 1996. (Photo: John Lee)

ways. Why would they want to forego all their personal benefits? Real change will not be possible until the middle-level bureaucracy is taken over by the next generation. And as Teacher Yuan pointed out in her letter, perhaps not even then.

Yuan's friend said she was thankful that at least she did not have to live on campus. The family's apartment, which belonged to her husband's work unit, was situated in the center of town. "It is less modern than the new apartments at our university, but I feel so much more free this way. I only go to the university on days when I have to teach or to attend political study. And I can earn extra money by privately tutoring high school students. Even that would be difficult if I lived on campus because some catty neighbor might find out and report me to the school authorities. Officially, you are not allowed to have a second job."

It is almost impossible for someone brought up in the West to comprehend how anyone can retain their sanity amidst all the rules and regulations in China. One is constantly reminded that something has to be accepted "for the good of the community." Just the size of apartments in China dictates that one hardly has any personal space at all. And some people have less than others. On numerous occasions I have heard acquaintances sigh in relief when they had managed to move from a one-story dwelling in an old courtyard house to an apartment building, simply because "at least the street committee women and the neighbors can no longer poke their noses into every single matter."

But I understood what they really meant only when, by chance, I got a tiny glimpse of some people's everyday reality. I was visiting friends in their dilapidated one-story apartment when suddenly the most awful argument broke out outside. "What on earth are they shouting about?" I asked. My girlfriend went out to investigate. About ten yards down the alley, a divorced man lived with his young son. His ex-wife's mother, the boy's grandmother, had come to see the child, but the man was quite adamant about not letting his former mother-in-law into his room. "You no longer have any right to meet the boy; you haven't given one *fen* (penny) toward his upbringing," the man argued. Through the thin walls, the neighbors could hear the woman pleading with the man. So they went out to try and persuade him to let her in. The man became all the more enraged and told them to mind their own business. Gradually, more and more people from adjoining homes gathered outside his door. Everyone was yelling at one another at the top of their lungs. I wondered how they could all fit outside his door because the alley was only a few yards wide.

My friends laughed in embarrassment when they saw my horrified expression, as the ruckus went on and on. "This sort of row erupts every now and again. It's no wonder, considering our crowded conditions," my girlfriend's husband said. The couple shared a single small room with their twelve-year-old daughter. "Sometimes I think it's only natural that people find a way to vent their frustrations," he sighed. My girlfriend added with a wink, "He's right. And that out there is much better than picking an argument with one's own family members."

"Where are the street committee members?" I asked.

"Probably in the middle of it all, screeching to their hearts' content. Or maybe they don't happen to be at home," my girlfriend replied. She said that the authority of the street committee was nonexistent in a case like this. "If someone were to commit a crime, they would be the ones to fetch the police. But the police can't possibly deal with all the family arguments in a city of this size. In the old days, we were all frightened by the street committee, because no one wanted to be accused of any political wrong-doing, and if the street committee felt so inclined, they could label almost anything that way. Nowadays they have very little to hold against us. Anyway, we all work in different work units. It would be awful to have one's workmates as neighbors."

That is precisely the situation in which my former students live. For this reason, I was careful not to broach the subject of working part-time, since Yuan's friend had told me that it was not permitted. But as the evening wore on, I got the hint when they started asking me about what opportunity teachers in Beijing have to earn extra money.

"These days everyone tries to do two jobs, if they are lucky enough to find suitable work," I answered. This applies not only to teachers, but to almost anyone working in the state sector. There are dozens of night schools and occupational institutes where teachers can seek additional employment. "And as far as I know, it is not illegal in Beijing, or so I've been told," I added. Some teachers also find part-time work in companies owned by relatives or friends.

"We would like to earn extra money too, but there aren't many possibilities in Jinan," said Teacher Su, a round-faced lady, whom I remember as a conscientious student. "Jinan does not have that many part-time institutes. Accounting teachers tend to find additional work in private companies, but not many of our fields and specialities are sought after in the business world. Who on earth would want to employ me?" Teacher Su smiled and I noticed everyone in the room trying to stifle a giggle.

For a moment, I did not catch on. Then I remembered: Su taught the history of the Communist Party.

Prominent Mao statues have become rare sights in the 1990s. One of the few such statues that remains stands in central Shenyang, the capital of Liaoning province. It was built when Mao's nephew, Mao Yuanxin, was the Party Secretary of Shenyang during the 1960s. In 1995, a group of disgruntled unemployed workers attempted to burn down the statue to protest against the city's "capitalist leaders." Photo taken in November 1995. (Photo: Linda Jakobson)

2

Red Youth

"Mao Is Part of the People's Subconscious"

When I felt like talking about politics, I sought the company in Jinan of my friend, Guo Hairong. She is one of those well-read people who loves intense debates and always puts forward thought-provoking arguments. I never tire of listening to her, or her family members, reminisce about the past. If Guo Hairong had been born in another society, or in China fifteen years later, she could have become a writer, a philosopher, or perhaps a historian. In any case, she certainly would be doing something other than working in the accounting department of a state-run department store.

"When I was born in 1952, China was full of hope. That is why I was given the name Hairong, which means Glorious Sea," Guo Hairong said. "It reflected the prevalent mood of optimism and my father's hope that a ray of glory would follow both my life and the future of our motherland. That turned out to be wishful thinking."

Guo Hairong embodies China's many contradictions. At home, she was taught classical Chinese, but in school she memorized the quotations of Mao Zedong. When she was twenty, everything she believed in was crushed by the realization that the revolution she had sacrificed her youth for was but an illusion, and she has never since found a new faith. Still, she is deeply patriotic, though the picture she paints of her country's future is dark and dismal. Despite her pessimistic view, she has a sunny disposition and inexhaustible energy which she uses to further her knowledge on a whole range of subjects. She is widely read in both Chinese and world history. When we argue about the future of China, she refers to Confucianism and Daoism as easily as to Marx, Hegel, or Heidegger. Though we do not always agree, little by little I have begun to understand the Chinese way of thinking, thanks to our many discussions. Guo Hairong has a wonderful ability to explain the endless allegories and idioms which the Chinese love to use to explain the present in terms of the past.

We got to know one another in Jinan in 1987, when she was among the handful of close friends who made my life there so memorable. Over the years, we have made a point of continuing to get together, sometimes in my home in Beijing, at other times in Jinan. My only regret has been that the visits have always been too short and the hours in the day too few for our marathon discussions. The evenings were still warm during the month I spent in Jinan in 1996, so we took to meeting at a small Chinese-style snack bar on the sidewalk outside Guo Hairong's apartment building. We sat on tiny plaited stools around a low table, sometimes nibbling on roasted peanuts and grilled beef on a skewer, or indulging in a bowl of steaming hot noodles. Meeting outside meant that we could talk as long as we wished without disturbing Guo Hairong's family. Every room was occupied in the crowded apartment which she, her husband, and their teenage son shared with her in-laws. Actually, her son slept in the hallway on a cot which was folded and put away every morning.

That autumn Guo Hairong was miserable because of her son. He had just started his last year of senior high school, but did not seem to be too worried about the university entrance examinations which lay ahead of him. "I can't say that he's a bad boy. He's kind and obedient, but he simply does not study enough. He has no idea about the realities of life," Guo Hairong sighed. "It's my fault, I know. I have mothered him too much. Remember how I even started studying English just to be able to help him with his homework?"

She is not the only mother I know who has studied English because of her offspring. Before I moved to Jinan, I became friends with a woman who worked in a textile factory in Beijing. Zhou had attended my English classes at a private evening school simply in order to be able to monitor her eleven-year-old daughter's homework. She and her husband, also a factory worker, used every extra penny to further their daughter's education. "The changes in China came too late for us. There's no way we can improve our lives. But it's worth trying for her sake," Zhou had replied, when I called her an admirable mother. Seven years later, I received an invitation to attend "the most memorable dinner this family has ever had." Zhou's daughter had passed the university entrance examination by the skin of her teeth. Her best results were on the English exam. "She is our family's first learned member," said her illiterate grandfather, his eyes glowing.

Education and scholarship were highly valued in Imperial China. The most prominent social class was comprised of civil servants who had passed a grueling examination requiring years of study. The oldest examination paper that has been excavated dates back to the year 408 A.D. Actually, there were three levels of examination. Very few men ever had the chance to take the most demanding one, but simply passing the first level elevated a person to the status of a gentleman and freed him from corporal punishment or serving in the army. When a young man managed to move into the ranks of the educated, his whole clan basked in glory.

From the fifteenth century on, the examinations were, in principle, open to all, but the lengthy period of preparation naturally favored only the wealthy. But the many tales of great men who rose from humble conditions to pass the examinations illustrate the admiration learned men enjoyed in society. When Mao Zedong wanted to destroy the old and make room for the birth of "a new socialist human being," he turned his vengeance on the educated class (especially after 1957).* But respect for education is deeply imbedded in the Chinese soul, integral to Chinese identity.

Competition for university admissions is extremely intense. As a result, the elimination process starts at an early age. Everyone complains about the amount of homework children are given, and also about the teaching methods, which are based on memorizing texts by rote. Still, scores of mothers and fathers I know do their utmost to find a good tutor for their child or to persuade a relative to help them out. "I think it's terrible that my child has no spare time, but I want to give him every possible chance to make it to university," is a statement I have heard time and time again. Others, like Guo Hairong, want their children to fulfil their own broken dreams.

Today, the Chinese school system is structurally similar to the American one. There are twelve grades: six elementary, and three each of junior and senior high. But unlike the American system, a child must pass an examination before moving on to the next school, and test results determine the kind of school he or she can attend. It is extremely difficult to be accepted into any senior high school, let alone a good one. Statistics for the whole of China give a rough idea of the situation: In 1996, 17.6 million children graduated from elementary school to attend regular junior high school, but only 2.8 million children went on from junior high school to regular senior high school. Instead, 15.2 million teenagers were admitted to other kinds of specialized high schools. Only 505,323 students were accepted into university on the basis of the national entrance examination—a staggeringly low figure for a country of almost 1.3 billion people.[1]

* In early 1957, intellectuals were encouraged to speak out about the failings of the Party during the Hundred Flowers campaign. However, the breadth and depth of the crtiticism shocked Mao Zedong, reinforcing his initial mistrust of the educated class, and he clamped down on them later in the year during the Anti-Rightist movement.

Above: The Shanghai government invests heavily in education; according to the deputy mayor, 25 percent of the city's budget goes to promote education and culture. In this high school, Jia Ping Middle School, situated in the Pudong Special Zone, every classroom is equipped with a television, and the school boasts a modern computer laboratory. Photo taken in 1995. (Photo: John Lee)

Right: Rural schools lack proper funding. Even in Yan'an—a name all Chinese are familiar with because it is considered the cradle of the Chinese revolution—the conditions in the schools are primitive. Mao Zedong's headquarters were situated in Yan'an in Shanxi province from 1937 to 1947. Even today, Chinese are encouraged to abide by the "spirit of Yan'an." Photo taken in village school near Yan'an in 1994. (Photo: John Lee)

Only 2 percent of the population over age twenty-five had attended tertiary level education in 1990; this contrasts with 45 percent of the population over age twenty-five in the United States in 1990.[2]

Every city has its own so-called key schools, where the quality of teaching is better than in other schools. Roughly two-thirds of the students in these key schools go to normal senior high schools and then to university. Already in the 1980s, parents had to pay substantial sums to get their children into a good school, and the practice has continued in the 1990s. Using the "back door" nowadays can require thousands of yuan. An acquaintance from my student days, an administrator working for a state petrochemical factory, managed to transfer his nine-year-old daughter to a reputable elementary school in the autumn of 1996. "The school is very popular, because the teaching methods are modern," Lu explained. "Children there are not spoon-fed phrases like 'Love the Party.' Instead, courtesy and personal responsibility are emphasized from the very first day." The entrance fee was 20,000 yuan ($2,455) and, on top of that, Lu had to pay out an additional 4,000 yuan ($490) in "back door fees." But he assured me that he was "a very happy man." His daughter was on a university track.

Sometimes it seems that there is absolutely no limit to how far people are willing to go in order to educate their child. One night during my visit to Jinan, I struck up a conversation with a female *miandi*-cab driver, who told me that she and her husband were from the countryside. She proudly described the apartment that they had recently purchased, in addition

to their three Jinan residence permits. When I heard that she and her husband had driven the taxi in two shifts round-the-clock seven days a week for the past four years, I asked her why on earth they both still slaved away twelve hours a day. She did not hesitate before answering: "So that there will be enough money for our son to study. All of this will be worth it if he gets into university."

Children of overly ambitious parents have to cope with pressure which borders on the inhumane. Some simply cannot cope. Reports about children committing suicide or running away from home are as common today as they were ten years ago. There are frequent articles in the Chinese press warning parents not to beat a child who has failed a test.

Guo Hairong and I never have any difficulties seeing eye to eye when discussing the sorry state of the Chinese educational system. Chinese leaders make grand public statements about the importance of education for the reforms and to realize the "four modernizations" program, but, in reality, the state has invested less and less in education with each passing year. Even official statistics show that the sum allocated for education has diminished in proportion to GNP; and in September 1996, the vice minister of education admitted that the proportion was one of the smallest in the world.[3]

In 1985, the money which the government allocated for education comprised 2.5 percent of the country's GNP. Five years later, it had dropped to 2.3 percent, and by 1993 to a disgraceful 1.9 percent. Even in India, which also has an enormous population problem, education was allocated 3.7 percent of GNP in 1993. (In the United States, 5.3 percent of GNP was spent on education that same year; in Finland, the figure was 8.3 percent.)[4] When I skimmed through the news bulletins of the official news agency, Xinhua, I noticed that the "grand old man of Chinese sociology," eighty-six-year-old Fei Xiaotong, in comments to a session of the Standing Committee of the National People's Congress in October 1996, had cautiously criticized the government for neglecting education. He referred to the education law which stipulates that the government's economic input in education should "rise gradually" and pointed out that, in reality, this had not occurred.[5]

"Only a man of that age can afford to be so blunt in public. He has nothing to lose. Not that it has any effect anyway," Guo Hairong retorted, dismissing my information with a wave of her hand. That is the way most Chinese react when assessing an individual's chances to influence public matters.

The government's education policy has pushed the economic burden onto the individual schools which, in turn, have had to increase tuition fees. Just ten years ago, people like engineer Song and my godchild's father, Xiao Ping, studied all the way up to their master's degree without paying a cent for their tuition. Neither of them had attended a key school, but as talented and conscientious pupils, they had always moved on to the next level, purely on the basis of their examination results. By eating the cheapest possible food in the university canteen they somehow survived on the 49 yuan ($13) monthly stipend and grain coupons which they received from the government. When they returned home, they would be lucky to get an extra 10 yuan or so from their relatives. In contrast, the female students whom I met on the train to Jinan in 1996 said that their parents had paid the China College of Politics and Law 860 yuan ($104) for one year's tuition and, in addition, about 700 yuan ($84) per year for a dormitory bed, books, electricity, security, and so on. Both girls received extra money from home to cover their food expenses because their monthly stipends lasted only through the first week of every month. To an American, an annual fee of 1,560 yuan ($188) does not seem like much, but to a Chinese it is a lot of money. Despite the rise in living standards, the average net annual income of a city person was 5,160 yuan ($629) in 1997. A person living in the countryside earned on average less than half of that, or 2,090 yuan ($252).

The decision to permit private schools and universities has only made the situation worse. These places of learning are colloquially called "aristocracy schools," because the tuition fees alone can amount to tens of thousands of yuan.

"The government is always boasting about the financial support it gives to students from poor families, but they are exceptions," Guo Hairong said. "In reality, a child's chances to make it to university no longer depend on talent and ability, as was mostly the case in the first years of the reform policy, nor on political considerations, as in Mao's time. Money is the crucial factor. Even if a child from the countryside or from a poor urban family is both intelligent and diligent, and does well on the examinations without attending a key school, the parents don't necessarily have the 1,500 yuan per year needed to fund his studies. It's a horrible system. This is how it was in old China. Even my father said the other day that it seems like everything he fought for and sacrificed his life for has been abolished. The Communists have not stuck to their principles in a single matter."

Guo Hairong was born in Nanjing in Jiangsu province. She grew up in a cultured family and remembers her early childhood as a very happy time. "I was always the best in my class. I had the highest test scores in the whole province when I was admitted to Nanjing's most distinguished middle school (junior high)," she said, when I asked her to tell me about her youth. Her parents both worked in a theater troupe which belonged to the army.

"My father even had a small role in a film which later became famous because Mao praised it. But because of his background, my father's career could never advance beyond a certain stage. You see, my parents both fought with the Guomindang troops in the war against the Japanese. Later, they moved to Nanjing and joined the Communists in the civil war. But because of their Guomindang past, they were always looked upon with a degree of suspicion and they were never permitted to become Party members. Both of them longed to join the Party. They believed that Mao was China's savior. And none of us children could become members of the Communist Youth League for this same reason. We had the wrong family background."

After coming to power, the Communists investigated every person's background and divided the population into categories: poor peasant, middle-income peasant, rich peasant, landlord, and so on. In the cities, there were dozens of different classifications. A person's political reliability, one could even say, his or her worth, was based on the classification. So-called counter-revolutionaries were thrown into jail or executed. Other "bad elements," like the relatives of Guomindang followers or former capitalists, were vulnerable each time a new political campaign was launched.

When, for example, the political campaign to discipline intellectuals began in 1957, it was decided ahead of time what percent of the population was suspected of being "rightists" and every work unit had to fulfill its quota. If not enough guilty people were found, a person with a "bad background" qualified as a suitable scapegoat, on the most whimsical of pretexts. Being labeled a capitalist not only meant that you were sent off to work in the countryside, with full knowledge that your career was doomed, it also threw a dark cloud of uncertainty over the future of your children and the rest of the family. They, too, were made to suffer.

"Actually, it was not just my parents' former Guomindang connections which were held against us. A much more aggravating factor was my uncle, who fled with Jiang Jieshi (Chiang Kai-shek) and his troops to Taiwan," Guo Hairong admitted. In other words, her father and her uncle had fought on different sides of the civil war. "Over the years, my uncle rose to a prominent position in the Guomindang Party. My father never mentioned this brother of his, not once. Later on, I discovered that my father did not even know if he was still alive. We received the first letter from him in 1991." But the Communist Party was well aware that Guo Hairong had an uncle in Taiwan. His shadow followed her when she, at age fifteen, left the city and moved to the countryside, as did millions of Chinese teenagers at the beginning of the Cultural Revolution.

"When I was seventeen, our brigade leader encouraged me to apply for membership in the Communist Youth League," she explained. "He said that I had proven myself to be an upright and trustworthy person despite my bad family background. One day, I was called into the Party office and criticized severely for having lied when filling out the application forms. Why had I not mentioned my Guomindang uncle, they demanded." Guo Hairong shook her head in disbelief, even though twenty-five years had passed since the incident. "I immediately wrote to ask my father, and he replied that I really did have a Guomindang uncle. Unbelievable, isn't it? The Party cell knew every detail about the background of one insignificant teenager all the way out in Inner Mongolia."

Though class labels were done away with during the 1980s, they still arise spontaneously in conversations. One afternoon Lao He, a pensioned factory worker who has cleaned my apartment once a week, sat on the sofa and poured out her heart as she recalled "the psychological agony" she has lived through all her life because of her bad class background. Her father was an educated man who had worked for the Guomindang regime during the 1940s. "I am just a poor worker. My biggest dream was to be accepted by the [Communist] Party. But it did not matter how often I volunteered for extra work or dirty jobs, or how hard I studied Mao Zedong Thought. I could not get rid of the shameful stain on my past. The Party members in our factory always regarded me with disdain. I was the daughter of a Guomindang bureaucrat. No one took into consideration that I was only six years of age when China was liberated."*

Mao believed in political indoctrination and the power of the mobilized masses. The revolutionary spirit of the people had to be kept kindled at all times. "The people, and the people alone, are the motive force in the making of world history," Mao said in his political report of 1945.[6] He believed that all inequality would be eradicated as long as the ideological struggle against the "three olds" (old institutions, old habits, and old beliefs) was continued with utmost zeal. Anything that remotely resembled Western thought or capitalism was to be condemned. Political study

* The founding of the People's Republic in 1949 is still referred to as "Liberation."

sessions were held everywhere, and each person had to probe his or her own soul and make self-criticisms about any heretical thoughts. The nation was kept in a perpetual state of fear of a military attack from all sides. At one point it was the Soviet Union, the next moment the United States. People were told to be constantly on the lookout for counter-revolutionary elements and disguised enemy agents, who were only waiting for their chance to sabotage the Communist revolution.

Even ordinary factory workers, who did not suffer significantly from political persecution, recall that life was an endless stream of consecutive political campaigns. I could not help smiling when *Laolao*, the grandmother in my godchild's family, was once telling me about her sister's wedding in the 1950s and suddenly stopped in the middle of the story. Half-muttering to herself she said, "Now I wonder who we were struggling against that year. Was it the counter-revolutionaries or the rightists? I can't remember, but in any case, the wedding took place in the midst of one of those campaigns."

Surveillance penetrated every facet of life. The Party kept strict control over the media. "You could develop into a noble citizen only by trusting the Party and by obeying orders from above," Guo Hairong said. "If you were not of the same opinion as the Party, it meant that you were against it and you would be branded a counterrevolutionary." In her book *Wild Swans*, Jung Chang writes: "Many people had been reduced to a state where they did not dare even to think in case their thoughts came out involuntarily."[7] On the other hand, Jung Chang's attempt to explain the loyalty of Party members strikes me as tame: "In China, one was accustomed to a certain amount of injustice. Now, at least, it was for a worthy cause," she writes of her mother who was trying to persuade herself that she should not resent the Party's methods.

Mao, the extremist, wanted quick solutions. He urged the masses to try harder, to strive ever more vigorously to achieve greater accomplishments. Mao became a god-like figure, comparable only to the Emperor. His personality cult reached such absurd proportions that people did not dare throw out old newspapers which carried his photograph.

In 1981, the Communist Party decreed that the Great Proletarian Cultural Revolution, which had lasted from May 1966 to October 1976, was "responsible for the most severe setbacks and the heaviest losses suffered by the Party, the state and the people since the founding of the People's Republic."[8] In fact, a far greater number of people had already perished because of the large-scale campaign launched by Mao in 1958. Known as the Great Leap Forward, this movement aimed to raise productivity in both agriculture and industry to completely unrealistic levels, and led to an economic disaster: Between 20 and 43 million people are estimated to have starved to death in the years 1959 to 1962, a horror described by historians as "the worst man-made famine in history."[9]

"In the cities, food was scarce and there was severe rationing. But, according to my parents, people had no idea how alarming the situation was in the countryside," Guo Hairong said. Urban dwellers still received ration coupons and the newspapers continued to publish ecstatic articles about record grain harvests and glorious feats achieved in industry. Revolutionary cadres did not dare to report the true situation. Instead, they sent reports with inflated statistics to their superiors.

The harrowing truth was unraveled two decades later when demograghic data became available and specialists started to piece together the horrid truth. Details of the consequences of the Great Leap Forward are still not discussed in public in China.[10] They are only referred to by catch phrases such as "the three years of natural disaster" or "the three difficult years." A thorough analysis would undermine the authority of the Communist Party, which is, after all, still in power. There has also been no public disclosure of the cannibalism which took place then and in the decade which followed. British journalists Jasper Becker and John Gittings have both probed the subject in their books, published in 1996, as has the Chinese writer, Zheng Yi, in the more detailed *Scarlet Memorial: Tales of Cannibalism in Modern China*. Reading Zheng Yi's book is a shocking experience. The flesh of "class enemies" was devoured in the Guangxi Autonomous Region during the Cultural Revolution. Thousands of people were randomly slaughtered.

After the Great Leap Forward, Mao refused to admit his mistakes and drifted even further from the other top Party leaders. But he knew that he still had the unwavering and blind support of the people. The Cultural Revolution was, in fact, Mao's attempt to suppress his own political opponents under the guise of ideological purity. As historian Paul Johnson has noted, there was later some misunderstanding about the Cultural Revolution. It was portrayed as a revolution of intellectuals. In fact it was quite the reverse. It was a revolution of illiterates and semi-illiterates against the intellectuals. It was led by ferocious young Red Guards, whom Mao had encouraged to rise up and rebel. Johnson describes it as the "greatest witchhunt in history."[11] Chinese dissident writer Liu Binyan, who was well known by many of his fellow countrymen in the early 1980s for his investigative reporting, maintains that "the absurdity in Mao's ideology was pushed to such an extreme that chaos resulted. Both Mao's authority and leadership went bankrupt. The idealistic illusions he had thrust upon the Chinese people turned into nihilism and cynicism."[12]

Unlike a war, there was no clear-cut strategy or even a specifically defined enemy. China was turned upside down.

No written analysis of the Cultural Revolution has impressed me as deeply as hearing the personal experiences of a few close friends. It is impossible to grasp fully the sort of repercussions the insanity of the Cultural Revolution has had on the human psyche. Occasionally, I meet someone whose whole being exudes nervousness and fear. Slowly it comes out that he or she suffered at the hands of frenzied Red Guards.

I still find it hard to fathom how my godchild's father, Xiao Ping, and his elder brother, *Gege*, grew up into such exceptionally well-mannered and considerate adults—they spent the greater part of their childhood and youth alone at home without adult guidance. Their father, a low-level ministry cadre, was seriously injured in an accident while working at forced labor in the countryside. Xiao Ping was seven and *Gege* thirteen when their partially paralyzed father was sent back to Beijing. For the next four years, the boys went to the hospital every day to wash and feed him.

"He had been branded a 'stinking capitalist roader.' Such people did not receive any care. Month after month we watched helplessly as his pain grew worse and his condition deteriorated," said Xiao Ping, the only time he has spoken about his father's ordeal. In 1976, his father was deemed "a hopeless case" and sent home, where he died two years later. "It's quite possible that Father would still be alive today if the doctors had tried in earnest to cure him. You see, Father was a man of will." Even as an adult, Xiao Ping becomes a bit nauseous when confronted with a hospital environment. When Tongtong was born and we went to the hospital to see her, I saw his face turn dead white as we stepped into the ward.

Xiao Ping and *Gege*'s mother was also ill during the Cultural Revolution. I knew that she had died at the age of forty-four, only nine months after the death of her husband, but after I learned about his fate I never dared to ask about the details surrounding her death. Years after I got to know the family, the subject came up by chance when *Gege*, his wife *Saozi*, and I were discussing the effect mental well-being has on a person's physical health. "My mother's nerves simply could not stand the continuous criticism sessions, and she broke down mentally. Of course she was also worried sick about my father. One day her kidneys gave out. Though the official cause of death was a physical illness, I would say

Mother actually died of a nervous breakdown," *Gege* said. Upon hearing this, *Saozi* immediately added, "That's exactly what they said about my father, too."

I looked at *Saozi* in bewilderment.

"My father was beaten to death on the sixth day of the Cultural Revolution," *Saozi* went on. "He was the leading doctor in one of Beijing's main hospitals, where the Red Guards were especially violent from the very first day. The official cause of his death was a heart attack. According to my mother, that might even be true. My father lost his mind and went into shock when the Red Guards tortured him. It is possible that his heart simply stopped."

I had no idea that *Saozi*'s childhood had also been marred by tragedy. She had once sarcastically remarked that, in contrast to her husband's parents (who were intellectuals), her parents had the best possible class background—in other words, they were both from poor working class families. At the time I had thought her comment quite tactless considering what had happened to her husband's parents. It is true that *Saozi*'s father was never mentioned in my godchild's family, but I always thought it was because her mother, *Laolao*, had remarried. I had presumed that everyone was being considerate to her, though I knew that *Saozi* did not get on too well with her stepfather. He never came to visit the family with *Laolao*, who, before the family hired a maid, sometimes spent days on end in their home caring for her grandchild.

"I always took it for granted that Xiao Ping had told you about my father," *Saozi* said. "I suppose he is such a sensitive soul that he still can't talk about those days." All of a sudden, I understood *Saozi* a lot better. There is a bit of a hard streak in her and at times I have found her a bit callous, even heartless. She was six years old when she lost her father. For the next ten years, she had to bear the stigma of being "a counter-revolutionary brat."

"But you must have heard us saying that no one, regardless of class background, was spared after Mao ordered the Red Guards to destroy the four old elements in society and to turn against authority," *Saozi* said.

I nodded. I had heard those words, but I had not understood that she had been referring to her own father.

"My father was the son of a poor rickshaw driver. He studied hard and became a doctor; then he went to fight in the Korean War. You couldn't find a more loyal and exemplary young Communist."

"But because of the Cultural Revolution, he was killed just the same as my father, the intellectual," *Gege* added.

In China, a thorough assessment has not been made of the Cultural Revolution either. I remember how amazed a history lecturer at Beijing University was when he heard that at Harvard University, young Americans majoring in modern Chinese history take a whole course about the Cultural Revolution.[13] "We are Chinese, but the years 1966 to 1976 are touched upon only in passing," he said.

Though the Cultural Revolution is officially referred to as "the ten years of suffering," and hundreds of articles and books depicting individual plights were published in China after Mao's death, the tyrant Mao is too sensitive a topic for the Communist Party. Deng is said to have understood that the people's cries of distress had to be given an outlet, and that is why he permitted the so-called "scar literature" to be published. (Deng also used the bitterness ordinary people harbored toward the leaders in power during the Cultural Revolution to strengthen his own position.)

In 1986, a year that intellectuals look back upon as the golden year of the 1980s, some leading academics and scholars gingerly debated questions of guilt and responsibility. But the Party has not tolerated an outright repudiation nor has it permitted public analysis of Mao's real intentions when he launched the Cultural Revolution.[14] An all-out assault on Mao would undermine the fundamental power structure in China. "China does not have a Khrushchev who could strip Mao of his heavenly cloak," my girlfriend Guo Hairong once remarked.

In the West, Mao's period has been interpreted in numerous ways. During the Cold War, leftists in many Western countries venerated Mao and turned a blind eye to his atrocities. Reliable information was scarce at the time. Even widely respected Western sinologists, who had personal ties to individual Chinese and to China in general, wanted to see things in the most advantageous possible light. Some later admitted to having worn blinders for too long. In his last book, John K. Fairbank describes his own views, as expressed in an October 1972 article in *Foreign Affairs,* as "an outstanding example of sentimental sinophilia." He had written "that in a certain context the Maoist revolution was 'the best thing' that had happened to the Chinese people in many centuries."[15]

The Cultural Revolution is remembered in millions of Chinese homes as a period of terror, torture, and political persecution.[16] Millions of urban Chinese were forced to move to the countryside for years or—in some cases—for the rest of their lives. This era is still talked about and referred to in everyday conversation as the period when part of China's cultural heritage was destroyed forever. The Chinese Communist Party to this day has not recovered from the loss of prestige and authority it suffered during the last ten years of Mao's life. A decade is a short time in China's history, but the upheaval was, to quote Harvard professor Roderick MacFarquhar, "indeed the Communist Party's 'most severe setback' since 1949—and the beginning of its demise, brought about ultimately by Mao, the man who led the party to power."[17] The Cultural Revolution still casts a cloud on China's present and will darken its destiny well into the next century.

It is impossible to use reason or logic to understand Mao Zedong's personality cult. According to Fairbank, "an outsider's understanding of Mao requires a feat of imagination." Because authority in China traditionally came from the top down, the leader of the Communist Party became "sacrosanct, above all the rest of mankind."[18]

To my knowledge, no book about the Cultural Revolution—whether by a former Red Guard, who describes his or her cruel behavior or by a victim, who tells of his or her inhuman fate—has been able fully to answer the following questions: What made people become monsters? What made children turn against their parents? Hundreds of thousands of people were murdered in the name of Mao and the Cultural Revolution. Certainly, part of the answer lies in mass hysteria, as well as in the fear that if you did not attack the class enemy mercilessly you would yourself become a victim.

In his book *The Search for Modern China*, Yale professor Jonathan D. Spence notes that "the rage of the young Red Guards against their elders suggests the depths of frustration that lay at the heart of Chinese society." For years, Chinese youth had been told to sacrifice themselves for the revolution and adhere to absolute obedience to the state. Overnight their idol, Mao Zedong, gave them the green light to turn against their parents, their teachers, and the Party bureaucrats. "To rebel is justified," was one of the leading slogans of the day. Spence points out that the political system bred fear and compliance.[19] People lived under strict surveillance in tightly knit surroundings where the word of one's superiors was law. Grudges abounded. Undoubtedly, the brutal measures of the totalitarian state and the complete control which the state exercised over the media were contributing factors.

Of course, it is important to remember that there were stoical Communists who, despite the risks, opposed the violence and tried to appeal to Mao, either in person or in writing. Many paid for this courage with their lives. There are hundreds of memos and documents, many available in English, which bear testimony to unrelenting leaders attempting to talk sense into their torturers.[20]

"The Cultural Revolution is the shameful stain of the Chinese Communist Party," the former deputy editor of *Renmin ribao* (People's Daily), Wang Ruoshui, said when we met in December 1996. "If the Guomindang or the Japanese had caused the Cultural Revolution, the Communists would have declared, 'Never forget your past,' and we all would be studying every detail of that frightful decade. But the Cultural Revolution was the Party's own crime. The Party is guilty and that is why it would like to see the people simply forget that whole period. This year was the thirtieth anniversary of the start of the Cultural Revolution, but the Party forbade the media to focus on it."

I looked up the seventy-year-old Wang Ruoshui on the advice of many older intellectuals. "He is one of the few people who still is a genuine Marxist," I was told. In 1986, he took part in the public debate that demanded the Cultural Revolution be thoroughly assessed. Like many other intellectuals of his generation, he felt that it was a necessity so that people could learn from the fateful mistakes of the past. He not only criticized the Party for failing to prevent the Cultural Revolution, but he also directed his words at the people who did not have the strength to fend off the catastrophe.[21]

Wang Ruoshui was convalescing when I finally met him. He had recently been operated on and treated for lung cancer. Though he was physically weak, his mind was as sharp as a razor, and he spoke in a clear voice. A slightly built man with bright piercing eyes, he had taken part in the activities of left-wing organizations as a student of philosophy at Beijing University in the 1940s. For the following three decades, he was a fervent supporter of Mao. He said that at the beginning of the Cultural Revolution he was "very enthusiastic about the new democratic mass movement." At the time, he was working in the theory department of the People's Daily, the mouthpiece of the Communist Party, and was responsible for overseeing the paper's editorials, a politically charged job to say the least. But when in 1972 he wrote a letter to Mao conveying his support for the moderate Prime Minister Zhou Enlai, he suffered the wrath of the so-called radical Gang of Four, led by Mao's wife, and was sent to work in the countryside for three years.

"Mao was a great Machiavellian," Wang Ruoshui said. "But he succeeded in deceiving many people. He caused immense suffering and widespread disaster to our country, but he still commands the respect of the majority of ordinary people. And the Party does not dare attack him head-on. He is the symbol of the People's Republic. He is the symbol of the Chinese Communist Party. He is the symbol of our revolution."

Wang's stance that the "leaders of even a socialist country do not necessarily conform with the people's interests" caused him in 1983 to lose his job as deputy editor-in-chief, the post he had been promoted to after his rehabilitation in the aftermath of the Cultural Revolution. The notion that "the Party is the country," which drew on the traditional concept of unity, was (and still is) the only acceptable dogma despite the more relaxed atmosphere after Deng Xiaoping's rise to power.[22]

When I asked Wang if he still believes in communism, he paused for the first time during our discussion. "I don't think I'm a Communist any longer, I'm a democratic Marxist," he answered after thinking a while. "I still have great respect for the doctrine of Marxist humanity. In that sense I am a Marxist, but in other ways I am not."

I wanted to hear Wang Ruoshui's views about the revival of the Mao cult which had gained strength in the run-up to the 100-year anniversary of Mao's birth in December 1993. Though it was already waning, people still spoke of Mao as a saint. On numerous occasions I have received the same answer when I persisted in speaking of Mao's responsibility for the chaos of the Cultural Revolution: "You can't blame Mao alone for the Cultural Revolution. The real culprits are people like his wife, Jiang Qing, and the Gang of Four, who acted in the name of Mao." People often refer to an ancient saying which implies that the holy Buddhist scriptures are not at fault, but rather the monks who interpret them. Many say that "Mao was too old to understand what was going on," and that "Mao was kept in the dark." It's evident that the Party has been successful in instilling its message.

It is easier to understand Mao's continuing appeal in the countryside, since tens of thousands of villages escaped the violence. It is the Mao cult among urbanites that I have found most baffling despite the fact that it undoubtedly is symptomatic of the deep dissatisfaction with today's society. "The nostalgia is understandable," Wang Ruoshui said. "Mao penetrated into people's souls. They are enchanted by him. He bewitched them. All their memories from their youth are associated with Mao and with the songs which they sang in his praise.[23] Mao is part of the people's subconscious. Already, at a young age, they lost the ability to think independently. That is our nation's weakness—people know how to criticize, but they do not know how to think."

Mao Zedong is revered as a saint by hundreds of millions of Chinese. Every tourist arriving in Beijing for the first time wants a photo taken in front of Mao's portrait at Tiananmen Square, preferably together with a People's Liberation Army soldier. According to Wang Ruoshui, such Mao nostalgia is understandable: "Mao penetrated into people's souls. He bewitched them." (Photo: John Lee, 1996)

Guo Hairong is an intelligent, forty-five-year-old who, in every sense of the word, fits the description of "an independent-minded" woman. But even she has told me that she had loved Mao and believed in everything he said.

"I was delirious with happiness when I was given permission to join my comrades, despite my parents' bad class background, and heed Mao's call to go to the countryside to spread the word of the revolution. According to Mao, the intellectuals were to learn from the peasants, and it never occurred to me to question any of his thoughts," Hairong said. She reminded me, as she has on many occasions, that the first years of the Cultural Revolution were a wonderful period in her life. She is not the only one who feels that way; nostalgia for the Cultural Revolution has experienced a renaissance of sorts among various groups during the 1990s. I have found it quite perplexing, though my instincts tell me that it is—like the Mao cult—a sign of the ideological void as much as a reflection of the uncertainty induced by the rapid transformation of society.

About twelve million youth were sent down to the countryside during the Cultural Revolution.[24] Now, at middle age, they wistfully reminisce about the solidarity and innocence of their younger days. "The nostalgia has nothing to do with the monstrosities of that decade," Guo Hairong said quite vehemently, when I accompanied her and her two sisters to a "Cultural Revolutionary restaurant." These ascetic restaurants, which are decorated with imaginative Mao memorabilia, have become popular in a few big cities. "Many of the so-called lost generation feel as I do. It makes us cringe to see the extent to which materialism is revered today. Sacrificing oneself for the good of a noble cause is an unknown phenomenon among the youth of the 1990s. Simplicity and purity are alien values. It's very sad. Everyone remembers the Cultural Revolution from his or her own perspective."

Guo Hairong spent fifteen years in Inner Mongolia. "I was a naive fifteen-year-old little girl when I left the city in 1967, and a cynical, tough-skinned grown-up woman when I returned in 1982. I worked with the Mongolian herders on the steppes for nine whole years. We were far away, truly far away. When we left Nanjing by train it took us more than a day to get to Baotou. From there we traveled three hours by bus to a country town where we boarded trucks and drove another five hours to our brigade headquarters. We had to walk the last twenty kilometers." In spite of the harsh conditions, Guo Hairong said she enjoyed her life among the herders. "They were very friendly to us city kids and there was plenty of food. Every day we ate mutton or beef in addition to the grain rations provided by the state. We had butter and cheese, too. But what I remember most is how excited we were about our mission. Every morning we faced toward the East and recited Mao Zedong's sayings. In the evenings, we studied Marx or Engels and discussed Mao Zedong Thought. We did not fantasize about romance. We knew nothing about sex. We believed in the revolution with all our hearts and we were overjoyed that we were allowed to be a part of it."

We were sitting at a table in the "Black Earth" restaurant in Beijing under a huge portrait of Mao. "Serve the People!" was splashed in big red characters on the opposite wall. It felt somewhat reassuring to notice that Guo Hairong's two sisters listened to her muse about her youth with the same look of disbelief that I was doing

Parents still often dress their children in army fatigues, even though it became less common in Beijing after the bloody suppression following the 1989 Tiananmen demonstrations. Photo from a village school near Yan'an in 1994. (Photo: John Lee)

Guo Hairong as a teenager in Inner Mongolia during the Cultural Revolution. (Photos: Guo Hairong's album)

my best to conceal. Their own experiences had been so very different. They had been sent to separate villages in their home province of Jiangsu. Hairong's eldest sister was raped by the village chief's brother one month after she arrived. Afterward she was allowed to return to Nanjing. "As far as I know, the whole matter was covered up and that man was never punished. My mother today still does not know what happened," the eldest sister said quietly. At the time, her parents were both in the countryside themselves, in a so-called cadre school where, in addition to doing manual labor, they were forced to study Mao Zedong Thought.

"In my village, the peasants had a hostile attitude toward us city kids from the very first moment," Guo Hairong's second sister recalled. "It was not surprising really. We were a burden to them and they had to feed us. We scraped by somehow, but I still remember that gnawing feeling of constant hunger that never disappeared. But in a way the mental torment was even more difficult to cope with. I lay in bed at night wondering how our revolution could be so wonderful if just eighty miles from Nanjing, people did not have enough to eat. We urban Chinese knew nothing about rural conditions. Gradually I realized that our entire lives had been based on a huge lie. The poor peasants were not the least bit interested in our revolution. Of course I dared not utter my thoughts out loud, but I wrote to a friend of Father's and asked him to help me. Finally, after spending four years in the village, I was transferred to a factory in a small city."

Guo Hairong said it took years before her eyes were opened, not until 1972, when she read in the newspaper that Lin Biao had died while attempting to escape to the Soviet Union.* Many people have told me that this episode was a psychological watershed. "I was shocked," Hairong said. "Lin Biao was Mao's closest comrade-in-arms. Now we were told that

* Lin Biao died in 1971, but his death was not made public until 1972.

he was a traitor who had tried to grab power. I started to suspect that the whole Cultural Revolution had been the result of a power struggle. We were the victims of dirty politics. We city kids discussed this among ourselves. We all had similar backgrounds—we were from educated families. We became lifelong friends in Inner Mongolia. Each year, when one of us received permission to go home for a visit, he or she would bring back news and share it with the rest of us. I had completely lost my faith in Mao by 1976. When I heard the news of his death, I felt terribly empty, but I shed no tears."

The same year that Mao died, Guo Hairong bid farewell to her life as a herder. At the age of twenty-four, she was at last given a chance to study at a teacher's institute in a small city in Inner Mongolia. Upon graduation she was assigned the job of mathematics teacher at the county middle school. There she met her future husband, also a sent-down youth. After numerous attempts, they managed to be transferred in 1982 to her husband's hometown of Jinan. "I spent all my spare time reading during those years. A colleague of mine had a relative in quite a high position in the Party's city branch. He had access to many books which were labeled 'for limited distribution only'. The more I read foreign literature, the more disillusioned and bitter I became. It was a very painful process. Everything that I had believed in was an illusion. I realized that for thirty years the Chinese people had toiled for nothing."

The Cultural Revolution was a turning point for Guo Hairong's generation. For the next generation, the events in the spring of 1989 were similarly epochal. The Cultural Revolution and the Tiananmen demonstrations of 1989 are not comparable. The former stretched over a period of ten years and was launched from above, on orders of the country's paramount leader. It became a violent movement because Mao himself specifically emphasized that no means were out of bounds in pursuing the revolution's ideological goals. The more recent incident in 1989 lasted a mere six weeks and started spontaneously. The Tiananmen demonstrations of 1989 began as student protests which later turned into a broader movement, involving city residents from all walks of life, and it was nonviolent in nature. But the Tiananmen events cannot be fully understood without taking into account the Cultural Revolution because it was during that decade that the Communist Party began to lose its grip on power. In 1989, the Party once again undermined its own position of authority and embittered a portion of the population. As Guo Hairong put it: "One more generation joined the ranks of those who have lost faith."

The "Goddess of Democracy"—reminiscent of the Statue of Liberty—was designed and built by art students, and unveiled in Tiananmen Square on May 24, 1989. Though it was crushed by army tanks in the early hours of June 4, the statue is still remembered as a symbol of the Beijing spring of 1989. (Photo: Marja Sarvimäki)

Tiananmen's Spark of Hope

Chinese Journalists Stoking the Fire

On May 18, 1989, I was about to set out for Tiananmen Square with a few friends. As always during that spring, the television was on. Suddenly a special news broadcast interrupted the regular program. Party Secretary Zhao Ziyang, Prime Minister Li Peng, and several other "leading comrades" appeared on the screen, entering a hospital in Beijing. Besides Zhao Ziyang and Li Peng, I recognized Politburo Standing Committee member, Qiao Shi, who was said to be in charge of state security, and propaganda chief Hu Qili.

China's highest leaders were visiting hospitalized students, who had fainted as a result of their hunger strike at Tiananmen Square, the broadcaster informed viewers. About two hundred students were now in the fifth day of a hunger strike and hundreds of thousands of other students were camping out in Tiananmen Square to show their support.

After a close-up of the Party secretary and prime minister hovering over several patient-demonstrators, the camera jumped to Hu Qili and other leaders talking to a young man, clad in striped pajamas. "We must re-establish the Party's prestige among the people," said the hunger-striker. "If the Communist Party has hope, China will have hope. Right now, some people think the country has no hope. The Communist Party has no hope."

My friends grinned and cheered upon hearing the student's comments. The atmosphere in the room was electric, as it had been throughout Beijing for weeks. The mood in the capital was exuberant, as if the whole city were high on hope. People believed that the students' actions were justified.

The young man in pajamas continued his sermon to Hu Qili: "Therefore, I think that, as in the United States, we should restore the people's confidence that the state can do a good job. Do you agree?"

Hu Qili and the other leaders nodded and said: "We fully agree with you."[1]

This broadcast is among the handful of powerful images from that incredible spring of 1989 that remain vivid in my mind. A month earlier, no one could have imagined such a scene on state-run television. What did hundreds of millions of Chinese viewers think when they heard a twenty-year-old student tell the country's leaders that "the Communist Party has no hope?" For forty years there had been no hope in China except the Communist Party, at least according to every officially sanctioned media report.

Astonishing events had begun appearing on Chinese television on April 30, when the government allowed student representatives to meet with the mayor of Beijing in a televised session, as the students had demanded. I had watched in utter disbelief as the students badgered the mayor to reveal his income. They challenged him about the problems in the education system. Never in the history of the People's Republic had a government official in power been humiliated in such a way by "ordinary people" before millions of television viewers.

My friends accompanying me to Tiananmen Square had a copy of that day's *Renmin ribao* (People's Daily), the official mouthpiece of the Communist Party—the *Pravda* of China. Details of Soviet leader Mikhail Gorbachev's much-awaited historical visit had been pushed down to the bottom corner of the front page, while coverage of the hunger strike and demonstrations—six page-one articles with photographs—dominated the top. "Save the Students, Save the Children," pleaded one headline.

"Imagine the impact this front page will have," my thirty-five-year-old journalist friend Li said excitedly. He waved a copy of the People's Daily at me when we met later that afternoon at Tiananmen Square. "It's like a bomb. We journalists are making history!" Li's hair shot out in all directions. He looked even skinnier than usual, as if he had hardly slept or eaten for weeks. But like so many people during those days, he was brimming over with a vitality which required neither food nor sleep.

Many outside observers compared the mood at Tiananmen Square to a carnival, and so it was. People gleefully released their feelings of emancipation like puppies unleashed from their chains. But behind the scenes serious-minded people, bent on pushing for political reform, labored 'round-the-clock to achieve their goals.

Reporter Li worked for a national newspaper, *Keji ribao* (Science and Technology Daily), which, despite its name, soared to prominence for its political coverage in the spring of 1989. It was the first newspaper to publish a summary of the student demands, as well as a factual account of the student demonstration of April 18, a march that proved to be the start of the movement.

"Now other journalists can point to our editor-in-chief when they try to persuade their own bosses," Li told me, the day the student demands appeared in his paper. "You'll see. The others will follow suit. The dams will break." He was right. The students' epoch-making march of April 27 was covered by all major Chinese media organizations. Even the official news agency, Xinhua, which enjoys ministerial status in the Chinese bureaucracy, broke its silence to report that tens of thousands of students had marched in Beijing, "carrying streamers and shouting slogans." That was the Chinese media's first flirtation with press freedom. Unfortunately, no serious relationship ever developed.

Western observers labeled the Tiananmen Square demonstrations an extraordinary event in Chinese history, because they took place in full view of the international media. In the United States, they were nicknamed "the first TV-revolution." It was true. CNN had drastically changed news coverage around the globe. The events in Beijing caught the attention of millions of people worldwide because so many foreign journalists and television crews happened to be in Beijing to cover the "meeting of the decade" between Deng Xiaoping and Mikhail Gorbachev. In the end, Gorbachev's visit became a secondary story. Public opinion abroad was especially strong after the massacre because the Chinese students had won the sympathy of millions. Day after day, images of young men and women standing up for "democracy" and "freedom" beamed into American and European living rooms.

However, the role and impact of the Chinese media during the Beijing spring of 1989 have received little attention in the West. The Chinese press was able, briefly, to report with relative truthfulness on an anti-government protest. This short-lived media freedom helped to turn the student protest into a more widespread citizens' movement. Television viewers all over China watched the same footage of hunger-striking protesters and idealistic youngsters appealing to their government that television audiences saw in the West. This was unprecedented.

By 1989, most Chinese knew that their newspapers did not necessarily print the truth. Media conveyed only "the official Party line." Since the founding of the People's Republic, news coverage was not intended to open minds, but to shape them. Readers trusted the People's Daily to tell them not what was real, but what was "permissible." When the state-run media reported on the students' demands at the end of April, it seemed to signify that the students had the blessing of someone in the top leadership. And because it became apparent that the country's highest leaders were divided about how to react to the student movement, ordinary Chinese imagined that they could influence the outcome by demonstrating their support for the students.

Of course, residents of Beijing had reason enough to vent their own frustrations. Student demands that inflation and corruption be curbed struck a responsive chord. But the citizens' actions would hardly have grown to such proportions had the media coverage not been openly encouraging it. When the newspapers and television started to report on the student protesters, without branding them troublemakers, the protests appeared to be officially sanctioned. As the political scientist Yang Yulin noted, "It was like giving people the green light, showing them that it was as good as permissible, certainly not risky, to support the students."

Thanks to the Chinese journalists' steadfast efforts to publish and broadcast their stories, word of the student demonstrations spread quickly. During the first three weeks in May, articles about the events in Beijing and demonstrations elsewhere in support of the students were published throughout China. According to the Chinese government, protests were held in a total of 84 cities.[2]

The presence of foreign journalists obviously did have some effect on the actions and self-confidence of the Chinese students. The students presumed that international media attention would make the Chinese leadership hesitant to use force to curb the demonstrations. Also, thanks to Voice of America and BBC Chinese-language radio broadcasts, news of the first student protests reached millions of Chinese in cities beyond Beijing. In early May, the Chinese were all the more delighted when they noticed that their own media organizations were reporting the same news. Nevertheless, Westerners are sometimes inclined to overestimate their own influence in China. A lengthy report funded by the Ford Foundation and published by Harvard University in 1991, examining the role of American journalists during the Tiananmen events, provides a detailed example of this tendency. The foreign journalists' overall impact was not comparable to that of the Chinese journalists.

In the spring of 1990, I was a fellow at the Shorenstein Center on Press, Politics, and Public Policy at Harvard's Kennedy School, which conducted the research project on the American media's role during the Tiananmen events. At the first meeting, I suggested the project also focus on the key role the Chinese media played in the crisis. My proposal received scant support and, as a result, I wrote a separate paper on the subject.

Though no research on the role of Chinese journalists in 1989 had yet been done, various U.S.-based academics, analyzing the events of the Beijing Spring of '89 from their own disciplines, backed my views. "The Chinese media mobilized the man on the street," political scientist Yang Yulin agreed. Yang, a research fellow at the Fairbank Center at Harvard, had worked in one of Party Secretary Zhao Ziyang's think tanks before the massacre.

American professor of sociology at Harvard Universty at the time, Andrew Walder, a China specialist, asserted: "The Chinese journalists were absolutely essential in stoking the fire. Their reportage helped to magnify public sympathy and involvement, and for a pivotal period, made it appear that the demonstrations might succeed in toppling the hardline leadership."

Student leader Li Lu, whose official title during the protests was "deputy commander of the hunger strike committee," told me: "The impact of the Chinese media was extremely important. It brought the movement onto a national scale." Li Lu was one of the many student leaders who fled to the United States after June 4, 1989.

The Chinese journalists' impact on the Tiananmen events was twofold—as reporters and as participants. On May 4, the journalists were the first nonstudent group to join the demonstrations with their own set of demands.

"We are thoroughly ashamed of the restrictions that we are forced to accept in our work. Now is the time to push for a new press law," reporter Li explained, when he phoned the day before the march to tell me of his decision to participate. "My father is furious. He has begged me to consider my future and that of my daughter. He is certain I will end up in prison. 'Don't compare yourself to the students,' he keeps telling me. 'They are in a class of their own. They are allowed to be pure, they can stick their necks out; that's the way it has been in China for hundreds of years.'"

Li's professor-father was referring to one of the special roles of students in Chinese society. Students have traditionally been a distinct group—on the one hand, they are looked upon as "children" who sometimes do not know better; on the other hand, they are also privileged members of the community who can claim a right to idealistic views.

"But I am a child of Mao who was taught that it is right to rebel," Li exclaimed jokingly, referring to his generation brought up during the Cultural Revolution. He quoted one of Mao's famous poems, "Swimming":

"I don't care how the winds blow and waves strike.
This is better than strolling in a courtyard."[3]

For all of Li's playfulness, I could sense that he was nervous. Only a week had passed since the People's Daily had published a harsh editorial (April 26) condemning the students' activities as a conspiracy against the socialist state and as an attempt to create "national turmoil." It was widely known that the editorial had been written according to explicit instructions of Deng Xiaoping himself. The word "turmoil" has explosive connotations in the Chinese context. To be accused of stirring up chaos is an offense punishable by death. Li's father had every right to be worried.

We all knew that the government's worst nightmare was a scenario in which the student movement would spread to the ranks of the working class. The next step would be a Chinese version of Polish "Solidarity." The day after the editorial (April 27), over 150,000 students defied the authorities in an unparalleled show of civil disobedience. Their ten-hour march from Beijing's university district to Tiananmen Square was historic. To counteract the editorial's accusations and to emphasize their loyalty to the Party, the students had carried banners proclaiming "Support the Communist Party!"

On May 4, Li and about two hundred other journalists joined the long stream of demonstrators as a distinctly separate group. Once again, the march was reported by the media. Once again, the awaited crackdown did not materialize. Five days later (May 9), a media delegation delivered to the government a petition demanding a dialogue to discuss press reform. It was signed by 1,013 journalists.

The journalists' boldness served as a catalyst. Other intellectuals felt inspired and encouraged that responsible adults, who also had families to support—people any educated city-dweller could relate to—had summoned enough courage to speak out about their frustrations. One by one, determined individuals representing other intellectual groups started to come forward and openly express support for the students' request to have a dialogue with the government. This was the students' primary demand. But from the point of view of the totalitarian government, negotiations with an illegally branded student organization were unthinkable.

The actions of the Chinese journalists in the spring of 1989 were the result of a long process. Soon after the reform policy was launched at the end of the 1970s, intellectuals started to speak out gingerly in defense of a more open press and public discourse. Simultaneously, a loosening of control was taking place in all areas of society. Theater directors were testing the limits, as were painters and poets. The Chinese were tasting *glasnost* well before Mikhail Gorbachev made the expression famous in the Soviet Union in 1985.

In 1977, Deng Xiaoping chose sixty-one-year-old Hu Jiwei to be editor-in-chief of the People's Daily, the flagship of the Communist Party. Hu Jiwei was not only a loyal Communist Party member, but an intellectual and devoted patriot. Traditionally, intellectuals in China have acted as intermediaries between the ruler and the ruled. They were expected to inform the Emperor of the needs and moods of the people, and were encouraged to put forward suggestions. In a system which lacks checks and balances this was a significant task, but also a delicate and risky one. Because Confucianism stressed the importance of harmony, a true political opposition, in a Western sense, has never taken root in Chinese society. Rebelling goes against the grain of Chinese tradition. Loyalty was paramount. Opposing the Emperor was equivalent to defying God.

"We intellectuals feel that we are the conscience of the nation," Li's professor-father once remarked. "We bear the burden of the country's fate on our shoulders. Foreigners don't really understand our dilemma. They feel we worry ourselves sick, but don't act. But we are born with the conviction that it is better to work from inside the system. If you are cast outside the establishment, you are powerless." Before the bloody suppression of the protest movement in June 1989, the overwhelming majority of intellectuals felt that they should collaborate with the government and not oppose it.

Even the students' cry for "democracy," held aloft on their banners, was directed at Communist Party reform. The students were not calling for a multi-party system as many in the West envisioned, but only for the democratization of the Party. The vast majority of the demonstrators had little real understanding of the meaning of "democracy." Though press freedom was one of their demands from the start, their definition of that concept was hazy, too. Like the intellectual community, the students hoped the Party would reform itself from within. It was only at the end of the protest movement that the most radical factions of the demonstrators advocated overthrowing the Party altogether.

Like so many intellectuals in leading positions, editor-in-chief Hu Jiwei had to come to terms with the endless tug-of-war going on in his soul. Should the People's Daily blindly follow the Party, or should it represent the voices of the people? On the whole, it opted for the latter course, and the paper's reporters were permitted to probe and write about abuses of power. Hu Jiwei is considered the Father of Chinese Investigative Journalism, though another man, Liu Binyan, is better known as the author of the most provocative articles.* But without Hu Jiwei, the work of Liu Binyan and others would never have been published. One article led to the resignation of the minister of petroleum, another described a senior official's wining and dining at public expense, and a third revealed that the "model people's commune" of Dazhai was anything but a model. These all might seem like tame subjects to an American, but it is worth remembering that after Mao lashed out at intellectuals in 1957, the media had ceased to function as a forum for differing opinions. Like my fellow passenger on the train had noted: "There was only one view on any given issue, and that was Mao's view."

Other newspapers followed the People's Daily's example, and with the exception of two brief campaigns against "spiritual pollution" and "bourgeois liberalization," the Chinese press slowly opened up during the 1980s. Men like Hu Jiwei and deputy editor Wang Ruoshui lost their posts as a result of these campaigns (Wang Ruoshui and Liu Binyan were also later expelled from the Party), but there were always new journalists of conviction who shared their principles to step into their shoes.

Hu Jiwei, who continued on as president of the Federation of Journalism Societies despite losing his position at the People's Daily in 1983, also argued publicly for a new press law to protect freedom of the press. But this was too radical a move for Party Secretary Hu Yaobang, who emphasized the sense of "social responsibility" to which every Chinese journalist should adhere. According to Hu Yaobang, journalists needed always to consider the possible negative effects their work might have on society. Wrongdoings could be written about only if it was in the interests of the general public, but there should not be an overabundance of unpleasant and unhealthy trends.

"Our newspapers should give 80 percent of their space to reporting good things and achievements, and give the remaining 20 percent of their space to criticizing the seamy side of things and to exposing our shortcomings," Hu Yaobang declared in a major policy speech in April 1985. In an irony of history, it was the death of this former Party secretary which first ignited the democracy movement in April 1989. After his abrupt dismissal in 1987 by Party conservatives for his more liberal views, the students revered him as a symbol of tolerance. They demanded that the work of Hu be reevaluated *post mortem*. "Liberal" is a relative notion in the Chinese political vocabulary.

* Today, Liu Binyan is one of the foremost Chinese dissident writers living in the United States.

When I first moved to China in 1987, I was impressed by the degree of openness and diversity in Chinese urban society. Newspapers published reports of Party officials indicted for embezzlement and profiteering. Letters to the Editor described the unfair treatment by Party members of ordinary people. In general, many commentaries and editorials touched upon the failings of society, frankly and pointedly. Younger journalists especially were influenced by foreign publications and by the Western correspondents resident in the country. They would test the limits of the permissible whenever they could.

Naturally there were some subjects such as Tibet which were not reported on, and newspapers ran frequent long-winded commentaries filled with ideological liturgy. But people were more informed about the goings-on in society, and they knew much more about the outside world than I had expected. This, however, was not solely due to the Chinese official press. The Voice of America and BBC broadcasts, in both Chinese and English were, and still are, popular, especially among younger city residents. In addition, many urban Chinese regularly saw a variety of the so-called "for internal use only" publications.

The Chinese propaganda apparatus has many levels. Anyone may purchase or subscribe to official newspapers like the People's Daily and *Beijing wanbao* (Beijing Evening News) or the numerous magazines put out by the national news agency, Xinhua. But there are also a number of publications produced for restricted consumption only. They contain direct translations from foreign newspapers and broadcasts, as well as uncensored articles written by Chinese journalists about sensitive issues. What one is allowed to read depends on who one is. The higher one's position, the more access one has to confidential and polemical material. By the end of the 1980s, the general breakdown of control had led to more and more people becoming exposed to a wider range of information.

I learned how censorship works in an official newspaper from reporter Li and a few other Chinese acquaintances who worked in the media. There is no central censorship bureau which checks articles before publication. Instead, every journalist is supposed to bear in mind the Party's policies, though, it is not always altogether clear what the policy on a certain issue is. At the end of the day, it is the editor-in-chief who has the last say concerning what is printable—no enviable task because one miscalculation can mean the end of a career (in Mao's days the consequences were even more severe). The editor simply has to have the right gut feeling about the political barometer at any given time. The whole system breeds cautiousness and self-censorship. "If I write about, let's say, a county boss who has misused funds intended for flood control, the article must first be approved by my section chief. If he wavers, the story is sent to a higher boss, and so on, all the way up to the editor-in-chief. Any article of importance ends up on his desk," reporter Li explained, in the winter of 1989.

More daring editors have, at various times during the reform period, permitted controversial stories. "A timid chief never takes a risk. He reprints articles already run by the People's Daily or Xinhua News Agency. They are both under the strictest surveillance, so copying them is always a safe course of action," Li said.

During the student demonstrations of 1989, heated debates took place in many newspaper offices. Younger reporters appealed to the "intellectual conscience" of their bosses and demanded that the protests be reported. "After Hu Yaobang's memorial service, a terrible argument broke out at our editorial meeting," Li recalled. "We wanted to tell our readers that, in addition to the official memorial service, 100,000 students had held their own mass meeting to honor Hu's memory at Tiananmen Square. Our editor-in-chief was in a terrible dither. Of course he supported us in his heart, but he had to take the Party's position into consideration." Though the stormy meeting ended in victory for Li and his colleagues, and the story about the students' activities was printed, the authorities tried to stop the normal distribution of the newspaper by mail. "We journalists delivered bundles of newspapers ourselves to smaller post offices all around the city and made sure that they were stamped and sent off. The staff at the post offices were very sympathetic to our cause. They actually helped us."

The editors of the most important publications are regularly summoned to meet with the Politburo member in charge of propaganda, who gives them instructions and guidelines concerning press coverage of important upcoming events. These briefings about major policy decisions and ideology are supposed to cue editors about where the Party stands on any given issue. When Hu Qili, the Politburo member in charge of propaganda, met with a group of leading editors in early May 1989, he let it be known that Party Secretary Zhao Ziyang approved of the opening up of the press. The editors were not criticized for permitting coverage of the student demonstrations. From then on, Chinese newspapers and television were flooded with news about the events at Tiananmen Square. That coverage, in turn, emboldened greater numbers of demonstrators to join the students. One work unit after another marched in support of the students camped in Tiananmen Square. Teachers, doctors, government officials, local Communist Party subdivision employees, and many average workers continued to rally behind the students even after martial law was declared

The charismatic student leader Wu'er Kaixi (center, white shirt) was a favorite among the press corps during the spring of 1989. (Photo: Marja Sarvimäki)

in Beijing on May 20. For the first time in the history of the People's Republic, elite intellectuals were joining a demonstration. I even saw reporter Li's gray-haired professor-father among the jubilant protesters. He was carrying a placard which declared: "More funds for education!"

I knew that the government was paralyzed but I was still surprised when I called the Ministry of Foreign Economic Relations and Trade to speak with a deputy department chief. "Call back next week," the voice at the other end answered. "He's out marching."

Despite its heady liberalization, the Chinese press was not prepared to report on every facet of the protest movement. Just as the students' definition of "democracy" left much to be desired, the Chinese journalists' interpretation of "press freedom" did not correspond to the Western notion of "objective reporting." On several occasions that spring I argued with friends and acquaintances who did not agree with my view that the Chinese media should also report the less flattering aspects of the student movement. For example, the journalists did not wish to mention the heated quarrels among the student leaders, or the accusations that the structure of the student organization was, with each passing day, beginning to resemble that of the Communist Party.

Reporter Li and I witnessed an ugly event that brought the issue to a head. Two student leaders had come to blows on the Square. As a foreign press photographer began to shoot photos of the fight, a group of "student guards" rushed to the scene and dragged the photographer away. I told Li that since the Chinese students were demanding that the government permit freedom of the press, they should at least heed the principle themselves. But he disagreed, vehemently.

"We are on the students' side. We can't start criticizing them."

"But don't you support freedom of the press?" I asked Li.

"Of course I do. But a picture like that could be used against us by the government," he answered. "We can't have photos like that made public."

To be honest, most foreign journalists were also so sympathetic to the students' cause that their reporting was not totally objective either. Many foreign reporters knew that Wu'er Kaixi, the charismatic student leader hero, was eating during his "hunger strike." Scores of correspondents were well aware that many student leaders were guilty of elite tendencies similar to those of the Communist leaders of whom they so disapproved. Different rules applied to the leaders and the masses, both for the students and for the Party. But to these weaknesses and others, most of the Western press turned a blind eye.

In sum, the Chinese journalists broke free from restraints thanks to their own determined efforts and to the ongoing power struggle among the Chinese leaders. From the start of the protests, the Chinese leadership was split on the question of how to deal with the students. Party Secretary Zhao Ziyang, the leader of the more liberal camp, felt cornered. He calculated that public opinion could help him win the duel with the conservative Prime Minister Li Peng. He was wrong.

In 1989, Deng Xiaoping was still very much alive. Though retired from day-to-day politics, Deng remained China's most influential man. He was that even officially as chairman of the Central Military Commission. Deng had sacrificed his entire life to build a socialist China. He was not about to allow his life work to be threatened by rebellious twenty-year-old college kids.

In their book, *Crisis at Tiananmen*, Yi Mu and Mark V. Thompson note that the Chinese leaders were educated in the sort of socialism that reinforced traditional Chinese views that the state must control all facets of Chinese society. "To some extent, these leaders really do believe that independent student organizations and independent unions are not simply a threat to their power, but a crack in the foundation of socialism as they understand it," Yi and Thompson write. "The real tragedy involved here is not that Deng Xiaoping and his allies were clinging to power, but that they ultimately believed that their views and their actions were fully justified."[4]

In the West, Deng was known as the great reformer. Thanks to him, China was joining the ranks of responsible nations. But Deng had never changed his staunch view that the Party must have absolute power. Nor had he ever been squeamish about using force to achieve his goals. Unfortunately, he had lost touch with his own people. The reform policy which he had set into motion had led to higher standards of living, but had also unleashed a whole new set of problems. People had many more demands than ten years earlier. They felt it was only natural that they should have a say in matters which concerned their personal lives. Bitterness over widespread corruption, rising inflation, and increasing injustice in the system was much deeper in all sectors of society than the conservative old leaders imagined. Deng took it for granted that his thunderous editorial in the People's Daily would frighten people into a retreat. Quite the opposite occurred. The people of Beijing were furious, indignant. China had changed in a way that Deng could not grasp. Deng, on the other hand, had not changed, a fact which many on the streets did not take into consideration.

Deng Xiaoping's personal experiences during the Cultural Revolution could not but have some effect on the way he viewed the student demonstrators. Though he came through "the ten years of madness" relatively unscathed, compared to other leaders (such as President Liu Shaoqi, who was tortured to death), his eldest son, Deng Pufang, a twenty-five-year-old physics major at Beijing University, was beaten severely by fanatical Red Guards who demanded that he declare his father a traitor. Deng Pufang was barely conscious when his tormentors dumped him in a bare fourth-floor dormitory room. The window and window frame had been ripped out, leaving a gaping hole open to the ground. "That is your only exit," he was told. To this day he does not remember if he rolled out by accident or was pushed. When he hit the ground his spine and legs were fractured, paralyzing him from the waist down.[5]

When Deng heard of his son's fate, he was in far-off Jiangxi province with his wife, doing forced manual labor in a tractor repair shop. He, too, had undergone humiliating self-criticism sessions, in which he was accused of being a "capitalist roader." Deng repeatedly asked the authorities to allow his son to receive medical treatment, but all requests were denied. Deng Pufang remains an invalid today. Since 1988, he has been the chairman of the China Disabled Persons Federation.

In the spring of 1989, when the eighty-four-year-old Deng Xiaoping was told that hundreds of thousands of students were camping out in Tiananmen Square and that some demonstrators were demanding his resignation, he must have been horrified that a new Cultural Revolution was underway. It is highly improbable that any of his aides stressed the peaceful nature of the demonstrations or described the admirable way in which the students were maintaining order. During the six weeks of the movement, there were almost no public disturbances in Beijing, a city of 10.3 million people. According to the police, even petty crime declined. Beijingers were bound together by an exceptionally strong sense of solidarity. It is evident that Deng Xiaoping did not personally venture into the city center to review the situation.

Deng panicked and resorted to the means he knew best—military force. It is quite conceivable that the Deng of 1979 would have masterminded a brilliant compromise to dampen the crisis at Tiananmen Square. During the tense six-week face-off, the government and the students each had two or three clear-cut opportunities to defuse the bomb. A ten-years-younger Deng might have adeptly grasped the situation, some observers say. All the more tragic is the fact that by the time of the massacre, the democracy movement was already dying down. There were no more than a measly five thousand or so students camped out in the Square, and most of them were from cities other than Beijing. They were in no hurry to return home. They had just embarked on their great adventure. On the other hand, the exhausted Beijing youths had, for the most part, already returned to their campuses. The majority of them supported pulling out of Tiananmen as victors. Nearly all of the original student movement leaders had lost their positions and, together with a group of prominent intellectuals, they advocated vacating the Square. Unfortunately, the student leaders who were in power toward the end of the movement were the most radical. They knew they would be the targets of disciplinary action whatever were to happen, so they tried to reignite the movement by urging the students to continue their activities.

After the massacre, it was pitiful to hear the emotional statements made by the tearful Chai Ling, the so-called commander-in-chief of Tiananmen Square, in a taped interview with an American journalist on May 28. From her statements, between fits of hysterical crying, it was clear that she had lost touch with reality. Bloodshed might have been avoided if she and the other prominent student leader at the time, Li Lu, had decided to persuade the last diehard students to leave the Square. The Chinese government was bound to enforce a heavy-handed crackdown. Hundreds of people would have been arrested in any case. That decision was irrevocable. But the lives of hundreds of Beijing citizens could have been saved.

During the night of June 4 tens of thousands of Beijing residents—ordinary working people—tried desperately to block the tanks and soldiers from reaching the students in Tiananmen Square. They built barricades, they attacked the soldiers with iron rods, and they formed human blockades at the major intersections in the city center. The column of army vehicles was hundreds of yards long. The battle went on for hours.

For this reason, it is more accurate to speak of the "Beijing (not Tiananmen) massacre." No more than possibly a handful of people died in the Square itself. Many Western media reports failed to point out that, after the first armed vehicles arrived at the edge of the Square in the predawn hours, the army commander permitted the last group of dogged students to leave the Square. But, on the "Avenue of Eternal Peace," the wide boulevard which runs east-west through the center of Beijing, soldiers randomly shot down unarmed civilians without hesitation. They fired point blank at their fellow countrymen. Tanks drove into human walls, crushing bodies under them. The majority of victims were not students, but mothers and fathers, aunts and uncles, even grandmothers and grandfathers who were trying to stop the approaching onslaught of soldiers heading for Tiananmen Square.

I stood with my friend Marja Sarvimäki a few hundred yards from Muxidi intersection on the west side of Beijing. "They're killing people! They're using live ammunition!" people around us screamed as the tricycle carts went past, trailing blood. Usually these carts transport vegetables. Now they were taking the wounded to the hospitals and the dead to the crematory. I will never forget the shock and genuine disbelief of the people in the streets when the gruesome truth unfolded: the "People's Army" was killing its own people.

All spring, people had assured me that "Deng Xiaoping will lose his Mandate of Heaven if blood flows at Tiananmen Square." These words pounded through my brain the entire night. This reference to the Mandate of Heaven derives from the traditional Chinese worldview in which the ruler is the son of Heaven. His power is based on Heaven's authorization. Though Confucianism emphasized the importance of harmony and hierarchy, it also stressed righteousness and benevolence. The Emperor was the absolute sovereign, but virtuous behavior was expected of him (and of officials exercising power in his name) in order to retain Heaven's mandate.

Reporter Li's younger brother was also at Muxidi intersection on that fateful night, though I did not know it at the time. He was a student at Beijing Normal University. To the very last moment, he was adamant that the strength of the democracy movement lay in its pacifist nature. Together with a few classmates, he tried to persuade the enraged citizens to refrain from violence when opposing the approaching army. He was one of the first to be hit when the soldiers opened fire. A bullet ripped through his lungs, and he died in a hospital on June 7.

How many died that night? That question will probably forever remain unanswered. The Chinese Red Cross, whose representatives were in contact with hospitals throughout the city, gave an estimate of 2,600 dead before the authorities insisted that they retract the statement. That figure might be high, but not by much, especially if it includes those who died of wounds in the aftermath. Skirmishes between soldiers and citizens took place all over the city in the days following June 4.

On June 5, reporter Li saw a group of angry Beijing residents literally tear a young soldier apart with their bare hands. As so often happened after such incidents, nearby vengeful and terrified soldiers shot randomly into the nearby crowds. In her book, *Red China Blues*, Canadian correspondent Jan Wong describes the fate of an eight-year-old boy who taunted a group of soldiers two days after the massacre. One of the soldiers took aim with his AK-47 and shot off a round of bullets. Though the wounded child crawled, bleeding, along the road, the soldier would not allow anyone to go near him. A frantic bystander finally managed to talk sense into the soldier and was allowed to take the boy to the hospital; he lost his spleen, a rib, and one of his kidneys.[6]

That same day, I was on my bicycle miles from Tiananmen Square, in the northern part of the city, when a patrol of soldiers appeared suddenly from around the corner, nervously shooting in all directions. I followed my fellow bicyclists' example and threw myself on the ground. The man beside me was shot in the arm.

Residents of Beijing have not forgotten the Tiananmen events of 1989, or their catastrophic outcome, though people seldom speak of them nowadays. The overwhelming majority of Beijingers will tell you that they will never again take an interest in politics. Still, when the moment is ripe, they will demand that the memory of the victims be honored and the "counter-revolutionary rebellion," as the leadership labeled the episode, be acknowledged as a patriotic and nonviolent movement. Of course, it is possible that at some point China's leaders will do this of their own accord. There is precedent for such a turnaround in the turbulent history of the People's Republic. When Deng Xiaoping rose to power at the end of the 1970s, he decreed that the names and reputations of victims persecuted during the Cultural Revolution be cleared. For millions vindication was *post mortem*, as in the case of my godchild's grandfather. But as long as Deng was alive, a reevaluation of the Tiananmen events of 1989 was not possible.

"It will definitely happen one day, but whether I'll be alive to witness that moment is another matter," Professor Ding Zilin said quietly, when I visited her in January 1997. Ding is one of the most tenacious and admirable women I met during my years in China. She has kept her resolve despite years of harassment by the authorities. Her phone is tapped, her mail is confiscated, her every move is watched. When Secretary of State Warren Christopher arrived in Beijing in March 1994 for talks with Chinese officials, a police car appeared outside her apartment building. When the Fourth World Conference on Women was held in China in September 1995, she was put under house arrest.

Her crime?

She has refused to be silenced about her son, who was killed on June 4, 1989.

"I'm a mother. Why is it a crime to grieve for my son openly?" the fifty-seven-year-old Ding Zilin asked, when I interviewed her for the first time in 1994. Five years had passed since the tragedy, but the mention of her son's name still brought tears to her eyes. A heartbreaking silence engulfed the room, the kind that made me wish I had chosen some other occupation.

Ding's health had visibly deteriorated in the two-and-a-half years since we had last met. But in 1997, she was even more forthright and expressed her indignation in even stronger words than before: "We have the right to voice our opinion. Freedom of speech is guaranteed by Chinese law."

Still today, Ding Zilin is just about the only relative of the victims of June 4 who has consented to speak with foreign journalists. The other next-of-kin were pressured into silence by the authorities after the Beijing massacre. Even the seriously injured were told to lie about the origin of their wounds. The Chinese leadership wanted people simply to forget the bloodshed. The police have used every means possible to obscure the events and people have been frightened into submission. For example, reporter Li's father sent me a message that I was no longer welcome to visit their home.

"My father's soul was crushed by my brother's death," reporter Li said. "He just cannot cope with any kind of tension. He starts to shake uncontrollably even when just the street committee members come by."

Ding Zilin and her husband Jiang Peikun, both former professors of philosophy at the People's University, are exceptional individuals. The pressure has at times been next-to-unbearable, but they refuse to be quiet. "I have never been politically active in my whole life," Ding said. "Can you imagine that before June 4 I had never even listened to a single foreign radio broadcast? I was a Party member, and I believed in our government."

For two years, Ding grieved for her son in silence. Then, one day in 1991, she happened to watch a televised broadcast of a press conference and heard a foreign reporter ask when the government planned to make public the names of those who were killed on June 4. Prime Minister Li Peng answered that "the family members of the dead are reluctant to have their names disclosed because they view the event as an anti-government riot. We must respect their wishes."

Professors Jiang Peikun and Ding Zilin keep the urn containing their son's ashes in their home in Beijing; in the background is a portrait of their son, painted on the basis of the last photo taken of him as he marched with his high school classmates. When this picture was taken in January 1997, Ding Zilin's health had visibly deteriorated. (Photo: Linda Jakobson)

"I was stupefied," Ding Zilin recalled. Two weeks later she gave her first interview to a foreign television reporter. "I looked straight into the camera and said that I was very proud of my seventeen-year-old son, who had marched for democracy. My son was at the top of his high school class and he wanted to take part in developing his motherland. We tried frantically to keep him at home that night. But he slipped out the bathroom window and went downtown with a classmate. He wanted desperately to stop the troops from reaching Tiananmen Square. He died in the morning hours of June 4. He had been shot in the back."

After the interview, the People's University forbade Ding from teaching and the Communist Party expelled her. When her husband, Jiang Peikun, made similar comments in an interview with Voice of America, he, too, lost his job.

Ding began to write articles about her son for publication abroad. She no longer had anything to lose. When donations started arriving from all over the world, she passed them on to other families of victims. She also decided to compile a list of the dead and injured. "This is humanitarian work. There are families who lost their only breadwinner. Many of the injured don't have enough money to finance plastic surgery or new limbs," Ding Zilin said. By 1997, she had tracked down the families of 150 victims. The majority still wish to remain anonymous.

When the Academy of Sciences in New York awarded Ding Zilin its human rights award in 1995, the police put the couple behind bars. For the first time since the Beijing massacre, sixteen family members of victims stepped forward and appealed to the government for their release. "The more uncertain the authorities feel, the more merciless their actions become. But their behavior evokes all the more contempt," Ding said when the couple was once again set free. "In the past, people who have been treated inhumanely suffered in silence and humiliation, waiting patiently for the government to correct its wrong judgement and restore their reputation. This must end."

Ding read me a part of the letter she had sent to the Academy of Sciences in New York:

"In the years since the tragedy, I have simply done what a mother's love and an intellectual's conscience drove me to do. Every citizen living in this land should not only have freedom from fear, but should also have the right to choose the kind of society, political system, and individual lifestyle that is compatible with human dignity. These were the dreams of those who gave their lives at Tiananmen Square. These are the goals for which we, the living, strive."

People remember the spring of 1989 in different ways. Over the years, some people have changed their line of thinking and adopted if not quite the government's view, at least the position that politics should not be allowed to threaten "stability."

A dark cloud hung over Beijing for more than two years. The despairing Party tried to indoctrinate its subjects with political correctness by increasing ideological education in schools and workplaces. In so-called key universities, first-year graduates were given ten months of military training, a practice that continued for several years at the "Harvard of China," Beijing University, where many of the democracy movement activists had studied, and at Fudan University in Shanghai.

Beijingers turned a deaf ear to Party rhetoric that attempted to justify its actions. Already, years before the Tiananmen demonstrations, many Chinese had privately mocked and ridiculed Communism and the Party. After 1989, the Party was criticized vehemently and with a new intensity. Hate, however, gradually turned to apathy. When economic growth took off in 1992, after Deng Xiaoping's famous southern tour, political indoctrination took a back seat and even in the capital, people began to devote their energies to raising their standard of living. Reporter Li, who was detained for four months after the massacre, became a businessman, as did many of his colleagues. "It's absolutely useless trying to work for change in society as long as Deng Xiaoping is alive. I'm better off concentrating on my own life. I want to earn as much money as I can," he justified his change of career to me in 1993. Millions of Chinese share his views.

Elsewhere in China, the Party was much more successful in spreading its message about the "necessity of stability." When I traveled in the southern and central regions of the country in the autumn of 1989, even young intellectuals expressed their annoyance at Beijingers for "irresponsible behavior" and "endangering the stable environment."

"Now we all have to suffer because the people of Beijing went too far. Foreign companies have left and the economy has stalled. China is not ready for democracy yet," a physics lecturer in Shanghai lamented. "We are too poor, and the majority of the population is not sufficiently educated." I heard similar comments in Hangzhou and Guangzhou. When the Soviet Union collapsed, the Chinese media focused its attention on the dismal shape of the Russian economy and the chaotic state of the country. The former Soviet example exhorted the Chinese leadership even more to emphasize the "need for stability," a phrase that is still continuously referred to in everyday conversations.

The Chinese leadership was acutely aware of the central role of Chinese journalists in the spring of 1989. Since its founding, China's Communist Party has attached great importance to the media. There are not many countries in the world where the Minister of Radio, Film, and Television has a habit of personally dropping by the studios before 7 P.M. to review the main evening news broadcast. As Party Secretary, Hu Yaobang used to check the editorials of the People's Daily himself; Zhao Ziyang delegated the job to Hu Qili.

It surprised no one that Hu Qili was dismissed after the Tiananmen events. The same fate awaited the director and editor-in-chief of the People's Daily. Three of the deputy editors-in-chief were forced to retire or relocate. In addition, more than forty of the paper's reporters were "disciplined"—fired, suspended, or transferred to other units. Reporter Li's two highest superiors at the Science and Technology Daily lost their jobs. Afterward, the deputy editor-in-chief admitted that he knew when that first daring issue of Science and Technology Daily was published that the paper would suffer a political purge and he would be one of the first to go. "But a person has to act according to his conscience. People had the right to know what was happening," he maintained.

The media was put under strict control. The grip of the propaganda authorities remains tight even today, nine years after the massacre. Though newspaper kiosks now sell dozens of glossy magazines, this is merely a reflection of the commercialism which has overtaken Chinese media organizations. The smiling pin-up girls and football stars can be misleading. Journalists still must "shoulder the important task of propagating the line, guiding principle, and policy of the Party and state" whenever they touch upon political issues. Jiang Zemin, who replaced ousted Party Secretary Zhao Ziyang, has repeatedly stressed the sense of social responsibility of the media. Journalists are constantly advised to emphasize socialism and patriotism, and resist the influence of decadent ideology and culture. When Jiang rallied support for his Spiritual Civilization Campaign in 1996, he reminded the press corps that a journalist is "an engineer of the people's minds."[7]

In the countryside, girls are taught to serve their brothers at a young age. Photo from Guizhou province in 1996. (Photo: John Lee)

五

A Peasant Woman's Hard Lot

"Bring a Little Brother after You"

Chinese living in the countryside hardly noticed the Tiananmen events unfolding in the cities across the country. Whenever I brought up the subject with people living in rural areas, they shrugged their shoulders and said laconically: "City folks making a ruckus as usual."

"That doesn't mean that country people don't understand politics," my girlfriend, Dr. Feng, reminded me. "But they're not the least bit interested in national politics. And they don't care about grand theories. But they know a lot more about current events than arrogant city people think they do. And they certainly have their own opinions about such matters."

Feng, a doctor of traditional Chinese medicine, was brought up in a middle-sized village in Shandong province. Thanks to her, I was able to get more than just a superficial glimpse of life in rural China, a feat I had deemed impossible because of the regulations restricting a foreign correspondent's movements outside the big cities. Cadres of local information departments, who acted as "guides" during my various reporting trips to the countryside, were careful to ensure that I did not encounter anything "too dirty," "too poor," or "too primitive." Even as a teacher in the 1980s, when I spent occasional weekends at the rural homes of some university students, I never felt that I had seen real life. A foreign teacher was treated like royalty by just about the entire village.

So in August 1996, when Dr. Feng invited me along on a visit to her "old mother" in the village where she was born, I eagerly accepted. We had planned this trip many times, but one of us had always had to cancel. I began to wonder whether my tagging along might, after all, be inconvenient.

"Are you sure that this is not going to cause your family any trouble?" I asked one last time.

Dr. Feng shook her head. "How many times must I tell you that I am the only one in the whole village who has gone off to school in the city?

As a doctor, I'm a privileged member of the community. Anyway, I'm on good terms with everyone. You can just imagine how many requests for help I get each time I go back home. My family has heard so much about you. And they were very disappointed that you didn't come last Spring Festival. It's high time they finally meet you.

"I know what you're worried about, but there's no need," she added. "If you wanted to write a sensational article, I might think twice. Not that there isn't plenty to write about. Our village chief is a real villain and the other members of the village committee are all his running dogs. But since you're writing a book, I think it's important that you see for yourself what peasant life is like. Don't fret about having to register. The village officials all come to me with their ailments, and I always remember to bring them medicine from the city. Of course, I never charge them for anything. They leave my family alone. You'll see, they won't bother us. If anyone asks who you are, I'll say you're my colleague."

Dr. Feng clearly knew what she was about. The villagers grew accustomed to my presence surprisingly quickly. Besides the respect that Dr. Feng commanded as a doctor and the only formally educated member of the village, it was obvious that she was well liked for her sweet personality and kindness. Just as she had predicted, one village official after another came to consult her for medical advice, and none of them asked to see my work permit or my passport, as is usually the case. I was introduced as a friend from Beijing, and that sufficed. It was a worthy reminder of how *guanxi* can open doors in China. Had I appeared in the village in the company of someone less prestigious, I am sure I would have been approached by the authorities in no time at all.

Indeed, I had been involved earlier in one such embarrassing incident, when I accepted an invitation, on the spur of the moment, to look up the uncle of an acquaintance in a village near Beijing. My acquaintance, Yu, had been driving the magazine's photographer, Petri, and I around the outskirts of the city. Yu said that his uncle's village would be well worth a visit because of the prosperous small cannister factory the villagers had collectively founded. (Petri was in China for a month to work with me on a series about changes in rural life.)

We had not even properly settled down in our chairs at the uncle's home—his wife was placing the obligatory tea mugs in front of us—when a policeman knocked at the door. After examining Yu's I.D., he apologized for the intrusion and said that a neighbor had come to his office to report the presence of two foreigners. Luckily, the policeman believed Yu's explanation that the foreign guests were his former English teacher and her husband, and that, unfortunately, we did not have our passports with us. As working journalists, we should have applied for permission from the county officials to conduct such an interview in the village. When we returned to Beijing an hour and a half later, Yu's somewhat annoyed wife already knew all about our visit. The policeman had phoned the street committee in Beijing to check the authenticity of Yu's I.D. Needless to say, the old lady in charge of the street committee office had run right over and chided Yu's wife about the call.

But in Dr. Feng's village, I was able to accompany her wherever she went. The only thing that caused a commotion each time we stopped to greet anyone was my ability to speak Chinese. Several villagers greeted Dr. Feng by saying: "Really, Dr. Feng, you are diligent. On top of everything else, you've gone and mastered a foreign language!" Upon hearing this, Dr. Feng giggled girlishly, as is her habit, and explained that she still could not speak a word of English, but her friend here had learned Chinese. Initially, I always had to say everything at least twice because, in addition to being unaccustomed to my "foreign way" of pronouncing Chinese, no one even attempted to understand what the "big nose" was saying. They just instinctively looked to Dr. Feng, expecting her to translate. The children caught on the quickest and exclaimed, "The foreigner really is speaking our language!" After that, the conversation gradually picked up. Once it did, we had a hard time continuing on our way.

Most of the villagers had never had any contact with a foreigner. They asked the same types of questions as the travelers I meet on trains—anything and everything about life in the West. Whenever we visited someone's home there was always at least one talkative member of the household who wanted to know how much farmers earn in the West, how much they are taxed, what kind of opportunities their children have to go on to high school, and so on. One by one, other younger and middle-aged relatives forgot their shyness and joined in. In numerous homes, I heard people mumble that "socialism has been of no use." And then someone would explain, "Previously, we were told that the peasants in capitalist countries went hungry, but in reality, your farmers drive around in their own cars and their houses have running water." Once, a middle-aged man, who said he had been as far as "the big city of Jinan," retorted, "We've seen on the television how fat the Western farmers are. Of course they're better off than we are!"

The only time I said anything that really took the villagers by surprise was when they asked about a farmer's right to move from place to place. It took quite a while for many to digest the fact that, in the West, not only a farmer, but also his whole family, can choose to settle down in a city. People spoke bitterly about the Chinese system of residence permits.

Elderly people always stayed in the background. In any case, I could only communicate with them with the help of Dr. Feng because I could not understand their strong accents. From their point of view, I must have seemed like a strange creature who had just landed from outer space. Elderly women never ceased to comment on my fair skin or the thin texture of my hair. The older generation's feelings toward me were summed up by one grandmother who turned nervously to Dr. Feng and inquired: "Am I supposed to give the foreigner tea just out of this cup?"

"Of course. What else is she supposed to drink it from?" Dr. Feng laughed.

"Well, you never know how foreigners drink their tea," the woman replied. I once overheard engineer Song's elderly aunt pose the exact same question, and she had lived in Jinan for more than fifteen years.

Dr. Feng had wangled a ten-day leave from her work unit on the pretext that she would gather various hard-to-come-by plants and roots, which her research institute needed. I tried my best to help her with this task, which in practice meant that I did the carrying. We trooped along the edges of fields and on the ridges of hills gathering the weirdest-looking roots, twigs, and plants. A group of children followed in our footsteps. "Put this in Auntie Linda's herb bag. Take this to Auntie Linda's food bag. This you can put in the bag for the rabbits; they'll love it," Dr. Feng commanded. The children ran back and forth, delighted to be included, ecstatic that they had acquired a "foreign auntie."

The villagers could hardly contain their laughter when I trudged home behind Dr. Feng, the bags swaying from a branch I had slung over my shoulder like a coolie. The scorching August sun had beaten down on our backs all day and I am sure that my face, stained with dirt and sweat, was quite a sight. In China, an intellectual traditionally never engages in manual labor. Dr. Feng's unorthodox and sprightly manner was already a source of great amazement among the villagers, not to mention what they thought of the foreigner following her up and down the hills.

In the evenings, Dr. Feng sorted the contents of the bags and cleaned the roots with a sharp pen-knife. It reminded me of the work my mother does after she has picked mushrooms in the woods. As a teenager, Dr. Feng had studied the basics of Chinese traditional medicine from her father and the village doctor. Later, she was trained in Western medicine and worked as a general doctor in the city. These days she conducts research on combining Western and traditional medicine to treat chronic illnesses.

My visit to Dr. Feng's home village was an unforgettable experience. Though I had driven through or wandered around much poorer, more squalid villages, I was left with a by far keener sense of the harsh realities of peasant life after being a part of Dr. Feng's household. We were only seventy miles away from Jinan, but conditions were extremely stark.

According to official statistics, urban residents earn on average twice the annual income of country folk, but, in reality, the gap is much wider. Zhu Qingfang of the Chinese Acadamy of Social Sciences estimates that the real difference is a ratio of four to one.[1] Living in Beijing and using that as a base measure for the economic development taking place in China, it is easy to forget the primitive conditions in which most Chinese continue to live.[2] Yet all the peasants with whom I spoke in Dr. Feng's village assured me that life is a lot better now than it was twenty years ago. Things have improved, I was told, over and over again.

But even more than the harsh circumstances, I was struck by the attitudes of the villagers. The influence of centuries of feudalism was almost palpable. I have often written that tradition is deeply embedded in Chinese thought, despite the Communists' attempts to eradicate it. Now I was experiencing the influence of tradition firsthand.

The name of the village, "Behind the Ponds," indicates its location. To get there, one must walk the last five hundred yards or so along a wide path that wends its way between two ponds. The nearby road is quite new. Ten years ago, the closest road was two miles away.

In the Chinese custom, houses are surrounded by walls, making the courtyard the center of all activity. The gate remains open in the daytime, and children run to and fro, from one courtyard to the other. Most of the neighbors are related, so that nearly all the kids in the vicinity are either first or second cousins to the children in Dr. Feng's family. The little ones passed the time of day jumping in mud puddles or playing with sticks and stones. During my visit to the village, I did not see a single toy. The bigger boys took turns riding around on two dilapidated bicycles, evidently discarded by the adults, and they went fishing with the men on Sundays. Children too young for school, and even some of the older ones, craved attention and seemed overjoyed when I showed them some simple games with my hands, or drew pictograms in the mud with a stick.

The lives of these village children differ drastically from those of my urban friends' offspring. In the city, an only child is the constant center of attention and generally spoiled to the core—with shelves crammed with the latest toys. In Dr. Feng's village, I never saw any adults playing with the children, as city parents so often do. The women toiled from dawn until bedtime, while the men would sit together smoking cigarettes or disappear inside to play mahjong, after the day's work was done.

"Men have an easier life than women," Dr. Feng said. "Just look at *Dimei* (younger sister-in-law). She helps my younger brother all day long in the cotton mill. On top of that, she alone tends to the family's small plot of farmland and also helps Mother with the household chores and preparing the meals."

When analysts note that the income level in the countryside has risen fourteenfold during the reform period, they seldom point out that women are often bearing even heavier burdens than before. During the 1980s and 1990s, in scores of rural families, men found work in light industry or went off to seek employment in the cities, leaving the responsibilities of both the farm work and the household to their wives.

Deng's revolution began in the countryside, as did Mao's. While Mao believed in collectivism, Deng freed the peasants from the central government's stifling control.[3] China's economic miracle has depended upon the industrious, entrepreneurial energies of its people, characteristics for which Chinese immigrants in the West have become famous. In the early 1980s, the communes were abolished, and each family was contracted a plot of land to farm. A farmer can now sell his produce on the free market, as long as he first hands over a certain quota of grain to the government at below-market prices.

Motivated by the incentive to earn money for themselves, production soared. The output of major farm crops rose by 30 percent, 50 percent, and in some fields even by 100 percent. The average annual income for rural workers increased from 191 yuan ($95.50) in 1980 to 397 yuan ($156.90) in 1985. After the communes were disbanded, a huge work force found itself with nothing to do, since the family plots were, for the most part, very small. Slowly but surely families, sometimes entire villages, joined together to start workshops and small factories. This process sparked a boom in light industry which still continues today. By 1996, privately or collectively owned factories accounted for 56.9 percent of China's industrial output.

Western media estimates that about 70 percent of the Chinese population (864 million people) live off agriculture are misleading because Chinese statistics lump rural industries together with agriculture. In 1996, less than half the population made their living solely from agriculture or animal husbandry. Because of this industrialization and the growth of small cities, the rural population has been declining year by year. Taking into account that 120 to 180 million rural residents are "temporarily employed" in cities, it is impossible to pinpoint accurately how many people actually live in the countryside. History's largest migration is now underway. Demographers predict that within twenty-five years, nearly half of all Chinese will live in urban areas.[4]

Besides Dr. Feng's younger brother, his wife, and their two sons, ages seven and eleven, the Feng household includes Dr. Feng's seventy-two-year-old mother, a tiny frail lady, who seems nevertheless to have an abundance of energy in spite of her wobbly legs.

The house has three rooms: two chambers and a middle room, which functions as a hallway, pantry, and dining room, all in one. The actual cooking is done in a shed at the end of the building. Dr. Feng's brother and his wife slept in the smaller chamber, while the rest of us all clambered up onto the *kang* in the main chamber. A *kang* is a raised platform, under which there is a stove. In the old days, a family both slept and ate on the *kang*, which often took up the entire room, the only one in the house.

On my first evening as I prepared to settle down on the *kang* with a row of heads beside me, I recalled my childhood experiences at summer camp. When Dr. Feng's husband and their teenage son arrived for the weekend, they took our places on the *kang*, and Dr. Feng and I moved into the smaller chamber. Her brother and sister-in-law, *Dimei*, took refuge at the cotton mill, which was situated about half a mile away.

All the houses in the village have electricity and nearly all the courtyards have access to a water pump. But none have a toilet, a shower, a washing machine, or a phone—amenities which have already started to become commonplace in more affluent villages nearer Jinan or Beijing. In some homes I saw black-and-white televisions, though the set Dr. Feng had brought the family from the city had been broken for a year and *Dimei* told me that there was not enough money to have it repaired. According to official statistics, nearly every other household in the Chinese countryside has a television. In city homes, there is at least one per family.

The village chief and the Party secretary both have phones at home, but they are off-limits for use by the villagers; the closest public phone was nearly two miles away. So unable to phone ahead, we arrived unannounced just as the family had sat down to their evening meal. In addition to some tasteless millet porridge, there was a cabbage dish with a few shreds of pork thrown in, as well as a plate of delicious leek-filled pancakes, which looked a bit like crepes.

The family's diet is largely made up of carbohydrates and vegetables. "We always have enough to eat nowadays, but we can't afford meat more than once, or at most, twice a week," *Dimei* explained halfway through our stay, apologizing for the monotonous menu. Every meal was the same: rice, porridge, or some kind of pancake, served with a stir-fried vegetable. When *Dimei* turned thirty-two, we feasted on chicken prepared in a black iron pot, three different kinds of vegetables, and traditional birthday noodles made by Dr. Feng's mother (noodles symbolize long life). In honor of Dr. Feng's husband's arrival, we had our first serving of pork, and on the two last days of our stay we had fresh fish. Dr. Feng's husband and son were avid fishermen.

About six hundred families live in Dr. Feng's village, approximately 3,000 people. The average income level of the residents is just below the national average, though Chinese statistics are best taken with a grain of salt. "Only the size of the grain harvest is reported to the government, and even then, one tries to bring the figures down to a round sum," Dr. Feng's brother told me. "Because of taxation, everyone keeps as quiet as possible about any additional sources of income, for instance, from growing vegetables or from a small workshop."

Whenever we came home, Dr. Feng's sister-in-law, *Dimei*, would take the big enamel bowl from its rack and pump fresh water into it, for us all to wash our hands and faces. In the evening, the children bathed in a metal tub placed beside the pump. We adults took turns going outside in the dark of night to splash a bucket of water over ourselves. After the roasting hot day, the ice-cold water felt heavenly, but it would be a nightmare to have to wash that way in the winter. Even during this dry week in August, it seemed that life was an endless struggle against the dust and the mud.

"*Dimei* likes clean and tidy," Dr. Feng said approvingly at least a hundred times during our stay. When I visited other homes in the village, I noted that the clothes of my host family's sons did, indeed, appear to be cleaner than those of other children. "My home has always been poor, but even in my childhood I remember that my parents paid a lot of attention to cleanliness," Dr. Feng said. "My father was the village doctor. He learned the profession from his grandfather, who in turn had been his uncle's apprentice. This village has been around for the last five hundred years, and there's always been at least one member of our family who has been some kind of a doctor. I was the first one to receive formal training, though because of the Cultural Revolution, I don't have a university degree. But I made up for it afterward by taking a series of courses at a medical college."

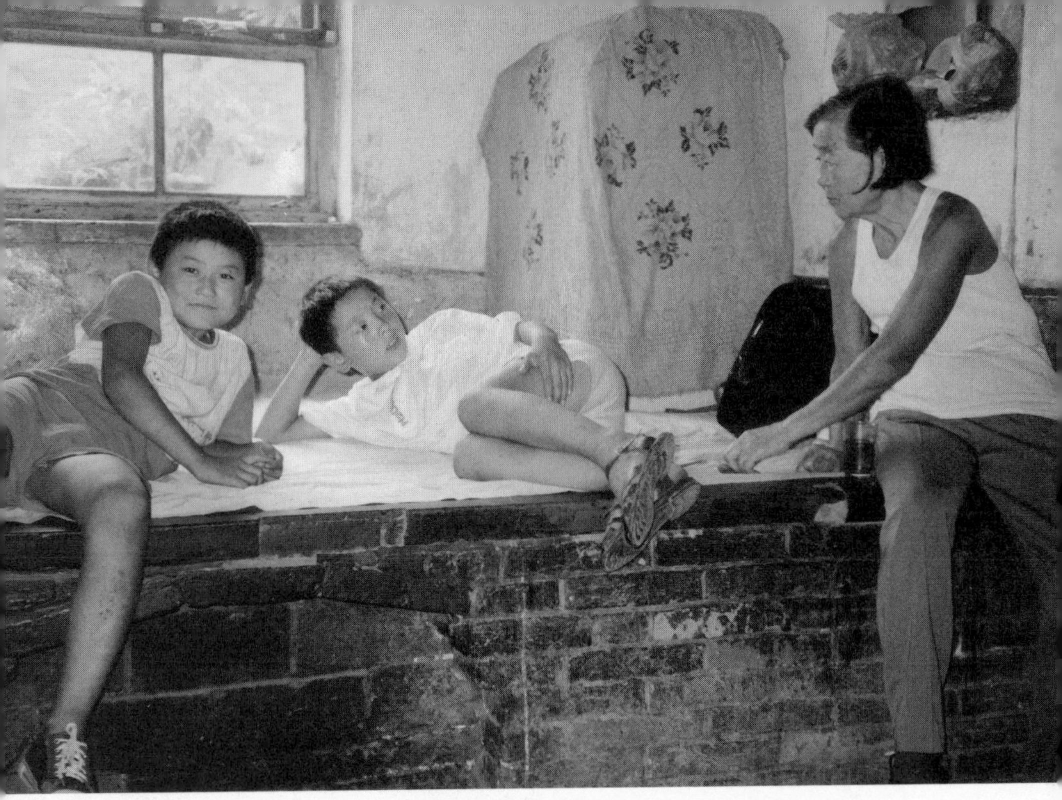

Doctor Feng's mother and her nephews on the kang. *During the daytime, the family's bedclothes are stacked in the corner and covered with a sheet. (Photo: Linda Jakobson)*

Dimei was not idle for a single moment. If she had nothing else to do, she would sweep the courtyard or squat beside the pump to wash some clothes. Even during meals, she often stood to eat, using her chopsticks to pluck a piece of cabbage into her bowl of rice from over her husband's shoulder. Or, if she did sit down at the table, she would be up again in a flash to fetch a cup of water for her children or more rice for her husband. She was constantly yelling at her sons: "Just look at the mud on your shirt," "Don't leave your shoes in the middle of the yard." But it was a good-natured type of scolding, and it seemed that an inner harmony prevailed in the family. Dr. Feng said the family had been lucky. Her brother is a good-natured fellow, and her mother and sister-in-law are on good terms. I hate to think what it would be like to live in a house where mother and daughter-in-law do not get along. This is the fate of millions in China.

"*Dimei* takes such good care of Mother. One couldn't hope for a better daughter-in-law in the house," Dr. Feng said. One evening she even remarked to her brother: "I wonder if you realize what a good wife you have." The poor man was at a loss for words. His ears turned scarlet with embarrassment. Showing affection is completely unheard-of among adults. On the other hand, everyone—even various male relatives—patted the children on their heads and Dr. Feng stroked their arms when they went to sit beside her. Dr. Feng's brother was reserved in my company, and it was obvious that he is the shyest member of the family, a quiet, but kind man. *Dimei* is an extrovert with a sunny disposition. She chatted happily with both her urban sister-in-law and me from the very first evening.

Dr. Feng's mother did not seem the least bit bashful in my presence either. She hobbled around the courtyard tending to her chores, proudly showing me every detail of her domain, including the stone enclosure she had built for the geese and hens. She had covered the top of the short stone wall with potted plants. Compared to the other homes I visited in the village, our courtyard was neater and better cared-for. Even the outhouse was tidier than many I have seen in Beijing. In the cities, a crude outhouse is often shared by all the residents on a lane of many one-story houses. Still today, only 54 percent of homes in the capital have their own toilets.

Doctor Feng's sister-in-law, Dimei *was never idle for a moment. The yard was a lot tidier than the others I visited in the village. (Photo: Linda Jakobson)*

A rural home's outhouse definitely has its advantages: One is at least blessed with the luxury of privacy. In the cities, there are often only walls a yard high to separate three or four holes. Sometimes there are not any walls at all. A Swedish friend, whose godchild lives on a crowded lane in Beijing, will never forget an experience in the nearby outhouse. She had just squatted down when she heard a familiar voice cry out: "My, isn't that Nini's godmother! We haven't seen you in ages. Have you just returned to China?" Privacy is a foreign concept in China. There is not even a good word for it in the Chinese language.

Dr. Feng's mother told me she had grown up in a nearby village. "But once I moved into this home, I only went to visit my parents once a year, on the second day of the Spring Festival. It isn't more than three *li* (about a mile) to the village of my birth, but in those days, it wasn't considered the right thing to do. After marriage, I belonged to this family. But I always urge my daughter-in-law to go and see her mother at least once a month."

According to Chinese tradition, a woman leaves the family of her birth upon marriage and becomes a member of her husband's household. Her most important task is to bear a son, who will continue the family line. In addition, she must care for her in-laws when they grow old. Classical Chinese literature is full of tales of women who have suffered the scorn of the whole family, but in particular the spiteful mother-in-law, if she does not succeed in producing a male heir.

"Still today, the law decrees that children must take responsibility for their aged parents. There is no social security in the countryside," my friends always remind me when the subject of favoring boys comes up. Though the law does not explicitly say that it is the son's responsibility, in reality, the task falls upon the son and his wife, in the countryside. A rural daughter abandons her own family when she moves to her husband's home.

I found Dr. Feng's mother quite a modern-thinking elderly woman, especially after I had heard the views of her neighbors. She told me that she had not opposed Dr. Feng's elder sister's divorce and that she accepted the younger sister's decision not to have children. Though there are more and more young people in the big cities who feel that these are private matters, the option not to have offspring is still widely frowned upon, as is the woman who chooses to stay single. Old ideas die slowly.

Attitudes toward divorce have changed greatly during my years in China. In 1987, a quarelling couple was under pressure to settle their differences, even when it was next to impossible. Family members, friends, workmates, even the street committee—almost the whole society—had a say in the matter. Ten years later, the majority of my city acquaintances agree that couples should not be forced to stay together against their own wishes. But in the countryside, a woman is tied to her husband's family. Often a wife's only plausible way out of a bad marriage is to move alone to the city and find employment in a private restaurant or workshop.

"My mother's attitude has a lot to do with the fact that both my sisters now live in the city," Dr. Feng reminded me. "Mother has spent the winters with us in Beijing. She knows that life in the city is completely different from that in the countryside. She's still old-fashioned in many ways. For example, she won't let my son work in the fields when he spends his summer holidays here, though I always tell her that manual labor would do a teenage boy some good. 'No,' says Mother. 'Your son is an intellectual. He must not be lowered to the status of a peasant.' But Mother is strict about making all his cousins work on the fields. 'They belong in the countryside,' explains Mother."

Differences between an educated person and an uneducated one, literally in Chinese "one who has no culture," are constantly stressed in China. Westerners find it strange that many educated Asian men let the nails of their little fingers grow long to indicate that they do not do manual work. On the other hand, Chinese find it equally odd that a Western professor or business executive might enjoy yard work and fixing the car, or feel that strenuous exercise is good for one's health.

One can never sufficiently emphasize the great gulf that exists between urban dwellers and those who live in the countryside. Rural women especially live in a world entirely different from that of their city sisters. By the 1990s, equality of the sexes had come a long way in the cities. Though only a small percentage of women rise to posts that wield genuine political power, city girls attend school as boys do and, on the whole, female wages are nearly comparable to those of males.

The grandmother in my godchild's family, *Laolao*, enjoys making a fuss over her equal status in society. "I know how popular it is to criticize socialism nowadays, and rightfully so, too. But don't forget that women are a whole lot better off today thanks to Mao," *Laolao* has said on many an occasion. *Laolao* is the daughter of a rickshaw-driver who never earned enough to support his family. "I would be an illiterate third-class citizen and totally dependent on a man if the Communists had not won the civil war. Just after I turned seven, I was allowed to go to school for six months.

Then, my mother managed to get the odd sewing job and I had to mind the younger children. After Liberation, the Communists educated me and I became a nursery school teacher. Today I have a pension, and I'm not dependent on anyone."

Laolao is the paragon of a strong-willed woman. Had she not taken an immediate liking to me, I doubt whether my godchild's family could have taken me under their wing so easily.

An educated urban woman is, generally speaking, an equal member of the household. A woman with less schooling tends to withdraw into the kitchen and can seldom be persuaded to sit down to a meal together with the men and visitors. I always feel awkward when, in the childhood home of my Jinan girlfriend, *Jiejie*, her mother slaves away in the kitchen and refuses to eat with us, even after all the dishes have been cooked. Then again, *Jiejie*'s mother-in-law, the opera singer, always joins us younger people at the table. *Jiejie*'s mother, a retired factory worker, is illiterate while *Jiejie*'s mother-in-law is an educated woman. Yet, despite her lack of formal schooling, I find *Jiejie*'s mother far wiser than many so-called intellectuals.

Young urban Chinese believe that a sufficiently headstrong and industrious woman can pursue a successful career. I have met dozens of women who have not studied beyond the ninth grade, but who run their own prosperous companies. When I interviewed women of different backgrounds before the Fourth World Conference on Women in 1995, many women under thirty laughed when I asked them about gender equality. "Why of course we're equal to men. Why wouldn't we be!" they cried out indignantly. On the other hand, when I spoke with their husbands, some of them mused: "I suppose men and women are equal, though my career is more important than that of my wife. Otherwise we're equal." Two or three men, whose wives were not within hearing distance, added: "In his heart, every man wants his wife to serve him. But it's not something you say out loud."

Despite the great improvement in the status of urban women, only about one-third of the country's scientists and technicians are women, and far fewer of the genuinely powerful political posts are held by women. For all its rhetoric, even the Communist Party has not embraced females wholeheartedly: 86 percent of its members are men.[5]

In nearly all the urban homes I know, spouses squabble about the housework, just as they do in the West. Chinese men are always amused when I tell them about Western expressions like "a hen-pecked husband" and "a nagging wife." "It's somehow consoling to know that a man in the West also has to put up with a pestering wife," my friend Guo Hairong's

husband once remarked with a wink. Actually, elderly men in the cities seem to be more active in sharing the household chores and caring for their grandchildren than their counterparts in the West. But in the countryside, such matters are not even discussed. The man is lord and master in the house, and household matters are no concern of his. The feudal way of thinking is still dominant. A rural woman's lot is certainly not an enviable one.

In many places, the status of women has actually deteriorated during the reform period because gender equality is no longer stressed in the way it was during Mao's time. In recent years, the traditional role of women has made a comeback, especially in poorer areas. The official press regularly describes "the grave problem in backward regions": the sale of wives.* Prostitution has also become a serious plague during the 1990s. Whenever I have traveled in the countryside in recent years, I have seen young women sitting on stools along the road, outside gas stations and inns, looking for clients. In a city like Jinan, where prostitution was next-to-nonexistent back in 1987, there were women selling their services at every single well-to-do nightclub I visited in the autumn of 1996. Even at a suburban dancing hall, I spoke with more than a dozen rural girls who were working as prostitutes.

Confucianism stressed hierarchy to uphold order and harmony. A son heeded his father as a subject served the ruler. A woman was obliged to obey the male members of the family throughout her life—first, her father, then her husband, and, when he died, her eldest son. Though Dr. Feng's brother gave the impression of a timid, shy man, I have no doubts that he still has the last say in the family in any matter of importance. Dr. Feng, on the other hand, is most definitely the one who makes the decisions in her family, as do both my godchild's and her cousin's mothers.

"I'm the one who carries the responsibility for the family. My husband doesn't do anything in his free time other than drink and gamble," a visibly distraught Dr. Feng once complained. That was years ago when we were first getting to know each other and she was trying to decide whether or not to seek a divorce. It was the only time I have ever seen her so upset. "Now I've stopped tormenting myself. I'm resigned to my fate," she said during our visit to her home village. "In the end, I just couldn't do it. It would have upset my son to no end. My husband is not a bad per-

* Before 1949, over 95 percent of marriages were arranged on a monetary basis. According to official statistics, today about three-fourths of young couples make the decision to wed or do so after consultation with their parents. This implies that about one-fourth of all Chinese marriages are still mercenary.

Left: City women live in an entirely different world than women in the countryside. Photo taken in Beijing in 1995. (Photo: John Lee)

son. He's simply an irresponsible husband and father. You never know if he'll come home after work or go out to play mahjongg with his friends. I have had to bring up our son on my own."

One seldom hears complaints about alcohol abuse in China. Even Dr. Feng was more annoyed about her husband's gambling than his drinking. The Western custom of spending an evening with friends over a bottle of wine is foreign to most Chinese. Alcoholic beverages—beer, sweet wine, or clear rice liquor called *baijiu*—are popular, but they are almost always consumed with meals. Sometimes rowdy groups of inebriated men in restaurants make a loud racket playing various kinds of games, but on the street one rarely encounters someone who is drunk. Western businessmen have recounted horrendous drinking sessions which take place during the course of a banquet, but Chinese businessmen do not spend their free evenings leaning on bar counters. Every Chinese who has visited me in Finland has been genuinely astounded at the amount of alcohol young Finns drink. Drinking is still associated with holidays or special occasions in China. Lots of Chinese are content to spend entire evenings in a karaoke bar or a disco sipping on a Coke or a beer.

The poor relations between Dr. Feng and her husband appeared to be the only flaw in the otherwise harmonious household. And if Dr. Feng had not confided her marriage problems to me, I probably would not have noticed them. The rest of the family seemed to get on well with "Old Tiger," as her husband is called. Even Dr. Feng's reserved, almost cold, manner when talking to her husband is not at all uncommon for a forty-year-old wife. Chinese are adept at concealing their inner feelings. It has taken me years to interpret the subtle gestures and remarks made in passing by the members of my godchild's family or a few close friends. Chinese seldom openly express their affection in words. They prefer showing that they care by their deeds.

Dr. Feng actually spoke well of her husband when we were discussing family relations. "Old Tiger is very fond of my family and he's always kind to them," she said. "Even when his own parents were still dependent on him, he was very generous toward my family. Now that my parents-in-law have become city people and can manage financially without us, he helps my family out even more. He bought the new furniture for the little chamber when my brother and *Dimei* got married, and he's always buying my mother's favorite foods when she stays with us."

Nearly all of my urban friends give a portion of their salary to their parents each month. As engineer Song explained, in the cities one takes care of both one's own parents and one's in-laws. But this new way of thinking has yet to catch on in the countryside.

From the very first day, I noticed the villagers' nonchalant attitudes toward girls. When a new child appeared in our courtyard, Dr. Feng's mother immediately told me which family the lad belonged to, if the child was a boy. If the child was a girl, she made no comment. Likewise, when we went to say hello to the nearby neighbors, the grandmother of the house was quick to point out her grandson proudly. Little girls stood at arm's-length, but no one mentioned them. The situation is totally different in the cities. Both father and grandfather smother a little girl with as much love as they do a boy. At his wedding, engineer Song announced that he hoped for a daughter. Though my goddaughter's father, Xiao Ping, had wanted a son, he has been an indulgent and adoring father from the very first day.

On a previous visit, Dr. Feng had promised to bring a camera to the village so that she could photograph her relatives' kids. It was heartbreaking to see one lady of the house after another pushing a little boy in front of the camera, without any regard for the little girls prancing around her. Every single grandmother wanted a portrait of herself holding her grandson in her lap. Dr. Feng tried to be impartial, but it was an impossible task because time and again I heard the older woman say: "Save your film, you can take pictures of the girls another time." And when the children followed us on our plant-hunting expeditions, ten-year-old girls dutifully carried their tired younger brothers on their backs. But I never saw anyone lend a helping hand to a younger sister. The given names of many girls are indicative of their status in the family. They are called "Zhao Di," "Yun Di," or "La Di," all of which express the wish that the next child in the family be a boy, names which mean "Bring a little brother after you."

When the school term began during our visit, I asked why there were so many girls wandering around during the day. "The family doesn't necessarily have enough money to pay for a daughter's tuition," Dr. Feng's mother answered. An annoyed Dr. Feng intervened: "And not every family thinks that it's essential either." After her mother

A proud grandmother with her grandson (Photo: Linda Jakobson)

objected, Dr. Feng continued: "In all fairness, most people these days do want their daughters to receive an education, too. But the school fees are unreasonable. If faced with a choice, parents deem their son's education more important. There are poorer villages where parents don't have enough money even to send their son to school."

The fee for one year at the local elementary school in Dr. Feng's home village is 250 yuan ($30). Since the Feng household's (three adults) joint annual income is 5,000 yuan ($600), school fees for two children make up 10 percent of the family's earnings. It is no wonder that educators speak so pessimistically about the future. The country's leaders speak gallantly of the importance of pursuing the "four modernizations," but they are not willing to invest in basic education. Though the central government has issued directives concerning the maximum sum that can be charged for schooling, in reality these matters are decided at the county, and sometimes even at the village level. In addition to tuition fees, Dr. Feng's brother pays an extra 20 yuan ($2.40) per child for books, and, as of that autumn, an additional 25 yuan ($2.90) for "security."

"That is outrageous," *Dimei* cried, when the boys came home on the first day of school and announced the new security fee. In the evening, a heated debate took place among the neighbors, Dr. Feng's relatives, in our courtyard. The village chief had decided that the school needed a security guard and appointed his younger brother to the post.

"That brother is a vile man. He's plain lazy and on top of that he terrorizes everyone with the authority he thinks he has because his brother is the village chief," one neighbor explained.

"There is absolutely no one threatening our children's safety. The new post is just a way to extort our money to support his brother. We ought to give the man a good beating," declared Dr. Feng's elder cousin, a bald man with a bushy moustache.

"Now just calm down," his wife cut him short. "It would only make for trouble."

When the others had departed, Dr. Feng's brother sat down on the steps and lit yet another cigarette. The smoke he exhaled seemed to express his frustration. He muttered something about how often the villagers find themselves in this same helpless situation. After a long silence he finally spoke again, in a clear, but disheartened voice: "Where can we escape to? We are bound to the land, and we have to put up with that rotten village chief. That's been the destiny of the Chinese peasant for thousands of years."

Dr. Feng told me that the village chief had fired two qualified teachers a year earlier and appointed his relatives in their places. "The new teach-

A rural girl's chances to receive an education have deteriorated as school fees have risen during the 1990s. If parents cannot afford to send all their children to school, they choose to educate their son. The photo was taken in a village school near Yan'an in 1994. (Photo: John Lee)

ers have no competence whatsoever," *Dimei* lamented. "Our older son's notebook is full of writing errors that no one has corrected."

Despotic county and village leaders, who arbitrarily impose new fees and taxes, are subjects of frequent official press articles. Occasionally, the central government even reports on peasant riots against these autocratic local officials. Such articles always quote central government officials who promise "resolute measures" to make the local officials heed the rules. In 1994, it was stipulated that peasants should not be forced to pay more than 5 percent of their net per capita income in various levies and taxes. When I asked Dr. Feng's brother to add up all the payments he had to make to the village, starting with road, water, and land taxes and ending with the welfare benefits paid to the "revolutionary veterans," he calculated that, all in all, he doled out about 32 percent of his and his wife's joint net income in obligatory fees.

The large number of children in the village also caught my attention. There seemed to be at least three or four kids in every household. I knew that the so-called one-child policy had, even officially in many rural areas, become a two-child policy. I also knew that, as a result of rising incomes, some families were prepared to pay the heavy fines for having more than the officially sanctioned number of offspring. But I had thought that these were exceptions. In this village, oversized families seemed to be the rule. According to Dr. Feng, this was true throughout the region.

"Rural parents are prepared to do anything to have a son," Dr. Feng reminded me. "It is not only an ancient tradition, it is the key to survival in the countryside. If you don't have a son, you have no security in your old age. Because anything can happen to a child, it is always safer to have two sons." (Contrary to the widely held assumption, however, Chinese generally did not have large families in the old days. The plots of land were so small that no one wanted too many heirs.)

Dr. Feng's otherwise reticent brother suddenly blurted out: "I would love to have a third child, so that we could have a baby girl. You foreigners shouldn't think that a Chinese peasant doesn't want a daughter. But if the number of children is restricted, a son is essential. Who would take care of my wife and me if we had two daughters? They would never be able to find husbands if they had the burden of caring for two old people. It's as simple as that."

His wife *Dimei* added: "Now we are told there won't be enough wives for all the men. But everyone has to look out for their own well-being first. There is not a couple alive who is willing to forfeit the most crucial security that exists just for the good of the nation."

Everyone agrees that there are too many people in China. Also, no one denies that the status of girls in the countryside has declined due to the strict family-planning measures which began to be enforced in the early 1980s. But there the consensus ends. How to control population growth is a very painful question. There are no easy answers.

In the late 1970s, with the beginning of the reform policy, the authorities tried to enforce a strict one-child-per-family policy. Rural opposition to the policy eventually led to modifications which, in over half the provinces, allow families to have a second child if the first is a girl. In 1994, when I conducted interviews in Yan'an, the cradle of the Chinese revolution, even the county official in charge of family planning told me: "We have accepted that one [child] is unrealistic. We strive for two, and we only fine families for the third." As with any regulation in China, enforcement varies greatly from place to place.

In the cities, couples have been strictly kept to one child. Every street committee and every work unit has a baby quota. A woman must acquire a baby permit in order to be admitted into a maternity hospital or to ensure that her child is given an I.D. When I was working on a story about population control in 1994, I learned that millions of children, born without baby permits, are growing up "unaccounted for" in the Chinese countryside. Rich parents can sometimes "purchase" an I.D. with the help of bribes, but a woman who has fled to another location to give birth or who bears a child while temporarily working in the city lacks the means to purchase such legitimacy.

The authorities decide not only how many children a person may have, but also when those children may be born. In women-dominated work units, such as textile factories, there are never enough baby permits to go around so they are fought over fiercely. Dr. Feng had at one time been in charge of family planning at her work unit. She said it was an awful task. The pressure was relentless. Though she had no say in determining the unit's baby quota, it was her duty to see that the quota was not exceeded. There were always a few married women who got pregnant without applying ahead of time for a baby permit. "Sometimes I managed to put away a few permits for that sort of situation. But if the permits ran out, I had no alternative but to persuade the women to have an abortion."

Women in China talk about abortion as openly as people in the West might speak of an ear infection. I have never grown accustomed to a girlfriend's offhand mention that she had just had an abortion. It is rare that a fetus stirs any emotion. Before leaving the mother's womb, the fetus is not considered a human being, and thus is not entitled to any rights under the law. It is not unusual for dating couples to "have an accident" that necessitates an abortion. Only a married woman is eligible for a baby permit.

In Dr. Feng's home village, intimate details about every married woman of childbearing age were posted on the outside wall of the "Family Planning Service Center." Doctor Feng told me that just a few years earlier, even menstrual cycles were registered on the chart. "Now, only the type of contraception she uses and how many pregnancies she has had are put on display. But the woman in charge of family planning in the village still keeps track of each woman's menstruation cycles, so that she can watch out for an unplanned pregnancy."

By the late 1990s, most urban residents have accepted the one-child policy, albeit grudgingly. Some support it genuinely, others concede that it is sensible because of the crowded living quarters. Still others just shrug their shoulders and say "*mei you banfa*," infamous words denoting helplessness and resignation when confronting the authorities.

In discussions about China's population problems, rarely does anyone mention the immense disservice Mao Zedong did to the nation by forbidding all family planning programs. Mao actually encouraged his countrymen to have as many children as possible. Middle-aged acquaintances often quote Mao when I bring up his policy's devastating effects: "Let us drown our enemies in the sea of people!" Mao believed that human beings were the driving force of the revolution. He reminded the masses of a famous Yuan dynasty saying, according to which the strength of people grows like a fire. The bigger the fire, the more magnificent the flames. When the People's Republic was founded in 1949, 540 million people lived in China. Less than forty years later, the population had doubled.

During my years as a correspondent, population control has perhaps been the most contradictory issue (of China's many irreconcilable challenges) to write about. Government attempts to curb population growth are understandable. Every year, the Chinese population increases by at least 13 million people. Space is limited. Only 7 percent of of the world's arable land is located in China, with about 25 percent of the world's population. In terms of cultivated land, China has only one-quarter of an acre per capita (in the U.S. the comparable figure is 2 acres per capita). In any discussion of the problems in China, you will inevitably hear the remark, "There are just too many Chinese."

The higher authorities constantly remind foreigners that the law forbids the use of force as a means of enforcing birth control. But force is indeed used. I have been appalled by the reports of baby girls being abondoned or killed. My urban Chinese friends are just as shocked. When the British documentary "The Dying Rooms" caused an international stir in the summer of 1995, it was nearly impossible to explain to people in the West that urban Chinese, and many who live in the countryside, condemn the abandonment of baby girls as strongly as we do. I still recall the comments of engineer Song, the doting father of a six-month-old girl, after watching my videotape of the documentary: "Parts of this country are so underdeveloped that you can produce as horrifying a documentary on just about any topic, for example, wife-beating or the selling of women. There is plenty of material. But it does not portray the whole truth about China."

Occasionally I have read secret "internal reports," written for the benefit of Chinese authorities, that describe the brutal measures of local family planning officials who were punished for their actions. These officials defended their behavior by saying that they had to fulfill the baby quota, which was decreed at a higher level, in order to hold on to their jobs. My visit to Dr. Feng's home village stunned me. I had naively imagined that the shocking measures I had read about were, by the mid-1990s, a severe problem only in remote, impoverished areas. But Dr. Feng's village is only three hours by bus from Jinan. There, just recently, two women, both eight months pregnant, had been hauled off to the county hospital for forced abortions. I learned about the incident when we came across a razed house on one of our daily excursions. We were walking on a plateau, with a full view of the battered building. The windows had all been broken, the door was hanging by a single hinge, and bits of broken furniture were scattered around the courtyard.

"The work of villains," Dr. Feng whispered, with a meaningful look. When we returned home, she asked her sister-in-law about the house.

"There were six women in the village who got pregnant at the end of last year, after the baby permits for this year had already been distributed," *Dimei* recounted. "The village chief, the Party Secretary, and the official in charge of family planning were absolutely panic-stricken. They started to pressure the families of the six ferociously, but only two of the women consented to have abortions. Two of the families offered the village chief and Party Secretary big enough bribes, so they looked the other way when the women disappeared a month before they were due to give birth. Both of them have relatives in villages not far away. There's gossip that one of the husbands paid 7,000 yuan ($840) altogether. Can you imagine? That's more than our whole family earns in a year. The last two women tried to hide."

Dimei took a deep breath and paused for a moment. "But they were found and taken, kicking and screaming, with their hands tied behind their backs, to the county hospital. Just think, they were in their eighth month of pregnancy."

Dr. Feng shook her head in dismay. "Something like that should never be allowed to happen. But what can an ordinary person do?"

I asked why the house had been ransacked.

"The husband of one of the women who had been dragged off threatened to go to the county leaders to complain about the two women who had managed to flee. They both returned quietly with newborn baby boys about a fortnight ago. They will have to pay some official fine, but, anyway, they're now the mothers of healthy babies. The village chief had his thugs beat up the man who had threatened to file a complaint. They confiscated just about everything the family owned. I heard the family has now taken refuge in another village. I'm not quite sure where they went."

A peasant in central Xian in 1995. (Photo: John Lee)

THE BATTLE AGAINST DESPOTISM.

"There Is No Justice in China"

The cadres in Dr. Feng's home village are not unique. By allowing the peasants to work for themselves, Deng Xiaoping revolutionized one sector of rural life. But though the communes were disbanded, cadres, often the same ones as before, continued to implement Party policies as they saw fit, albeit under a revised organization of local government. The Chinese media often report cases of village chiefs, local Party secretaries, court officials, and police who have abused their power, each covering up for the other.

One evening, Dr. Feng's cousin sat on the *kang*, unburdening his heart about his twenty-six-year-old daughter. The young woman had been detained for seven months, accused of embezzling 1,500 yuan ($185) from the bank where she used to work. She maintained her innocence.

"I'm in no position to say if she is guilty or not," said her father, a man in his fifties. "I just wish her case would be brought to court. It's agony not knowing how long she'll have to languish behind bars. But I have no *guanxi* among the county officials, and I'm not on good terms with our village chief. I went to see him, but he wouldn't even promise to take the matter up at the county headquarters."

When someone remarked—for perhaps the hundredth time—that the village chief was a good-for-nothing scoundrel, I asked whether elections for the post of village chief had been held in accordance with the new electoral law.

The chamber went dead quiet. Everyone looked at me bewildered. I realized that these people had not yet heard about this significant reform launched six long years earlier.[1] Sometimes China is truly a depressingly large country.

At last Dr. Feng's brother spoke up. "What are you talking about?" he asked.

I told them about my trip in March 1995 to Liaoning province in the Northeast, where I had witnessed free elections in several villages. About 60 percent of the incumbent village chiefs in Liaoning lost their posts as a result of elections that year. Based on what I had seen, I was hopeful that local government reforms gradually might win out in the long struggle against despotism and injustice. At least it is a beginning step toward establishing a system of checks and balances at the grass-roots level. In the weeks preceding the elections, candidates had the opportunity to state their platforms publicly and to explain their plans for developing the village.

In the West, the project is referred to as "village democracy reform" and numerous Western countries donate money to train local officials in the practicalities of the electoral process. One of the project's first sponsors was the International Republican Foundation in the United States. The ideological background of the donor does not seem to matter much to the Communist regime, as long as it pays in dollars.

Elections for the post of village chief are held every third year. Each adult has one vote. More importantly, there must be more than one candidate running for the post, and he or she need not be a Communist Party member. According to the regulations, the organizers must ensure that there are secret ballots. In many villages, there have already been as many as three or even four rounds of such elections. So far, the reform has been most successful in middle-income villages where residents earn their living from both agriculture and industry. Because the majority of rural factories are collectively owned, the villagers care about how local revenue is allocated and therefore who the local officials are.

The person in charge of implementing the reform, an open-minded man called Wang Zhenyao, had studied the election process in the United States, several European countries, and in India, Asia's oldest democracy. When I interviewed Wang in January 1997, he estimated that more than half of China's villages had elected a non-Party member as village chief. If that is not a revolutionary reform, what is? The Communist Party abdicated its right to appoint the village chief, conceding that better results can be achieved if the villagers take part in the decision-making process. A person who opposes a Party member is no longer called "an enemy of the people," as was the case in Mao's days.

"Some of the newly elected village chiefs, about 20 percent, later applied and were accepted into the Party," Wang Zhenyao said. "This way the Party recruits younger and more able members, who also command respect among the villagers."

One recently elected village chief in Liaoning province thought it strange when I asked why he wished to join the Communist Party. The Party had twice before rejected his application, but because of his overwhelming electoral victory, he felt confident that the next time he would finally be accepted. "We only have one Party. Its members are all leading citizens of society," answered the burly man, a former truck-driver. "Isn't it only natural that a person wants to feel respected?" (Communist Party members are indeed an elite group, making up only 4 percent of the population.)

In the cities, people look upon Party membership differently. Even during on-the-record interviews, I have been told that one joins the Party purely for utilitarian reasons, to benefit one's career advancement or business opportunities. Otherwise membership is referred to quite offhandedly, even mockingly. A friend of mine was horrified when her boss encouraged her to apply for membership. "Who wants to be a member? You have to sit in meetings all day long," she said. With a grin, she added, "Thank goodness my mother-in-law taught me the correct way to refuse that kind of an offer: 'I don't think I yet have enough of the virtuous qualities required of a Party member. Let's wait a while.'"

Those who are skeptical about village democracy are quick to point out that the Party secretary, not the village chief, is still the most influential man in the village, though the Village Council, headed by the village chief, is supposed to be responsible for the village's economy. No doubt such claims are, at least in part, true, though the situation varies greatly from village to village. According to Wang Zhenyao, electoral reforms have strengthened the position of the village chief. "If the village chief and the Party secretary disagree, the village chief can say, 'The residents of this village have chosen me for this job. Next time, you can stand for elections.'" The notion of secret ballots is spreading within the Party itself. Usually county officials appoint the Party secretary in each village, but, according to Wang Zhenyao, Party members in numerous villages have started to demand (and, on occasion, have been granted) the right to choose the Party secretary by voting among themselves.

China's top leadership is well aware that Party authority has been eroded by officials who abuse their power.[2] The experiment with village democracy is one of many reforms initiated in the 1980s. Some Western observers were puzzled to discover that the reform had the strong backing of Peng Zhen and Bo Yibo, both known as old-guard conservatives. These two revolutionary veterans were deeply worried about the Party's loss of prestige, legitimacy, and the resultant arbitrary control by clans, religious groups, and secret societies in the countryside. Grassroots political institutions had ceased to function after the Cultural Revolution. Village leaders were either unwilling or unable to fulfill their paramount obligations: gathering the grain quota, collecting taxes, and supervising birth control. A State Council report in early 1992 warned that 30 percent of the Party cells in the countryside had collapsed; another 60 percent were extremely weak and disorganized.[3] The central government needed competent and trustworthy officials to ensure the success of the reform policy in the countryside.

Peng Zhen and Bo Yibo had no intention of letting the democratic election process spread beyond the village level. When I asked the fifty-two-year-old deputy mayor of Shenyang if he envisioned free, multicandidate elections in the cities, he answered without hesitation: "Not in my lifetime."

Wang Zhenyao, a man in his early forties, is an exceptional cadre. He had thrown himself into the village democracy experiment heart and soul in 1988, traveling around the country to persuade and advise local officials. He is known for his strong will, but also for his ability to compromise—a mixture of qualities rare for a Chinese bureaucrat. Our numerous conversations during the 1990s always left me thinking that if all Chinese leaders were as competent and broadminded as he, the country's future certainly would look a lot brighter. He abhores sanctimony and does not let his subordinates bow and scrape before him. I am not alone in my respect for him. I have heard many people, both Chinese and Westerners, say that Wang is the only higher-level cadre they have encountered who appears to be totally incorruptible.

Wang Zhenyao's task was never-ending. About 4.2 million officials needed to be trained in how to arrange a multicandidate election with secret balloting. Even more important, local leaders had to be persuaded to accept the changes. Village chiefs who had held their posts for years, even decades, were not enthusiastic about measuring their popularity in open elections. Because the people in charge of overseeing free elections were county and provincial officials, the success of the village democracy reform depended on whether Wang Zhenyao and his team could win their support. The fact that the residents of Dr. Feng's village had not even heard about the reform shows that Wang and his colleagues have not always been successful. Dr. Feng's relatives listened in disbelief as I explained how village chiefs had been elected in Liaoning. They were not in the least bit impressed. They all took it for granted that I had been shown rigged elections.

"Sure, we have elections," Dr. Feng's cousin snorted. "There is one candidate for the post of village chief, and he is our Party Secretary."

"Don't forget, our village chief did indeed change last year," his wife said teasingly. "The new man is the old one's nephew."

Dr. Feng made no comment. I did not expect a city resident to be familiar with the notion of village democracy since official newspapers had—in 1996—only mentioned it in passing.[4] For several years the government was cautious about spreading word of the village electoral reform; many leaders evidently were not eager to let the urban population get too excited about representative democracy. Foreign journalists did not learn about it until Wang Zhenyao took us with him on expeditions to the countryside. After 1995, the subject became so popular in the Western media that the Ministry of Civil Affairs decided to downplay the politically explosive term "village democracy," referring instead to the "local governance reform" being carried out at the village level. Actually, this appellation is more in line with reality—the Chinese leadership is pursuing a means of implementing good governance, not democracy.

The way my godchild's family reacted when I prepared to go to Liaoning reflected the typical urban view. "Now don't go thinking that genuine elections are being held in the countryside. It's all just put on for your benefit," Xiao Ping's brother, *Gege*, warned me. *Saozi* was outspokenly indignant. She assured me I was being taken for a ride. "How could country bumpkins possibly understand anything about democracy. Nonsense!"

When I returned and described what I had seen, at least they did not accuse me of concocting tall tales. I told them that the organization of the elections was far from perfect, with many details yet to be worked out. For example, in one village I saw two young women squeeze into the voting booth together. "We always have the same opinion anyway," they giggled when the election official reprimanded them and tried to get them to enter one by one. Others did not want to stand in line. They filled out their ballots in the open air, using their bicycle seats for support. In another village, the younger challenger complained that his opponent, the incumbent village chief, had been given far more time to present his views at the village assembly meeting. In spite of these shortcomings, I was impressed that multicandidate elections were truly being held. Wang Zhenyao did his best to keep the local officials at bay when we three Western journalists were permitted to wander around on our own. The majority of those under age forty with whom I chatted seemed enthusiastic about the reform. "At least this is an attempt to make the officials more accountable," was a comment I heard more than once.

Though the members of my godchild's family did not question my experiences, they remained dubious as to the overall effect of the election reform. "The heads of the more important families can decide the candidates among themselves. Or a rich farmer can pay off voters the same way he now bribes the village chief," my godchild's mother pointed out. "And how much power does the village chief have anyway?" *Gege* added. "That reform will never be allowed to spread further than the villages."

When I met Wang Zhenyao in early 1997, I told him about my experiences in "a village in Shandong," meaning Dr. Feng's ancestral home.

"The villagers' ignorance doesn't surprise me. As I've told you, this is a long, slow process. There are nearly one million villages in this country," he said, unfolding a map of China. Three rounds of elections had already been held in twenty-two provinces.[5] "Six provinces have been exemplary. In other words, voters cast their ballots in secret, there was more than one candidate for the post of village chief, and all candidates were given a chance to explain their views at a public meeting. In about ten other provinces, progress has been sporadic. Shandong is one of them. In some parts of that province, the villagers were so active in arranging public meetings that officials had to curtail the campaign. Beyond these are a dozen or so counties which still have not had a single proper election, like your friend's village."

Wang Zhenyao and his colleagues have their work cut out for them. In Northeast China, I once heard him vent his frustration: "How can we teach people about the noble concept of democracy when they can't seem to learn how to form a line?" When he saw that the local officials with him thought he was joking, he became even more distraught. "Really, I'm talking about a serious matter. Why is it that in India uneducated citizens line up patiently and wait for their turn at the polls? But here in China it seems like an impossible task."

Wang was not exaggerating. People rarely line up for anything in an orderly fashion in China. I sometimes tease my friends that pushing and shoving are national habits. Even when an empty bus approaches a bus stop and no more than fifteen people are waiting to get on, everyone tries to squeeze through the door at exactly the same moment. I have always thought it was only natural in a country where there is not enough of everything for everybody, but Wang's reference to India, which has as severe a population problem, proves my theory wrong.

However, Wang Zhenyao had far greater worries than impatient voters. In some provinces, the governors informed him in as many words that village democracy reform was too much of a bother. What they meant was that incumbent village chiefs, and their relatives, were vehemently opposed to it. There are also groups within the central government who have their doubts about the project.

But Wang is not one to give up easily. "The more frequent the peasant uprisings and the more serious the problems become in the countryside, the more willing the higher authorities will be to endorse the village election process," he predicted. The advocates of village democracy always refer to the spread of hooliganism and crime in the countryside.

When I started to research the subject I discovered a lively, longstanding debate about the pros and cons of village democracy. Though little had appeared in the general newspapers, a wealth of material had been published in legal journals and so-called "restricted" publications. Numerous articles begin with vivid descriptions of murders and robberies or attacks on corrupt village chiefs. Clearly it was the fear of outright chaos that led to local government reform. The leaders of China were not trying to implement democracy, they simply were being pragmatic. The villages need leaders capable of overseeing the Party's interests (collecting grain and taxes, and overseeing family planning). If elected leaders are more effective than those appointed by the Party, "village democracy" might well become permanent in China. It is well to remember that the elected village officials have no power to change central government directives. They only have the authority to find the best possible means of implementing them.

When I accompanied Wang Zhenyao to Liaoning in the spring of 1995, he mentioned that the election reform had not yet been carried out in his own home village. He said that giving out high-handed orders to impertinent officials in one tiny village was not his way of doing things. The whole country was full of stubborn and backward-thinking leaders, he reminded me. It was wiser to carry out educational work step by step. The reform process was supposed to proceed from county to county. In addition, he wanted to be considerate of his relatives in his home village.

When we met in 1997, I asked him how things were progressing in his home village.

"Don't talk to me about that. They're an utterly hopeless lot," Wang answered curtly. It suddenly dawned on me that his somewhat embarrassed and pained expression reflected one of China's many paradoxes. The person in charge of the nationwide implementation of village democracy is an intelligent and influential man, who is genuinely and tirelessly trying to reform his country. But the obstinate cadres even in his own home village oppose him.*

* When I was preparing to leave China in the summer of 1997, I heard that Wang Zhenyao had been relieved of his duties and transferred to the Department of Disaster Relief under the Ministry of Civil Affairs. The official explanation for the transfer was that after nine years at one job it is healthy to do something else for a change, but the unofficial grapevine in Beijing offered a number of alternative reasons for his transfer. "Wang was probably just too competent, and that upset his superiors," one of his subordinates reckoned. Unfortunately, this is the fate of many able cadres in China.

The West considers China a totalitarian country. The term accurately fits a government that imprisons or even executes anyone deemed "a threat to the state" for simply voicing an opinion. When an individual gets on the wrong side of the authorities, the consequences are nearly always disastrous. But the "totalitarian" label may be misleading to those who presume that the orders of the central government are obeyed in every corner of the country. That is not the case. During the Deng era, the central government delegated part of its power to lower levels to ensure the success of the economic reforms.

In a country the size of China, the remarkable development of the last two decades would not have been possible had the leadership in Beijing kept a tight rein over all facets of the economy. Innovation and enterprise had to be encouraged. But, as a result of the successful economic experiments, county and even provincial leaders have become much more independent. By the 1990s, many local leaders were taking the initiative and making decisions that did not always accord with central government policy. A constant tug-of-war goes on between the central authorities and those at the provincial level. It is a bit like bartering over the price of a watermelon at the marketplace in Beijing. Both parties have to give a little until a mutual agreement is reached. Central government directives are often amended and modified in various ways before they are actually implemented and enforced in the provinces.

The growing income gap has increased the friction between city and rural residents. This yuppie couple in Beijing (right), leaving the upscale Lufthansa Department Store, has little in common with a peasant couple from Guizhou (left), on their way home from the nearby village market. (Photos: John Lee)

Acquaintances and friends who live outside major metropolitan areas like Beijing often compare their local leaders to the warlords of the pre-Liberation period. The economic reforms have given rise to a new class of autocrats with little, if any, respect for the law. One such "little dictator" is a factory director who was introduced to me by my economist friend, Chen.

"Because of his business success, Director Lin has soared to a position above the law," Chen claimed. "His brother is the village Party secretary, his cousin is the police chief, and he has bought off all the important leaders in the county and the nearby city, starting with the mayor himself."

"Little dictator" Lin runs his own privately owned factory in the countryside. Officially, he has employed economist Chen by "borrowing" him from the city university for a fee. This is a common practice in the 1990s. Private factories badly need the know-how and foreign language expertise of university graduates, while the overstaffed university welcomes the extra income. As for Chen, he earns 2,400 yuan ($295) a month instead of the 600 yuan ($75) salary he received as a lecturer. But he is still on the books as a university employee, which offers him a safety net of sorts.

I met Chen when we were both studying in Beijing in 1987. Upon graduation he won a government-funded scholarship to do research at a European university. Then he moved back to the city of his birth in Henan province where he was assigned a job at the university. In a matter of years he went from being an underworked lecturer of economics to a thick-skinned deputy director at Lin's factory. In his student days, Chen did not have enough money to buy a two-dollar train ticket to attend his brother's wedding. For years, he could not afford to eat anything but the dreary grub at the school canteen. The first time he invited me to dinner at the Sheraton Hotel in Beijing, I could not help but chide him a bit: "You're no longer the skinny economics major, happy to wear hand-me-down sweaters with patches at the elbows." Like many of my old acquaintances, Chen had been transformed into a fashion-conscious, suave businessman who was quite proud of being teased about his large belly.*

Over the years, Chen has recounted such incredible tales about the goings-on at the factory that every now and again I have felt the need to check their authenticity. Once I looked up a forty-year-old engineer, whom, according to Chen, Director Lin had beaten up and then fired. When the man arrived for our appointment, I took one look at his swollen, bruised face and realized Chen had not exaggerated. Another time I phoned the Beijing representative of a European company to confirm another story about Lin. The executive was aghast when he realized what I was calling about, but, with a little prodding, he admitted that he had indeed been shamelessly cheated by Director Lin. The European had sold Lin high-tech cable machines for approximately half a million dollars. The contract stipulated the terms of payment in detail. But Lin had decided long before signing the contract that he was not going to pay the last installment of $100,000.

"Director Lin felt he was paying too much for the machines in the first place. He knew the last shipment of equipment would be installed in the factory before the last payment had to be made," Chen said. The European engineers were forcibly hustled from the factory to the airport the moment the last test was run. Chen's description of the incident reminded me of a scene in an American "Wild West" movie. Accounts of similar situations appear frequently enough in the Hong Kong press that China has begun to be called the Wild East.

The European company that sold the cable machines to Director Lin first tried on its own, then through its embassy in Beijing, and after that through its Vice Minister of Foreign Trade, to get what rightfully was its due. All to no avail. The company's chief representative said Director Lin

* Skinniness is associated with poverty; body-fat with good health and prosperity. Often when I return to Beijing after being away for more than a week, the woman who runs the elevator and the older relatives of friends greet me: "You're fatter than before!" It is meant to be a compliment.

was like a piece of soap which always managed to slip out of reach. At last, the Europeans turned to the highest authorities in the province.

"The European ambassador and Vice Minister were invited to a grand banquet, hosted by a vice governor of the province," Chen told me. "When the foreigners left they were told that the matter would be sorted out in no time. But nothing ever happened. Why? Because Director Lin has very good relations with another vice governor, and the vice governor who had hosted the banquet was not willing to get into an argument with his colleague just because some foreign company wanted to be paid. So the matter dragged on and on until the foreigners simply gave up."

I started to understand why the Chinese government has such difficulties getting the producers of pirated CDs and video cassettes to toe the line. I remember the sarcastic comment made by the general manager of a multinational company after dining with a Chinese vice minister. The vice minister had tried to explain why the trade row between the United States and China could not be easily resolved. "Of course, the leaders in a totalitarian state can make their subordinates abide by the regulations if they want to," the general manager exclaimed haughtily. "Mao only had to whisper, and his word would be heeded in every village in the country." Such a claim was an exaggeration even for the 1960s; it is totally out of touch with today's reality.

Director Lin is only one among thousands of wealthy, unscrupulous sharks in China. Their patrons are often the most powerful civil servants in the county, or the city, or even the provincial government. These cadres, in turn, receive generous kickbacks for their protection.

I was eager to meet "little dictator" Lin. To my surprise, my friend Chen said it would be easy to arrange. "At present Director Lin is going through a phase where he's interested in everything foreign. We'll invite you to pay a visit to our factory," Chen said with a grin.

The factory is located in Henan province. The two-lane road leading out of the city is the kind you see all over China. Every vehicle we passed was either a truck, a tractor, a bicycle, or a horse-drawn cart, and the surface of the road was full of potholes. Corn fields and shabby-looking houses whizzed by, along with the occasional small factory or workshop. In China, drivers honk their horns before they pass you, they honk again while they are passing you, and they honk whenever they feel the need to warn anyone of their existence. Traveling by car is often an endless, movable cacaphony.

After about twenty-five miles, we turned off the poorly maintained highway onto a road with a surface so smooth that we might have been speeding along the brand-new airport motorway in Beijing. Except that we were in the middle of nowhere!

Chen had portrayed his boss as a ostentatious type, so I had anticipated that the drive leading to Director Lin's kingdom would be "the finest road in the province." But nothing had prepared me for the view which opened up in front of my eyes after another fifteen minutes. A rectangular building the size of a football field stood out on the horizon. When we came a bit closer, I swallowed hard. Behind this ultramodern factory, which resembled an enormous box, stood half-a-dozen brand-new high-rise apartment buildings and three Western-style luxury villas. A bit further on, I could see a white-tiled office building with large, blue-tinted windows and beside it, a four-story hotel. The dilapidated old factory off to one side looked quite out of place among the mowed lawns and trimmed bushes. "Wait until I show you the goldfish pond," Chen chuckled.

My visit began with a lunch hosted by Director Lin. His appearance betrayed no hint of his monstrous reputation. He was about fifty, balding, with unusually small eyes that seemed out of proportion with his large round face. If I had not heard so much about Director Lin, I would have thought he was a typical self-made businessman who was well aware of his stature as the wealthiest man around. I had met many similar men in my travels through the provinces; most of whom, like Lin, sported a sizable paunch. He wore gray slacks, and the sleeves of his white shirt were rolled up. His short welcoming speech was full of friendly, superficial phrases, typical for such an occasion. Though I do not approve of my Chinese friends' habit of evaluating a person purely on the basis of education, I have to admit the word "uncivilized" is an apt description of "little dictator" Lin. But, in contrast to his coarse manners, he came across as a businessman with acute financial instincts. He had a single-minded focus: money, and only money, makes the world go 'round.

"Now where is that brandy bottle which we received as a gift in Europe?" Lin asked Chen, halfway through the lunch. "Go and ask the waitress to fetch it." Then he turned to me and said, "Do you know how much that bottle costs in a Chinese department store? 2,700 yuan ($330). I asked my son to check."

The way Lin talked about money is not unusual in China. "How much did you pay for that?" and "How much do you earn?" are standard questions. But Director Lin's obsessive bragging about his wealth far exceeded any normal discussion of prices. I decided that his other guests must be better at acting impressed than I could bring myself to be, as his pomposity grew with each new dish that was brought to the table.

"Next time you come, we'll send a helicopter to pick you up at the airport. We could build a helicopter pad over on the west side, couldn't we, Little Chen?" he exclaimed when, to my relief, the soup was served. The arrival of the soup is a signal that a Chinese banquet is about to end. "I got the idea of buying my own helicopter when we spent some time in Europe last year. I'm sure you've heard about our trip."

I had a hard time keeping a straight face as I recalled Chen's hilarious account of the trip. Director Lin had never been outside of China. The European factory he had been negotiating with to purchase the cable machines had invited him and Chen to pay a visit. The day before they left, Lin had marched into Beijing's finest department store to buy his first Western suit and proclaimed in a booming voice: "I want the most expensive suit you have in this shop. I'm going to Europe."

The tour of Europe turned into a nightmare for poor Chen. He had to take care of Director Lin as if he were a small child and show him how to behave every step of the way. In addition, Chen had to put up with his boss's fits of anger whenever the host company's arrangements did not please him. "What could I say to our hosts? That my superior is worse than a spoiled brat and that if you want us to sign this deal you had better treat him like the Emperor himself?" an exhausted Chen had sighed upon his return. Mealtimes were the worst. Director Lin often sat sullenly, muttering to himself about the rotten-tasting Western food.

After that first trip, I saw a lot of Chen. He always came through Beijing before setting off on expeditions to different corners of the globe. In the beginning, Director Lin accompanied Chen. Then, one sunny day Lin declared: "Now I've seen all the richest countries in the world. There is no more need for me to travel."

As Chen became more and more indispensable to Director Lin, he started to squeeze more benefits out of him. First, he asked for a car, so that he could return home to his family in the city at the end of the day. Other city employees had to spend the work week at the factory. They were driven to town by a factory bus on Saturday afternoons. Next, Chen set his heart on his own apartment, an impossible acquisition on a monthly salary of 2,400 yuan. "I'm probably the only person Director Lin respects," Chen once mused as he described the complicated apartment negotiations which had taken place. "He knows that with my university degree and foreign language skills, I can get a decent job in the city any time I want. No other city boy has put up with him for more than six months." Finally, Director Lin agreed to purchase a three-bedroom apartment in the prime central city district. Through a maze of intricate (and illegal) maneuvering, the apartment was transferred to Chen's name. One day, in the spring of 1997, Chen called me and said that he had just become the happiest man in China. "Every Chinese dreams of this moment, but very few ever experience it," he said.

Chen, to my surprise, did not become a snob or a show-off in Director Lin's company. He is still the same down-to-earth guy I knew ten years ago. He is also one of the few Party members I know who does not go around blasting the Party. "I was chosen to be a member because I was at the top of my class in university. You know that I'm not at all interested in politics, but why should I mock the Party? The state paid for my education and funded my studies abroad. I'm a boy from a poor family," Chen answered, when I commented on his unusual attitude. "On the other hand, the Party is no longer important. There's really no single part of society that looks up to the Party these days. It sounds crazy to say this but from the point of view of ordinary people, money has substituted the Party. Money gives you a sense of security, and money is a good reason to work hard."

Chen said that his new apartment was worth every minute of the suffering he had endured during the last six years at Director Lin's side. He assured me that after a few more years he will have paid off his gratitude for the apartment with his work. "Then I can return to the university and live the quiet life of a lecturer for the rest of my life," he claimed, though I do not believe for a minute that he will ever again be satisfied twiddling his thumbs as a cadre.

After I spent the day at Director Lin's factory I realized that, had I not known how he had acquired his wealth, I would have painted a somewhat different picture of the man. He is a remarkably successful entrepeneur. He employs three-fourths of the population of two nearby villages. Thanks to him, every family has earned enough to build a new brick house, with running water and even a telephone. Though the factory is a private enterprise, it recently paid for a new high school in one of the villages. In the other village, a new health clinic was being constructed. The area I called "Lin's kingdom," about 100 acres all told, is conspicuously neat and tidy. In addition, Lin arranged scholarships for thirty young villagers to study at a technical institute in the nearby city, something they never could have afforded on their own.

Lin was born into a farmer's family in 1943. "We didn't starve, but still, I don't recall ever having enough to eat as a child," Director Lin reminisced. "In school I only went as far as eighth grade because my father had a serious accident when I was fourteen. After that, I had to work full-time with my mother in the fields."

His parents are still both living. His father, a frail man in a faded Mao-suit, moved around the factory grounds in a motorized wheelchair. I only caught a glimpse of his mother before she was taken in the factory Mercedes to the city hospital for treatment for her rheumatism. Director Lin can certainly not be accused of neglecting his family. According to Chen, the smarter family members held various posts in the factory and the "stupid" ones, or those whom Director Lin did not get along with, were paid to stay away. "After all, someone has to take care of the farming," Chen quipped.

Lin's background is typical for a countryside magnate. When the reform policy was launched in 1979, he quit the army where he had worked as an electrician for twelve years.

"I was thirty years old and fed up with just scraping by. We Chinese are intelligent people; why should we be poor? I had lots of ideas about how to make money."

Lin tried a number of enterprises until he got the idea of assembling television tubes. "It was a sure bet back in the early 1980s. I'm sure you know that at first every family had its heart set on the 'four things that go round'—a clock, a sewing machine, a fan, and a bicycle. After that they would save for a television.[6] I talked the county leaders into investing some of the local revenue into a television tube factory. Of course, I promised them their own personal share of the profits. And then, when the competition got too tough, I switched to cables," Lin said. He proceeded to recite mind-boggling figures to prove how much industrial and phone cable was needed in Henan province alone.

When I visited Director Lin, he was already contemplating his next move. The last of the new cable machines had not yet been fully installed, but he had already determined that the cable industry would only yield big profits for three or four more years. "I'm looking into the computer business. You've always got to be one step ahead of your competitors. Now that I have Little Chen, I've come into contact with foreign investors. We can get rich together."

When I dropped by to see Chen again two and a half years later, the cable factory was no longer operating at full capacity. On the top floor of the huge building four hundred young workers sat tapping away at computers, working in three shifts around the clock. "Our customers are all in America. They send us, let's say, the phone books of a whole city or state or an entire set of law texts by express freight, and we input them into the computer," Chen explained. "After our employees have punched in the text, we send it back to the U.S. via modem, and our American partner makes a CD-ROM out of it."

"Are you telling me that all these young villagers have learned English?" I asked incredulously. ("Villagers" is a misleading term in this case. These twenty-something workers cannot be compared to the young people in, say Dr. Feng's village. They were all as neatly dressed as high school graduates you might find in Jinan, Manchester, or Detroit.)

"Of course not," Chen answered, laughing at my simple-mindedness. "All they do is copy the text into the computer letter by letter. The people in that glass office over there do the final proofreading. Actually though, a computer program provided by our American partner does most of the work. The proofreaders are all university graduates from the city who majored in English. Also, the computer engineers are from the city."

It was difficult to keep in mind that we were in the middle of the Chinese countryside, that some twenty miles away less fortunate Chinese still lived in primitive dwellings with straw-thatched roofs. The only sound in this meticulously clean computer hall was the tap-tap-tap of keyboard keys. The employees were so engrossed in their work that they hardly glanced up at us. They were paid according to the amount of data they entered. Chen said that many did not even stop for a meal break.

"You have to be kidding!" I said, amazed. One thing I have learned in China is that mealtimes are not to be taken lightly. Chen assured me he was not kidding. I was even more astounded when he told me that food was served free of charge three times a day in the factory canteen. Each employee was entitled to one free meal per shift.

Computers humming away in the Chinese countryside. (Photo: Linda Jakobson)

"Don't forget, this is not only a worthwhile operation for Director Lin," Chen said. "The more experienced employees are earning about 500–600 yuan ($60 to $75) a month, the same as university lecturers who have held their jobs for nearly ten years. Without this work, these kids would all be unemployed. Every morning there is a long line of hopefuls at the gate who I have to turn away."

Over the years I have had many chances to speak at length with Director Lin. I have not changed my opinion that he is a despicable braggart, but he is, admittedly, an interesting man to talk to when he is in a good mood.

"You are just as hopelessly idealistic as Little Chen when I first met him. You intellectuals really don't understand society," Director Lin told me once, shaking his finger at me. The three of us had eaten in the dining room of his Beijing hotel, and then had gone up to his room to continue our discussion over a cup of green tea. At dinner he had quizzed me about doing business in the West. From there we slipped back into his favorite topic, doing business in China. That evening it was mostly Lin who spoke:

> *You tell me that people like me take the law into our own hands. You're right, we have to because we if we don't, we can't survive. You tell me that by tinkering with the bookkeeping, I evade taxes. That's also true. Why should I pay taxes to the central government? What do I get in return? It's much more effective to pay bribes to the local officials who keep my interests in mind when decisions are made. I would be happy to do business in a fair and just society where one wouldn't have to dole out money for every damned official every single time one wants to take care of even the most insignificant matter. But there is no justice in China.*
>
> *You have no idea how tiring it is to sit at banquet after banquet wining and dining these cadres, feeding them shark's fin soup, goose liver, and all the most expensive dishes money can buy. I have to buy them cigarettes and cameras and video recorders—whatever they fancy. The vice mayor of the city drives around in a car I bought him. The son of the director of the patent office lives in an apartment I renovated. But you can't just blame the cadres. Their salaries are ridiculous. They make their living off us businessmen. Otherwise they, in turn, wouldn't survive. I use tens of thousands of yuan each year just to take care of my* guanxi. *But if I didn't, I wouldn't be granted an export license, I couldn't get a bank loan, I wouldn't even have the electricity and water I need to run the factory. All these matters are decided by local officials. They're the ones I have to stay on good terms with, not the guys in Beijing.*

Everything Director Lin said is probably true, from his point of view. I could not help remembering the fatalistic remark I hear every now and again from my Chinese friends: "China has no hope." Usually I am more optimistic than they are, but on this evening, my mood was as gloomy as the dark autumn night. To top it off, outside the hotel I flagged down a taxi driver who had just had a nasty run-in with the police.

"It's obviously the start of one of those fine-gathering campaigns again. Every district has a quota of fines to fill," the driver spat out, cursing his rotten luck. "A fine is a fine, and I can pay it, though I'm certain I didn't go through the red light. But the policeman took my driver's license. He told me to stop work for tonight and come and see him in the morning. That can only mean one thing. He wants money. Otherwise I won't get my license back."

"Can't you file a complaint?" I asked, though I could guess the answer.

"Complain? Who should I complain to? His colleagues at the police station? Huh! It would be of no use. All I would do is get myself into even deeper trouble."

Outside my apartment building as I paid him, he added: "You foreigners have no idea how we Chinese detest this society!"

I trudged up the fifteen floors to my apartment (the elevator stops running at 11 P.M.) feeling thoroughly nonplussed. Why have I written that China is gradually taking the necessary steps toward becoming a civil society governed by law? Am I blind to reality? At each passing floor I thought up new arguments, both for and against China's progress. At the tenth floor, pausing to catch my breath, I realized I would reach the top of the building long before I could come up with a conclusive answer.

During the past decade, legions of new laws have been passed. Ordinary people now are much more aware of their civil rights than they were ten years ago. Newspapers tell their readers how to file for divorce or how to complain about shoddy goods. Phone lines which provide legal counseling are so jammed that it is hard to get through. Likewise, call-in radio shows that advise people on legal affairs are immensely popular. Since enforcement in October 1990 of the Administrative Litigation Law, allowing citizens and organizations to sue the government for legal violations or grossly unfair procedures, over 160,000 people have brought suit against the government. In nearly 20 percent of these "citizen versus state" cases, the citizens won.[7] Even the cynical said this was groundbreaking progress, I reminded myself.

But new laws and public awareness are only a small part of what it takes to build a society based on the rule of law. As long as the courts are not independent of the Party, genuine progress cannot be made. Pei Minxin of Princeton University notes, in his assessment of the Administrative Litigation Law: "It makes no provision regarding administrative actions taken by the CCP (Chinese Communist Party), giving the ruling party immunity from judicial review."[8]

Many Chinese employees are subject to the whims of their bosses, no matter how unjust, with no recourse to higher authorities. My girlfriend, Guo Hairong, was denied an obligatory letter of recommendation by her immediate superior to pursue a master's degree because she had refused his sexual advances. Another friend never went to the United States though he had been awarded a fully funded scholarship—a jealous professor refused to sign the paper needed for the passport application. Neither of these people had any realistic means of making a complaint. Director Lin is right when he says that there is no justice in China.

Close friends of mine, a doctor-scientist couple who live in a small city in central China, suffered a spine-chilling experience. Their elder son, Tang, a twenty-four-year-old engineering major whom I nicknamed "the exemplary citizen" during one of my first visits with the family, was their pride and joy. He respected the traditions of his intellectual family, studied hard to become a chemical engineer, and was chosen chairman of his factory's Youth League department. The family's harmonious life was turned upside down one night in 1993 when a policeman knocked on the door after midnight with the news that their son had been arrested.

Tang had argued with his boss over a trivial matter involving the use of his stereo recorder at a party sponsored by the factory's Youth League. When Tang refused to accede to his superior's demands, the boss had him arrested. Tang spent a total of ten months behind bars. The officer in charge of the police station told Tang's parents straight out that if they were willing to pay 5,000 yuan (in those days about $870), their son would be freed. "Giving a bribe is as illegal as accepting a bribe," Tang's mother said, when she told me of the couple's decision not to give in to the police officer's demands. "We're both cadres and, on top of that, my husband is a Party member. Initially, we wanted to settle the matter according to the law. In any case, we had no guarantee that 5,000 yuan would have been sufficient. Maybe they would have blackmailed us for more, who knows? Five thousand yuan is about half of all our savings."

For three months, Tang was not allowed any visitors. The shock of imprisonment and the guards' apparent bullying began to take its toll. Tang elapsed into a deep depression and showed signs of mental instability. Only after relentless efforts by his parents was he finally transferred to a mental hospital. At this point his parents used every penny of their savings, and borrowed even more from relatives, to bribe the prison officials. Their younger son quit university to work in a private factory to help fund his parents' crusade to save his elder brother. When I visited the family in the spring of 1994, Tang had just been released from the hospital and he was slowly recuperating at home. But he would be incapacitated for a long time to come.

Tang himself had no recollection of the preceding months. "All I know is that my father's thick black hair has gone gray and there are dark rings around his eyes," a visibly tense Tang said. His left hand still shook uncontrollably in the presence of a visitor.

I nodded quietly. His father looked like a feeble old man with sunken cheeks, though he was only fifty-two. When we had become friends seven years earlier, I could never have guessed that he had spent years doing forced manual labor in the countryside. His upright stature and, above all, his overall optimism, were hard to associate with a man who had been kept locked up in a pig shed that was only a yard-and-a-half high for seven months during the Cultural Revolution.

"I'm an intellectual and also a Party member. In the past that has been a fateful combination," he said. He was telling me about his life as we traveled by train through Siberia in March 1987. I was moving to China; he was on his way home after a year on a research project in Europe. His eyes had shone brightly as he painted his vision of China's rosy future. "I'm convinced the Party has learned from its mistakes and is capable of reforming itself. The open-door policy is going to make our country strong again. China has put its dark past behind it." Now, in 1994, as he glanced at his sickly son, he lowered his voice and declared: "Our society is thoroughly rotten."

Despite his poor health, Tang's father was not prepared to give up. He and his wife were determined to use the new law permitting citizens to take government institutions to court to pave the way for Tang's return to society.[9] "Though no charges were ever brought against our son, he'll never be employed by the state as long as there is a mention of his arrest in his personal dossier.* The private sector offers a chemical engineer scant opportunities in a small city like this," Tang's father explained. "We're

---

* A personal dossier (*dang'an*) exists for each and every citizen. The file includes information about employment, family background, and possible misdemeanors or crimes. In the Mao era, a mention of a person's "political unreliabilty" could mean the end of his or her career. Citizens have no right to know the contents of their files.

I have always regarded Tang (left) and his younger brother as model sons of intellectual parents—they did well in school, they treat their parents with respect, and are willing to sacrifice everything for the good of the family. This photo was taken when Marja Sarvimäki (right) and I visited Tang's family in 1988. (Photo: Linda Jakobson)

going to take the factory to court. We want our son's reputation restored. And we intend to demand that they pay him compensation for his suffering and for all the months he spent in prison and in the hospital."

When three years and three months had passed from that fateful knock on the door, Tang's parents were informed of the court decision. When I phoned Tang's mother she told me that the official who delivered the decision had greeted her with the words, "You have won."

"I answered that there can be no victors. Our son's life was destroyed," Tang's mother said matter-of-factly. "The official didn't say anything at first, but then he exclaimed, 'Yes, yes, but for that you will be paid 10,000 yuan (in 1996 about $2100).'"

The line went silent. I was at a loss for words.

Suddenly I heard Tang's mother break into a sob. "But we have been given justice. That should be a consolation, shouldn't it?"

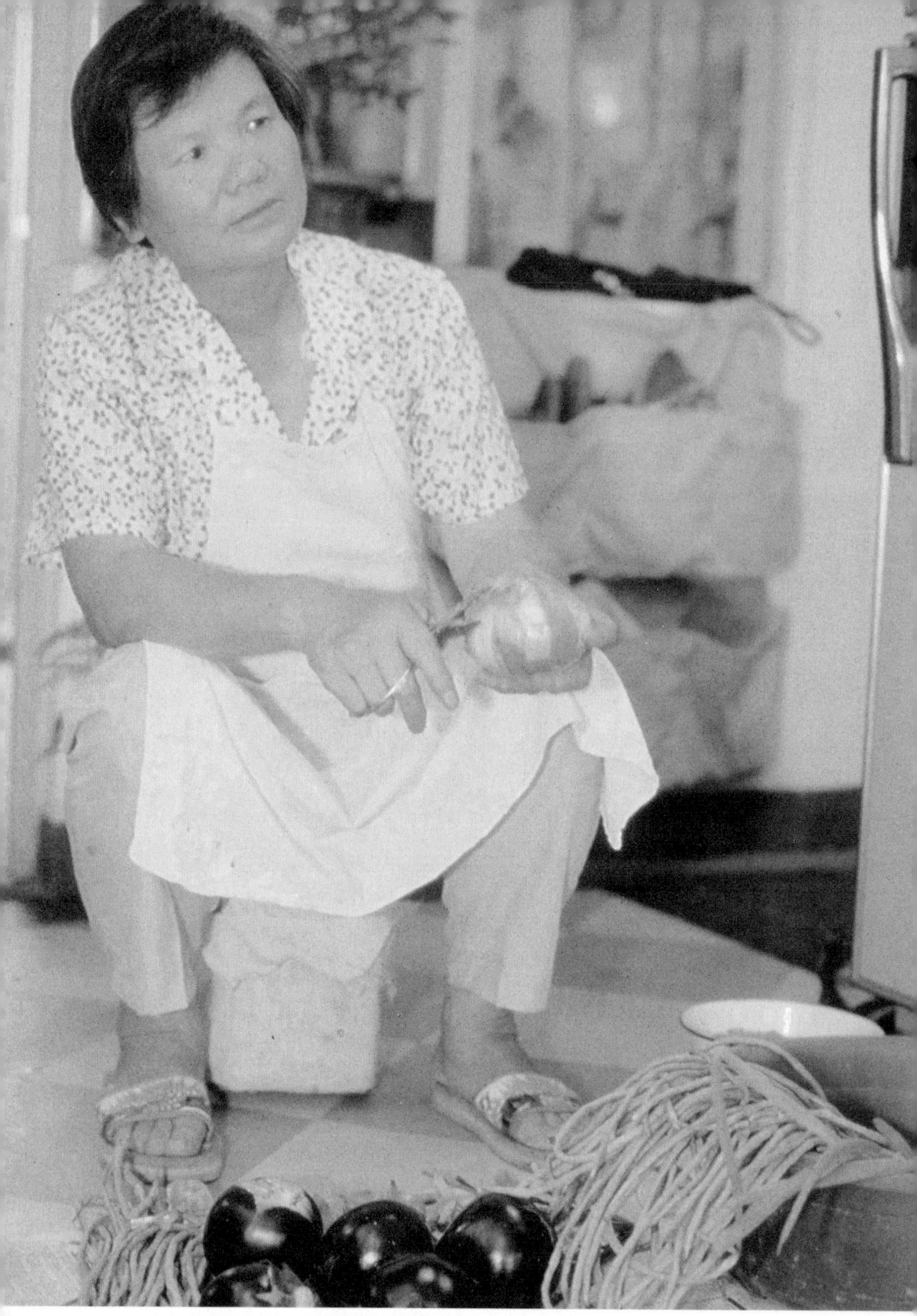

John Lee's mother washing vegetables in her living room in 1995. (Photo: John Lee)

七

Optimists and Individualists

"We Learn to Lie as Kids"

Despite the despotism, China is full of optimists. That is one of China's fundamental contradictions—amidst all the bad there is so much good. Hearing all the terrible tales of human suffering one might think that people go about their daily lives with scowling faces, cursing the authorities and moaning about their bosses. Of course some do, but in the major cities I have met at least as many individuals with positive attitudes and a real zest for life. They are just as fed up with corruption and arbitrary justice as the grumblers, but they seem to take it all in stride, as an unfortunate but inevitable nuisance. I admire the undaunted spirit and tenacity of my Chinese acquaintances. Rather than optimists, one could call them persevering souls. They do not necessarily have such an upbeat view of China's future as a whole. But they do believe that by hard work and ingenuity, they can improve their own lots in life. They have faith in themselves and their own possibilities.

In his book *Megatrends Asia,* John Naisbitt describes one of the many differences between the Western and Asian ways of thinking. When an Asian bus driver looks out the window and sees a Rolls Royce, he thinks, I may never sit in that car, but someday my son will. A Westerner in the same situation tends to be defensive and look upon the situation as unfair.[1] Asians work long days, save money, and feel optimistic, acccording to Naisbitt. Of course this is a gross oversimplification, but it contains a grain of truth. A Westerner tends to insist on his rights, while an Asian rolls up his sleeves and gets to work, believing in a better tomorrow.

On the other hand, the tendency among Chinese to grub for money with a fervor bordering on hysteria can be taken as a sign that they really have no faith at all in tomorrow. Considering recent Chinese history, it is easy to understand why many people believe it is best to take what one can immediately, before conditions change.

Western analysts often erroneously lump all Asian countries together. Asia's twenty-plus nations are home to numerous cultures at vastly different levels of development. China is not really comparable to, for example, the Asian "tigers"*; because the generations who came of age in the People's Republic during Mao's regime received a socialist education, they are at a disadvantage to compete in the world economy. For example, initiative and responsibilty were not prized in a society where everyone ate from the same "iron rice bowl." Standards of service and quality control suffered and are still serious problems, as is the mentality—"that's no concern of mine." Economic growth will also depend on the government's willingness to free the prices of basic food, as well as its ability to reform state-run factories and the banking sector, just to mention a few of the major problems. There are no guarantees that the reform efforts made thus far will be successful.

Several other determinants separate China from its neighbors, starting with the sheer size of its population. In 1990, 29 percent of the population aged twenty-five and over in China had no schooling at all, not even a primary education, while in South Korea the corresponding figure was 11 percent. And only 2 percent of Chinese adults had a university education, as opposed to 14 percent of South Koreans.[2]

One feature that China does have in common with the so-called Asian tigers is its rising middle class. I agree with optimists like Naisbitt that the growth and vitality of the middle class will have a profound effect on China's future. Middle-class families fill their apartments with household appliances and electronics, sport trendy clothes, and still have enough cash left over to spend on leisure activities. In addition to consuming, they invest in the education of their offspring.

My godchild's family members are typical urban residents who have moved into the middle class in the past ten years. But they always contradict me when I call them a middle-class family. "Oh no. We're just ordinary Beijing people," they claim, to which I answer: "Yes, exactly. More and more people in Beijing are just like you." The term "middle class" is still unclear to most Chinese. Officially, citizens are classified only as workers, farmers, cadres, soldiers, and intellectuals.

One day, in the autumn of 1996, my godchild's eleven-year-old cousin, Yaoyao, phoned and asked me to come over "as soon as possible." His mother had bought him a computer, and he was having some trouble understanding the English-language DOS-terminology. That afternoon I stood in the doorway of his room watching him sort out all the cables and

---

* The Asian "tigers" or "dragons" refer to Hong Kong, Singapore, Taiwan, and South Korea.

plugs with the air of a professional. He looked so happy and proud that I was almost moved to tears.

I recalled the day Yaoyao started preschool. I had brought him a Disney pencil case from Finland. It was a first for him. "I don't think anyone in this neighborhood has such a rich aunt," I remember him saying. Who could have imagined at that time that the family's standard of living would soar to such high level in just five years? The pencil case cost more than his mother or father earned in a week in those days. Understandably, the family did not want him to take it with him to school. Better not to cause "red eye disease," as envy is colloquially called in Chinese.

After we read through the manual together and the computer was working fine, I asked Yaoyao if any of his classmates had computers at home. "At least half of them do," he answered. "After all, we have a class called computer training." He had already promised a few of his buddies that they could come over the next day to see his new computer. Then I understood what the rush had been all about. Lavish presents are no longer a source of embarrassment.

My godchild's family started saving for a holiday in Finland, a plan too farfetched even to joke about ten years ago. Today, it is actually plausible, though still too sensitive to discuss in front of Yaoyao's grandmother, *Laolao*. I was told not to mention the matter in her company. She has made it clear that she does not approve of her daughter's and son-in-law's (*Saozi* and *Gege*) extravagant and frivolous ways.

"Mother, we will never ever have enough money to buy our own apartment even if we save and save and save. So what is the harm in making our lives a little bit more comfortable and enjoyable?" I once heard *Saozi* fend off her mother's criticism when she brought home an ultramodern aquarium. "The aquarium makes the room much more colorful. I love to sit in the dark and watch the fish swim around in the reflection of the lights."

Gege took no part in the conversation. Afterward he whispered to me with a smile: "My mother-in-law can never accuse me of being wasteful because she knows how little I earn working for the state." *Gege* is stuck in his job because it entitles him to the apartment which he, Saozi, and Yaoyao share with Tongtong and her parents. Like all apartments assigned by a state-run unit, the rent is nominal. "So it is my wife who brings the money into the family," *Gege* continued gleefully, "and all the consumer goods we have acquired are things she has bought."

The trip to Finland depends on whether Yaoyao does well on the entrance examinations for junior high school, the family told me. If he misses the magical boundary by just a few points, his parents will have to pay 30,000 to 40,000 yuan ($3,700 to $5,000) to get him into a respectable school through the "back door." "If he does poorly, no amount of money will be enough. We'll have to think seriously about enrolling him in a private school," *Gege* explained. "The entrance fee for a mediocre private school is about 40,000 yuan ($5,000). On top of that, school costs 10,000 yuan ($1,230) per term. But, we couldn't bear for him to go to a third-rate state school. The teachers are lousy and so are the pupils. It would mean that he would have no chance at all to make it to university."

We were talking about astronomical sums. *Gege* earns a bit less than 1,000 yuan ($123) a month, while *Saozi* brings home a monthly salary of about 4,000 to 5,000 yuan ($500 to $615) from the private travel agency where she works. Sending Yaoyao to a private school would mean tightening their belts for at least the next three years and lowering their standard of living to what it was in the 1980s.

The family's dilemma reflects the great importance attached to education. But I found the situation appalling. An eleven-year-old should never be put under such extreme pressure.

Regardless of the fantasized trip to Finland, the upcoming junior high entrance examination caused tension in the household for months. I have always held *Gege* and *Saozi* in high esteem for being sensible parents. In China, that means that they have not spoiled their son rotten. Most of my other friends' children have become more self-centered and badly behaved with each passing year. The media talks about little emperors and empresses. I call them little terrorists. Actually, it makes me uncomfortable sometimes to see how strict, and even cold, *Saozi* can be toward Yaoyao, especially as there seems no limit to the loving attention she gives little Tongtong. For this reason I was not prepared to see both *Gege* and *Saozi* worrying themselves sick for many months over Yaoyao's education.

"Every evening we sit around trying to figure out different alternatives. His teacher warned us that he'll have trouble making the mark in Chinese grammar and composition," *Gege* said about three months before the fateful exam. "We've put off thinking about a trip to Finland for at least another year. First things first." We were in my apartment for a change. I was in bed with a bad cold, and *Gege* and *Saozi* had come over with Chinese herbal medicine and a basket of food. Chinese can be the most caring of friends.

Yaoyao's weakest subject was Chinese language, one of the two subjects tested on the junior high school entrance exam. The other was mathematics, in which Yaoyao topped his class. To make it into a relatively good school—not even a key school—he had to get at least 191 points. "Even if he scores the maximum 100 points in math, his teacher says there is no way he'll manage 91 points in Chinese," *Gege* said. He looked miserable. I had not seen either of them so unhappy since Tongtong had fallen ill after birth. At home they tried to keep their spirits up, for Yaoyao's peace of mind, but here in my apartment they felt free to indulge their anxiety.

"If Yaoyao ends up in an inferior school, he'll be among the dregs of society. Classmates have such an influence at that age. He'll never even make it to upper middle school (senior high)," *Saozi* said. "In that case," she cried out, "our son will become a *liumang*." According to the dictionary a *liumang* is a hooligan or a gangster, but perhaps the word "scoundrel" might be a more appropriate translation.

Gege and I could not help bursting into laughter, which relaxed the taut atmosphere for a moment. There was something absurd about *Saozi*'s shrill voice and the word *liumang* in connection with Yaoyao. It was hard to imagine their adorable, well-behaved son turning into a little gangster. But I do not mean to belittle their worries. With the exception of Chinese language, Yaoyao is an excellent student. It would be a shame if his chances for a proper education were cut short at the age of twelve.

Many families endure similar mental torments every year.

"Soon this agony will come to an end. We're going to move into our own apartment next autumn," a girlfriend of mine once exclaimed, after a dreadful row with her mother-in-law. "That is, if Tingting can get into junior high school on her own accord." My friend groaned. "Otherwise we'll have to put off buying our own home for another three years. I just can't bear the thought."

Four adults and eleven-year-old Tingting shared a tiny two-room apartment.

Besides the ascent of a middle class in the 1990s, individualism has become a significant social factor. When I moved to Beijing in 1987 there were few individualists, not counting a handful of long-haired rock musicians, artists, and bohemian types who eagerly hung out in the foreign community. Many of them were offspring of high-level cadres and they did, admittedly, like to talk about the freedom of the individual. But they were a miniscule group, on the fringe of society. The vast majority of city residents viewed them with suspicion. I still remember the reactions of my godchild's family when I dropped by to inform them of something-or-other, and I had a rock 'n' roll enthusiast named Youdai with me. (None of my friends had phones in the 1980s, so such spontaneous visits were normal.) The next time I saw *Saozi*, she told me bluntly: "Don't trust that guy. He seems suspicious." She had formed her opinion solely on the length of Youdai's hair and his place in society as a freelance artist. There is not even a word for "freelance" in Chinese. My godchild's father, Xiao Ping, was clearly quite impressed that I knew Youdai because he was an avid fan of Youdai's radio programs, but even he said: "You had better be a bit careful in Youdai's company."

Today, the majority of city youth have adopted at least some traits that are considered individualistic in the West. They are less and less prone to accept the Confucian tradition, which requires unquestionable adherence to the wishes of the older generation. Nor have they embraced the Communist doctrine of sacrificing oneself for the benefit of society. By the 1980s, the younger generation was making fun of socialism, but they were not openly and purposefully flaunting their views as they do now. On the other hand, young people are still very patriotic and family-oriented. Such contradictions are part of today's China. Many young city residents do not consult their parents when they decide to change jobs or start a new business, as they would have fifteen years ago, but they still go to great lengths to see to their parents' well-being.

Pluralism has become a defining facet of society. It is popular to be a bit different. Because of the explosive increase in opportunities, talented young adults pursue their dreams in the cities much the same way as their counterparts do in the West.

The photographer with whom I have worked as a correspondent is a new breed of young urbanite. In the 1980s, John Lee would have been considered a radical bohemian simply because of his decision to quit his work unit. Now in Beijing alone there are thousands of graphic designers, writers, artists, actors, film-makers, and advertising professionals who earn their living from freelance work. Not all of them drive around in their own Volkswagen Jetta, as John Lee does, nor do they all own a Nokia mobile phone, but their standard of living is certainly comparable to that of my godchild's family. Actually, John will not belong to the middle class for much longer. It is only a question of time before he will be able to hand over the equivalent of 50,000 U.S. dollars in cash to purchase an apartment and thus fulfill the last condition to be considered rich.

The first time I met John Lee, I would not have predicted his future success. Nor did I envision that one day we would work seamlessly together. I found him a bit cocky and childish, with his idolatry of all things

Western, so typical of many young Beijingers. That was the autumn of 1991, when John was twenty-three. He introduced himself as a freelance photographer. Gradually I realized that the only experience he had had was sporadic photography work at his former work unit, a joint venture hotel. He had been an independent freelancer for only six months. In reality, he was unemployed.

John said he had requested a job assignment in a four-star hotel after graduating from high school because he thought the international environment would be exciting. "Aren't the waitresses in first-class hotels supposed to be beautiful?" he quipped. "I wanted to go to university, not because I was interested in studying, but just to move away from home. I wanted freedom. A life with friends in a dormitory appealed to me as a fun alternative. But I was a lazy student and didn't pass the university entrance exams."

The hotel to which he was assigned sent John to an English-language training course for ten months. Thereafter, he went to work in its public relations department, where he was given the name John Lee. Having an English name became a status symbol of sorts among young urban Chinese in the 1980s.

Years after our first meeting, John told me he decided to become a freelancer on the spur of the moment. "I had my first real girlfriend, and we were living together. I hated getting up in the mornings to be at work at eight. Anyhow, the work at the hotel was boring."

John started to hang out with an American photographer working in Beijing, volunteering to work as his assistant. Though he gradually received a few jobs of his own, his first year as a freelancer was tough. "Some months I didn't earn more than 160 yuan ($30). I had to borrow money from my mother to buy food."

His frugal life evidently had a positive effect because I met a very different John Lee when I returned to Beijing two years later to take up my post as a correspondent. Especially during our long and exhausting trips together to the provinces, I have been thankful to have such a sympathetic and hard-working colleague. Spiteful tongues claim that I have been responsible for John's successful career. Few people realize how much my own assignment benefited from our teamwork.

At first, the fees he earned from my employer, the weekly newsmagazine, made up about one-third of his yearly income. But by our final two years together, the magazine work provided only about one-tenth of his total earnings. John makes most of his living from commercial photography, shooting interior designs, new technology, and exhibition stands. His clients include major hotels in Beijing, advertising agencies, and multinational firms. His fees have grown with his reputation. In the spring of 1997, he was charging the Hilton Hotel the same fee as a Western photographer, 600 U.S. dollars per day. His clients are apparently pleased with his work, since he has many more offers than he can handle.

John went into business for himself at precisely the right moment, just like fax repairman Zhang. After 1992, the advertising business boomed. And John has a charm that I can well imagine appeals to hotel directors in need of fancy brochures. He has a natural knack of being polite. He is outgoing, a quick study, and a good talker. He also has the advantage of speaking good English. Though we speak Chinese together, I have often admired the ease with which he communicates in English when he speaks with other foreigners.

Because so many Chinese befriend foreigners in the hopes of finding a way to go abroad, John's reluctance to visit Finland at my invitation was unusual. John had often said that he would willingly invest all his savings in any venture that would enhance his skills as a photographer. So I arranged for him to work as an apprentice with the magazine's staff photographers in Helsinki for a month in the summer of 1994. I knew he had enough money to pay for the trip himself, and I thought it would do him good as he still had a lot to learn as a photojournalist. But the money John was earning as a commercial photographer had started to go to his head. When I noticed he kept putting off applying for a passport, I concluded that he could not bear to be away from Beijing, where his income had shot up to about 2,000 dollars per month. A mutual friend of ours made a catty, but probably accurate statement when he commented, "John thinks he is a professional now just because dollars fall from heaven every time he presses the button of his camera."

Fortunately John came to his senses. He had a great time in Finland, adapting easily to life in the West. He charmed my family and everyone at the magazine with his bright and engaging disposition. Afterward, he told me that he had not imagined how different it would be to work with professional news photographers in Finland. "I learned a lot. It felt like I was charging my batteries every minute of the day," I heard John tell his friends back in Beijing. He was even happier when he started receiving compliments from colleagues about his news photography.

Two years later, as we drove a thousand miles to the Northeast in his first vehicle, a Beijing Jeep, John brought up his visit to Finland. He mentioned his initial hesitancy. When I told him my own interpretation, he laughed out loud and said there was probably some truth to it. "But, also,

I didn't ever want you to think that I was obsessed with going abroad," he said. "The American I worked for as an assistant spread that rumor about me after I started to make a living on my own."

John was born in Northeast China, where he spent the first seven years of his life, with his mother and older brother. His father worked in Beijing and visited the family once a year during the Chinese New Year (Spring Festival).

"My brother and I were both born nine months after the Spring Festival," John told me with a grin, when I was on my way to meet his parents for the first time in the spring of 1995. It was pouring rain that day. I remember the weather because later John told me his mother had composed a short essay about my visit (meeting a foreign woman for the first time in her life). She wrote that she was delighted to see I had a wooden-handled umbrella.

"Why was that so special?" I asked John. I had grabbed a large umbrella I had received at some promotion event when John came to pick me up.

"In the old days, all umbrellas had wooden handles. Then came ones with plastic handles. Mother still associates a wooden-handled umbrella with the days of poverty. She thought it very interesting that a foreigner would use one," John explained. "She didn't expect you to wear such ordinary clothes either. She said that it helped her relax. She was very nervous before your visit." I had not noticed anything extraordinary about John's mother. On the contrary, I thought it was wonderful that she did not fuss, like so many other mothers whom I have met, but talked to me in a matter-of-fact way from the start.

John's mother was fifty-eight, with short-cropped hair. She wore dark cotton trousers and a white short-sleeved shirt. Her outfit was nearly identical to that of John's father, except that his slacks were gray. I cannot imagine John's mother in a flowery, frilly dress, though John says she used to wear skirts in the summers when he was a child. She belongs to the generation of women taught to rebuff the slightest feminine nuance. The new socialist woman in Mao's time was neither frivolous nor romantic, a dramatic contrast to the women in John's life. His girlfriends favor tight-fitting miniskirts and open-necked tops. They paint their fingernails a shocking red and expect John to bring them gifts of Yves Saint Laurent perfume or Revlon mascara when he returns from work trips to other cities.

But when John's mother told me about her childhood home in the countryside I realized that, in fact, she had much more in common with

John Lee's maternal grandmother (middle) continued to live with her husband as a "second wife" after giving birth to four girls and after her husband found a new wife. In this photo from 1995, John's grandmother is eating dinner with her husband's son from the second marriage and his family. John's grandmother lived with them in the village of her birth until her death in 1996. (Photo: John Lee)

her future daughter-in-law than with her own mother. At least both mother and girlfriend consider themselves very much equal to men. The same can not be said for John's grandmother.

"After my mother had given birth to four daughters in a row, my father changed wives," John's mother told me. "His second wife immediately bore a son, and Father was content. Father's outlook on life can be summed up by the old Chinese saying: 'You cannot build a wall out of dust. Parents cannot depend on a daughter for support.' But I proved Father wrong. I showed him that a daughter also can be a source of support to her parents. Thanks to Mao's policies, I went to high school and became a cadre. I still send part of my pension back to my home village." For all her austerity, John Lee's mother has a colorful personality. She definitely has her own ideas and opinions about a number of issues, though she has trouble getting a word in edgewise around her talkative husband and son.

John's father dominated my first visit. He was used to foreigners because he had worked as an interpreter. When it was time to go, I asked John's mother if she would consent to an interview for a longer article I was working on about Chinese women before the Fourth World Conference on Women, to be held in Beijing in September 1995. China was very proud to have been chosen to host this UN-sponsored event, and I figured talking with a foreign reporter in conjunction with the conference would not cause John's parents any trouble. I wanted to write about a retired rank-and-file female cadre.

"You don't know how happy Mother was when you said you wanted to sit down next time and talk with her alone," John told me when he phoned that evening. Once again, I had been oblivious to any emotional reaction. His mother had quietly consented to my request. What I did notice was his father's insinuation that his wife probably did not have much to say.

Things did not work out quite the way I had hoped. In the end, I did not interview John Lee's mother alone, but probably because of John's prodding beforehand his father sat on the sofa without saying a word during the entire interview. John, on the other hand, interrupted us at least twice, yelping, "Is that really true?" What hit him the hardest was the news that his mother had been engaged to another man before she had married his father. "Unbelievable!" John confessed the next day.

"My father promised me to the neighbor's son when I was only twelve. That was the year of Liberation (1949)," John's mother explained. "Then I did well in school and passed the test to go to upper middle school (senior high). That meant moving to the city. So I became a city resident and a cadre, while the neighbor's boy never made it further than middle school (junior high), and, like my sisters, had to stay put in the village. I couldn't bear the thought of becoming that man's wife. There was too great a cultural gap between us. Even though we were living in a new era of gender equality and, according to the new marriage law, I was supposed to be allowed to make decisions concerning marriage independently, I somehow felt that my father's promise obligated me. But I was very lucky. The neighbor's son was a fine man. He wrote me a letter freeing me from the contract made between our fathers."

After graduating from high school, the state sent John Lee's mother to a police academy for two years. After that, she was assigned a job in the library of a prison. A colleague, the wife of John's father's nephew, introduced her to John's father.

John Lee's parents' wedding photo from 1964 and a family outing in 1977.

"How long did you go out together before you married?" I asked. I could see John craning his neck to hear his mother's every word.

"We didn't really go out together. He worked in Beijing, and we wrote letters to each other for about a year. Then he came back to the Northeast to see his parents for the Spring Festival, and we met for the first time. Did he stay two weeks? Perhaps not even that. Anyway, in his first letter after his return to Beijing, he suggested that we get married."

Again, John cried out in disbelief. His parents were wed after getting to know each other for less than a fortnight. "That was normal in those days," John's mother said in her down-to-earth manner. "The main thing was to build a New China. Personal matters were secondary."

As John's mother relaxed, there was no need to pose questions. Her life story unfolded on its own: "I didn't answer his letter immediately. I wanted time to think. I knew we would have to live far apart for a long time, because transferring my residence permit to Beijing would take years. Also, I was a bit skeptical about the difference in our levels of education. He had graduated from university. I had only attended a police academy. I still think that spouses should have the same level of schooling. Now, I must admit, if I had known then how hard it would be to live with him, I would not have married him. After all, we were strangers when many years later I finally received permission to go to Beijing and we moved into our first home together."

I tried to keep my composure and concentrate on taking notes. Her words sounded so harsh, considering that John's father was sitting right beside her. He made no comment and, to my relief, John was in the kitchen fetching more hot water for the thermos bottle. Had he heard, he surely would have made some barbed remark to his father.

"Now we are used to each other," John's mother continued quietly. "Our work unit is financially sound. Our pensions are paid regularly and we have a spacious apartment. Both our sons have found work."

John's mother referred often to the 1960s and 1970s, reminding me that life was very different then. "Everyone worked as hard as they could for the motherland. One's own personal comfort was of no importance. Our wedding was held in the meeting hall of the prison where I worked. My work unit provided the sweets. There were no other refreshments, not even tea. We were all so poor."

John's mother lived with the children in the Northeast for a total of eleven years. "I saw my husband once a year. Then, when my residence permit was finally transferred to his work unit in Beijing, he was on the road working as an interpreter for the next three years. I hardly ever saw him. I was in a strange environment where I didn't know a soul. But it never occurred to me to complain. Our country needed our services."

I let the tape recorder play and forgot my notebook for a moment. I sat back in my chair and observed mother and son. I knew John was very close to his mother. She had encouraged him when he started out as a freelance photographer, in spite of his father's objections. "Mother has an open mind," John often says, when speaking of his parents. Like millions of Chinese women of her age, she was armed with that famous adaptability to which *Gege*, in my godchild's family, likes to refer. An unwanted daughter had come a long way from the home of her feudal father to being the mother of John Lee.

John's relationship with his father is complex. Though neither of his parents approve of their son's extravagant lifestyle, John's father relies on the traditional role of a patriarch in his interaction with John and he makes his views known even in the presence of visitors. The natural generation gap between father and son is even wider than usual because the China for which John's father has sacrificed his whole life no longer exists. John's father is a man who reads the newspaper regularly and is keenly aware of the changing times. He knows his son is not the only one who works hard purely for his own sake, but he still has a difficult time accepting it. He is proud of his son's success, but would like to see John save his money, or at least not to flaunt his wealth. Once when John was driving his father and a colleague from their work unit to the city center, John's father tried to hint that the car belonged to John's employer. "What are you talking about?" John growled. "I don't have an employer. I bought this car with my own money."

Because of his unusually high income, John can spend and consume to his heart's content. He and his friends regularly dine in restaurants and spend their free time in karaoke bars, discotheques, and bowling alleys. John can easily spend the equivalent of his father's monthly pension in one day.

By the mid-1990s, bowling was so popular that cadres happily accepted invitations to bowl instead of going to karaoke bars after dinner. Not even a high-level ministry official, with a salary of about 1,000–1,500 yuan ($120–$180) per month can afford a hobby which costs 100 yuan ($12) an hour. It is not unusual to see famous people trying for a strike on a neighboring lane. If I had not known this, I would have thought my American colleague was joking when she invited me to a bowling-dinner with the spokesman of the Foreign Ministry. In 1997, Shen Guofeng was well-known to television viewers all over the country because he headed

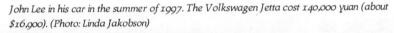

John Lee in his car in the summer of 1997. The Volkswagen Jetta cost 140,000 yuan (about $16,900). (Photo: Linda Jakobson)

the Foreign Ministry's weekly press conference. Whenever Washington upset Beijing, it was Shen who blasted the United States in public. Shen and his wife are avid bowlers.

Nothing could be more foreign than bowling to an old-fashioned cadre like John Lee's father. Like the majority of retired people living in a faraway Beijing suburb, John's parents live modestly and hardly ever venture outside the gates of their work unit. But they do not mind bicycling far out into the countryside in search of cheap vegetables. They save every *fen* (penny) they can.

"My parents are utterly hopeless about saving," John Lee often complains. As a responsible son he regularly buys them new clothes and delicacies like shrimp or honeydew melon. "I would like to see them eat better. They could easily afford to because they both have good pensions, but they refuse to waste money, as they call it, on food. I don't give them money, like other children, because they would simply put it in the bank and not spend one *fen.* They have a washing machine at home, but Mother won't use it because she says it is a waste of electricity. I tell you, they are hopeless."

Recently, articles in both the popular media and scholarly journals have indicated that filial duty, paramount in the Confucianist value system, is on the decline in the People's Republic. I disagree. It was encouraging to read about a survey, conducted in 1994 jointly by American and Chinese scholars in Baoding city, showing that "sentiments of filial obligation remain robustly intact."[3] Though the rapid transformation of society has widened the generation gap in many other realms (attitudes toward choice of career, sex, cultural preferences, etc.), I have yet to meet a male Chinese who does not consider it his obligation to care for his parents.

What seemed to annoy John's father even more than his son's jet-set lifestyle was his decision to break off with his first girlfriend. John's parents had grown very fond of the girl and accepted her as their future daughter-in-law. John's father reproached his son about the breakup often, even in the company of guests. That is why John no longer introduces any of his new girlfriends to his parents. In fairness to his father, John did act against tradition. Ten years ago, it was still customary for young people to have just one steady girlfriend or boyfriend, whom they eventually married. Major decisions were made in consultation with one's parents. John simply did as he pleased.

When I started to work with John in 1993, I was very surprised when he told me he was living with his girlfriend in an apartment separate from his parents' home, but in the same work unit compound. In the 1980s, only bohemians lived together in open marriage or spoke openly about sex.[4] Though the puritanical spirit of the Mao era still dominates public discussion of sexuality, young adults in the big cities are radically more easy-going and knowledgable about sex than their counterparts ten years ago. Long gone are the days when a twenty-five-year-old friend showed me his work unit's wedding present—a package of condoms—adding, "I'm not really sure what to do with these."

A decisive change in attitudes toward open marriage took place in the mid-1990s. Even so, I was surprised when engineer Song told me in 1997 that his conservative father had accepted that his younger brother was living with his girlfriend in Jinan. But, Song added, his father took it for granted that the girl was his future daughter-in-law. As had John's father.

It is tempting to portray John Lee's father as a stereotypical sixty-year-old Party member who has served in the same work unit his entire adult life. Whenever we meet, he is extremely friendly and hospitable. He can be absolutely charming, but there is something unnatural about him that makes it impossible to totally relax in his company. If the dinner conversation turns to current events, he starts to use official-sounding phrases. It is uncanny how precisely he can repeat the Party's catch-phrases from the People's Daily on just about any subject.

John never stops taunting his father when he hears him spouting off the official language. "My father does not have the ability to switch off the Party member inside of him," John once said straight to his father's face. His father remained expressionless.

John's annoyance with his father's official manner of speaking strikes me as ironic, since it is John's own different speaking styles that have caused the only problems in our otherwise harmonious working relationship. Especially in the first years of our collaboration, I found John's "official face" nearly unbearable. Of course, all human beings behave differently in private and in official settings. We vary our manner of address to different individuals depending on who they are and what our relation is with them. But I am tempted to venture that the Chinese have many more faces than Westerners. The demeanor of my Chinese friends and acquaintances changes drastically depending upon their company.

When John has to deal with cadres, a daily occurrence on our trips outside Beijing, he becomes so ingratiating and sanctimonious that I hardly recognize him. At first, I told him, with irritation, that his empty talk would reflect on me as well. He answered with his enchanting smile: "You don't understand. You cannot talk to cadres in any other way. Trust me. I know how to deal with the authorities." I have to admit that he does, though his sugar-sweet behavior still irks me. Not only does his whole being and body language change, his choice of words is very different from the language he uses with friends.

Over time, I have noticed that some people are more adept than others at alternating between official and unofficial language. At dinner with a group of designers in Jinan in 1996, Wei, an interior architect, said he had been appalled that morning when he chanced upon a former classmate in a meeting at the Housing Bureau. "My classmate cringed before his boss, the department chief at the Housing Bureau. I wouldn't stoop that low for all the money in the world—though of course I have to use all kinds of official phrases when I try to convince a potential customer of my abilities as a designer."

Both the official and the unofficial language have their own expressions and idioms to avoid taking a precise stand on a given issue. This is necessary in a culture which shuns direct confrontation. That is why translated Chinese can sound so ridiculous—because there are no corresponding expressions in English. Chinese often make frequent allusions to ancient proverbs, which are difficult to translate into a Western language. Unfortunate misunderstandings may also arise because, in Chinese, one word may have many meanings.

Sometimes in my work I have to interview individuals who spend hours on end spewing forth mere empty talk. But I have much less patience if a pleasant evening among friends turns stiff and boring because someone in the crowd stubbornly persists in using a formal manner of speech, which usually leads to everyone else following suit.

Though generalizing is dangerous, I would describe most Chinese as very suspicious of people whom they do not know well. Sociologist Fei's "rings on the surface of the water" and the loyalties those circles imply are instructive. Most Chinese are prepared to do almost anything for a relative or close friend, but one seldom sees anyone help a stranger who has taken a tumble on the street. Writing in the sociology journal *Shehui* (Society), Zhao Tiantang asserts that harmony does not necessarily concern those outside the circle; the traditional personality does not care about strangers.[5]

Engineer Song, despite his high level of education, is perhaps the most traditional-thinking of my close friends. He showed me how the theory of Fei Xiaotong's rings works in practice, during the harrowing days following the Beijing massacre in 1989. Many a friendship is cemented when the pressure is at its worst. I had to get in touch with *Jiejie*'s brother, Yang, because I had heard through a mutual acquaintance that he needed help to flee the country. In those days, most ordinary people did not have phones at home. And in order to dial long-distance from Jinan to Beijing, Yang would have had to go to the post office where it was highly probable that calls were being monitored. I suddenly remembered that Song's fiancee's family had a phone at home.

I hesitated a long time before dialing the number of Song's fiancée. I really did not want to get Song mixed up in this matter. He is totally apolitical, and I knew he would be taking a risk if I asked him to contact a democracy movement activist. Those were extremely tense times. On top of everything else, I knew there was no love lost between Yang and Song. "What an idler," Song had muttered after their first meeting. On the other hand, Song knew that also Yang was my close friend.

When I summoned enough courage to call Song, I cryptically asked him to find my "long-haired friend" and bring him to the phone at a designated time. Song and I spoke to each other in monotones. I trusted that Song understood the situation. Then the line went silent for a long while. I had to stop myself from pleading: Please, please, do this for me.

But I did not want to back Song into a corner.

It occurred to me to tell him that just that afternoon I had encountered firing soldiers when I went downtown to fetch his ticket to Europe. (Song had received a grant from his work unit to go abroad for research study long before the events at Tiananmen. Because of the chaotic situation in the capital, I had offered to take care of his travel arrangements.) But mentioning that would have been equally tactless. Besides, I could not start talking about shooting soldiers on the phone.

Finally I heard Song answer quietly: "I'll do this for you. I would not do it for him."

Years later, I asked Song about that fateful phone call.

"Do you know why I was silent for such a long time?" Song asked. "My fiancee, her sister, and my future parents-in-law were all there around me. You know that my father-in-law had to condemn the democracy movement in his capacity as a leader in his factory. I was sure that bringing Yang to their home would cause a bit of a commotion. Anyone can see that he is not just some ordinary guy. But when I said 'I'm doing this for you,' it made it more acceptable. You had met my future in-laws. They know we are old friends. They also think that one should always help a friend in need."

"Would you have agreed to the request if it had been, let's say, Yang's sister (whom Song had met a few times in passing) who had done the asking?"

"No," Song answered without hesitation. "At least I wouldn't have brought him to my fiancée's home. You know my point of view. Why should I help Yang? He's not my friend."[6]

In trying to understand the relationships among people who do not belong to the same interest groups, one must take into consideration the overall social effect of political surveillance. In the Mao era, the state did its best to make everyone, even family members, report on one another. In a tightly controlled society, no one wants to risk having heretical thoughts or unorthodox behavior being reported to one's work unit; an urban citizen's chances to lead a stable and harmonious life were, as recently as ten years ago, entirely dependent on his or her immediate superiors. It is only in the past few years that political surveillance has ceased to depend on tipoffs to the street committee or even to the police by callous neighbors and colleagues. But self-protection is still an important element in today's China, though less so in major cities and especially among younger people working in the private sector.

It was some consolation to learn that Chinese-American author Bette Bao Lord finds the suspicious attitude of most Chinese toward one another as off-putting as I do. Bette Bao Lord moved to America as a nine-year old and only returned to China in the 1980s as the wife of United States Ambassador Winston Lord. In her book *Legacies: A Chinese Mosaic*, she writes: "Chinese, unlike Americans, were wary of making new friends. Old ones were safe. New ones were risky: betrayal had been a daily occurrrence during the Cultural Revolution; caution had become habitual. Still, I never grew accustomed to how frequently, how sincerely, how urgently one good friend of mine would warn me about another good friend of mine.[7]

During my first years in China, I was foolish enough to try to bring together friends from different circles. Because they belonged to different interest groups, the atmosphere was always a bit strained, sometimes even nerve-wrackingly tense. Though I might have been considered a part of each person's "we-group," they were all circumspect of one another.[8] Mistrust for political reasons was seldom the problem. Among young people, politics are now much less of a decisive factor. Sometimes the reason was plain envy, or the desire of more than one person to be the constant center of attention. Sometimes, a few of my close friends with strong personalities were downright rude to one another.

"No Chinese wants another Chinese to have a better face than he does," John Lee once explained during one of our numerous discussions about the misgivings Chinese are inclined to have about strangers. An exhaustive explanation of his statement would fill an entire book. There are dozens of myths about the social phenomenon of face, and volumes have been written about it. "He didn't give me face" is a literal translation of a remark one often hears when a person complains of having been told off, or spoken to in some unflattering manner in front of others. A similar typical expression, "you have to give him face," refers to allowing for a compromise in business or how to approach an official.

My friend, Yang, who has studied abroad, says Westerners make too much fuss about face. He thinks that the Chinese habit of making sure one does not lose face, or making another person suffer a loss of face, is comparable to the Western notion of good manners. "You shouldn't hurt anyone's feelings and you should avoid tactless behavior," Yang summed up his outlook. Others who, like Yang, have lived in the West, ardently reject this comparison. They say the Chinese attach excessive importance to how things appear. The significance of ritual that was stressed by Confucius still dominates. Many of my Chinese acquaintances, returning from abroad, decry their countrymen for being pathologically oversensitive about personal self-esteem. I tend to agree. The importance of "face" in interpersonal relationships is critical, even among educated Chinese of the younger generation.

When explaining "face" and its consequences, one often appeals to Chinese cultural tradition, which dictates that one must avoid conflict at all cost, to safeguard harmony in society. For this reason a person's behavior should always be moderate and decent. According to Confucian thought, *li* is the basis of proper behavior. But *li* (which originally meant "ritual") is very difficult to translate properly. Many scholars use the term to convey "moral," "tactful," or "self-controlled." "Face" does not only entail a person's public self-image: "rather face is social capital and can be either thick or thin, weighed, contested, given, augmented, diminished, borrowed and so on." Since a Chinese person's identity and integrity are so entwined with that of others, face is also collective property.[9] I have often heard elderly Chinese warn younger people: "Don't lose our face."

"Saving face" can be more important than telling the truth. "Honor the hierarchy first, your vision of the truth second" is considered a basic rule of Chinese culture.[10] When I asked my close friends about this they affirmed that going around the truth is acceptable to save one's own or one's family's face. Honest or truthful interaction is not necessarily a priority in a culture where communication is based on yielding to the wishes of others.

Professor Perry Link discusses the significance that unofficial and official language, together with the importance of face, have on morality. He first compares moving from one mode of speaking to another to donning and doffing a cap. "Could it be that moving back and forth amounted to donning and doffing integrity as well as idiom?" he asks. And he concludes: "Sometimes, rather clearly, it did." Link points out that the proper way of expressing oneself has a long tradition in Chinese culture. "Proper" has often meant "morally proper," but "proper" can also mean "prudently proper, when the task is to reach one's goal more efficiently."[11] Confuciansim emphasized that righteousness can be achieved through correct or proper behavior, *li*. In other words, a person's actions (including a person's speech) are not only evaluated on the basis of how good they are, but also on the manner in which they are performed.

Norwegian socioligist Børge Bakken explores the structural "ways of lying" inherent in "an exemplary society that forces people to behave in prescribed ways, and to follow exemplary 'objective' standards." He writes, "Chinese conformity is often a surface conformity where individuals are not subject to serious pressures for consistency between inner beliefs and outer behavior." Instead of using the expression a "culture of hypocrisy," Bakken favors a "culture of simulation."[12]

I did not master all the rules of face in my ten years in China. It could well be that even a lifetime would not suffice. At some stage I noted, with a sigh of relief, that my close friends were indeed capable of relaxing if I invited them all to a joint dinner for a special occasion. When my parents, Max and Marilyn, visited Beijing in 1993, my godchild's family and a half-dozen of my other old friends joined us to celebrate Max's seventieth birthday, and the atmosphere was remarkably convivial. I concluded that perhaps my friends had matured or perhaps their long friendships with me had finally made them feel more comfortable in the company of my other close friends. John Lee interpreted the buoyant mood as a sign that my friends have all done well for themselves. There was no longer any need to eye one another enviously. "We all have face," was how he expressed himself.

To a person raised in the West, many rituals connected with "face" appear quite theatrical. Sometimes it is hilarious to watch two acquaintances going through all the motions of maintaining face while handling money. I was sitting on the bed in *Gege* and *Saozi*'s room at my godchild's family home one day when a neighbor came in with two boxes of computer disks he had purchased at *Gege*'s request because he could receive a special discount through a friend. When *Gege* tried to pay him for the disks, the neighbor first declined emphatically. "No, no, no!" the man cried out. After *Gege* persisted three or four times, the neighbor quite spontaneously produced the receipt from his pocket and willingly accepted the money *Gege* had been trying to give him from the outset. I have enacted this same ritual a million times. As have all my Chinese friends.

Political study sessions are a theatrical genre all of their own. In these weekly meetings at government offices, work units, and schools across the country, political correctness is the name of the game. Though the sessions have slowly transformed into gatherings where personnel matters and job-related issues are increasingly relevant, they are also used to explain national policy or a Party leader's key speech. Nowadays, industrial workers are being spared the ordeal as political study sessions are no longer held regularly in factories and enterprises.

Before beginning this book, I asked my godchild's family about the sensitive topic of "forced lying," as I call deviating from the truth in official situations. "We're so used to it that we don't even consider the morality of it," my godchild's mother said. She reminded me of the stern political study sessions she was obliged to attend in the months following the Tiananmen events in 1989. Everyone working at the university, one after the other, had to condemn the "counterrevolutionary rioters" who had taken part in the "turmoil."

"I would have lost my mind if I had thought about how many times I had to lie. Everyone mechanically mumbled the required phrases without letting their brains work. It was terrible. But anyone who refused to comply would have been dismissed. We had to lie." She described preparing to leave home for work with the expression: "I changed into a protective overcoat."

Gege said: "We learn to lie as kids. Look at our son. At home Yaoyao hears us complain about the failings of the Party, but in any situation that requires it he will recite: 'I love the Party as I love the motherland.' It happens automatically, for him, and for us."

"Not for me anymore," *Saozi* called out lightheartedly from the kitchen. "I haven't had to lie for years. That's one of the benefits of working for a private company—no political study sessions! I'm not forced to participate in any of that nonsense."

I glanced at Yaoyao. He was so immersed in his new computer game that he was not even listening.

Is this man a slave driver or one who gives women new lives? Zhang Yongda, the owner of a small factory in Panyu in 1996. (Photo: Linda Jakobson)

八

The South Is a World of Its Own

"A Good Communist Is a Rich Man"

This could be Victoria Station in London at rush hour, I thought, and laughed out loud. "After so many years I didn't think I could still feel culture shock in China," I told my girlfriend, Yuan. We were in Guangzhou, formerly Canton, sitting in a restaurant the size of a wholesale warehouse. At round tables that seated eight apiece, hundreds of people sat sipping tea and enjoying *dimsum,* small southern Chinese-style snacks. Perhaps "enjoy" was not precisely the term, considering the deafening clatter of plates, the din of voices, and the hurried, hectic atmosphere. Waitresses rushed back and forth between kitchen and customers, while others went from table to table filling teapots with boiling water, and still others went from table to table artfully pushing carts of delicacies, from which diners chose small pastries or pies with different fillings, served in round steamers of weaved bamboo. The service was incredibly swift and efficient.

Waitresses in the North would never be able to pull this off, I thought. The service would be sluggish. You would never dare pop into a place like this if you were in a hurry. By temperament, the Cantonese are the Italians of China.

"The southern Chinese really do cherish their morning refreshments," Yuan remarked, laughing at my stunned expression as I took in the scene. My northern friend had been transformed into an assured businesswoman, at home in the rush of modern life. In 1987, Yuan and I had both taught English at the economics college in Jinan. Two years later, she had taken the big leap and moved to the South with her husband.

I was still a bit dazed. This seemed like another world to me. I had just stepped off a "slow train," which had chugged along for forty-four hours from Yuan's hometown, a small city near Jinan, to Guangzhou. Most of my fellow passengers had been Shandongese. Except for a few young lads in search of adventure and half-a-dozen weather-beaten peasants, they were all entrepreneurs—both men and women. They were on their way south hoping to make their fortunes in China's richest province (Guangdong). As I glanced around the *dimsum* restaurant, everyone looked like foreigners, so different from the Chinese I was used to seeing. I had, after all, spent the majority of my time in China in the North. The other diners at our table were much shorter and slightly built than the Shandongese. Their skin was a shade darker and their hair much curlier.*

"Don't people start work at nine, like up North?" I asked Yuan. "It's a quarter after ten and this place is still packed. Who are these people?"

"The majority are businessmen and -women, and they're already working," Yuan answered. "Informal meetings are always held over *dimsum*. When someone has something to discuss with me, they'll phone my office around nine and make a date for *dimsum*. But, as you can see, there are also lots of retired people here, and young people, too. People escape their cramped apartments and chat over *dimsum*. It doesn't cost more than 20 yuan ($2.40) to order tea and a few pies." The Guangdongese spend a larger proportion of their salaries on eating out than other Chinese, I have been told.

"There's no place like this in Beijing or Jinan," I reminded Yuan. *Dimsum* is not part of the northern culture. Though the capital had its own teahouse tradition before 1949, it disappeared with the arrival of socialism. Meeting for a meal is always problematic in northern China, because one party has to pick up the check, while the other must accept the debt of gratitude. Sharing the bill is unheard of in China, except among the most Western-minded city youth. In Beijing, a handful of small teahouses have re-opened during the 1990s. The only other alternatives are the lobby bars of hotels, Western-style pubs in the area where foreigners live, or the increasing number of fast-food restaurants. But rank-and-file Beijingers, like my girlfriend, Dr. Feng, or the members of my godchild's family, would never suggest meeting in any of those places. In the North, people visit each other at their homes and socialize over endless mugs of tea. The elderly and the young often spend time with friends in parks.

Yuan could not understand my amazement. "Really, what is it with you? You've been to the South lots of times. I think you're just a bit muddle-headed after your long train ride," she smiled, shaking her head. "Don't you remember? We had *dimsum* last time you visited me in Hainan. Of course, that place wasn't quite as large as this one."

"It's not just the commotion," I tried to explain, though I could not really grasp what I was experiencing either. "Northerners are capable of making a racket too. It's not that. It's the way these people communicate with

* The division between North and South China is the Yangzi (Yangtze) River.

each other. They're all gesticulating so emphatically. And their clothes. They're dressed simply, not glamorously, but tastefully, though this is clearly not a fine restaurant. It feels as if I'm in some foreign land. But you're right, maybe two days on a train has something to do with it. And don't forget, I'm not coming from Beijing—I've been visiting your mother in your hometown, a sleepy little northern city."

"I know what you mean—inward-looking and lifeless," Yuan remarked and sighed. "I'm so happy we decided to make the move. Here in the South you feel alive. The cities throb every minute of the day."

As we were leaving, the woman sitting next to me turned to us and said: "I think the difference between Germans and Italians is similar to the difference between northern and southern Chinese." She could not have helped overhearing our conversation. She looked to be in her early forties, smartly dressed in a tweed blazer and brown skirt.

"I'm just back from Rome. On a previous trip I went to Mannheim, because I work for a Sino-German joint-venture company. Economically, though, the comparison works the other way round. In Europe, the South is poorer than the North, but here in China we in the South are more developed and much richer. But the difference in temperament is the same. The Germans and Italians like different food and speak different languages. When they talk to each other, they have to switch to English because neither speaks the other's tongue. The Italians aren't very fluent in English just as we Southerners don't like speaking Mandarin."

On a previous trip to Guangzhou, in the spring of 1993, John Lee lost his cool just about every time we entered a small restaurant or sat in a taxi. "Talk to me in *putonghua*," he would blurt out. "We're in China." Being a Northerner, John Lee didn't understand a word of Cantonese. *Putonghua* means "general Chinese" and is reminiscent of the Beijing dialect of Mandarin Chinese. General Chinese, or a dialect very similar to it, is spoken in the northern and middle regions, while numerous other dialects are used in the southern and southeastern areas of the country. Some dialects are as distinct as French is from Italian. *Putonghua* gradually became the official language in schools after 1949. It is used throughout the country on national television and radio broadcasts. (John is very easygoing, not one to lose his composure even when tired or hungry. It was the principle which vexed him: "In France, one must speak French.")

When Chinese from different parts of the country meet, they instinctively change to *putonghua*, though many speak it with a heavy accent. The least intelligible encounter I ever had was with a specialist of internal medicine at a Beijing hospital in 1997. In Chinese fashion, there were several other patients with me in the same room as the doctor. As I waited my turn, I noticed that the patient before me could not make head or tail out of what the doctor was saying. I started to understand why the receptionist had apologized so profusely about the doctor being from Wuxi in Jiangsu province. What a country, I thought to myself, with a smile. Two university-educated people (the patient before me had told me that she was a lecturer) cannot comprehend each other, though they are both speaking the same language. Our savior was the doctor's assistant, who literally repeated every word the doctor said, translating it into intelligible *putonghua*. The goodnatured doctor merely chuckled at his patients' inability to understand him. He, after all, could understand everything we said.

It is surprising how few Southerners feel comfortable in Mandarin Chinese. When I interviewed a fifty-year-old factory director in Guangzhou, he refused even to try to converse in *putonghua*. Instead, his assistant translated from Cantonese to Mandarin. "This is how we proceed with all our visitors from the North," the director said. He confessed that he had originally been chosen for the job because of his "good political background," but he was allowed to keep his post after the reform policy was launched because he had successfully overhauled the factory into a profit-making unit. "I never finished middle school (junior high), and anyway, *putonghua* wasn't taught in my hometown in those days," said the director, explaining his complete ignorance of Mandarin.

In 1997, a joke about Prime Minister Li Peng circulated in Beijing: Li Peng came home one evening looking depressed after an important meeting with the other top leaders. His wife asked him worriedly, "What's the matter? Did something happen at the meeting?"

The prime minister answered, "I don't know. I couldn't understand what they were saying."

Party leader and President Jiang Zemin, formerly the Party secretary of Shanghai, has promoted so many of his former Shanghainese allies to important posts in the central government that political circles in the capital speak mockingly of the "Shanghai gang."* Only the Shanghainese understand the Shanghai dialect.

It is difficult for a Westerner to comprehend that spoken Chinese and written Chinese are two separate means of expression. The system of written Chinese is not based on a phonetically structured alphabet. Rather, the characters are pictograms and conceptual ideograms. One has to memo-

* This is a play on words. Mao's wife and her associates, the radical political leaders during the Cultural Revolution, were colloquially known as the "Gang of Four."

rize each one by heart. The written language is the same for all Chinese, but the spoken language varies from region to region. In other words, the characters are pronounced differently in different places, though everyone can read the same newspaper.

Thanks to the characters, John Lee always managed to order what we wanted to eat in the South. He simply used his finger to draw imaginary characters in the palm of his hand. And if the first waitress did not happen to be literate she would run off, with a squeal and a giggle, and return with someone who was. I learned Chinese with the help of the so-called *pinyin*-transliteration system, using the Roman alphabet as an aid. As a result, I speak Chinese far better than I read or write. I can get along with spoken Mandarin in most situations, even when dealing with complications arising from an appendix operation. But I can only write three of the five characters depicting the expression "testing one's white blood cell count" (*jian cha bai xue qiu*). My friends tease me that I am one of China's 164 million illiterate or semi-illiterate residents.[1]

Writing Chinese characters is a feat all of its own. Even a university-educated person who is not required to write regularly in his or her work has difficulties remembering how to form more complicated characters. Some of my engineering acquaintances have told me how embarrassed they feel when they make mistakes in front of their children. One's ability to read does not decline, but one's writing skills get rusty with alarming speed, my friends tell me.

The diversity of local cultures in China receives scant attention in the Western media. From afar, China looks like a gigantic, but unified country. Politically, and also in terms of cultural tradition, it is just that. Also ethnically, the country is homogeneous. Han Chinese make up 92 percent of the population. But every province has, not only its own dialect but also its own subculture, which influences the way people eat, how they build their homes, how they communicate, and how they approach life. China is a country made up of twenty-two provinces and five autonomous regions.* If one wanted to write a book about all the different provinces and regions and spend a mere two months in each of them to learn about local customs, it would take 54 months just to gather the material. In

* Administratively, China is divided into twenty-two provinces, five autonomous regions, and four centrally administered cities (Chongqing, Beijing, Shanghai, and Tianjin). Because Beijing considers Taiwan a renegade province of China, one hears official references to "twenty-three provinces."

terms of population, Sichuan province alone would rank eighth among the world's most populous countries at the end of 1996; and Shandong province (of which Jinan is the capital) would rank eleventh.

In recent years, pride in the distinct local cultures has been revived through new films and biograghies about local heroes, through new museums and the renovation of historic sites, and through academic research. In the 1950s and 1960s, provincial cultures were heavily suppressed. But economic independence has led to a loosening of central government control in all spheres of society, especially in the more prosperous coastal regions. As a result, popular culture at the local level has become vibrant. When I visited Jinan (Shandong) and Jilin (Heilongjiang) during the autumn of 1996, the best-selling books and music were works by homegrown writers and singers.

A skeptic might look at the map of China and wonder whether you would really notice any difference going, say, from the province of Hunan to Jiangxi. Yes, definitely. The dialect is different, the cuisine is different, the folklore is different, and because of this, the way of life varies from place to place. In areas with many minority groups, there is even more diversity. Dr. Christina Nygren, who specializes in Japanese and Chinese theater studies, made numerous trips to small townships in different provinces during the 1995–1998 period to gather material for a forthcoming book about popular culture. It was fascinating to hear her describe the variations in the dance and theater performances she attended. China has more than 350 local theatre genres (*difang xi*). The performances and the music of each are remarkably unique.

In the West, we often speak mistakenly about "Peking Opera" when we mean traditional Chinese theater in general, an offense I have been guilty of myself. In reality, Peking Opera, or *jingju*, is the theater genre of the capital, merely one form of many. Its popularity has, admittedly, spread widely and *jingju* performances can be seen all over the country. Instead of "Peking Opera," Christina Nygren advocates the use of the more accurate term, "*jingju*" (theater of the capital), when speaking of this most famous form of Chinese theater. "Many a mix-up would be avoided, because there is also a Beijing-based Western opera troupe, as well as several groups performing local Beijing theater," she said. "Westerners have, after all, embraced many other foreign terms like 'taiji,' 'kabuki,' 'sushi,' and 'yoga.'"

In, for example, Jinan, both the *jingju*-troupe and the Shandongese local theater *luju*-troupe have their own work units and each stage regular performances. "Local theater, or *difang xi*, has come into existence because of

Left: Women of the Miao minority returning home from a performance portraying traditional arts in southern Guizhou province. (Photo: John Lee, 1996)

the wishes and needs of people living in that area," Nygren said. "Contrary to general belief, local theater is still very popular among ordinary people. I find it very sad that in the big cities one constantly hears people saying; 'No one is interested in theater anymore.' This is simply not true. In villages, townships and smaller cities, the theaters are packed. In addition to state-run theater troupes there are numerous private theater companies that tour the countryside."

Local theater troupes often perform on traditional Chinese holidays. Many of the themes of these plays are derived from local legends and popular beliefs based on ancient mythology. Popular beliefs, including ancestor worship and fear of the natural forces upsetting the harmony of the universe, have experienced a resurgence during the reform period. They are a more prevalent and vital part of the culture than they were ten years ago, though many acquaintances in Beijing still brush them off with the comment, "It's all just superstition."

Popular beliefs are stronger in the countryside than in the cities, though this generalization falters when one moves south. In Guangzhou (Canton), it is only a few steps from skyscrapers and flyover highways to narrow alleys and shops where small altars honoring goodness-knows-which deity abound. These altars usually have burning incense, flowers, rice, and perhaps some fruit placed in front of them. Modernity and tradition, existing in harmony side by side, have become hallmarks of Guangzhou in the 1990s, as they have been for decades in nearby Hong Kong.

My girlfriend from Jinan, Guo Hairong, who was educated in the puritanical atmosphere of the Mao days, once remarked contemptuously that life after death is an obsession in the South. "Southerners think that in order to be lucky and successful they have to honor and show respect to the souls of the deceased, and to hundreds of other spirits, both good ones and bad." During the Mao era, the Communists tried to eradicate these popular beliefs. Certain generations of mainland Chinese, especially in the North (like Guo Hairong who was born in 1952), are true atheists. Or they will tell you, as many of my younger friends do, that they only believe in one thing: "Money."

In the South, Mao's call to destroy all that was old and feudal appears not to have resounded with as much authority as elsewhere. In February 1997, I spent my first Chinese New Year (Spring Festival) among Southerners. In the past, I had always celebrated the holiday in my godchild's home in Beijing or with Yang's and *Jiejie*'s family in Jinan. This year I was working in the southernmost city in China, a small place called Sanya on Hainan Island, and my girlfriend Yuan and I received an invi-

A jingju*-actress preparing for the evening's performance. (Photo: John Lee)*

tation to spend New Year's eve with her friend, naval commander Pei and his family. As we rolled out the dough for the traditional midnight meal of *jiaozi** I noticed one member of the family after another disappear into the bathroom "for the last shower of the year."

Our host, originally from Hunan province, came back to the table in his pajamas and prodded his "ignorant northern guests" (Yuan and me) to hurry up and shower. "You can't take a shower on New Year's Day. Otherwise all the luck for the New Year will be washed away," this naval commander and Communist Party member decreed earnestly. His wife continued: "Furthermore you shouldn't sweep the floor on the first day of the year. And you must put on a pair of brand-new socks!" Yuan and I looked at each other. A new pair of socks is not the first thing that comes to mind to pack when one is invited to dinner, though I noticed that all of Pei's relatives were correctly equipped. Commander Pei saved the situation by ordering his younger brother to go out and buy us each a new pair of socks. In Beijing, this would not have been possible, because the whole city closes down for the eve of Spring Festival. In the South, street

* *Jiaozi* is a Chinese dumpling, a small ravioli-type pastry usually filled with a mixture of vegetable and ground meat. There are many traditions related to "knotting" the dumplings together, and it is usually an activity in which all members of the family participate.

hawkers were still doing business into the wee hours of the morning when we left Pei's home.

It is rare to see home altars in Beijing, nor do restaurant and shop owners have the habit of appeasing the spirits with offerings. But even in the capital it has become commonplace in the 1990s to hear people refer to old folklore and traditional beliefs, as well as to the importance of lucky numbers. Scores of car owners pay thousands of extra yuan for license plates with the triple digit "888" because it symbolizes wealth.* And I was astonished to see a bronze statue of a "good spirit" being hauled into my favorite restaurant on the small lane behind my apartment building in July 1997. The owner, a Beijinger in his forties, said it was a statue of Guang Gong, a historic figure from the Three Kingdoms period (A.D. 184–280), whose spirit is considered to protect people from evil.

Communist Party conservatives always point to the renaissance of popular beliefs as an example of the unhealthy tendencies that have emerged due to the reforms. The central government has urged people to refrain from ancestor worship. The authorities have also tried to stop the building of altars and temples to honor various deities, but perhaps this is the

* The number eight "*ba*" is considered lucky because it sounds like the word for prosperity "*fa*."

Folk beliefs are especially widespread in the countryside. Several dishes of food, prepared for the deceased, have been placed in front of this home altar—I chanced upon the funeral while visiting Dali in Yunnan province in the autumn of 1995.. (Photo: Linda Jakobson)

sphere in which the Party's loss of authority is most evident. Numerous sources attest to the widepsread reversion, especially in the countryside, to rituals related to popular beliefs. In recent years, local authorities have used increasingly aggressive measures to curb ancient customs. According to the main newspaper of Hubei province, *Hubei Ribao*, in the area of one city alone, Ezhou, 1,600 altars and temples were torn down in November 1996 on the orders of the Party secretary.[2]

My visit to the South in the autumn of 1996 forced me to scrutinize China from a totally new perspective. The days I spent in Guangzhou with my girlfriend Yuan reinforced my initial feeling that the gap between the province of Guangdong and the rest of the country had widened.

Three years had passed since my last visit. Even then the South stood out because the standard of living in Guangzhou, the capital of the province, was visibly higher than that of Beijing. Of course, the distinctly different southern culture—the Cantonese language, Cantonese cuisine, and the Cantonese style of architecture—and the faster tempo of life set it apart from Beijing at that time too. In the autumn of 1993, John Lee and I had spent a month in Guangdong working on a story comparing the province to the other Asian dragons, or little tigers, as they are also known. During his famous trip to the south in 1992, Deng Xiaoping urged the Guangdongese to strive for parity with these dragons within the next twenty years. The "dragon target" was a hotly debated topic.

In 1993, optimists predicted that Guangdong, and neighboring Fujian province, would form a dynamic Greater China Economic Zone in the near future, together with Hong Kong and Taiwan. The zone's GDP would surpass that of the United States and Europe by the year 2005, one Hongkongese bank director had told me. Others predicted that southern China would be as wealthy as southern Europe by the beginning of the twenty-first century. Though many assumed that twenty years was too short a time to reach the living and production standards of Taiwan, Hong Kong, South Korea, and Singapore, no one denied Guangdong's extraordinary rise as one of Southeast Asia's economic engines.

Seventy million people live in Guangdong. In 1996, they earned at least 60 percent more, on average, than Chinese in other parts of the country.[3] Of all the foreign investments utilized in China, over one-fourth were in Guangdong. Of China's exports, 40 percent came from Guangdong.

But by the autumn of 1996, it was no longer the prosperity of Guangdong which impressed a visitor arriving from Beijing. Though

Guangdong's economic growth was still rocketing (the volume of its foreign trade had tripled since 1992), the economies of the major cities in the North had also developed in leaps and bounds during those years. It was the difference in the attitudes and outlooks of the Guangdongese that was most striking, thus giving me the feeling of being in another country. Already in 1993, cadres in Guangdong were far less conservative than cadres in Beijing. Three years later, they were even more notably open-minded. Young people in Guangdong had formerly been proud that their province was more affluent and developed than the rest of China. Now they preferred to look outward, toward their Asian neighbors, to contemplate how much they still had to learn before their know-how would reach the level of the Taiwanese or the Singaporeans.

Employees in state-run work units in the South, especially managers in responsible positions, made the deepest impact on me in 1996. Dealing with them was entirely different than in the North, where one can instantly pick out the leader of a state-owned factory who is well-versed in the official language, with its evasive and circumlocutory answers. Of course, such officious types exist in the South too, but I did not meet any when I interviewed a half-dozen directors of state-run light-industry factories in Guangzhou and nearby Panyu city. These men were neither ostentatious nor pretentious, and they spoke about issues in a matter-of-fact way. They were professionals, coping with the same kinds of pressures and worries as factory directors in the West. Most had traveled abroad many times and were familar with Western business culture. The difference between them and their northern counterparts was like night and day.

Over lunch, the southern directors could discuss national politics or the tug-of-war over taxation between the provincial and national government as relaxed as private businessmen. "Of course the Guangdong government leaders want to keep as much of our revenue as possible for new investments in this province. They are interested in developing Guangdong. They don't care about the rest of the country," was a comment I heard on several occasions. This was not, in itself, very radical, but a northern director would not have been as straightforward about a sensitive political matter in the presence of a foreign journalist whom he did not know personally.

I remember one man, Zhao Rujia, in particular, perhaps because of a mix-up in the hotel lobby. When he came to fetch me for an interview, I mistook him for the driver. If the director of a state-run factory in the North arranges to have you picked up, it is always a secretary or a chauffeur who appears. I had never before met a man of his stature who took to driving himself. In the North, important people are chauffeured around in black cars. Zhao Rujia, the fifty-three-year-old director of a middle-sized factory which produces generators, had been introduced to me through the Chinese colleague of a Finnish businessman. He drove a bright red Mazda sports car. In the course of my stay in Guangdong, I met many other state enterprise directors who also enjoyed sitting behind the wheel.

"Your hotel is right on my way to work. No need to bother others," he remarked. Before we had cruised out of the gates of the hotel, he asked me what kind of information I was interested in. This was a new approach. An interview in a state-run factory in the North nearly always begins with what I jokingly call "a session on the laces." In the 1980s, most armchairs in the dowdy reception rooms of work units had lace covers. Though many reception rooms have now been refurnished with leather sofas, the way interviews are conducted has hardly changed. The host usually utters a few polite phrases of welcome, then proceeds to reel off a twenty-minute run-down of statistics about the work unit. The briefing does not necessarily contain any information the guest is looking for.

I decided to answer with equal frankness. I told Zhao Rujia that I was writing an article about the working conditions in different types of factories. For my forthcoming book, I also wanted to find out how a Communist Party member coped with the pressures of supervising a factory in a market-oriented economy.

"Whose interests are more important, the factory's or the workers'?" I began.

Zhao chuckled before answering. "To begin with, what makes you think that I'm a Party member? Nowadays there are many directors of state-owned factories in the South who are not members. Times have changed. I am, I joined as a young man. But let me answer your question. Of course, the interests of the factory are the most important. Otherwise I couldn't ensure work for my employees. We employ one thousand people. A good Communist has every reason to be a successful factory director. There is no contradiction."

I asked him to what extent his salary depended on the factory's profits, always a sensitive question in the North. In fact, no director has ever told me the exact amount of his bonus. It has always been someone else who has provided me with that figure, off the record. By the 1980s, a factory leader's income was tied to the success of the work unit. Complaints about corrupt bosses are understandably most common in money-losing factories where the extravagant lifestyles of the leaders irk employees, struggling to survive on downsized salaries or minimal benefits.

"Of course my income depends on the profits. My salary, including all the extras, is 4,000 yuan ($482) a month," Zhao answered, lighting a cigarette. "Last year was a difficult one. I only received 40,000 yuan ($4,820) as an annual bonus. My bonus the two previous years was 50 percent larger."

"How much do the workers make on average?"

"If you include their bonuses, about 800 to 1,000 yuan ($96 to $120) per month."

"So the director earns just under 100,000 yuan per year ($12,050) when times are bad, while the majority of his employees make at most 12,000 yuan ($1445)," I calculated out loud. "As a member of the Communist Party, don't you see any contradiction in the fact that the boss earns about ten times that of his workers? Isn't that exploitation?"

Director Zhao waved his hand in the air impatiently. "You've obviously spent too much time in the North. Soon you'll start asking me something about ideology or the like and I won't understand a word you're talking about. A good Communist is a rich man. Don't forget, the income of our workers, ten to twelve thousand yuan a year, is much higher than elsewhere in the country. Didn't Deng Xiaoping say that some people have to get rich first? That applies to individuals as well as to regions. We Guangdongese are the forerunners. The others will follow suit."

When we arrived at the factory, Director Zhao asked his secretary to show me the workers' dormitories. "See for yourself and compare them to the dormitories in the nearby private factories you mentioned. Half our employees are from other places. The rest live in Panyu and go home at night. When you're through we can continue our discussion."

Director Zhao knew how to pull the right string. The dormitories of the generator factory were simply furnished but conspicuously clean. The shower rooms were newly renovated, with white tiles from floor to ceiling. The workers who did not live in Panyu had at their disposal a spacious recreation room with karaoke equipment, televisions, and ping pong tables. Even the dining room was bright and airy. Facilities were just as modern at the nearby state-run clothing factory that employed two thousand people.

Before visiting the state-run factories, I had spent a few days touring a dozen or so private workshops. Panyu, fifteen miles from Guangzhou, is a satellite city, with one million residents, well-known as a center of toy, shoe, and clothing production in Guangdong. The employees of the private factories are all rural peasants, who have come from far-off places to find work in the rich South.

The South Is a World of Its Own

In the 1980s, foreign newspapers carried glowing reports about successful private enterprises churning out goods for export, proof of the Chinese economic miracle. As the controversy concerning workers' rights and working conditions became more heated within GATT and then its successor, the World Trade Organization, the tone of these articles changed substantially. Western countries accuse Asian countries of relying heavily on the exploitation of impoverished workers. Asians defend themselves by saying that the West went through a similar phase during its own industrialization process. Asians feel they have been targeted simply because they threaten the West's competitive edge.

Based on my reading, I was prepared to find the working conditions as oppressive and miserable as those of the early Industrial Revolution, as described by Charles Dickens in his novels. That is exactly what I encountered. The dormitory conditions of the small factories and workshops were appalling. In many places, twelve girls shared a room just big enough to squeeze in four three-tiered bunk beds. Young workers, some not yet eighteen, sat bent over sewing machines or alongside long wooden tables in primitive-looking halls. They were paid according to what they produced. In one small factory, owned by a South Korean woman, employees were not allowed to leave the area without special permission. About one hundred young adults produced leather handbags in three round-the-clock shifts. The area was fenced-in; the gate was kept locked.

"This is like a prison," whispered the young woman from Panyu, who normally put in an eight-hour day at a Sino-Finnish joint venture but was temporarily acting as my assistant. "We city people have no idea of these poor peasants' working conditions."

But when I spoke with the workers in the handbag factory, I was confronted with another kind of vision. "We work every day of the week, except Sunday evenings, so we have neither the time nor the money to go into town," a twenty-two-year-old man explained, when I asked him about the locked gate. It was his third year in the Korean woman's factory. "We are paid according to what we produce, and every one of us wants to earn as much as possible. Our bonuses are slightly better than those in other workshops. I couldn't care less if the gate is kept locked or not."

He said he was from a small village in Anhui province. He went home once a year for ten days to spend the Spring Festival with his family. That is the only time of year the factories of Panyu are quiet—when the migrant workers head home. When I asked the young man how long he planned to work for the Korean woman, he answered without faltering: "As long as she will keep me on. This is a dream job. I send home about 500 yuan ($60) each month. My family has already built a new house of real tiles with my income. I earn more than all the other family members together."

I remembered my friend Chen's remark about employees not even taking time off to enjoy a free meal. In a country where there are not enough jobs for everybody, it makes sense to work while there is still money to be made.

Another worker in the handbag factory was a talkative girl from Sichuan, who claimed to be eighteen years old, though she looked fifteen at most. She pointed to my assistant from Panyu and said: "Not even that 'elder sister' can imagine how dirty and poor my home village is. Here I eat three times a day. And I can take a shower. We don't even have running water in my village. I'm not going home until I've saved enough money for my own house. Then I won't have to listen to my father or my brothers and I can marry whomever I please."

I had heard similar comments from the waitresses in my favorite little restaurant down the lane in Beijing. They work just as long hours as the factory workers in Panyu and they sleep in a cramped room behind the restaurant. When they first arrive in the big city, they are timid country girls, but in the course of their stay they become independent-minded young adults. Once, when I asked about a specific girl after the Spring Festival, I was told: "She's not coming back this year. She saved enough money for her own house and got married."

In another Panyu workshop, which produces Christmas decorations for export to the United States, I had a long conversation with the Chinese owner, Zhang Yongda, thirty-seven, who struck me as a sympathetic fellow. The atmosphere was more relaxed than in the Korean factory. Nor was the gate kept locked. Still, for a Finn, it was shocking to see the state of the washroom and the make-shift dormitory room, not to mention the sign on the wall with the working hours: 07:30–11:00, 13:00–17:30, 19:30–23:00—in total, eleven and a half hours per day.

Zhang was genuinely perplexed when I told him the West sees his line of business as exploiting human labor. "I offer a hundred young women the chance for a new life," Zhang said, shaking his head in bewilderment. "Sometimes when there aren't too many orders and there isn't enough work for the whole weekend, the girls get very impatient. They complain that they don't want any extra free time. 'We've come here to work, not to rest,' they tell me. Every week I have to turn away new girls who beg me for employment."

When I said that the workers were completely at the mercy of their employers and that no one was looking out for their rights, he quipped: "I

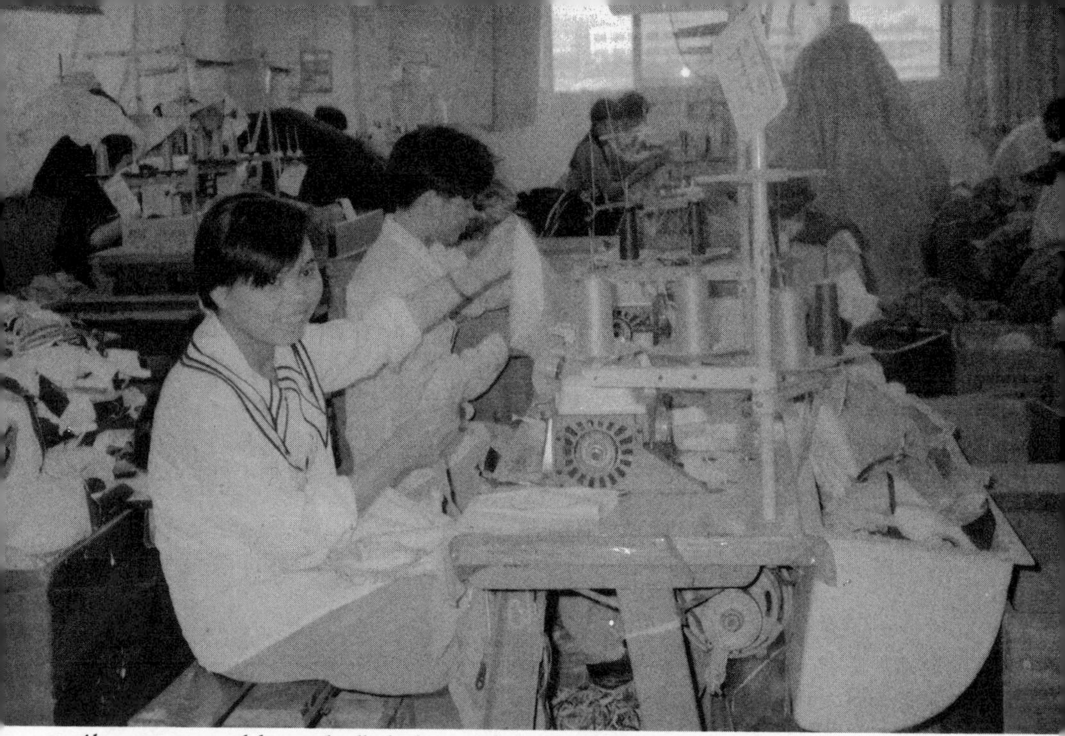

About 250 young adults, nearly all of whom are from the countryside, work in this private Hong Kong–owned clothing factory in Panyu. They produce women's wear for the American market and earn slightly more than the workers in Zhang Yongda's factory. In addition, they are paid extra for overtime—rare in China. (Photo: Linda Jakobson)

ask you, who looks out for their rights at home? Here, they can quit any time they want. A few have done just that when they've found better-paid work elsewhere. That is why some employers lock their gates and pay their workers only once a year. But that will soon change. That's not right—the competition must be free."

I took a photograph of Zhang Yongda in the middle of the production hall and wrote in my notebook: "Is this man a slave driver or one who gives women new lives?"

When I returned to the head office of the generator factory, Director Zhao showed me the work unit's calculated social welfare costs for 1996. "When you look at those figures you'll understand why it's so difficult to stay competitive with the private factories," he said. "I have to pay out pensions. I have to pay medical expenses. I have to pay for maternity leave. I have cut down on all the old-fashioned benefits of a state work unit. I don't invest in apartment buildings and I only offer my out-of-town workers a dormitory bed. I don't pay newspaper or barbershop bills either. But still, it's tough. A private factory has only a fraction of my expenses."

Director Zhao reminded me that state-run units only account for less than 25 percent of Guangdong's industrial output. "The reason is clear enough. State-run factories that are burdened with too high social welfare costs simply cannot survive in competition with the private sector. On the other hand, the state units that do operate are genuine business enterprises. Those famous plants that swallow up government subsidies are all elsewhere." Zhao took a deep breath. "Northerners still have a lot to learn. They go to the factory and think they're at a kindergarten where everything will be taken care of for them."

Zhao claimed he was not the least bit interested in politics. He assured me he never read the editorials in the newspapers. Yet, he continuously quoted the speeches of Deng Xiaoping. "Deng Xiaoping understood us Southerners. It was very wise of him to let Guangdong have a free hand to experiment with reforms. We are more interested in money than politics. I think that's probably the biggest problem in the state work units in the North. Even though the reform policy has been in force seventeen years now, they just can't seem to make their operations profitable. We Southerners think it's their own fault. Why don't they just get to work and stop talking politics? One must be flexible. One must be ready to move into different fields, to be constantly on the lookout for what's new and be willing to experiment."

Director Zhao made many references to Chinese history: "A feudal outlook is the biggest hindrance to economic growth. It constrains movement and stifles the process of learning. The cradle of Chinese civilization is the area around the Yellow River, but look at it today. It's China's most backward region." He also rebuked Confucianism for looking down on merchants (because they produced nothing new and merely moved goods from one place to another) and for disapproving of travel abroad (because it interfered with the important duties toward one's family).

Though official history texts describe the suspicion with which "greedy tradesmen" were regarded, recent research has revealed stories of merchants who occasionally rose to prominent positions in areas along the coast. Unofficial trade with foreigners was conducted to a far greater extent than one might conclude from the few mentions of it in official sources.[4] It is often joked that the Guangdongese and the neighboring Fujianese were born with the instinctive talents of businesspeople. "Trade and competition were a natural part of life in the South already in the times of our forefathers," Director Zhao said adding: "Without competition there can be no development."

Many rules were bent in the far-flung corners of the Empire, just as they are today in the People's Republic. According to Finnish architect Marja Sarvimäki, one can conclude from the designs of buildings that regulations issued in Beijing were ignored the further one went south. (Marja specializes in the history of Asian architecture. On her account, I have inspected nearly every nook and cranny of several historical buildings on our many excursions around China.) In previous centuries, both urban planning and the design of residential buildings were regulated by various norms which expressed the strict hierarchy of Confucianism—there were city areas which were meant only for people of a certain social status, just as rooms in individual houses were reserved for specific members of the household, based on their gender, age, and status in the family. There was even a custom that decreed that only in buildings for Imperial use could the gate be situated on the center axis—but the headstrong Southerners did not always adhere to this principle. In a residence where the owner wanted to emphasize his social status, the gates would be placed on the center axis, as an assertion of his power.[5] Imperial rules designed to indicate hierarchy extended even to dress. For example, common merchants were not supposed to wear the colorful silk robes which were reserved for bureaucrats. But, as Director Zhao told me, with a wink, the southern Chinese learned how to get around the rules hundreds of years ago. "In the South, merchants who were rich enough would indulge in silk robes on a par with the upper classes."

When I asked Director Zhao to what extent the Guangdongese were willing to heed Beijing's orders nowadays, he became serious. "Chinese want to avoid conflicts at all costs. Of course we don't flagrantly disobey Beijing's regulations. We just amend them to suit our needs. The economy doesn't develop in a straight line. It flows like rapids. There is never an even current. The water gushes out in torrents, but there are tranquil spots along the way. We Southerners are a smart lot. We always know how to change direction at exactly the right moment, as an accomplished boatman avoids hitting rocks by a split-second when he's shooting the rapids."

Director Zhao concluded with an old proverb which, literally translated, means: "Fish can't swim in water that is too clear." When I repeated it for my girlfriend Yuan that evening, she nodded approvingly. She said that Zhao was alluding to the innumerable loopholes in the system which offer an abundance of possibilities to those who know how to use them for their own benefit. "With that proverb he wanted to say that the economy would not prosper if the regulations were spelled out too clearly and the rules were too explicit."

By Western standards, Director Zhao had not said anything remarkable. But still it was different from what I was accustomed to in the North. When we parted I asked again, to be on the safe side, if it was all right to quote him by name. "Of course," he answered. "Everything I've said to you is my own personal opinion." Which is exactly what directors of state-run factories in the North tend to lack.

My girlfriend Yuan and another Jinan teaching colleague, Xiao Hong (which means "Little Red"), did not bat an eye when I recounted my conversation with Director Zhao. "He sounds like the same type of liberal-minded and smooth-tongued businessman as my father-in-law, who is the complete opposite of my own father," said Xiao Hong. She is interesting to talk to because she was brought up in the Northeast, but is married to a man from Guangzhou. They met when she was studying international business at a graduate school in Shanghai, where he was training to become a computer engineer. She had been devastated when she was assigned a teaching job in Jinan, but, in the end, she had not taught there for more than a year when she managed to have her residence permit transferred to a school in Guangzhou. The couple's five-year-old son spoke both Cantonese and *putonghua* fluently.

Xiao Hong said she had grown accustomed to life in the South surprisingly quickly. "People's relationships here are so much less complicated than in the North," she said. "Close friendships are perhaps more rare, but life in the South is more carefree and practical matters are easier to cope with. For example, in the North everyone gets terribly stressed out before the Spring Festival. They run from one acquaintance to another, making sure that each and every one receives a present according to tradition. And then they get terribly flustered when they've forgotten someone who might be only a casual acquaintance."

"What are you talking about?" Yuan interrupted. "It's exactly the same here in the South. All I do before the Spring Festival is tear around delivering presents to our customers. It's absolutely essential for business in the South too."

"Yes, I know, but I was talking about the relationships between friends and acquaintances, not the business world," Xiao Hong answered. "Here in the South we send one another a card, or perhaps just phone to wish a friend a Happy New Year. The actual holiday is often celebrated in a restaurant, not at home as it is in the North. The family is important in the South too, but somehow one's family ties are not as restraining and demanding as those in the North. Elderly people here are much more independent. They are not expected to take care of their grandchildren full-time. In the South, we employ nannys. Though my brother in the Northeast has a good salary and could easily afford a nanny, my mother feels it's her obligation to care for her son's child. When I suggested they employ someone, even my brother argued: 'How would it look if a grandmother didn't take care of her grandson? What would the neighbors think?' My in-laws here in Guangdong travel and eat out a lot. I think that's fine. We encourage them to enjoy their lives. But in the Northeast, my parents sit at home and save."

Xiao Hong added that a fundamental difference in attitudes concerned education. Generally speaking, the standard of education is lower in the South and one often hears the claim that education is not held in as high esteem as it is in the North. "In the South, a person is evaluated on the basis of his salary and, to some extent, his talents. Of course, as a teacher, I find it sad that education is not emphasized, but, on the other hand, I like the fact that a maid is not looked down upon in the same way as in the North. Northerners turn up their noses and say that Southerners are only interested in making money. It's true, they are, but in the North a maid or a nanny is not even considered a human being, just because she is an illiterate country girl. No one takes into account that she fulfills a necessary and, in many cases, worthy task. In the South, one appreciates a competent maid, even if she doesn't have a formal education."

"But in the South, money is so important that a rich person is respected even if he or she has made a fortune by dubious means," Yuan remarked. "I'm still a Northerner in the sense that I can't stand the shady, wealthy wheeler-dealers one often meets in the South."

"That's not necessarily true. Southerners don't think much of them either," Xiao Hong disagreed.

It was my turn to butt in: "I know at least two Southerners who have no respect for wealth that has been amassed dishonestly."

I told them about journalist Liu, one of the three main characters in my reportage about Guangdong's pursuit of "dragon-status" in 1993. The other two were the boss of a privately owned advertising agency, Director Han, and the managing director of a state-run paper mill, Xie Shuwen. I had chosen Liu, Han, and Xie because all three represented success stories, though they were very different from one another. But all three had flourished in the same milieu—Guangdong, the flagship of

China's open-door policy. Journalist Liu had arrived from the North with no money to her name just two years earlier, but she was already a millionaire. As an economic reporter, she had made skillful use of her good "relations" with prominent members of society to acquire her first apartment. (Bribes, which often entail exorbitant sums, are common in the Chinese media world.) Then she started speculating on the real estate market.

When I met journalist Liu again in the autumn of 1996, "the crazy years" in the real estate market had already passed, but she was apparently still living in the fast lane. She had married a wealthy Guangdongese businessman and was now speculating in the stock exchange. She had recently returned from Macao, where she had spent an evening with friends at the casino and had lost an astonishing 20,000 yuan ($2,400). "But," she assured me, "the trip was lots of fun."

"I'll never forget the look on Director Han's face at the advertising agency when I recounted journalist Liu's experiences," I told Yuan and Xiao Hong. This former art teacher, a gentleman with a wiry mustache, had founded the most reputable advertising agency in the province. "There are also honorable ways to make a fortune," was his wry observation. Director Xie made a similar comment.

"I suppose you understood what they were trying to say," Xiao Hong said with a smile. "Miss Liu had most probably nurtured her good relations in bed."

"That's what John Lee kept telling me," I answered.

One theme that recurs whenever the changes in Guangdong are discussed is the effect of Hong Kong on the province. Everyone tends to agree that Hong Kong's influence on the development of Guangdong has been phenomenal, not only economically, but also psychologically. In fact, Guangdong's and Hong Kong's economies were already integrated when Hong Kong returned to Chinese rule on July 1, 1997. Three-fourths of the so-called "foreign" investments made in Guangdong since 1979 were actually made by Hongkongese. Hong Kong companies employ five million people in Guangdong. All sectors of Guangdong society are familiar with Western goods and Western habits, thanks to Hong Kong television and radio broadcasts, which are far more popular than the Chinese state-run channels. By watching Hong Kong television, the Guangdongese have also been able to compare their own standards of living with those of other Asians.

Xie Shuwen, the director of the Guangzhou Paper Mill. (Photo: Linda Jakobson)

Now that Hong Kong is a political entity of China, ties between the two will further be strengthened. After the handover there was talk of building a bullet train which would enable Hong Kong residents to pop into Guangzhou in just an hour. The trains today are already packed with day commuters, though the trip takes three hours. Thousands of trucks loaded with goods pass daily across the border at Shenzhen, the first of the Special Economic Zones (SEZ) founded in 1980 to experiment with a capitalist economy. A superhighway runs along the Pearl River delta, connecting Shenzhen and Zhuhai, another SEZ, with Guangzhou. Directors like Xie Shuwen and Zhao Rujia visit Hong Kong regularly and have many friends in the former British colony. My middle-class friends, Yuan and Xiao Hong, have also been to Hong Kong.

"Nowadays, the people in Guangdong and Hong Kong understand each other perfectly," said Xie Shuwen, director of China's largest paper mill, in 1996. He was not merely referring to the fact that the Hongkongese and the Guangdongese both speak Cantonese, but also to their way of thinking. "The soft values that we have absorbed from the Hongkongese have been just as valuable as their money. We have learned what it means to be international. We have learned how to deal with Westerners. These are immeasurable assets."

Xie Shuwen is one of those extraordinary people one bumps into every now and again in China. He had just turned thirty-three when he was appointed managing director of the Guangzhou Paper Mill in 1987. He had only been employed at the mill for four years when he was promoted. His age alone is exceptional in a country where even fifty-three-year-old Zhao Rujia is considered young to be a director. Xie Shuwen is unmistakably brainy but extremely modest.

"Bashful to the degree that you'd think he'd be more at home as an economics researcher at some university," I wrote in my notebook during my first interview with him in 1993. He belongs to the generation who missed out on an education because of the Cultural Revolution. His youth was spent "making revolution," as he himself put it. In 1979, as a twenty-five-year-old worker in a truck factory, he passed the university entrance examinations and was accepted at the best school of economics in Guangdong. From there his career soared.

Director Xie has been to the West many times. During my first visit, new paper-making machines from Finland were being installed in one wing of the factory and he was in the process of acquiring a water-filter system from Austria. The factory employs 5,200 people and supports an additional 2,000 retirees. Family members of employees also live on the factory grounds. The actual production lines and warehouses make up only a small part of the entire work unit. There are also two schools, a kindergarten, a day-care center, a health center, a movie theater, a swimming pool, a library, and numerous shops and restaurants.

At age forty-two Xie still looked boyish, more like a university lecturer, in his unpressed pale cotton trousers and docksiders, than a factory director. But there was a new air of confidence about him. He gave me a detailed run-through of the mill's budget and debts, and the plans he had for the future, including construction of a second power plant. His manner and level of openness did not differ in any way from that of a general manager of an American company.

In 1993, his aim had been to increase the production capacity, to make the Guangzhou Paper Mill the biggest in China. By 1996, he had a new target, to be the biggest in Asia. Xie reminds me of Wang Zhenyao, the man in charge of "village democracy" reform. If all the state-owned factories were run by men like Xie, the future would look bright. When we met in 1996, he told me that in addition to running the paper mill, he had spent every weekend of the past two and a half years at his old university studying toward an international MBA degree.

Xie was shocked to hear that I planned to describe his paper mill as an exemplary state-owned work unit (the mill was, after all, making a sizeable profit), and he categorically forbade me to call him a model director. "We have the same problems with corruption as everywhere else in China," he said quite spontaneously. "There are endless intrigues when it comes to deciding who should be promoted and who will be allowed to further one's studies—we have to fight against corruption every minute of the day. The problems that arise between people in a state work unit are the most difficult to deal with. They give me a headache."

Considering that he is a Communist Party member in a high position, he said with surprising candor that the Party had made its greatest mistake by neglecting political reform during the open-door policy period. "That's why we have such a grave problem with corruption, and that, in turn, has started to slow down our economic growth. Government officials have a lot of power, but it goes unchecked. Hong Kong had a terrible problem with corruption back in the 1960s, but it was curbed after the British developed a sound legal system. We are going to walk down that same road," Xie predicted.

I asked him how he could be so sure that Guangdong will copy Hong Kong, rather than the other way round. A number of Western business acquaintances have predicted that the decay and rot of the Guangdong business world will seep into Hong Kong and slowly erode the rule of law which the British managed to establish over the years. Many Western businessmen curse South China for its flagrant corruption.

"Of course there is always that danger," Xie answered, but in that case, "the Party will be digging its own grave.

"China simply must start to implement laws in a trustworthy and convincing manner. Otherwise our economy will stagnate. We already have many plausible and good laws, but they are not enforced. But there have been signs that the civil servants of Guangdong are beginning to understand the precariousness of the situation. They are now pushing for more genuine legal reforms. The impetus will be even stronger with Hong Kong a part of China. You'll see, Guangdong will yet again be a forerunner."

Qigong (ch'i-kung) *has been compared to the hatha-yoga of India. It consists of breathing and meditation exercises that are said to improve one's health and cure various sicknesses. There are dozens of various types of* qigong, *some of which recommend the use of props to enhance the flow of* qi-energy, *as in the case of this musician in Xian. (Photo: John Lee, 1994)*

九

A Labyrinth of Ideas and Beliefs

Let Your Qi-Energy Flow Freely

The woman at the *dimsum*-table in Guangzhou, who had compared Southerners to Italians and Northerners to Germans, hit a politically sensitive nerve. Chinese have been taught from time immemorial that a unified China is strong and affluent, but if the Empire falls apart, chaos will prevail. In other words, China has always thrived under a single, powerful ruler, while the weakening of central power has meant instability and unrest. That is why it is treasonous—applying this ancient doctrine of unity—to compare China to Europe, with its numerous separate sovereign states. The unity of the country is constantly underscored in all official speeches by top leaders in Beijing. For President Jiang Zemin, street demonstrations are a minor concern compared to the prospect of provinces breaking away and declaring independence.

Outsiders who ponder the future of China often mention the possibility that China will fall apart like the former Soviet Union. Such observers naturally focus on border areas like Tibet and Xinjiang, where minority nationalities, such as the Tibetans and the Uighurs, oppose the supremacy of the Han Chinese.

More recently, analysts have called attention to the growing economic independence of the coastal provinces of Guangdong and neighboring Fujian, which are far more affluent than the rest of the country. Will these two provinces, with a total population of 100 million, continue to accept absolute rule by Beijing? At some point, will they not inevitably look upon union with China as an economic burden, especially as the central government policies must take into consideration the poorer backward regions of the country? In purely economic terms, some sort of loose federation with Taiwan and Hong Kong would appear to be a lucrative alternative. China-watchers pursuing this train of thought are quick to point out that these two southern provinces are culturally different from the rest of the country.

Those who see the possibility of future disintegration often back up their views with the traditional Chinese cyclical conception of the world. It is popular to quote the classical novel *San Guo Zhi Yanyi (Romance of the Three Kingdoms)*. It begins with the sentence: "Empires wax and wane; states cleave asunder and coalesce." But others argue that a weak empire does not automatically result in chaos. Central weakness may lead to disunity, but not necessarily to the break-up of the state. The Song (960–1279) was a weak dynasty, in terms of political control, but "it was the highpoint of intellectual and economic achievement, the pinnacle of China's artistic history."[1]

After the Tiananmen events in 1989, some people outside of China believed that the country would soon fall apart. The Communist dynasty was thought to have lost its Mandate of Heaven; in other words, its legitimacy. But critics lowered their voices after 1992, when eighty-eight-year-old Deng Xiaoping, though officially retired, persuaded Chinese leaders to believe in the magic of economic prosperity. Unprecedented economic growth diverted people's attention—at least for the time being—away from politics.

Distinctive local subcultures are hardly a new phenomenon in China. Throughout its long history, diverse local dialects and customs have varied from region to region. Nor have the provinces commanded equal influence. Economic inequality, now a crucial problem in the People's Republic, was already a fact of life in the days of the emperors. The coastal areas have traditionally been more prosperous than the interior. For centuries Guangdong, far from the imperial throne and the seat of power, served as a shock absorber for new ideas coming in from abroad. As early as the fifteenth century, Cantonese merchants were famous throughout East Asia. They returned from their voyages not only with new products, but also with new ideas and influences. The people of Guangdong today are merely following in the footsteps of their forefathers.

Natives of any particular region may cherish their distinctive lifestyles and attitudes which set them apart from other parts of the country. But local cultural identity would not tempt a provincial government to push their regional agendas at the expense of Chinese unity. That approach is taking the theme of diversity a step too far. Factory directors Zhao Rujia and Xie Shuwen both envision a more independent Guangdong that will be able to decide not only economic issues, but also questions concerning education and local governance, much like states in the U.S. But they have no aspirations for Guangdong ever to break away from China. "Absolutely not," was the indignant response from all the Guangdongese I met. "We're all Chinese."

Whenever I have broached the possible independence of Tibet or Xinjiang with anyone in Beijing, the idea was always rejected out of hand. Perry Link, professor of literature at Princeton University, who has a wide range of contacts of all age groups among the Chinese intelligentsia, notes that "the issue of Tibet generates little interest among Chinese intellectuals."[2] Even my friends who have had the chance to consider the Tibetan question from outside, while studying abroad, and who want to see China develop in a more democratic manner, do not accept the Tibetans' right to decide their own future.

"Tibet is a part of China. China will remain unified," is the attitude of artists, musicians, authors, and other independent-minded individualists with whom I have spoken. They use exactly the same arguments as those holding power to justify their contention that all areas inhabited by minorities still belong to China. On the other hand, when we discuss artistic freedom, these same people are highly critical of their country's leaders, accusing them of hypocrisy and of attempting to influence their creative work.

I once had a heated argument about Tibet with two painter friends, Mushi and Heiyang. Both of them mechanically repeated arguments from the official history texts. As both were liberal-leaning artists in their thirties, I had expected them to side with the oppressed Tibetans.

"Has it occurred to you that you have been given false information about Tibetan history?" I asked. I reminded them that only half an hour earlier, they had told me not to believe "the lies put out by the Ministry of Culture" regarding stipends granted to artists.

"No one has lied to us about the history of Tibet," a visibly perturbed Heiyang answered. "Tibet has always been a part of China."

This same nationalistic stance has been adopted by numerous Chinese dissidents whom I have met in the United States—people who claim to advocate broader political rights in China. Some of them do, however, admit that their position is purely tactical. They do not want to burden themselves with the issue of Tibet, which is explosively sensitive to the Beijing government.

It is hard to imagine the circumstances under which China's leadership would permit the Tibetans or Uighurs to form an independent state. But it is possible that they will be granted more authentic autonomy at some future date. The other fifty-three officially recognized minority groups living in China have much less hope of attaining self-determination. They are widely scattered, mostly in the western and southwestern parts of the country.

China cannot be compared to the former Soviet Union. Ninety-two percent of the population are Han Chinese, bound together by a cultural identity so strong and so ingrained that it is difficult for a Westerner to grasp. One continuously hears allusions to Chinese history and civilization, going back many thousands of years. "We're all the descendants of the rulers Huang and Yan," is a popular expression, which refers to legendary rulers who lived more than 4,000 years ago in the area around the Yellow River. Although scholars disagree about certain aspects of this claim, what is relevant here is that the saying is a common one.

Historical figures appear frequently in everyday conversation. "Three simple-minded tanners can outdo Zhuge Liang," my neighbor once exclaimed triumphantly, after he and his friends devised a way to acquire a license plate without the required Beijing residence permit. Zhuge Liang was a third-century military commander, famous for his intelligence and his accurate predictions. The moral of the story is that three average guys can outsmart even a great genius when they put their heads together to come up with the right solution. The Chinese stock of such legends is bottomless.

Many attempts have been made to explain Chinese cultural unity, their sense of belonging to a unique cultural identity. Not only the denizens of the People's Republic, but also many of the fifty million "Overseas" Chinese living elsewhere, some of whom have never set foot in China, comprise a distinct cultural group with deep emotional bonds toward the land of their ancestors.[3] Their input as investors has been instrumental during the open-door policy period.

Historian John K. Fairbank described Chinese "culturalism" as devotion to one's own way of life, "an across-the-board sentiment as strong as the political nationalism of recent centuries in Europe." At various times over the millenia, when barbarians from the north conquered China, the Chinese "found their refuge in their social institutions and feelings of cultural and aesthetic superiority."[4] (Mongols ruled the Middle Kingdom during the Yuan dynasty [1279–1368] and Manchus during the Qing dynasty [1644–1911]. The unity and flowering of Chinese civilization did not require a Han emperor.)

Social institutions and the importance of ceremony comprise the glue that has held the Chinese together, according to cultural anthropologist James L. Watson. A common written language played a significant role, along with an imperial center and a complex bureaucracy. But equally important was the fact that Chinese identity "involved no conversion to a received dogma, no professions of belief in a creed or a set of ideas." Rather, it stressed ritual form. In contrast, as Watson points out, the history of Christian Europe is very much "a history of fragmentation resulting from disagreements over correct belief."[5]

According to Confucianism, correct ideas follow from correct behavior, affirming the primacy of ritual (*li*), such as the proper way to act when dealing with one's next-of-kin or one's superiors, the proper way to marry, the proper way to bury the dead, the proper way to honor one's ancestors, and so on. In a huge empire with such a wide array of subcultures, it was functional to emphasize the form rather than the content of these rites. Orthopraxy became more relevant than orthodoxy. As Watson concludes, the strength of Chinese cultural identity was that it allowed great variations within the framework of a unified, centrally organized culture.

Watson's ritual approach to Chinese identity is no doubt one-sided. Both Confucian and Daoist thought stressed harmony. Therefore the distinction between form and content is difficult to draw when "the value of 'harmony' (*he*) is constantly promoted . . . as the proper form of all human relations."[6] In theory, Confucius held benevolence and love or kindheartedness (*ren*)[7] in as high esteem as rites and decency (*li*), but in practice, form tended to overshadow the virtuous dimension.

Whether or not one agrees with Watson's approach, it does shed light on the Chinese way of thinking which, still today, retains underlying elements of Confucianism, Daoism,* Buddhism, and earlier popular beliefs, all coexisting in relative harmony. A Westerner may find it hard to comprehend this blend of philosophies and religions. The question "What do you believe in?" usually provokes (if not the sarcastic rejoinder, "Money") the spontaneous answer, "I don't believe in anything." But if the conversation continues beyond superficialities, it often turns out that what the person actually believes is "a bit of everything."

Confucianism is commonly considered a single philosophy. In reality, different schools of Confucianism emerged over centuries. It became the predominant philosophy of the Chinese court during the Han dynasty in the first century B.C. The process was slow, and the "Confucianism that won over was a curious synthesis of ancient philosophies and current superstitions, and not at all the pure, ethical teachings of Confucius. . . ."[8] The same can be said of the Confucianism which later became official dogma during the Song dynasty (960–1279), which was strongly influenced by Daoism, Buddhism, and earlier animistic beliefs. This Neo-Confucianism, as it became known, encompassed a metaphysical dimension distinct

* Daoism can also be written as Taoism.

from earlier Confucian thought. Thus, to equate the original teachings of Master Confucius with "traditional Chinese thought" is misleading and inaccurate, though it is often done.

The philosopher Confucius,* who lived about 500 years B.C., actually never wrote down his thoughts. They were compiled by his disciples (after his death) into a text called *Lunyu* (*Analects*), which consists of the master's enigmatic statements, anecdotes, and short dialogues with students on a wide range of subjects. Because the text is often abstract and the fundamental contentions of Confucius are open to interpretation, over the course of history they have been read and understood in numerous different ways, most of which reflect the biases of the interpreter.

When, in recent years, the Chinese Communist Party began trying to fill the ideological void left behind by an increasingly irrevelant Marxism by adapting elements of Confucianism, it was merely continuing an ancient tradition. Rulers have habitually remolded Confucianism to suit their own purposes. In the foreword of his translation of *The Analects of Confucius*, China scholar Pierre Ryckmans (Simon Leys) notes:

"Karl Marx once warned overenthusiastic followers that he was not a Marxist. With better reason, one should say that Confucius was certainly not a Confucianist. Imperial Confucianism only extolled those statements from the Master that prescribed submission to the established authorities, whereas more essential notions were conveniently ignored—such as precepts of social justice, political dissent, and the moral duty of intellectuals to criticize the ruler (even at the risk of their own lives) when he was abusing his power, or when he oppressed the people."[9]

For this reason the sense that ordinary Chinese have of Confucianism does not necessarily reflect the thoughts of Master Confucius as expressed in the *Analects*. "We can thank Confucius for this country being so backward," my engineer friend Song once observed, repeating a constant theme of the Cultural Revolution. All the revolutionary movements in twentieth-century China have been staunchly anti-Confucian. In 1993, I nearly had to force Song and his wife to accompany me on an excursion to Qufu, the birthplace of Confucius. Although they had lived in Jinan their entire lives, neither of them had ever visited this historic temple and residence, built in honor of Master Kong. Qufu is only a three-hour bus ride away from Jinan. In their childhood memories, Mao Zedong was exalted as the "Reddest Red Sun," while Confucius was deemed the blackest of black Satans.

---

* Confucius's name in Mandarin is Kong Qiu. After his death he was bestowed with the title of "Master" (*fuzi*), and he became known as Kong Fuzi or Kongzi.

Nearly all the Chinese I know who were born in the 1950s and 1960s associate Confucianism with feudalism and stagnation. They even make contemptuous remarks about the canonization of Confucius as the Great Teacher. "Because of Confucianism, generation after generation of Chinese children were compelled to learn everything by heart," my economist friend Chen scoffed, after he returned from his studies abroad. "Confucianism suppressed creative thinking."

Yet numerous scholars, both Chinese and Western, admire the philosopher Confucius for his "modern" outlook. They claim he was wrestling with many of the same social problems confronting us today.

It was ironic to hear a professor of philosophy in Beijing bemoan the Communists' attempts to restore Confucianist values in the 1990s. In 1958, this same gentleman had been sent by the Communists to do forced labor because he had defended Confucius's "progressive thoughts" in an academic paper. "Now they are hysterically attempting to find something to counterbalance the overemphasis on materialism. As a result, the teachings of Confucius have become even more blurred, even among intellectuals," the retired professor complained. "The leaders are simply picking out thoughts to suit their needs, as if plucking flowers for a floral arrangement they had designed ahead-of-time."

I had looked up the professor prior to the international symposium held in Beijing in October 1994 to celebrate the 2,545th anniversary of Confucius's birth. Several older intellectuals I spoke with felt that Party sponsorship of the conference was grotesque. Even more than the Party's change of heart vis-à-vis materialism, they found the official turnaround toward Confucianism hard to stomach.

But the Confucius symposium did not lack its entertaining moments. Li Ruihuan, a member of the Standing Committee of the Party Politburo Central Committee, gave an exhilarating speech about Mencius, a disciple of Confucius, whose book of thoughts is second only to the *Analects*. Li Ruihuan spoke spontaneously, without notes, which is quite rare for such a high-level leader in China. The King should not think he is a good King just because the men around him say so, Li Ruihuan told his audience. "Mencius taught us that there is no way to become a true King except by providing for the well-being of the people and thus winning their support." Li Ruihuan also referred to the writings of Mencius regarding the obligation of citizens to speak out about social injustices. A noble citizen is not silent.

The atmosphere in the auditorium was electric as the audience leaned forward in their chairs to take in Li Ruihuan's each and every word. Li's references were clearly intended to be a jab at Party Secretary Jiang Zemin and acknowledgement of the people's needs to voice their opinions about shortcomings in present-day society.

The debate surrounding the essential nature of Confucianism will continue as long as there are Chinese. Despite the many contradictory interpretations, Confucius's thoughts are intimately linked to Chinese identity. No book has affected the Chinese way of thinking more profoundly over the past two thousand years than the *Analects.* The family-oriented approach to life, respect for education, emphasis on authority, and the inclination to put the needs of the collective before those of the individual are all part of the Confucianist legacy.

Though Confucianism was mainly a code of ethics and civics, the official cult of Confucius was vested with what a Westerner would call religious trappings. It became a sort of state religion. As early as 58 A.D., all government schools were ordered to make sacrifices to Confucius. Confucius Temples were built throughout the Empire, with prescribed rites to honor the Great Sage. Statues of Confucius, Buddha, and Laozi (the mythical founding father of Daoism) stood side-by-side in sanctuaries built in homage to popular deities. The Chinese concept of religion does not entail the exclusivity of Christianity, for example, which acknowledges only one true faith. Chinese religious beliefs complement and supplement one another much like the forces of *yin* and *yang*.

Even before Confucianism and Daoism, Chinese thought emphasized the collective. According to the earliest traditional beliefs, only the ruler could make sacrifices to the most supreme of gods, Heaven, on behalf of the people. Man did not have what Christians would define as a personal relationship with God.

The reform policy period has seen a strong revival of all forms of religious beliefs, especially Buddhism. A February 1996 internal Communist Party document estimated that there were perhaps 70 million religious believers in China. Christianity evokes interest among several different circles of Chinese, young and old, reflecting, to some extent, the curiosity many people have about anything Western. But this interest may also indicate the insecurity many feel in the absence of any credible ideology.

Christmas, in its most commercial form, is the one Christian holiday most urban Chinese are aware of, due in large part to the department stores in major Chinese cities. But most of those who now buy Christmas decorations or send Christmas cards to friends have no idea why the holiday is celebrated. Only a handful of my friends have ever asked me what it means to be a "Christian," "Catholic," "Protestant," "Jew," and so on. And those few cannot understand how people who all believe in one God can differ to the extent that they do not naturally drop in to one another's churches to pray. But then, it is not easy to explain to Western friends why a Chinese acquaintance, a woman in her fifties, who prays at a Buddhist temple at least twice a week, also buys a small Christmas tree every year and decorates it with shiny little stars and matchbox-size pictures of the Crucifix. "It can't hurt to pay respect to the foreigners' gods as well," she once explained.

Officially, less than one percent of the Chinese population are Christians; approximately 6.5 million Protestants, and 4 million Catholics. However, church organizations and Western observers estimate the numbers to be much higher; up to 20 million Protestants and 8 to 10 million Catholics.[10]

My Jinan friend, Guo Hairong, who spent her youth on the Mongolian grasslands, is exceptional because she strives to understand Western customs from a historical perspective. She is the only Chinese friend I have who is well-versed in European and American history. Usually people only want to know: "How is this done in the West?" They do not care to know why. In May 1995, Guo Hairong recounted a conversation she had overheard on the train to Beijing. Three representatives of a medical research institute were reminiscing about a recent trip to Europe. They were perplexed as to why their innovative birth-control capsule had been so well received in Germany, but totally rejected in Italy and Spain. "They knew it had something to do with religion," Guo Hairong said. "One of the men even exclaimed, 'It's really strange. There must be a lot of Christians in Germany, too. We saw just as many churches there as in Italy.'"

Guo Hairong said she could not wait to describe this encounter to her nephew, who works as an interpreter for a Sino-German joint venture. "My nephew says his German bosses are always complaining that we Chinese are obsessed with our history. They often tell him sarcastically that their knowledge of history suffices to sell their products all over the world. They don't seem to understand that we have our own way of looking at things. It's because our distinctive culture developed over thousands of years with little influence from abroad." Guo Hairong was visibly agitated, upset by the attitude of her nephew's employers. "Foreigners who have never heard of Confucianism and Daoism are as lost in China as those three Chinese who went to Europe to sell birth control pills, without a clue about the Roman Catholic doctrine regarding contraception."

Forming a precise picture of Chinese cultural identity today is a formidable task. Much of the legacy of the past—though certainly not all of it—has indeed been swept away by the dramatic political changes of this century. But I was quite astounded when a Finnish businessman who lives in Beijing said he thought traditions had all but died out in China. "No one cares about anything else but money," he claimed in all earnestness. If he had been a casual traveler, I would not have been surprised. A short visit can certainly leave one with such an impression. But this man, married to a Chinese, had lived in Beijing for ten years.

"How can you say such a thing?" I asked in astonishment. It was mid-December. The topic of tradition came up at dinner when the Finn was enthusiatically describing Finnish Christmas traditions to his wife, implying that the Chinese had no reverence for anything similar. I felt like telling him that his wife—an independent, modern woman in her thirties—might well have a nonchalant approach to tradition, just as many career-oriented wives in the West do not bother with all the trappings of a traditional Christmas holiday. But it was nonsense to say that tradition was dying in China. The reform policy has certainly brought on an identity crisis. First, so much was destroyed during the Cultural Revolution, and these days a portion of urban youth only wants to copy blindly everything Western. But every day the majority of Chinese either consciously or subconsciously continue centuries-old customs—in their eating habits, their interactions with family members, their attitudes toward birth, marriage, and death, their means of expression, and, without question, in the way they observe important holidays.

For seven years in a row, I have celebrated the Spring Festival either in my godchild's home in Beijing or in *Jiejie*'s and Yang's home in Jinan. For both families, the holiday consists of three full days of following traditions. The whole family gathers for an elaborate dinner on the eve of the Spring Festival, feasting on special dishes prepared according to time-honored recipes. We play mahjong and various board games, many of which originated in ancient times. We make traditonal *jiaozi*-dumplings, which have to be eaten at midnight regardless of if we are hungry, and we shoot off firecrackers in the street (to scare away the evil spirits). The next morning we join the crowds at the nearby Daoist temple, to throw coins in the fountain and patiently wait our turn to stroke the ear on a statue of a famous deity, all for good luck. The children are given *hongbao*-packages which, according to tradition, are wrapped in bright red paper and contain money. On the second day, we visit the parents of the female members of the family, and on the third day we visit close friends and more distant relatives, as tradition dictates. Considering the long list of things we do purely because "it's tradition," the claim that traditions are in danger of extinction seems ridiculous.

Southern Chinese tell me they observe many more traditions than Northerners do during the New Year period. Many families in Guangzhou, no matter how modern-thinking, faithfully smear honey on the lips of the "Kitchen God" ten days before the start of the Spring Festival (to ensure that this deity of moral behavior will tell others only of the sweet and good deeds of the family when she flies off on her annual heavenly escapades before the start of the new year). In contrast, most northern Chinese I know do not keep a picture of this goddess in their kitchen. When I have asked, I have been told it's "all part of the superstitious nonsense Southerners believe in." But even in Beijing, many more traditional wall coverings, with graceful strokes of calligraphy wishing a prosperous and lucky new year, appeared during the 1990s than there were in the 1980s. These strips of red silk paper are often stuck on doors and gates by the entrance to buildings.

Renewed cultural awareness has even begun to attract members of the younger generation in the 1990s. Young educated urbanites seem to hold a slightly more balanced view of Western culture than people their age did ten years earlier. In the 1980s anything Western was idolized without reservation. (In some cases, such adoration has now turned to outright scorn because of the recent rise in nationalist sentiment.) As in modern Japan, where many traditional customs still dominate the way of life, educated young people in China are realizing that modernization and Westernization are not necessarily synonymous. A higher standard of living does not mean abandoning one's own cultural traditions. Today an increasing number of modern Chinese artists, theater and film directors, writers, and musicians are exploring their own rich cultural heritage in their creative work.

I could have mentioned all this, and more, to the Finnish businessman who had written off Chinese tradition, but I did not want to spoil a pleasant dinner, especially since his wife did not object to his comments. I wondered why not, until I recalled that she was born in a city in northern China at the start of the Cultural Revolution in 1966. During her childhood, all tradition was held in contempt. After graduating from university, she immediately went to work for a European company, thus assimilating into the "foreigners' world" of the capital.

The Finnish businessman's words were a forcible reminder of China's numerous faces. Many Chinese, like his wife, who have spent all of their

Even the most modern of Chinese art has gradually absorbed features from China's traditional culture. Performance artist J.G.[2]*, a friend from my student days in Beijing, is one of the most daring and radical in his artistic expression, but thus far, he has only performed abroad. The makeup is similar to that of a traditional jingju-performer; however, nudity is still taboo in China. The text in the background advertizes medicine for sexually transmitted diseases.*

adult lives mingling in foreign circles in Beijing, have turned their backs on the ideology they were taught in school, but they do not have that natural devotion to "their own way of life" that Fairbank described. That way of life was destroyed and thoroughly disparaged during their youth in the 1960s and 1970s. Such individuals have scant knowledge of their own traditions. And the westernized environment to which they have become accustomed tends to increase their ambivalence. Many foreigners living in Beijing encounter Chinese with a similar lack of interest in Chinese customs. The language barrier alone makes it difficult to reach the China where tradition still flourishes.

In everyday conversations Chinese commonly refer to ancient philosophers or popular beliefs. Daoist influence, especially, underlies many situations, though overt allusions to Daoism are rare. Many sayings or attitudes are justified simply as "being Chinese." Most of my Chinese acquaintances know surprisingly little about the theories of Daoism as a philosophy or a religion, though most Chinese heed Daoist principles in their everyday lives. The Chinese diet, *taiji* (*tai-chi*), *qigong*-meditation (*ch'i-kung*), the month of rest after a mother gives birth, and Chinese traditional medicine are all, to some extent, based on Daoist principles, or older popular beliefs. Even Chinese yuppies, who dismiss *qigong*-meditation as rubbish and do not believe in traditional medicine, instinctively follow the principles of the "five elements" in their diet. There are five tastes—salty, sour, bitter, spicy, and sweet—and a well-balanced meal must include all five.

In the elevator in my apartment building, when I once complained of having the flu, the elevator lady glanced at my shopping bag and remarked: "You mustn't eat tangerines if you have a sore throat. Tangerines bring out the fire." "And don't eat anything cold!" a neighbor advised. "Boil slices of pear together with ginger and sugar. Then drink the fluid. That will remove the fire from your body." Such folk knowledge is second nature to a Chinese. To a foreigner it is usually inscrutable, especially if one is not familiar with the basic principles of Daoism. For example, the term "cold" does not refer merely to items that are stored in a refrigerator, but also to bananas, cucumbers, or soft drinks kept at room temperature.

Sometimes advice is contradictory, not surprisingly, since Daoism does not profess absolute rules. Every human being must find his or her own "way" (*dao*) to good health. And every family tends to advocate its own unique way, as grandmothers in the West may have a "one-and-only" remedy to nurse a sick child: bouillon perhaps, or hot chicken soup. Lao He, the woman who cleans my apartment, always chastises me for drinking too much green tea. But my godchild's family advises me to drink it in abundance, except on days when I have to take Chinese herbal medicine. My girlfriend, Dr. Feng, has yet another approach. She says I can drink as much green tea as I want as long as I abstain half an hour before and after taking my Chinese medicine.

Daoism is the the second most important component of Chinese thought after Confucianism. (The third is Buddhism, which spread to China from India and was "sinified" over a period of five centuries, starting from about A.D. 300, absorbing elements of Daoism and other, older Chinese popular beliefs.) Daoism focused on the relation between man and nature. Originally, it was antithetical to the ideas of Confucianism, which addressed man's relation to society. Though Daoists, from time to time, suffered the wrath and persecution of the rulers (as did Buddhists), generally Daoism and Confucianism have complemented each other and developed side-by-side in harmony for the last 2,000 years. In the West, they are seen as two separate schools of philosophy (or religion). Actually, they correspond to each other in many ways. Both traditions looked to the Emperor as the mediator between man and the forces of the cosmos, a principle which derives from early Chinese beliefs. Both (especially Neo-Confucianism) drew upon ancient classics and, especially, the classic *Book of Changes*, which expounds on the theory of the mutually reinforcing forces of *yin* and *yang*.

It is said that a civil servant in Imperial China was a Confucianist at work and a Daoist at home. The Daoist approach to life was the "cheerful and carefree side of Chinese nature," balancing the moralistic, goal-oriented Confucianist way of thinking.[11] The Daoist approach to sexuality was straightforward: Male and female sexual pleasures were held in high regard, as attested to by numerous Daoist paintings and sculptures.

Confucianists regarded citizen participation in society as an obligation, while Daoists tended to prefer to retreat and withdraw from society. A Daoist had to discover his personal liberty and harmony from within, not to expect it to come from above. Daoism, in fact, served as a balance to the dominant concepts of Chinese culture. While Confucian morality and insistence on social conformity were restrictive, in Daoism "the individual could achieve self-expression; his intellect was free to wander at will." Since neither Confucianism nor Daoism were exclusive religions in the Western sense, the individual, and the whole society, could be both

Confucian and Daoist at the same time, "achieving perhaps a healthier psychological balance on these two bases than could have been achieved on only one."[12]

According to Daoism, man achieves peace of mind by living in harmony with nature. But this is not a static relationship, because all forces of nature are in a constant state of motion. The "eternal cycle" is regulated by the cosmic forces of *yin* and *yang*, and balance between the two has to be maintained at all times. *Yang* represents masculinity, activity, and light, while *yin* is associated with feminity, passivity, and darkness. The two forces complement each other. Interaction between the two is the foundation of all matter. Without *yin* there can be no *yang*. All elements in nature (including human beings) consist of both *yin* and *yang*, as well as of *qi*; that is, energy. In the West, *qi* is also translated as the "vital energy" or "force of life."*

Because Daoist philosophers grappled with issues of longevity and immortality, they devised certain methods to preserve good health. When a person is healthy, the *yin* and *yang* forces are in balance and the *qi*-energy flows freely through channels (also called medians) which connect the organs and tissues. A person can strengthen his or her *qi* by eating cer-

* *Qi* is the pinyin form of the older *ch'i*, or *chi*. *Qigong* is also written *ch'i-kung*.

Morning exercises at People's Square in Xian in 1994. (Photo: John Lee)

tain foods in the right combinations and by practicing various breathing exercises and *taiji* (*tai-chi*). The basic nature of traditional Chinese health care is prophylactic.

Today, tens of millions of Chinese practice *taiji* or do *qigong* exercises every morning, either in public parks or in their own yards. Every day people flock to hospitals specializing in traditional medicine to consult doctors who examine the flow of *qi* through their patients' bodies and then prescribe medicinal herbs. Or they look up an acupuncture doctor or a *tuina*-masseur who will try to open their blocked *qi*-channels or stimulate the flow of *qi*-energy in specific organs.* Medical texts describing these treatments date back more than two thousand years.

There are three forms of *qi*-energy: the *qi* one inherits from one's parents, the *qi* one receives from the environment—including the food one eats and the air one breathes—and the *qi* produced by the body's inner organs. These organs (heart, lungs, spleen, liver, and kidneys), which produce and nurture the *qi*-energy, represent the so-called five elements (water, wood, fire, metal, and earth). Ensuring their friction-free interaction is as important as maintaining the balance between *yin* and *yang*. Everything has a bearing on everything else. That is why traditional Chinese medicine is considered a holistic approach to a person's well-being. The effect of treatment is usually slow because the initial aim is not to eliminate the symptoms of the illness, the pain, fever, or nausea, but to correct the source of the symptoms. That is why a human being is seen in his or her entirety, in terms of one organ's effects on the others, previous illnesses, emotional state, diet, and even the effect of the environment.

I had my first encounter with Chinese traditional medicine after taking a tumble off my bicycle in Jinan in 1987. A deep cut on my hip refused to heal, though I had used the salves and taken the antibiotics, all familiar brands in the West, prescribed by the doctor at the hospital of Western medicine. So my friends decided to take me to a hospital of traditional Chinese medicine. There, a charming female doctor named Lin first doused a gauze in a disgusting-looking dark green fluid and then placed it on the wound. She also gave me seven brown paper bags to take home. Each bag contained an assortment of dried herbs, roots, bark, and goodness-knows-what. The contents of each bag were to be boiled according to explicit instructions, and I was to drink a big mug of the extract twice a day.

* *Tuina*, literally translated "push-and-pull," is one of the most general forms of traditional Chinese massage.

A pharmacist making my prescription at the Central Hospital of Traditional Medicine in Beijing. There are well over a hundred different kinds of herbs in a standard Chinese pharmacy. Usually a doctor of traditional Chinese medicine prescribes a mixture of twelve herbs, each one precisely weighed by the gram. (Photo: Marja Sarvimäki)

"The herbal medicine will help heal the inflamed cut and enhance the recovering process of your body in general," Dr. Lin explained. "Your fall was quite a jolt to your whole system. If we don't look after your overall condition now, other problems will crop up later somewhere else in your body." I gradually learned that this approach is fundamental to traditional Chinese health care.

Now I can laugh at my shock when I swallowed the first gulp of dark brown extract. A group of university students who happened to be visiting at the time thought it hilarious that "Teacher Lin" had to rush to the bathroom to vomit. I literally discovered what it means to "eat bitter" (a Chinese saying which means to "endure hardship"). I soon invented a technique to get the terrible tasting liquid down: I pinched my nostrils together and poured the liquid down my throat without breathing. But I stopped complaining when I noticed that my wound was healing. I also started feeling much better.

Over the years, I have mastered the ability to imbibe Chinese traditional medicine. Twice during the 1990s, ancient methods of healing rescued me from ailments much more serious than the wound on my hip. In both cases, Western doctors had been unable to find the reason for my low-grade fever. Boiling herbs twice a day was a burdensome task, and the pungent smell spread from my kitchen throughout the whole apartment building. But both times I regained my health. In addition to the herbal medicine, I was treated with acupuncture needles twice a week.

My health problems began as a young adult when I suffered recurring bladder tract infections which were medicated with antibiotics. Over time, I became increasingly immune to even the newest antibiotics. Then my symptoms began to vary. Frequently, I suffered low-grade fevers for days on end, as well as feelings of out-and-out exhaustion. Laboratory tests and other examinations, at some of the best of hospitals in the West, revealed no signs of infection or other causes of the fever. After I moved back to Beijing in 1992, my friends implored me to try traditional Chinese medicine. "It can't hurt to try. Herbal medicine doesn't have any side effects," one friend after the other urged.

Finally, in the summer of 1993, my girlfriend *Jiejie* from Jinan put me in touch with Dr. Ye Peigong. In typical Chinese fashion, we went through the "back door" because otherwise, as *Jiejie* assured me, we would never get an appointment to see this well-known guru of traditional Chinese medicine, who specializes in chronic internal ailments. I was introduced to Dr. Ye through the business partner of *Jiejie*'s sister-in-law, who, in turn, was the uncle of Dr. Ye's assistant.

Doctor Ye's consulting room resembled a run-down office of a government bureau. As is often the case in China, there was no privacy. His patients all sat in his room, waiting their turn. I learned a fair amount about traditional Chinese medicine in the next few months, just from sitting in line. "You must have a frightful temper; I can feel it from your liver," I heard Dr. Ye exclaim more than once. Each main internal organ is coupled with an emotion. Anger or irritation corresponds with the liver. Emotions, in turn, have an effect on the flow of *qi*-energy and on the functioning of the organs. The message, expressed in everyday language, is clear enough: A positive frame of mind affects one's health, as good health bears directly on one's spirit.

There was not a single medical instrument in Dr. Ye's office, not even a thermometer or a blood pressure cuff. The assistant sat opposite the doctor with fountain pen and pad of prescription forms in hand. This was all that was needed. During my first visit, I did not say a word about my low-grade fever. I simply let Dr. Ye examine me. *Jiejie* had told me that doctors of traditional medicine do not usually require background information.

Dr. Ye placed three fingers on my right wrist and kept them there for a few minutes, concentrating deeply. It reminded me of a Western doctor taking my pulse. In traditional Chinese medicine, it is called "observing the *qi*-energy channels." His first words were: "You certainly have taken a lot of antibiotics in your life." Then he placed three fingers on my left wrist, asked to see my tongue, observed my complexion, and inquired about the color of my urine. Next he spoke of poor blood circulation, due to my susceptibility to wind (cold). This hindered the *qi*-energy from circulating freely in the area around my kidneys, he said. He also mentioned the inability of my lungs to intake oxygen properly and the inclination of my lower limbs to amass cold and dampness.

"But first of all we must do something about your sore throat," he said and proceeded to call off the names of different herbs to his assistant.

"But my throat isn't the least bit sore," I objected.

"You're about to come down with a bad flu," Dr. Ye said placidly. "Let's try and stop that before we start dealing with your other problems." I

Doctor Ye Peigong observing a patient's qi-energy channels. (Photo: Petri Kaipiainen)

remembered his words later that afternoon when I suddenly had a sneezing fit, and swallowing became painful.

Every morning for the next six months, I faithfully boiled the most peculiar looking mixture of herbs, grass, and roots, and drank the extract twice a day. I packed my brown paper bags, even on trips out of town. Along with my portable computer went the bags, my portable cooker, and two big mugs. (The malodorous aroma caused quite a commotion in some hotels, I must confess!) Every Thursday I went to see Dr. Ye. He would observe my *qi*-energy channels for a minute or so, then dictate a new prescription to his assistant. Slowly but surely, life with herbal medicine became a routine. From the start I was resigned to the notion that this was going to be a protracted process. There was no point in venturing into it if one was not prepared to be patient, I told myself.

My periodic low-grade fever disappeared altogether three months after my first herbal medicine prescription from Dr. Ye. The strange infection stayed away for the next three months (while I was still drinking the extract) and also for the following half a year after I stopped boiling the herbs. I have no doubt that my health also benefited from the Daoist exercises I regularly practiced to strengthen the muscles in my lower back (the area near the kidneys) and from my general positive frame of mind. Of course, the elation over not having a recurring low-grade fever is enough to enhance anyone's spirits. This all fits in well with the Daoist approach to good health.

Then, the familiar symptoms started to reappear. I first blamed pressure at work as my excuse to fall back on Western antibiotics. Herbal medicine is such a bore to cook every day, I told my friends. The antibiotics helped, but only temporarily. When I finally decided to return to Dr. Ye, two years had passed since my first visit. The second time around, the herbal medicine started to work after a mere three weeks. This time I only had to take the cure for three months. My low-grade fever was kept at bay for just under a year.

Two years later, when Dr. Ye agreed to be interviewed for my magazine, I persuaded him to try to use Western terminology to explain his diagnosis of my case: antibiotics have weakened my power of resistance. The area around my bladder is susceptible to inflammation whenever I catch cold or am overly tired. I am prone to come down with the flu because my lungs are weak and that, in turn, affects the functioning of my kidneys. With herbal medicine he had tried to remove the dampness from my body and to increase the circulation of my blood and *qi*-energy; in Western terms, to strengthen my power of resistance. When I asked Dr.

Ye if I could rid myself of this curse altogether, his prognosis was dismal: "It's very difficult to cure the problem of dampness completely because whenever you are tired or stressed your body absorbs moisture."

By Chinese standards, Dr. Ye Peigong is quite young to be so accomplished a doctor. (He was fifty-seven when I interviewed him in 1994.) He had already turned thirty when he began to take an interest in traditional Chinese medicine. Before that he had graduated as a mechanical engineer: "I felt a natural pull to this field," he said. "During the years of the Cultural Revolution, I had a lot of time on my hands to read and research the classic medical texts. Later I studied with several old masters."

Doctor Ye stressed that no amount of studying or experience is a guarantee that one can practice traditional Chinese medicine successfully. He blatantly criticized numerous colleagues, who profess to call themselves doctors, but who are not necessarily the right people in the right occupation. "This field requires a special kind of intuition, the ability to internalize the actions of another person's body. The vast majority of people simply don't have this knack." He recalled that he had been just as severe in his judgment toward his daughter. She had wanted to follow in her father's footsteps, but Ye had told her that she was doomed to fail. "She isn't the right type. Better she becomes a respected computer engineer than a lousy doctor," Dr. Ye said with a hint of a smile.

Ye has lectured about *qi*-energy channels in the United States and in Switzerland, so he is well aware of the controversy that ancient healing methods have provoked in the West. In spite of this he said quite deliberately: "Traditional Chinese medicine can cure a number of illnesses which Western medicine cannot. Traditional medicine is at its best when treating chronic illnesses, heart problems, internal diseases, and gynecological ailments. But it is slow. Many people don't have the patience to cook the herbs on a daily basis."

Like others with whom I have discussed traditional Chinese medicine, Dr. Ye readily acknowledged the superiority of Western medicine for treating acute illnesses or serious wounds. And he did not deny that he had suffered setbacks during the course of his career. "Every doctor faces disappointments. Of course I have also had patients whose illnesses had already deteriorated to the point that I was not able to help them." Doctor Ye's patients include some of China's highest-ranking civil servants. His father (Ye Jizhuang) was one of Mao Zedong's loyal generals, who served as the People's Republic's first minister of foreign trade.

From this account, one may conclude that I consider Ye Peigong a miracle worker or that I believe traditional Chinese medicine can perform wonders. I do not. Health is an extremely personal matter. Each of us must find our own way to optimum health.

Every doctor also has his (or her) bad days, an unfortunate fact of life I discovered personally in the spring of 1997, after complications arose from an appendix operation. My side ached and the thermometer was stuck for days on end at 99.5 degrees. Western medicine seemed to have no effect at all, though I had never before been examined so thoroughly (blood tests, x-rays, CT-scan, ultrasound, etc.) in three hospitals of Western medicine in Beijing and Hong Kong. When the CT-scan pictures failed to provide a clue as to what was causing my discomfort, the Dutch doctor in charge of my case was at a loss for words. The Chinese professor of Western medicine, who had supervised my CT-scan examination, also conceded defeat. He took me aside to suggest that perhaps I should consult a doctor of traditional Chinese medicine: "In obscure cases involving internal inflammation, it is often the best option. After this examination I am confident that the problem is neither an abscess nor a growth."

So off I went to Dr. Ye again. But this time the herbal medicine he prescribed did not seem to work. After ten days, I still had a fever and a pain in my side. I felt utterly frustrated. "Ye Peigong is a specialist in chronic illnesses. You have a problem related to an appendix operation," my friend Dr. Feng said, in her typical determined manner. She arranged for me to go to Beijing's largest hospital specializing in traditional Chinese medicine. Unlike the hospital where Ye works, this hospital uses Western methods of examination to supplement the traditional examination of a patient's *qi*-energy channels. Dr. Wu Junyu, the man who spoke unintelligible Mandarin, is reputedly an "appendix problem specialist." After observing my *qi*-energy, Dr. Wu diagnosed my problem as a slight inflammation of the gall bladder (though numerous ultrasound examinations had shown nothing abnormal whatsoever about my gall bladder). The herbal extract Dr. Wu prescribed tasted totally different from Dr. Ye's concoction. Both the pain and the fever disappeared after two weeks.

Traditional methods are mainstays of health care in both urban and rural areas. Some Western scholars attribute this to the government's poor health care facilities and weak social welfare benefits—herbs and needles cost much less than Western medicine. I paid 40 to 50 yuan ($5 to $6) for a week's prescription of herbal medicine. Antibiotics would have cost at least twice as much. On the other hand, Dr. Feng has told me that even the wealthiest peasants prefer to seek out doctors of traditional Chinese medicine though they could easily afford to go to the county hospital of Western medicine. The same can be said about urban residents. Every now and again I notice *Saozi*, in my godchild's family, downing a mug of herbal extract. My Jinan friends *Jiejie* and Yang usually choose an herbal cure over a Western prescription.

Most Chinese alternate between Western and traditional medicine as naturally as they accept various religious and philosophical influences. My own acquaintances always emphasize what Dr. Ye did: it is crucial to find a talented and experienced doctor of traditional medicine with sensitive vibes. There are hundreds of different herbs. Choosing among them and knowing how to combine them is a unique skill.

During my years in China I have met many Europeans and Americans eager to try ancient health care methods. A Finnish woman who had suffered nerve-wracking migraines for years was relieved of her pain after five sessions of acupuncture. When I heard from her two years later, she was still enjoying a migraine-free existence. An American friend's aunt had a terrible allergy which caused incessant itching. Herbal pills rid her of the nuisance. Traditional Chinese medicine should always be taken as an extract even though, to the relief of travelers, many herbal medicines can now be purchased in pill form. Dr. Ye, however, does not approve of these ready-made cures.

Personally, I am convinced that the best alternative is to combine the best of both cultures. Harmony, above all, would be a Daoist's comment.

If a general concensus prevails among "the broad masses" about the benefits of traditional health care, the same cannot be said about attitudes toward *qigong*-meditation. *Qigong* is a divisive issue for the Chinese. Some of my friends and acquaintances write it off as "Nonsense!" and have warned me not to believe the blizzard of recent literature attesting to the supernatural powers of *qigong*. Others feel that *qigong* breathing, gymnastics, and concentration exercises are beneficial to one's physical health and mental well-being. But even proponents are skeptical of claims made by some *qigong*-masters. These masters are able—so they say—to use their own *qi*-energy to treat another person's illness. Published articles describe *qigong*-masters helping the blind to see and curing cancer-ridden patients previously diagnosed as hopeless.

Qigong has experienced a tremendous revival since the end of the 1980s. *Qigong*-courses are held all over the country. Solitary people standing by a tree, deep in thought, or performing slow-motion gymnastics are a common sight in many parks. The deputy chairman of "China's *Qigong* Scientific Research Association" Guan Qian told me in an interview in 1994 that over 60 million Chinese currently practice *qigong*.

Qigong was banned in the Mao period, along with another pseudo-science, *fengshui*, or Chinese geomancy,* based on ancient methods of divination to determine the favorable locations for everything from a house to a grave, or even a city. Both *qigong* and *fengshui* were deemed feudal superstitions during the Cultural Revolution, supernatural phenomena to be avoided by "the new socialist human being." *Fengshui* has also made a comeback during the past two decades, though mostly in the countryside and in southern cities. *Fengshui* not only affects the choice of the correct site for a building or for a grave, but may also influence health issues and business transactions. In rural society, *fengshui*-masters are sought out by officials, entrepreneurs, and ordinary peasants alike. They are consulted when a pregnant woman wants to know the sex of her fetus, when a businessman needs advice about the most auspicious day to start a company, or family members wonder why so many of their next-of-kin have been struck with sickness. In June 1997, a village *fengshui*-master in Longsheng, a mountainous area north of Guilin, told me that the local government tolerates his practicing his profession as long as he does not advise his clients to break the law.

What should one make of *qigong*- and *fengshui*-masters?

John Lee offered a Chinese answer: one cannot really say that one fully believes in them, but, on the other hand, it is best not to say that one does not believe in them at all. I tend to agree with him, especially after the experience of a Finnish businessman named Kari Aaltola. This gentleman, well past fifty, was not the type to believe in supernatural occurrences—quite the contrary. Kari's leg started to bother him in the spring of 1994. The pain became so intense that he had trouble walking. He was examined by a number of different specialists in Finland, all to no avail. Then he arrived in Beijing on a business trip, limping and complaining of his misery, until the Chinese secretary of a business associate asked if he wished to consult a *qigong*-master.

"I reckoned it couldn't do any harm, since the Finnish doctors hadn't been able to help," Kari reasoned and went on to describe his encounter with master Zhou, a man a few years younger than himself: "First he told me to stand in the middle of my hotel room. Then he asked me to close

* Geomancy is a means of prophecy based on the forms of nature and cardinal points. *Fengshui* literally translates as wind (*feng*) and water (*shui*).

my eyes and just relax. After awhile I lost consciousness. The next thing I knew, I was lying flat on my back on my bed. I could feel myself lifting the sore leg up and down as if there were no pain at all." Before taking his leave, master Zhou spread a sticky essence on Kari's calf and said he had driven away the infection with his *qi*-energy.

"I stood up and walked normally down to the hotel bar," Kari recounted. "Since then my leg hasn't bothered me a bit." He laughed and said, if anyone asked him how he cured his leg, he would not know what to say. "If I tell people the truth, they'll think I'm absolutely nuts."

I decided to look up master Zhou. In a matter of minutes after I asked him to "guide his *qi*-energy" toward me, I fell into a mesmerized state, presumably what it feels like to be hypnotized. Unlike Kari Aaltola, I had no specific ailment that needed attention, but I left master Zhou's home feeling immensely relaxed and refreshed.

When I was researching a story about *qigong* for my magazine, I toured public parks in Beijing to interview ordinary *qigong*-enthusiasts. They concentrate solely on cultivating their own *qi*-energy. Only masters use their *qi* on others. I met a sixty-year-old man who told me he had practiced *taiji* every morning for the past eighteen years. Now that he was retired he was taking up *qigong*-breathing exercises. He was in visibly excellent health.

"One mustn't confuse *taiji* with *qigong*," noted this composed gentleman, who introduced himself as Yu. "*Taiji* is a form of physical exercise. It has taught me to have complete control of my body and limbs. *Qigong* focuses on the mind. One learns how to concentrate and relax."

In the course of our chat, I realized that Yu had been a high official in the Ministry of Machine-Building Industry. In his youth, he had been a fellow student of the present Party Secretary, Jiang Zemin, at university in Shanghai.

I asked if he did not find it a bit ironic that he was now practicing *qigong* when he presumably had participated in condemning it twenty years earlier. From the smile on his face, I could tell he knew what I was getting at. "*Qigong* is part of China's cultural tradition," he answered. "It was a mistake to try to eradicate something that is a natural part of being Chinese."

More than fourteen million Chinese had purchased mobile phones at the end of 1997. The Chinese government estimates that mobile phone sales will reach thirty million by the year 2000, putting China second behind the U.S. in market size. Photo from Shanghai in 1995. (Photo: John Lee)

Jumbled Misunderstandings

"Everyone Wants China to Become Strong"

Coupled with the omnipresent Chinese culturalism is a resurgent nationalism. Patriotic fervor has intensified during my years in China, due in part to the dramatic rise in living standards. Many Chinese have begun to feel that perhaps China will, after all, be lifted up from its state of abasement to join the respected nations of the world. During the 1990s, I seldom heard ordinary people spontaneously bemoan, "China is so poor!" a common refrain of the 1980s. The recent surge of nationalism is also partly a result of Party propaganda. Communist Party leaders, realizing that it is now far more effective to appeal to feelings of patriotism than to a belief in socialism, lean all the more heavily on nationalism to bolster their own legitimacy.

Hong Kong's "return to the motherland," as China saw the event, was considered a prophetic sign by many ordinary Chinese. Though most people I spoke to conceded that Chinese media were only mouthing the government line, they also genuinely felt that the return of Hong Kong symbolized the end of a disgraceful era in Chinese history. "Of course, we want to see China grow strong and affluent again," is a popular sentiment, regardless of a person's social status or political views.

The Chinese date the decline of their civilization from the first Opium War (1840–1842). By the terms of the peace treaty after the Middle Kingdom's humbling capitulation, the Chinese were forced to give up Hong Kong island to the British. Naturally the return of the island in 1997 provoked deep emotions. Not that my friends blame China's degeneration entirely on greedy and militaristic foreigners. Other factors, they are quick to point out, also played a part; the Confucianist tendency to favor the status quo instead of reform, the corrupt Manchu bureaucracy, the pressures of immense population growth, dwindling farmlands, and so on. But the shame of the humiliating military defeats and the treatment of Chinese as second-class citizens in areas controlled by foreigners linger in people's minds, smoldering just under the surface. Chinese are highly sensitive to the slightest gesture that might connote imperialist superiority. This is surely true in any country where outsiders once ruled, but the Chinese are perhaps especially sensitive (some say overly sensitive) because of their ancient civilization, stretching back thousands of years.

In a discussion about relations between Chinese and Westerners, Mao Lingen, deputy general manager of a Nokia joint venture in Beijing, said bluntly: "The most serious problems arise when foreigners behave in haughty or disparaging ways toward their Chinese counterparts. Of course the Chinese employees have a lot to learn from foreigners. But that doesn't mean a Western engineer has the right to treat a Chinese engineer as his lowly assistant."

Having lived in the United States and worked alongside Europeans from a number of countries, fifty-five-year-old Mao Lingen is well-placed to judge cross-cultural cooperation. After graduating with a master's degree from China's most prestigious technical university, Qinghua, he studied at the University of Illinois from 1981 to 1984. Both Chinese and expatriates working for Nokia urged me to look him up to learn more about the human dimension of joint-venture operations. He was described as "sympathetic," "understanding," and "a man who knows what he's talking about." The international telecommunications company, Nokia, and the joint-ventures it partly owns employ about 1,500 Chinese and 100 expatriates in China.

Mao Lingen clearly wished to be as objective as possible. He admitted that the attitudes of the Chinese employees also left room for improvement. "Our foreigners do their utmost to get things done 'well,' while our Chinese tend to make do with 'pretty well.'"

Because of my special interest in cross-cultural cooperation, I have interviewed dozens of general managers and employees in joint-venture companies over the past decade. Every time I speak to a Chinese employee, he or she complains politely, as did Mao Lingen, that many foreigners consider themselves superior to the Chinese. If the interview is off-the-record, their appraisal is more forthcoming: The biggest problems are caused by the racist attitudes of some foreigners—many foreign employees in fact concur with this view.

Nandani Lynton, a German consultant in Beijing, arranges seminars and courses for companies striving to improve communication among a multinational work force. Nokia is one of her clients. Like most people, Lynton avoided the word "racism" when she described her experiences, but a straightforward question received a frank answer: "Yes, racism is clearly a subtext in the most serious cases involving poor communication between colleagues. It's often the Westerners with the worst attitudes who won't even agree to attend the courses."

Mao Lingen has given a great deal of thought to the misunderstandings between Westerners and Chinese. He advises Westerners coming to China to realize that: "Poor is not synonymous with stupid. A person with a different way of thinking is not necessarily wrong." I recalled his words six months later, when I heard the comments by a Nokia manager, flown in from Helsinki, at a company meeting before the International Telecommunications Fair in Beijing. After introducing the Chinese person responsible for Nokia's exhibit at the fair, the Finn switched into his native tongue and added: "By the way, she's really quite smart."

"Surprise, surprise. She's really quite smart, even though she's Chinese," spat out one of the Chinese employees present, recounting the incident. The Finn, having just arrived in Beijing, had not realized that some of Nokia's Chinese employees have learned Finnish.

Mao Lingen emphasized that Chinese have their own methods for handling problems and their distinct way of thinking. A joint-venture company would do well to adopt a blend of customs from both cultures. "Foreigners should not think they can decide everything. They often forget that here in China there are situations that we know how to cope with better than they do." Other joint-venture employees agree with Mao Lingen. On the other hand, I have heard many foreigners complain about how difficult it is to work in China, that Chinese employees do not know how to do this or that, nor do they want to learn. Unanimity appears to prevail about one thing: a single racist employee has a devastating effect on the whole group's teamwork.

Tensions arising from biases must be addressed in any multicultural environment. In China, one needs to raise one's level of awareness by a power of ten because of the events of the past 150 years. The Chinese I know do not complain about the racism of foreigners, but rather about the foreigners' "condescending way of approaching us, because they are so much richer than we are." When Chinese acquaintances working for European or American companies criticize the "imperial attitudes" of their superiors, I sometimes wonder whether these foreigners might not simply be ignorant or boorish. After all, many Western employees have to put up with ill-tempered and badly behaved bosses too.

Everyone mentions problems arising from the language barrier. It is no exaggeration to say that I have witnessed hundreds of misunderstandings between foreigners and Chinese because of inadequate language skills. The

English spoken by many Chinese leaves much to be desired. But the varying accents of Americans, British, Australians, New Zealanders, and Canadians are often tough on those for whom English is a second language.

More important than mere language proficiency is the different manner in which Westerners and Chinese express themselves. The numerous proverbs, sayings, and allegories that Chinese quite naturally use in everyday communication are often incomprehensible to people who have never studied the Chinese language. An American working for IBM once showed up at a dinner date with the greeting: "Could you explain to me about the old man and the dragon?" During meetings that day, his interpreter had twice referred to this famous Chinese fable. It is about an old man who boasts of his love for dragons. As proof he keeps pictures of dragons throughout his house. Hearing of this, the dragon decides to pay the old man a visit. But instead of welcoming the dragon, the old man runs away in fright.

I had heard the story of the dragon when some friends were mocking the Communist Party leaders who claim they want democracy in China, but at the same time do nothing to pursue democratic reform. In business negotiations, a Chinese might bring up the story of the old man and the dragon as a hint that the other party should not make promises that cannot be kept.

Though I think that this particular saying is simple enough to explain in any language, the same cannot be said about the difficulties political analysts face trying to decipher what is happening on the Chinese political scene from the roundabout intimations printed in the official media. I would never have known that rumors of a vice-mayor's suicide in 1995 were as good as confirmed when the Beijing Daily printed an article about a famous poet, Qu Yuan, who lived in about 300 B.C.

"Don't you see?" my assistant asked quite indignantly. "Qu Yuan threw himself into the river after being banned from the capital in disgrace. It's quite obvious that this article is referring to the vice-mayor's suicide." The article also alluded to doubts about whether the poet really killed himself or whether he was murdered by conspiring court officials, an implication that the vice-mayor might have been knocked off for political reasons. My assistant was right. A few days later, Xinhua news agency reported that vice-mayor Wang Baosen had committed suicide because of allegations of his involvement in an unfolding corruption scandal.

Western businessmen are forever being told that knowledge of Chinese history and culture will benefit their relationship with Chinese counterparts. On the other hand, Chinese civil servants and engineers visiting

One sees foreign advertisements in cities all over China. Foreign brands and foreign customs are especially popular among well-to-do urban youth. For example, thousands of Chinese women have undergone an operation to "straighten" their eyes to make them look more Western. Photo taken in Shanghai in 1995. (Photo: John Lee)

Western countries tend to have little interest in Western history or culture. American and European businessmen frequently tell of Chinese delegations who do not care to acquaint themselves with the technology of the host company or even to see any of the tourist sights. Once they pose for the obligatory tourist pictures in front of Capitol Hill or the Eiffel Tower, their only interest is to purchase items to take home or watch pornographic movies—all at the expense of their hosts.

"But if you criticize them, you're accused of speaking contemptuously about the Chinese," a British businessman told me with a sigh, after an especially tiresome trip home with Chinese clients. His guests, cadres from a city "out in the sticks," spent their whole visit moaning about either the second-rate hotel, the inedible food, or the boring program. "You can't imagine the pomposity of these officials, who consider themselves the highbrows of a tiny city in China," the Englishman recounted. "I really don't understand why you choose to live in this country." Many businessmen I know have made similar remarks. I always answer that I probably would not have, if I had to associate exclusively with businessmen and bureaucrats.

The slice of China most Western businessmen encounter is admittedly one of the least appealing—and their frustration is understandable. At every stage of a negotiation process, someone demands a bribe, either in cash or in the form of a paid holiday abroad (officially called an "educational trip"). There are countless ingenious ways of demanding compensation for "ensuring that the negotiations proceed in a favorable manner." A son might need funds for education in the West. A daughter might need a job. The mistrust arising from suspicion that Chinese salesmen are "always looking to make a buck on the side" is allegedly one of the greatest sources of friction between Western bosses and Chinese employees in joint-venture companies.

Not only do business delegations give their foreign hosts headaches. In Cambridge in 1996, a Harvard University professor worried aloud about a group of Chinese visitors, mostly middle-level cadres from the Ministry of Defense and Chief of Staff. They were in town to prepare for the visit of a group of high-ranking military officers who had been invited to attend a two-week intensive course about American society. "I really don't know what will come of this experiment," the American professor said. There was no mistaking his skepticism. "Some of the Chinese officials smoke in the lavatory though it is strictly forbidden, and I've seen a few of them spitting in the corner of the lobby downstairs." He too wondered out loud why I had chosen to spend so many years in China.

But this story, at least, had a happy ending. Some weeks later, I received an e-mail from Cambridge: "What a delightful bunch those Chinese colonels were—charming, civilized gentlemen, the whole lot!"

The rise of nationalism in recent years has certainly not eased communication between Chinese and foreigners. Especially among urban Chinese of the younger generation, I have noticed an inclination to rebuff all judgments perceived as "foreigners' attempts to put down the Chinese." During trips in 1996 and 1997 to Shanghai and Guangzhou, I felt continually confronted by self-assertive, even conceited and obnoxious, twenty-somethings. (Of course my Beijing friends say all Shanghainese are born arrogant, that is nothing new. There is no love lost between Beijingers and the Shanghainese—a source of numerous jokes.)

The most distasteful incident I experienced took place in Beijing in the spring of 1995. I was bawled out by a Chinese man in the bank near my apartment. The remittance I expected had not arrived and I groaned: "How can it take so long just to transfer money from the head office in

Beijing to this local branch." I am sure I sounded irritable, but I had not raised my voice or directed my words at anyone in particular. I was leaning on the counter, whining about this unfortunate state of affairs when, from behind me, this man, about sixty, in a gray, pin-striped three-piece suit, started to shout that I had no right to criticize China and that it was high time that foreigners learned to respect the Chinese people. From what he said (or yelled), I understood that he had lived in the United States for close to ten years. The clerk behind the counter was as stupefied as I was. She even tried to interrupt the man, telling him that I had been a client in the bank for years and that I was not "that kind of a foreigner." But it had no effect. He just kept bellowing. In the end, I also lost my temper.

After I calmed down, I realized how it must feel when a Chinese secretary or interpreter has to endure the erratic fits of foreigners who vent their frustration at innocent assistants when something goes awry. Such scenes play out every now and again at airport check-in counters or in hotel lobbies. Traveling in China can fray even the calmest of nerves.

Nearly every foreigner has, at some point, what I have come to call a "China fit." Engineer Song and our mutual British friend still enjoy teasing me about our train trip to Jinan from Qingdao in 1987. I had a fierce argument with the ticket conductor because she refused to let Song sit with us in the corridor of the empty first-class wagon, insisting that it was reserved only for "foreigners and Chinese who purchased first-class tickets at the train station." The Briton and I refused to leave engineer Song on his own in the second-class compartment, which was crammed full. In those days it was next-to-impossible for an ordinary Chinese to purchase a first-class ticket. They were meant only for Party officials and the nouveau riche who could use their money to butter up the ticket sellers. Raising my voice did not help, as it seldom does in China, and the three of us stood squashed among fellow travelers in the second-class compartment for the six-hour trip to Jinan.

The pace of change in China has been so rapid that it is easy to forget how different circumstances were only a few years earlier. When I first moved to Beijing in 1987 there were two, quite segregated, worlds: the Chinese world and the foreign world. In addition to first-class train compartments, finer hotels, restaurants, and the Friendship Store (the sole department store with imported goods) welcomed only foreigners and privileged Chinese. But even these Chinese were usually treated as inferior clients. Similarly, in the Chinese world "big noses" were shut out of numerous situations.

Until 1994, there were also two currencies: FEC (Foreign Exchange Certificates) meant for foreigners, and the so-called people's money. Already a year or two before the FEC was abolished, hotels and department stores began to remove restrictions regarding Chinese. Some businesses even advertised that "we serve our Chinese customers as well as our foreign ones." It did not take long before well-to-do Chinese became their best clients. On Sundays, restaurants serving *dimsum* brunch or buffet lunch in Beijing's finest hotels are now packed with wealthy Chinese families, the kind who live in my apartment building.

Though Chinese people knew very well that the authorities wanted to keep them apart from foreigners for political reasons, many of the regulations in the 1980s and early 1990s evoked memories of the days when foreigners lived in China as a class above the law. "The Chinese law has to be obeyed by foreigners too," an elderly policeman taunted, lecturing me with relish in public one afternoon. John Lee and I were "in the middle of nowhere" in November 1996, driving toward the Northeast. Like a dozen or so drivers before me, I had fallen into the policemen's trap by wrongly passing a vehicle. (One of those notorious fine-gathering campaigns was evidently under way.)

The dozen or so other drivers who had been pulled over, along with a group of peasants from the nearby village, all crowded around to hear a Chinese policeman castigate a foreigner. I could see a younger policeman and John Lee breaking into amused smiles as the elder officer embellished his sermon for the benefit of his audience. I decided the best thing to do was nod humbly and keep quiet.

That same evening I got into a row with a man from Shenyang who adamantly claimed that Western children are taught in school to look down upon Chinese.

"Where on earth did you hear that?" I asked.

"This is something I know for certain," the thirty-five-year-old man answered. He owned a garage in Shenyang, a Northeast industrial metropolis of about eight million people. "It's all very clear. Of course it's in the interests of the West to teach their kids to hold Chinese in contempt. Every nation wants to be better than the others." It was a complete waste of time to debate the issue with him. The only result was my blood pressure rising to an intolerable level.

Because we had to spend several hours in this garage, waiting for the car's generator to be repaired, I had no choice but to listen to many other "truths" about the West which Manager Fan eagerly expounded. The garage, ultramodern compared to the rest of dismal Shenyang, "was superior to any garage in the whole of the United States." Another assertion I distinctly remember was that "the governments in Western countries enforce a strict family-planning policy to curb the growth of the population." That is why we do not have a population problem in the West.

Manager Fan told us he was a former policeman. Officially, he still belonged to a work unit under the supervision of the police corps. After Deng Xiaoping's famous southern tour in 1992, he was given a free hand to come up with ways of earning money for his unit. In practice, he professed, the money he made for the unit went straight into the pockets of his superiors. He began his career as a businessman by speculating on the real estate market, then he wisely pulled out before it crashed and he used his profits to invest in the high-tech garage. Later he founded a small hotel that, I have to admit, had some of the more tastefully renovated rooms I have seen in China.

Manager Fan had spent one week in Osaka and another in Los Angeles. On the basis of these two visits, he knew everything he needed to about Japan and the West, including our educational system and family planning policies. I, on the other hand, could not possibly understand any-

The Nasa-discotheque in Beijing is like any other high-tech disco, whether in Paris or New York. But in China, only the wealthy can afford to frequent such places. The entrance fee is 60 to 80 yuan ($7.20 to $9.60); the average Beijinger earns 573 yuan ($69) a month (1996). (Photo: John Lee)

thing about Chinese society, though I had lived in China for seven years. I was a foreigner!

"Isn't that so?" he said to John Lee, who responded by mumbling something unintelligible. John has often found himself in similar predicaments when someone we meet emphasizes the difference between a Chinese and a foreigner. Even in this garage, though we were chatting informally, it was futile to expect a Chinese acquaintance to side with a foreigner against another Chinese. Of all my close friends, only my former teaching colleague, Yuan, has the spunk to agree with a foreigner, or to admonish another Chinese by saying, "But isn't that an outdated way of thinking?" or "Have you ever considered looking at things from another point of view?" And Yuan has never been to the West, unlike John Lee, engineer Song, economist Chen, bohemian Yang, and several other friends. They all, in the true spirit of Confucianism, try to wangle their way out of any contradictory face-off. If forced to choose, they will always take the Chinese side.

I had never before heard anything resembling the outlandish allegations of Manager Fan. But they reminded me that the strange notions that many Chinese have of the West have not disappeared just because thousands of foreigners now travel about the country. It was not all that long ago, as Jung Chang recalls in her book *Wild Swans*, that children thought all Westerners had horns and were terrifying. Manager Fan is not a stupid man. He had been abroad twice. I can well imagine the assurance with which he aired his views about the West to his unknowing friends and acquaintances.

Just as I tire of hearing Western friends generalizing, "All Chinese are short," or "Chinese don't love their daughters," I find the fixed ideas Chinese have about us quite exasperating. I do not know how many times someone has told me in all seriousness that Western grandparents do not love their grandchildren (because they do not take care of them full-time after retirement) or that the family is not considered important in the West (because young adults move away from their parents' home even if they are still single). Whenever someone who has not previously visited my apartment sees the photo I keep on the desk of my parents, my brothers, and their children, they turn to me in surprise and make some remark along these lines.

There are copious myths about the Western value of individualism. Even John Lee, who has several American and European friends, gave me a stereotypical answer when I asked him how Chinese and Western customs might differ in everyday life: "If a Western man makes a date with his girlfriend to go to the movies and a close friend then phones him, asking for help, the Western man will apologize and say 'Sorry, I'm busy.' In the West, one gives first priority to one's own personal life and aspirations. In China, the man would cancel his date and go right off to help his friend in need."

When Lao He, the woman who cleans my apartment, wished me a good trip to Finland in June 1994, she added: "I'm happy for you that you're going back to your own country for a vacation. But I'm worried about what will happen to your health."

"Why is that?" I asked. I could not help thinking that the clean air in Finland would do my health a world of good after living in polluted Beijing.

"Because one can get AIDS abroad," Lao He answered.

It was not until the beginning of the 1990s that Chinese media broached the subject of AIDS—"love capitalism disease," as it is translated into Chinese. Based on comments I have heard, many Chinese think one can catch AIDS from the food one eats or even the air one breathes.[1]

Men with ideas like those of the garage owner, Manager Fan, are not uncommon, especially in provincial cities. His nationalistic stance made me shudder. "If we could only put politics aside, it would take us Chinese a mere ten years to accomplish what it took the West a hundred years," he declared at one point, adding: "Chinese are so much more intelligent than Westerners." He ventured that if it had not been for Mao and his endless political campaigns, "we would be mightier than the United States is today."

Nearly all my Chinese friends assure me that such attitudes, and incidents like the one in the bank, are passing phenomena. They belittle Western media reports that Chinese are becoming ultranationalistic. The recent and rapid rise in living standards has produced a defiant arrogance, they say. As more and more Chinese are lifted from poverty and as education improves, these inflated sentiments will calm down to a more rational level of patriotism. Many of my younger friends are optimistic about the future, whereas scientist Bao, the man who stayed in China when the Communists took power despite his family's objections, is pessimistic. He is afraid that foreigners will become the targets of his countrymen's discontent.

"In a country where criticizing the government is not permissible, people might start to take out their pent-up anger on the foreigners," he predicted in the spring of 1997. I tend to agree with him, not that I foresee a return to the days when all foreigners were the "running dogs of imperialism." But Chinese, increasingly frustrated with the slow pace of social and political change, and with more knowledge than ever before about how people live in other countries, could well decide to blame their problems on the outsiders. Even in the apartment building where I live, relations between the Chinese tenants and the growing number of foreign residents have not been wholly harmonious. The elevator ladies have more than once blurted out: "There are too many foreigners here." And when a rowdy party in a Chinese musician's apartment dragged on into the early hours of the morning, I heard neighbors muttering about the "foreigners causing trouble as usual." In fact, there had been only three foreigners among the twenty-odd guests.

If economic growth stalls, foreign businessmen should brace themselves for expanded protectionism. Articles in the official press already claim that certain state-run factories are encountering troubles because Western products dominate the markets (for example, soap powder, toothpaste, chocolate, and soft drinks). As scientist Bao said, since it is a punishable offense to attack the authorities, foreign companies are much safer scapegoats.

Not that the Chinese leadership encourages any sort of public expression of opinion. A demonstration for whatever reason could easily ignite into an anti-government protest. There is a time bomb ticking away in places like Shenyang and other northeastern cities. Laid-off workers from unprofitable factories in the heavy-industry sector cannot be expected to endure unemployment silently forever. There have been a number of demonstrations in Shenyang during the 1990s. According to eye-witnesses, in April 1994, tens of thousands of people marched through the center of the city chanting "We support the Communist Party, we want food!" No one controls events like these. Nationalistic sentiments are in the air.

In everyday life, it is impossible to differentiate deep feelings of culturalism from patriotism or nationalism. These emotions and perceptions overlap and are interlocked in human hearts and minds. In the 1990s, I began to compare the relation that a Chinese citizen has with his native country, the People's Republic of China, to a layer cake. The firm cultural identity is the base of the cake, upon which are piled layers upon layers of patriotism, and it is topped off with a nationalistic icing.

Few people analyze their feelings as deeply as scientist Bao, an intellectual approaching the age of eighty: "From the time of the Opium Wars we have been humiliated and ordered about, by the Japanese in particular, but also by Westerners. In Mao's days, we were looked upon with suspicion by the outside world. Of course I am proud to think that Chinese could once again belong to the respected and leading peoples of the world. Thanks to the reform policy we are regaining our self-esteem, and that is a positive development. This has nothing to do with the fact that I detest our present government. For today's youth, China is equivalent to the People's Republic, but there is no such clear-cut distinction in my mind—China could just as well have remained a republic had the civil war ended differently. People of my generation still remember the heated debates regarding what kind of a nation we wanted to build."

The notions of "nation" and "national identity" became the focus of a discourse among intellectuals in China much later than in the West—not until the turn of the twentieth century and then, only under pressure from the outside. Modern terms like "the Chinese people" (*Zhongguoren*, people of the Middle Kingdom) and "Chinese nation" (*Zhonghua minzu*) were introduced in writings which warned of the "danger of national annihilation under external invasion."[2] Before that, perceptions of "the state," "culture," and "the world" were all intertwined in the concept of the "Middle Kingdom" (*Zhongguo*, China). Beyond China's borders lived the barbarians. An illuminating story is the one about the viceroy of Canton, Deng Tingzeng, who in 1839 became confused when a British trade official urged him to settle the differences between "the two nations" by peaceful means. Deng Tingzeng mistook "the two nations" to mean England and the United States. It did not occur to him that China was a "nation" as well.[3] More than 150 years have passed since this incident, but misunderstandings still arise over interpretations of specific terms.

The decay of the Manchu court, the growth of Western and Japanese imperialism, and widespread hunger gave rise to numerous rebellions in the 1800s. Reformers and revolutionaries alike wanted to save the country. Despite differences of ideology and method, they all aimed at creating a strong unified state. One of the best-known revolutionaries of the early twentieth century was Sun Yat-sen, regarded as the father of modern China. In "The Three Principles of the People," which later became the official ideological doctrine of the Nationalist Party (Guomindang), he spelled out the goals of achieving national respect, freedom, and equality in the international community. One of the principles was nationalism (*minzu zhuyi*), but that term, which carried the baggage of being anti-Manchu, was used in the struggle to overthrow the Manchu Emperor. Another concept, *aiguo zhuyi* (patriotism), which literally means "the ideology of loving the country," became a more acceptable, unifying term to describe loyalty to China.

Mao Zedong agreed that only a strong national state could save China. He was not bothered by the notion that a Communist was supposed to be an internationalist. Just as the original teachings of Buddhism had been adapted to suit Chinese cultural conditions, Marxism was also molded into a Chinese form. China was declared saved when, on October 1, 1949, Mao proclaimed the founding of the People's Republic with the famous words: "Our nation will no longer be an insulted nation. We have stood up."[4]

From then on, the identity of China has been linked to the Chinese Communist Party. This is a key to understanding the identity crisis in the People's Republic today. The Communists demanded (and still insist) that "loving the motherland" entails loving (and obeying) the Party. Civil war had ravaged the population for years. Loyalty to Mao's China called for complete repudiation of the previous Nationalist (Guomindang) government and its foreign allies (especially the United States). Already months before the end of the civil war, Mao declared that all Chinese "must lean either to the side of imperialism or to the side of socialism. Sitting on the fence will not do, nor is there a third road."[5]

Deng Xiaoping decided that such absolutism was not practical. When he came to power at the end of the 1970s, he pushed ideology into the background and appealed to "all Chinese patriots." This strategy lay the foundation for his reform policy's success. It was patriotism that motivated Chinese who lived outside the People's Republic to participate in the rebuilding of China. They felt no devotion whatsoever to communism. On the contrary, many of them had fled mainland China when the Communists won the civil war.

In the West it has become commonplace to speak of the significance of Western investments in China, without paying enough attention to the fact that it has been the Overseas Chinese who have been instrumental in bringing about the so-called economic miracle. Up to 75 percent of all foreign investments made in China since 1979 comes from "Chinese roots." In other words, though an investor might carry an American, Canadian, Indonesian, or Thai passport, he or she is ethnic Chinese.

Approximately 50 million Chinese live outside mainland China, and in several Southeast Asian countries the Chinese population dominates the economic sector. Mikhail Gorbachev did not have similar support to fall back upon when he launched his *perestroika* program in the 1980s. The Overseas Chinese are well known for having their own "bamboo network" that joins family members, distant relatives, and family friends living in different countries.

Mainland Chinese have absorbed indispensable know-how and information about Western business culture from the Overseas Chinese. It is impossible to measure the psychological effect of the Overseas Chinese; it is equally difficult to estimate the monetary value of the donations made by Overseas Chinese during the past two decades. A Chinese tends to have sentimental feelings toward his ancestral village, his *laojia*, whether he was born in San Francisco or Jakarta. Schools, hospitals, libraries, and research centers are built all around the country with Overseas Chinese money.

Of all the Overseas Chinese I have met, the one who has made the deepest impression on me is my friend Susan Lawrence's grandmother. Through her I have been able to, in a unique and personal way, sense the intricate maze of China's historic contradictions. In Chinese her name is Li Hsiao Li; in England she is Lady Lindsay; in the United States she is "just Mrs. Lindsay," and to us, the friends of Susan, she is plain *Laolao* ("maternal grandmother"). As a college student, she assisted, at first unknowingly, the Communists in their underground resistance movement against the Japanese invaders; she later marched loyally with the Communist Army during the war against Japan, and she got to know Mao Zedong and his wife in the good old days when "they were still friendly people." After that, she endured being shunned as an enemy of the People's Republic of China and a friend of the Communists' rivals on Taiwan. She spent nearly fifty years in exile, but a more compassionate Chinese patriot would be hard to find.

"There wasn't a day that I did not think about China," she said as she recalled her life abroad. This was in January 1997, when we sat down together in her apartment in Beijing to talk about the past. *Laolao* is an extraordinary and headstrong silver-haired lady who loves to watch *jingju*-theater performances and old Chinese movies as much as soccer games and weepy Western dramas.

The story of her life is in places as difficult to follow as is the history of China at the beginning of this century. "It's all a bit complicated," she apologized. At one moment she would recall a middle-school friend whose father was one of Chiang Kai-shek's closest aides; the men fled together to Taiwan after the civil war. The next moment her narrative would unravel further as she mentioned how shocked some of her fellow students at university were to discover that her roommate's father was the Japanese-installed puppet governor of Shanxi province.*

Laolao is a wonderful storyteller and though she has strong opinions about almost any subject, she does, every once in a while, remember to put

* Though troops of both the party in power, the Nationalists (Guomindang), and the Communists officially fought on one side together in the war against Japan (1937–1945), in practice the efforts took place on different fronts. In 1945, the civil war, which had already begun at the end of the 1920s, started anew. With the Communists poised for victory, the last of Chiang Kai-shek's troops in 1949 beat a retreat to the island of Taiwan, earlier called Formosa.

Li Xiaoli and Michael Lindsay on their wedding day in Beijing in 1941. The smaller photo is Li Hsiao Li, alias Laolao, *in 1996. (Photos: the Lindsay family album, Linda Jakobson)*

in a word or two about how the issue at hand was looked upon by others. Once she sighed: "History is really such a difficult subject; everyone has their own way of looking at it."

It was enchanting to hear *Laolao* reminisce about her childhood. She was born in impoverished and isolated Shanxi province in northern China in 1916, a time of new ideas and change. Her mother had bound feet, as did her elder sister. But *Laolao* was spared this excruciatingly painful process, one that young Chinese girls had suffered for generations. Besides her immediate family, the two people who are vivid in her childhood memories are an opium-smoking uncle, of whom her father very much disapproved, and her father's concubine.

"Father acquired the concubine on the spur of the moment because he was a bit annoyed with Mother. Afterward I think Father was ashamed of himself, but as a wife who strongly believed in observing tradition, Mother would not let my father send the girl off. Instead, she became a member of the family and, to me, the youngest of the children, she was a dear big sister," *Laolao* recalled. Like most women of her generation, *Laolao*'s mother did not have a formal name, nor could she read or write. "Father was influenced a lot by the changing times, but my mother was very old-fashioned."

Laolao's father, a reform-minded officer in the army of the Shanxi warlord, approved of his son going off on a scholarship to study at Harvard University in America, and he encouraged his younger daughter to study all the way to university—rare for a girl in those days. *Laolao* attended the American Protestant Yenching University in Beijing where she met her future husband, teacher Michael Lindsay. (The title of Lady derives from the fact that Michael's father, noted British educator A. D. Lindsay, was awarded a peerage in 1945, making him Lord Lindsay of Birker. Michael later inherited the title from his father, and Michael's wife, *Laolao*, became the first Chinese-born peeress in British history.)

If *Laolao* with her liberal outlook and independent mind was not a typical Chinese young woman, Michael Lindsay was certainly not an ordinary scion of the British establishment.[6] While he was working as a teacher at Yenching University, Michael Lindsay became involved in the activities of the Communist underground resistance movement. He recruited his student, *Laolao*, to help him. "I'm the one who wasn't interested in politics and I knew nothing about Communist guerrillas, not the other way round," *Laolao* said, explaining that many people took it for granted that it was she who persuaded Michael into assisting the Communists. During lengthy visits to Communist-held areas in 1938 and 1939, Lindsay saw for himself that Communist troops were putting up a wholehearted resistance to the Japanese invasion. "He was very impressed by the popular support the Communists enjoyed," *Laolao* said.

Though Michael Lindsay was inclined to feel that the Communists offered China a better alternative than the corrupt Nationalists (Guomindang), he himself was not a Communist, unlike so many of the other foreigners who decided to help the Chinese Communists during those war years. As Susan Lawrence notes of her grandfather: "Michael remained, to the puzzlement of some, a patriotic Briton and an acute observer and critic of China, sending reports about the Communist areas to his government and publishing anonymous articles in his country's leading newspapers."

Michael Lindsay and *Laolao* were married in June 1941. "My parents liked Michael, especially my father who valued his educational background," *Laolao* recollected when I asked if they objected to her marrying a foreigner. After war between the United States and Japan was formally declared in December 1941, the couple hurriedly left Beijing, escaping the Japanese secret police by a matter of minutes. They headed for guerrilla territory, where they spent the next four years as members of Chairman Mao's army.

Using his skills as an amateur radio technician, Michael Lindsay helped the Communists improve their communication network in the war against Japan. In 1944, he designed and supervised the building of a transmitter powerful enough to reach San Francisco, enabling the Chinese Communists to begin broadcasting news from their front of the war directly to the West, thus bypassing Guomindang censors. The transmitter launched the international service of the New China News Agency (Xinhua), and Michael thereafter became the service's English-language advisor.

Susan's mother came into the world in a mountain village where people had not yet heard that the Emperor had been dethroned thirty years earlier. In Yan'an, western China, where the Lindsays moved in May 1944, *Laolao* gave birth to a son, Susan's uncle, in a cave not unlike the cave where Mao lived. Half a century later, when this uncle inherited his father's peerage, a British newspaper reported the event with the headline "Cave Lord."

In Yan'an, Michael Lindsay found himself increasingly at odds with the Communist leaders with whom he had innumerable debates. He opposed the personal cult developing around Mao and was disappointed to see the Chinese Communists embracing an authoritarian and bureaucratic leadership style which relied heavily on the Soviet model. "They used Marxism to their own ends in the same way as Confucianism had been used by earlier people in power throughout Chinese history," *Laolao* said.

Not only was Lindsay increasingly disillusioned about the direction the Communists were heading, he also did not want to become involved in a civil war, so, in 1945, four years before the founding of the People's Republic, he left China with *Laolao* and their two small children in tow. They returned to England from where fate led them to Australia, Taiwan, and, in the end, to Washington, D.C., where Lindsay served as Professor of Far Eastern Studies at American University from 1959 to 1974. Throughout the 1950s and 1960s, Lindsay's criticism of Mao's regime earned him the wrath of the Communist leadership.

"Mao turned into an evil man, he nearly destroyed China," *Laolao* said. "The Communists did not turn out to be any better than the Guomindang in the 1930s; they killed people and, in addition, they wanted to control people's thoughts. I have always been such an independent-minded person that I could never have given up my soul to any organization. My brother suffered a lot, for the most part on account of his opinions and because he was a banker before 1949, but also because of me. I am sure that he committed suicide. He died during the Cultural Revolution."

It was not until the late 1980s that Michael Lindsay's name was rehabilitated in mainland China. Today he is looked upon as an "old friend of the Chinese people." A recent Chinese television documentary coproduced by the Central Committee Party History Research Office approvingly profiled Lindsay alongside left-wing American journalists Edgar Snow, Agnes Smedley, and Anna Louise Strong, and the Canadian doctor Norman Bethune. Old comrades from the days of Yan'an arranged for the Lindsays to be assigned an apartment in Beijing. Though Michael Lindsay did not live to enjoy that gesture in full, *Laolao* moved into the apartment in 1994, after his death. In addition to old friends and two nephews in Beijing, she also had nearby her granddaughter Susan, who was in China as correspondent for *U.S. News & World Report.*

Thanks to Susan and *Laolao,* I have caught a glimpse of a world previously unknown to me. Many of *Laolao*'s friends are members of the Communist elite and they live, as elites did in the days before the Communists took power, behind high walls in traditional houses built around courtyards—scrolls by distinguished calligraphers hang on the walls, and faithful servants are part of the household.

Laolao's amazing array of guests includes both old revolutionaries who survived the turbulent decades of the People's Republic and Overseas Chinese who fled to the United States or Taiwan; they, like *Laolao,* have returned to the country of their birth, either permanently or as regular visitors. In the whirlwind of politics they were all cast in varying directions, but when they meet now it no longer seems to matter. They are bound together by history, by their cultural heritage, and by their unwavering patriotism. *Laolao* and like-minded members of her age group of Overseas Chinese have embraced a Western style of life only up to a certain point, and they remain very much Chinese. In addition, they are all strong supporters of the open door and reform policy—the China that they love is finally moving in the right direction.

Deng Xiaoping needed support not only from the Overseas Chinese community to make his reform policy successful. Help from the country's intellectuals was also crucial. They too responded enthusiastically to Deng's call on their patriotism, eager that genuine knowledge and skills would once again be appreciated.

The principle of "saving the country" underscores the traditional role of intellectuals. In Imperial China, the educated had a moral obligation to "take responsibility for all under heaven" and to "be the first in the world to assume its worries, the last to enjoy its pleasures."[7] Throughout history, the intellectual community worked within the system to influence the development of society. They did not regard autonomy from official power as a moral asset, like their Western and Russian counterparts. In tune with their literati predecessors, Chinese academics, scientists, writers, and artists "regarded themselves as establishment intellectuals" after the founding of the People's Republic, and "assumed that their moral and political authority converged and was the same."[8]

Even after the chaos of the Cultural Revolution, despite their loss of faith in socialism and erosion of trust in the Communist Party, most intellectuals considered it their patriotic obligation to collaborate with the Communist Party because that meant serving China. Though the spiritual bond between the intellectual community and the Party-state was broken during the Cultural Revolution, the traditional view of the intellectual acting as a go-between between the people and the leaders persisted in the first decade of the Deng era. The vast majority of even the most progressive dissident intellectuals wanted to avoid direct confrontation with the state. Obviously, the brutal punishment awaiting anyone branded as "an enemy of the state" has also had great psychological effects ever since the founding of the People's Republic.

During the 1980s, the goal of serving the Party was transformed into the goal of changing Party policies. As the father of Tang, the young man who lost his sanity in jail, told me in 1987, he sincerely believed that the Party was capable of reforming itself. China had put its dark past behind it and was going to grow strong again.

The massacre following the Tiananmen demonstrations in 1989 was a turning point. After that, a number of members of the intelligentsia conceded in private conversations that they needed to change their outlook and form an unequivocal political opposition. Others still believed in the long-established way to act. As former minister of propaganda Lu Dingyi lay on his deathbed in 1996, his intellectual conscience would not leave him in peace, as he worried about his country's future to the bitter end. Lu had suffered an inhumane fate at the hands of zealous Red Guards in the first months of the Cultural Revolution. He was also one of the Party's old guard members who opposed the campaign against bourgeois liberalism in the 1980s. But instead of making a public statement, as a man in his position might in the West, he composed a biting letter to the Central Committee, asking why a thorough assessment of the wrongdoings during the Cultural Revolution had still not been made. Party Secretary Jiang Zemin is said to have been furious when he heard of the letter circulating among high-level cadres, but he could not punish the author. Lu Dingyi was already dead.

"We love our country, but we hate our government," was one of the more radical slogans splashed on banners during the Tiananmen demonstrations in 1989. According to the traditional Chinese view, the interests of the individual are inseparable from those of society. The line between state and society is blurred. In Mao's time, there was no question that "society" meant the Party and the state. Only after more liberal political winds began to blow in the first years of the Deng era, and individual sufferings in the Cultural Revolution became part of public discourse, did some writers gingerly allude to the notion that patriotism did not necessarily require loyalty to the authorities or even to the Communist Party. The vehement reaction of the Party was to be expected. During campaigns against bourgeois liberalism and spiritual pollution in the 1980s, "unpatriotic" became synonymous with "anti-Party." Besides the initial shock of the People's Army shooting its own people in June 1989, the residents of Beijing were especially outraged that the authorities accused the democracy movement of having been unpatriotic.

Since 1989, one Chinese after another has drawn a line of distinction between feelings of patriotism and Party loyalty. But patriotism is still not without its contradictions, because the notion of a nation-state, that of the People's Republic of China, is so closely intertwined with the Communist Party. No one under the age of fifty, or even sixty, has any recollection of China as anything other than the People's Republic, with the Communist Party as its leader. They have no alternative concept to fall back on. When a foreigner criticizes the Communist Party, it can be taken to mean speaking badly of China which, in turn, can be understood as thinking disparagingly of Chinese in general—this can make the blood boil of any Chinese.

Except in the company of three or four of my very closest friends, I have to be extremely careful when voicing my opinions of Communist Party policies, even if the people with whom I am talking are roundly condemning their leaders and the Party. In a corresponding situation in the United States, I cannot imagine my American acquaintances taking offense or thinking that I opposed America if I joined in when they carped about Bill Clinton's leadership style or the Democratic Party's course of action.

"We can criticize. You do not have that right," John Lee once confessed, as we discussed the sensitivity of his fellow countrymen. The words of a foreigner, even constructive criticism, are nearly always interpreted as "Chinese being put down by outsiders," thus immediately provoking a defensive response. Many foreigners working in joint-venture companies have complained of this reaction as a growing problem during the 1990s. In theory, the Chinese employees say they want to learn the Western style of business management. In practice, an American or European is often told: "This is the way we Chinese do things." And it does not do to disapprove of the Chinese way.

Princeton professor Perry Link poses thought-provoking questions in his book *Evening Chats in Beijing* about Chinese pride and their "worrying mentality" (*youhuan yishi*); in other words, the historic burden of "mission and responsibility"[9] that Chinese intellectuals bear. "The intellectuals themselves have made 'Chineseness' such a powerful category, with such strong moral connotations, that it obstructs normal lines of observation and reflection," Link writes. He, too, describes the inability of academics and other well-educated intellectuals he knows—"mature individuals and people who long ago had understood that I mean China well"—to accept criticism. He goes on to ask: "What limitations of vision result when so many issues must be conceived in part as matters of Chinese pride? As China faces complex and inexorable pressures to join the modern world, does it help to maintain such a profound distinction between 'Chinese' and 'foreign'? Must we acknowledge Chinese 'specialness'—which is a code for 'superiority' and, in turn, often a heartfelt attempt to banish the notion of 'inferiority'?"

Even the small group of Chinese who actively work to promote freedom of the press and other political reforms—despite the formidable opposition of the authorities and the risks of punishment—do not, as a rule, approve of Western countries condemning the Chinese government in the realm of international interaction. "Chinese leaders must be constantly pressured because 'keeping face' is extremely important to them. But they should never be outrightly denounced or excoriated. That would hurt the pride of all of us Chinese people too," said Dai Qing, China's most outspoken environmentalist, when I interviewed her in Beijing in 1996. Like just about every Chinese I know, she does not approve of economic sanctions as a method of pressure.

Dai Qing, a vivacious and talkative fifty-five-year-old writer, is known in the West for her staunch opposition to the Three Gorges dam project. She was a Nieman Fellow at Harvard University in 1992 and received the Goldman Environmental Foundation Prize for her environmental work in 1993. She is also famous for her candid views which she is not afraid to air to Western journalists: "A government that is unsure of its position is intolerant," she told me. "If one has nothing to fear, one is not afraid of criticism." Many believe that Dai Qing has special pro-

Environmentalist Dai Qing in 1995 (Photo: John Lee)

tection because she is the adopted daughter of one of China's ten marshals. Then again, she spent eleven months behind bars after the Tiananmen demonstrations.

In the West, human rights or, to be more precise, abuses of human rights are always mentioned in conjunction with China. In China, I have only heard the term "human rights" when people refer to the problems between China and other countries or when someone curses their own unjust treatment. Then, a person might snap: "There are no human rights in China!"

As I prepared to leave China in the summer of 1997, Beijing ruled with such an iron grip that there were few, if any political activists left. They had all either been imprisoned or exiled abroad. The eleven-year sentence handed out to twenty-seven-year-old former student leader Wang Dan in late 1996 sent shock waves through the dissident community. Wang Dan had already served a four-year sentence for his role in the 1989 Tiananmen democracy movement. After his release, Wang Dan continued to speak out in defense of freedom of speech. In May 1995, he and Xu Liangying, the seventy-five-year-old translater of Albert Einstein's collected works, organized a petition urging the Chinese leaders to show greater tolerance. The letter also demanded a reevaluation of the Tiananmen Square protests. It was signed not only by young persistent protesters like Wang Dan, but also by several older generation intellectuals—the mother who refuses to be silent about her dead son, Ding Zilin, and the former deputy editor of the People's Daily, Wang Ruoshui.[10]

As things turned out, Wang Dan served one and a half years of his second prison term before he was released on medical parole and exiled to the United States in April 1998, apparently as a concession to Washington before President Bill Clinton's trip to China in June 1998. At the time of Wang Dan's release, Amnesty International estimated that 2,000 people were still imprisoned in China for political crimes. Furthermore, some 230,000 political dissidents, human rights defenders, and members of religious and ethnic groups were believed to be held in labor camps.[11] The police still retain the power to sentence people to three years of labor reform without a trial. Torture is reported to be endemic.[12] The death penalty is used extensively and arbitrarily to instill fear. A 1996 Amnesty International summary of human rights in the People's Republic cites the case of two peasants executed in Henan province for stealing thirty-six cows and agricultural machinery worth $9,300.[13]

Every Chinese with whom I have broached the subject of human rights has said they dream of a society devoid of arbitrary justice and despotism, governed by the rule of law. They want their leaders to be accountable for their actions. But, on the whole, not even the urban Chinese who keep abreast of current events are familiar with the names of the dissidents who have received such acclaim in the United States. It is rare that anyone, without prompting, mentions the need for a multiparty system. Like Dai Qing, they say that Western pressure is very important so that the Chinese leaders are consistently nudged in the right direction. But I have never met anyone who approves of pressure too severe. "One mustn't hurt the feelings of the Chinese" is a recurring comment.[14]

It was interesting to hear an American friend relate her experiences of watching the opening ceremony of the summer Olympic Games in Atlanta in 1996 with a group of Chinese friends. One was a well-known dissident, freed from prison and bundled off to the United States, thanks to pressure from Washington. Also present was his wife, a strong-willed lady who had worked relentlessly to secure her husband's freedom. When the Chinese team marched into the stadium and the American television broadcaster mentioned China's dismal record of abusing human rights, the dissident's wife jumped up in fury. "What right does that American have to mix up human rights with sports?" she exclaimed vehemently.

I met this dissident in the United States in November 1996. He too thought it was unnecessary to blast the Chinese government in connection with the Olympic Games. The most effective way to influence events in China was to work behind the scenes; for example, by financing private law offices and supplying financial support to liberal-minded think tanks.

He stressed that he was very careful not to speak out against the Beijing leadership while he was in the United States. "That would be a shameful act. I would play right into the hands of the Chinese authorities. They would leap at the chance to claim I had allied myself with foreigners and turned against China. I would alienate many of my fellow citizens in China," he said.

The handful of courageous Chinese in Beijing who do work for an improvement of human rights are, for the most part, in favor of ongoing Western pressure on China's leaders, but they also want to see the West engage China, not isolate it.

Since the suppression of the Tiananmen demonstrations in 1989, Westerners have debated the morality of engaging in trade with a country like China. The more China opens up to the outside world and is integrated into the international economy, the more probable it is that reform-minded groups within China will succeed in making their voices heard. In addition, the growing amount of information that ordinary Chinese have about the West, as well as the Chinese economy's increasing dependency on the outside world, force the Chinese leaders, at least to some extent, to consider the consequences of their actions. For this reason, the leaders of the West should speak with one voice. It is also worth remembering that it is not only us Westerners who benefit from trade with China. China's continuing economic growth is heavily dependent on foreign trade. It makes up about 35 percent of the country's gross national product. Foreign direct investment projects employ more than 16 million Chinese.[15]

Another hotly debated issue is whether or not pressure on the Chinese leaders actually yields results. Up to a certain point, it does. I agree with environmentalist Dai Qing when she says that the Chinese leadership is acutely sensitive about its image. But Westerners should never be under the illusion that they can decisively affect Chinese politics. The crucial impulse must come from the Chinese themselves.

One of China's many contradictions—American goods are popular and American movies play to packed theaters, though the general feeling toward America has become more critical during the past decade. Photo from Beijing in 1996. (Photo: John Lee)

十一

America Is No Longer Heaven on Earth

What to Do about Taiwan?

The relationship between China and the United States is characterized by a complex mixture of infatuation and antagonism. Americans and Chinese tend either to romanticize or to demonize each other. As I prepared to leave Beijing in the summer of 1997, Michael Jordan's photograph adorned many covers of youth and pop magazines, hamburgers were consumed with rapturous delight (at a rate of 50,000 per day in the capital alone), and the American movies *True Lies* and *Twister* were playing to packed theaters in major metropolises. But when I asked friends and acquaintances how they felt about the United States, the response was often: "The United States wants to prevent China from growing into a strong and wealthy superpower."

For more than two hundred years, relations between China and the United States have been marred by "illusions, dreams, myths, prejudices and half-truths."[1] America enchants, America enrages—both politically and personally. Similar emotional confusion prevails on the other side of the ocean, too—China fascinates, China exasperates. There are as many American misconceptions of China as there are unrealistic Chinese perceptions of America.

When I moved to China in 1987, adoration of America among ordinary Chinese knew no bounds. Urban Chinese, at any rate, turned a deaf ear to official media warnings about the negative effects of capitalism or the less flattering facets of American society. Ten years later, the atmosphere is distinctly different. The basic tone of Chinese media reports has not changed, but now most Chinese I know speak about the United States much more critically, even malevolently. Where before there was only reverence and—at least from a European point of view—an exaggerated admiration for the United States, now contempt and an alarming resentment are prevalent. The pendulum has swung to the other extreme.

In the 1980s, I was constantly reminding my acquaintances that every country, even the United States, has its problems. To a Finn, the high crime rate and the disparity between rich and poor are repugnant features of American society. But by the mid-1990s, I found myself emphasizing the positive aspects of American life. During my first years in China, I was considered an America-basher. Now my friends chide me for being an American apologist. But my own views of the United States have not changed at all.

What has caused the dramatic shift in Chinese attitudes toward America? Above all, Chinese perceptions of themselves have undergone fundamental changes. As elsewhere in Asia, confidence and self-esteem have risen along with improved living standards. With their new self-image the Chinese are viewing other countries, especially America, in a different light. Also, many urban Chinese have access to much more information about the West than they had a decade ago.[2] In the 1980s, my Chinese acquaintances knew even less about European nations than they did about the United States. Nor were they all that interested.

Though opinion polls should always be viewed with some caution, the results of a 1995 survey indicate the conflicting attitudes of young urban Chinese toward America. According to the poll, 57.2 percent of the respondents (aged fourteen to thirty-four) named America as the country they disliked the most, and 90 percent felt Washington had taken a "hegemonist and unfriendly attitude" toward China in recent years.[3] But, according to the same survey, the United States also topped the "favorite country" list.[4]

It is essential to differentiate between Chinese attitudes toward the United States as a political entity and attitudes toward Americans as individuals. When dealing personally with Americans, whether in business or education, many Chinese still express their enthusiasm about America. They remain as warm-hearted and curious as ever about the country. Among the tiny number of city-dwellers who have regular contacts with Westerners, Americans are often praised as "easy-going people" compared to the "stuffy" British or the "reclusive and shy" Finns. Thoughtful Chinese do, for the most part, distinguish between the American people and the American government and media, of which they are so critical. But in casual conversations, Americans tend to be lumped together so that all Americans, not just Capitol Hill politicians, are accused of arrogant and condescending behavior. As a Finn, I have perhaps heard more unchecked anti-American outbursts than an American would.

America Is No Longer Heaven on Earth

My most vivid recollection of being a non-American in China was the day I stood before my class for the first time at the economics college in Jinan (September 21, 1987). The twenty-odd students, who had all beamed with gleeful anticipation at being taught by an American, went dead silent when I told them I was a Finn. No one tried to hide their disappointment.

"We thought we were going to have an American teacher. We want to hear about American customs and life in America," one young man blurted out. The others nodded in agreement. Only after I told them that I had spent seven years of my childhood in New York and promised to devote one class each week to a lesson about America did they finally cheer up a bit and resign themselves to their unlucky lot.

Later in the term, I asked the class to name the country they would choose to visit, if they could travel anywhere in the world; twenty-one out of twenty-two chose the United States.* The frenzy to find a way to go to America led to ironic moments: One day a student told me she was trying everything to have her application accepted for Communist Party membership.

"Why?" I asked her in surprise. In previous conversations, she had not concealed her cynicism about the Party.

"Because it will help me get to the United States," she answered. "The majority of government-funded scholarships for study abroad are reserved for Party members."

I was well aware that almost everyone under age forty-five with a high school education considered America "heaven on earth." During the previous term, when I had studied Chinese at a university in Beijing, the Americans on campus were—for better or for worse—the center of constant attention. Chinese students were more than eager to help the Americans practice their Chinese, but the Americans were also bombarded with requests for assistance in obtaining a visa or a scholarship to study in the U.S. America was seen as the land of hope, where everyone drove a big car and made lots of money. "Americans are more exciting than other Westerners," explained an associate professor in Chinese history, aged forty-three, "Because America is the most powerful country in the world. Also, no other nation is as free. In America, everyone can do as he pleases."

Most Chinese I spoke to in 1987 knew next-to-nothing about *mei guo*, the "beautiful country," as America is called in Chinese, but they longed to go there, either to study or to emigrate. It was futile to point out that

* Officially, my class had seventeen pupils, mostly recently graduated teachers, but an additional half a dozen or so students of the economics college also regularly attended my lectures.

not all Americans are millionaires, that not everyone lives in a big house. No one wanted to hear anything negative about America.

I made the mistake, a few months into the term, of using statistics to help describe American society. My claims that 32 million Americans were classified as living below the poverty line and that more than 21,000 people were murdered in the United States in 1986 met with disbelief and utter indignation.[5] One of the female students stood up and said, "Teacher, I feel you are repeating the propaganda of the Communist Party." A few of my students were so outraged by my presentation that, after class, they headed for the dean's office, where they demanded that I be fired. The episode was resolved when I promised to resume lectures on American customs. In practice that meant endless explanations about how to eat a hamburger, countless demonstrations in the art of using a knife and fork, and detailed descriptions of the do's and don'ts when invited to an American home.

Today, there are still long lines of Chinese citizens outside the American Embassy in Beijing to apply for visas. To be honest, I doubt there are many Chinese who would not leap at the chance to visit America. An opportunity to study in the United States is as prized among educated Chinese now as it was ten years ago. The stream of illegal immigrants into the U.S. has not stemmed either. Every year, about 100,000 undocumented Chinese from mainland China, Taiwan, and Hong Kong slip into the United States.[6] American popular culture is also just as sought after as a decade ago, and there is lots more of it nowadays. Madonna and Michael Jackson are immensely popular among urban youth, as are books, in translation, by such authors as John Grisham and Sidney Sheldon. Numerous American fast-food restaurants have sprung up in over a dozen Chinese cities. Television series like "Dynasty," dubbed in Mandarin, had tens of millions of avid Chinese watchers. However, the general feeling about America, if there is any such thing in a country as vast as China, has become more critical in the 1990s, and in many cases has soured.

In private conversations with a wide range of people, from factory workers and university teachers to businesspeople and artists, I have heard America cited as a "bully," a country "afraid of China's economic and military development," and a nation that is "trying to obstruct China's growth" and that "has no right to act as the world's policeman." When, in 1996, I told Lao He, the woman who cleans my apartment, that I was going to Boston for a month, she spontaneously blurted out, "America is unfriendly toward China."

I heard similar views when I revisited Jinan in the autumn of 1996. One of my students at the economics college nine years earlier, a bright, charming young man, invited me to dinner at his home. Zhang now works as a teacher at another university, and, in Chinese style, he and his wife live with his parents. On the living room table was a copy of an old *Newsweek* Zhang had purchased on a recent trip to Beijing. The words "China—Friend or Foe?" were splashed across the cover photo, which depicted a stern-looking Chinese soldier holding a pair of binoculars.

"What does foe mean?" asked Zhang's father, a sixty-seven-year-old retired chemical engineer, as he idly picked up the magazine. When I told him, he shook his head in dismay. "Why do Americans want to see us as enemies?" he said. "What has China done to threaten them? America bullies us and criticizes us, but actually, I think it's because they want to stop China from developing into a great nation again."

Zhang's father is no supporter of China's present leaders. In private, he does not hide his disgust for them. Though at one time he believed the Communists offered the best available solution to the country's vast problems, his personal sufferings over the past four decades have dispelled any illusions about the morality or legitimacy of the authoritarian regime. But like many Chinese with whom I have discussed America, he feels insulted by what he sees as American attempts to stand in the way of China's development.

His son Zhang was much more vehement. "America looks down on us because Chinese have a lower standard of living," he said heatedly. "But America is afraid of us, afraid that we might become more powerful than they are. And so they want to make us look dangerous, like the image of that soldier on the cover of the magazine."

When I reminded Zhang that only a decade earlier he and his colleagues used to worship America and were very annoyed when I mentioned anything negative about the United States, his cheeks turned pink with embarrassment. Then he laughed good-naturedly and agreed. "Yes, that's true, but now we can distinguish among Western countries. Canada and Australia are free societies too, but they don't pressure China." And then he said something I have heard with increasing frequency since the mid-1990s, mostly from well-educated Chinese of his generation: "We are now much better able to evaluate other countries' relations with China, because our own media reports openly on foreign policy issues. When you lived in Jinan ten years ago, the Chinese government kept us citizens in the dark. That has changed."

Only a handful of Chinese I have spoken to admit that the official newspapers publish one-sided articles about Sino-American relations or that the manner in which the Chinese government presents Washington's actions has a bearing on their own views. When my friends and acquaintances debate domestic issues, they have an admirable ability to read between the lines of official statements and comments. But I always wonder why this talent for dissecting propaganda fails when we discuss issues relating to the United States, or, as previously mentioned, Tibet.

A number of people do concede that anti-American sentiments, and especially nationalistic fervor, play into the hands of the Chinese leaders, who face immense domestic problems. In June 1997, a senior government official told me that among the top leaders there were sharply divergent views regarding the surge of nationalism. "One group feels that nationalistic zeal is useful. But others worry it might damage our international relations," the official said.

A case in point is the best-selling book, *Zhongguo keyi shuo bu* (China Can Say No), a satirical jumble of anti-American and anti-Western slogans, anecdotes, and conspiracy theories. The five co-authors, university-educated writers and poets in their twenties and thirties, claim they want to instill a stronger feeling of national pride in the younger generation. When I met two of the authors in September 1996, a few months after the book was published, I was struck by their cockiness, their naïveté, and, above all, by their lack of knowledge about the West. None of them had been abroad.

"We don't pretend to be foreign-policy experts. We just want to warn young Chinese not to trust Westerners, and Americans in particular," said thirty-two-year-old Zhang Zangzang, the author considered the driving force behind the book project. He looked more like a self-made businessman—in his brand new black suit and flashy sunglasses—than a poet. He went on: "This book is to counterbalance all the anti-Chinese books written by Americans."

Song Qiang, the quieter of the two authors, added: "Our aim is to urge young Chinese to value their own culture. Chinese need to have a stronger sense of self-respect."

Both authors emphatically denied that any of the writers had connections to the government. "I disagree with our leaders on many issues," Zhang Zangzang assured me. But when I asked him why had he had not written a book critical of his own government, he shot back: "You know very well a book like that would never be allowed to be published."

This book was the first of a slew of anti-American books in China—"How China Can Say No," "Why China Can Say No," etc. This first one stood out because of the attention it received in foreign media and—partly because of that—among urban Chinese. On the whole, readers lamented the book's childish approach and errors of historical fact, but defended the anti-American theme. "A lot of what the authors say is true," is a comment I heard time and again. Only political scientist Jia Qingguo at Beijing University, and another acquaintance who teaches drama, expressed distaste for the authors' bigotry. Many friends said they enjoyed the straightforward way the authors poured out their feelings.

A thirty-seven-year-old chemical engineer-turned-factory owner, whom I have known since 1987, observed: "It was very refreshing to see people my age expressing themselves in a manner I could relate to. Don't forget, America stopped us from hosting the Olympics." China's failure to win the bid to host the 2000 Summer Olympic Games is still, more than four years later, a sore subject among Beijing residents. The United States is widely blamed for the setback.

Even my well-read friend Yang from Jinan, who fled to the West after the Tiananmen demonstrations in 1989 and has visited the United States, agreed with the authors' views that Washington is trying to block China from becoming a superpower. He is one of the few friends I can speak with as freely as I wish. Once, when we were arguing about the United States, I remarked: "You sound like a government representative. You even use the same expressions as [Prime Minister] Li Peng!"

"You don't understand because you're not Chinese," Yang snapped. "When we are talking about the way the American government treats China, I do, for the most part, agree with our leaders. We all want to see China grow strong and rich."

Chinese and American misconceptions of one another go back more than 150 years. From the start, China's image of the West and the American image of China were greatly influenced by missionaries. The first American missionaries went to the Middle Kingdom in 1830 and shared their experiences through publications and visits back home. Though the missionaries failed to generate much interest in Christianity, their contributions to education and health care were significant for the process of modernization in China.

In 1925, sixteen Christian colleges, run mainly by American Protestants, accounted for about 12 percent of the total college enrollment in China.[7] Among the most prominent was Yenching University, whose alumni include several distinguished citizens, such as former foreign minister Huang Hua, and China's former chief representative in Hong Kong, Zhou Nan. When Yenching alumni in 1994 celebrated the seventy-fifth anniversary of the founding of the university, members of some of the most influential families in China were present. Of course *Laolao*, alias Lady Lindsay, was among the guests.

America still plays an important educational role for China. Since the beginning of the open-door policy, tens of thousands of Chinese youth have attended universities and colleges across the United States.[8] Nearly every top Chinese leader has a son or daughter who has studied in America, including Deng Xiaoping's youngest son, whose wife gave birth to the patriarch's "American grandchild" while the couple was in New York—a source of many jokes among elite circles in Beijing. Chinese refer to the offspring of their leaders as "the princelings" or "the prince's party" because so many of them, through their well-placed connections, have amassed fortunes or have risen to the highest echelons of power during the reform period. A number of these princelings and their family members have acquired either an American green card or American citizenship. Not even the children of China's veteran Communists have complete faith in their own fathers' efforts to transform China.

The majority of the students who went to study in the United States during the 1980s have not returned. China lost nearly an entire generation of its best-educated youth in the aftermath of the crackdown on the Tiananmen democracy movement in June 1989. At that point, many Chinese who had left home during the first years of the open-door policy were about to finish their university studies abroad. When, in April 1990, President Bush issued an executive order allowing Chinese who were in America at the time of the massacre to apply for permanent residency, about 60,000 took him up on the offer.

The Beijing massacre caused the first major crisis in relations between Beijing and Washington since Richard Nixon's historic visit to China in 1972 and the resumption of official ties between the two countries in 1979. In those days, the U.S. and China had a mutual enemy: the Soviet Union. It was beneficial for both sides to downplay many of their differences. Deng Xiaoping visited the U.S. in 1979 and became the West's favorite Communist leader. Americans watched with fascination as Red China took its first steps "along the road to capitalism." *Time* magazine named Deng Xiaoping "Man of the Year" not once, but twice, in 1979 and 1986.

But after the Soviet Union fell apart, the relationship required a new basis. Mutual goals were harder to come by. As Harry Harding, one of the foremost scholars on Sino-American ties, writes, "What the Chinese saw as a partnership to promote their country's socialist reform, Americans perceived as an effort to encourage China's political and economic liberalization."[9] Professor David Shambaugh puts it more bluntly, attributing American sentiments to a "missionary complex": "For the United States, it seems that the issue is never whether to change China, but how."[10] Until the early 1990s, there was a general consensus among policy-makers in Washington that "China will inevitably become more like the West—non-ideological, pragmatic, materialistic, and progressively freer in its culture and politics."[11]

The road has been rocky, to say the least. President George Bush's China policy was a failure. In public he condemned Beijing's decision to use tanks against its citizens, but shortly thereafter sent his aides on a "secret mission" to negotiate with the Chinese leaders. Such missions hardly ever remain secret. I agree with Princeton professor Perry Link's assessment that "Deng Xiaoping thoroughly thrashed the president [Bush] in the symbolic Chinese game of face."[12] The vacillation which marked the Bush administration's dealings with China continued when Bill Clinton took office. Clinton first linked human rights to most-favored nation (MFN) status in trade relations, but that decision also backfired. When, in May 1994, Clinton reversed his campaign promises and the policy he had pursued in the first year of his presidency by delinking human rights and trade, Beijing scored a major victory. The Chinese were left with the image of a vocally defiant, but harmless, Washington.[13] In the end, Beijing received confirmation of what it had doubted all along: MFN was not a credible threat. Washington decided that jeopardizing American business interests is not a realistic means of promoting human rights.

Numerous contentious issues—human rights, arms control, trade policy, and, above all, the future of Taiwan—complicate relations between Washington and Beijing. As critical as any of these specific issues is the new way both parties have come to regard each other. China is suddenly the center of attention among security policy analysts in Washington. Since China's economy took off in 1992, American leaders have become progressively worried about Beijing's efforts to modernize its armed forces. As recently as the early 1990s, China's military capabilities were of marginal concern. Today nearly every analysis of American foreign policy mentions China as the biggest challenge—or threat—facing the United States.

Should economic and other relations be expanded to induce China to become a more responsible member in the family of nations; *i.e.*, should the U.S. seek "engagement"? Or should America pursue a policy of containment, to try to keep a rising China in check? These two questions lie at the heart of the heated debates about China. To China's leaders, the mere mention of the word "containment" is derogatory and infuriating. It is largely on account of this term that ordinary Chinese exclaim, "America wants to stop China from becoming a superpower."

The titles of two articles about China in the spring 1997 issue of *Foreign Affairs* highlight the problems facing decision-makers in Washington: "The Coming Conflict with China" and "Beijing as a Conservative Power." The former predicts that China will seek to replace the United States as the dominant power in Asia within the next decade or two. Its authors claim that China is no strategic friend of the United States, but rather a long-term adversary. "China's sheer size and inherent strength, its conception of itself as a global civilization, and its eagerness to redeem centuries of humiliating weakness are propelling it toward Asian hegemony," write Richard Bernstein and Ross H. Munro, both former China correspondents. They quote "influential Chinese planners" like General Mi Zhenyu: "For a relatively long time it will be absolutely necessary that we quietly nurse our sense of vengeance. We must conceal our abilities and bide our time," Mi reportedly asserted in 1996.[14]

In the second *Foreign Affairs* article, political scientist Robert S. Ross concludes that there is no "China threat" for the simple reason that China is militarily weak and will remain so well into the twenty-first century. He backs up his position with details of China's naval and air capabilities. "Chinese leaders remain committed to seeking constructive relations with all their neighbors," Ross writes, encouraging the United States to take advantage of the situation and pursue a policy of engagement.[15]

In off-the-record interviews, five Western military attachés based in Beijing confirmed Ross's view that China will not have the naval capacity to launch a full-scale war in the South China Sea for at least twenty years, if not more. They too emphasized China's intention to maintain the status quo and to use its military clout to "defend its own territories." This is the ambiguous term that Chinese leaders themselves also use. According to Beijing, both Taiwan and the controversial Spratly Islands—a group of disputed uninhabited islands in the South China Sea—are "a part of China."

After nearly four years of groping for a viable China policy, President Clinton finally took a firm stand in support of "comprehensive engagement" when he met President Jiang Zemin in Manila in November 1996, and formally invited him to pay an official state visit. Despite the general view in both Washington and Beijing that Jiang's trip to the U.S. in autumn 1997 and Clinton's visit to China in June 1998 were generally considered to be successful, the struggle between engagement and containment is bound to cause discord among American politicians each time China acts counter to Washington's interests.

The "productive relationship" that Clinton heralded during his trip to China is a shaky one. China and America continue to view the world quite differently, and Sino-American relations will inevitably continue to experience ups and downs. Though China was commended for its responsible behavior during the Asian financial crisis, the authoritarian government in Beijing has not substantially removed trade barriers, nor has it abstained from missile proliferation or from imprisoning political activists. Furthermore, Jiang Zemin stoutly defended the repressive regime when Bill Clinton was in Beijing.

Sino-American relations look very different from Beijing. China longs to be accepted as an equal in all areas of international cooperation. It is especially insistent that the United States treat China in an appropriate manner. Clinton's visit to China will be long remembered as a landmark—Chinese leaders and citizens alike concurred that the U.S. was finally according China the respect it so craves. Nothing could have delighted the Chinese leaders more than to hear Clinton say that China's course is "morally right," and that the United States does not have the right to impose its values on other countries.[16]

"Washington lectures Beijing in the manner of a teacher. But this is not a relationship between teacher and pupil. America should treat China as an equal," said Beijing University professor, Jia Qingguo, in 1996. To an outsider, Beijing's sensitivity borders on paranoia. Besides, Beijing only wants to be a first-class player in selective fields. In trade negotiations, China demands concessions as "a poor country."

According to Jia Qingguo, Western evaluations of China as an emerging economic superpower propelled Beijing to adopt a more defiant attitude toward the United States in the early 1990s. "Beijing no longer sees a need to justify why the United States also needs China," he said. American exports to China have grown at an annual rate of 16 percent during the 1990s, and American companies sold China 12 billion dollars worth of goods and technology in 1996. On the other hand, U.S. exports to China comprised only 4 percent of total U.S. exports, while China's exports to the U.S. made up 18 percent of China's total exports.[17]

Assistant Professor Jia Qingguo, who returned to China after ten years abroad, in the 480-square-foot apartment assigned to him by Beijing University. The floor is concrete. In the background, Jia's six-year-old son learning to use a computer. Photo taken in June 1997. (Photo: John Lee)

In 1981, Jia Qingguo attended Cornell University to write his Ph.D. thesis on Sino-American relations. After graduation he worked as an assistant professor, first in San Diego, then in Sydney. Altogether, he spent ten years abroad. Like most returnees, he said his son's education was a major factor in the decision to move back to China.

"Culturally, it is extremely important that my son learns to read and write Chinese characters. I want him to go to school in Beijing, and become a Chinese," forty-year-old Jia said. In the two years since his return he had not regretted the move, "at least not yet," though he readily admitted that library facilities at Beijing University are not comparable to those in the West. "But, thanks to e-mail, it is easy to keep in touch with other researchers in the field. I have also attended several international conferences since returning to Beijing."

Jia Qingguo belongs to a new generation of political scientists. He dresses casually in jeans and a sweatshirt. He submits articles to international English-language journals. Though free of Marxist jargon, his writing does not deviate significantly from the public speeches of China's leaders, but his interpretations of issues do shed light on Sino-American relations.[18]

Political scientists, both Chinese and Western, who are optimistic about China's future, point to signs of an emerging pluralism, even in the realm of foreign policy. "China no longer speaks with one voice, as in the past. Previously, officials didn't dare state their own interpretation on any issue in public," Jia Qingguo reminded me. "Now, many ministries have their own spokesperson."

The fact that a political scientist can sit alone in his apartment in Beijing with a foreign journalist discussing a sensitive issue like Taiwan is proof that China has indeed changed in the past ten years. No one checks Jia Qingguo's articles before they are submitted to foreign journals—he has to know himself what may get him into trouble. I first met Jia Qingguo in 1995 through mutual friends, and I have always had the impression that the opinions he expresses are his own, not dictated to him. He speaks in a relaxed manner and even offers a bit of criticism of Chinese policy. Talking about disagreements over copyright infringements and environmental issues, he said that Beijing "needs to take a more responsible approach. It cannot define China's national interests in a very narrow way, with no regard for international concerns."

Only when I asked Jia how he, a widely traveled and well-educated Chinese, felt about China's human rights abuses, did I hear an answer that repeated, nearly word for word, the official line: "Human rights abuses are directly related to a country's economic and social development. Though China still has many problems on this front, one has to bear in mind the positive progress that has been made over the past years. The situation will improve only if China continues to develop its economy and stays politically stable. An attempt to carry out a democratic revolution would lead to chaos."

Jia Qingguo did concede that he was troubled by the upswing in nationalistic sentiments. "People react so emotionally. They don't see things objectively," he said, referring to books like "China Can Say No." "This kind of book reflects the changing attitudes toward the 1989 Tiananmen events. At first, many people felt defensive [when criticized by outsiders] that their government had done such a terrible thing. Then came economic progress, and Chinese officials found a way to rationalize the whole process: Political stability had made economic progress possible."

Several articles published in China during the 1990s stress that the collapse of the Soviet Union was partly a result of Mikhail Gorbachev's soft stance toward the West and the Soviets "giving in" to the United States. Jia Qingguo agrees: "The Soviets bowed down before the Americans. That is one reason Russia is in such bad shape." After 1989, the term "peaceful evolution" became a dirty word in Chinese politics. Conservatives accuse more reform-minded officials of allowing liberal Western values to infiltrate the socialist system.

"Washington and Beijing approach our relationship in such different ways," Jia Qingguo mused. "In the States, one first brings up the question of human rights, problems of trade and arms control, and how to 'manage' China. Many politicians on Capitol Hill still feel that Washington's policy should be aimed at curbing China's growth. In China, we concentrate on how to manage the relationship without damaging political stability and economic development. My colleagues and I see a lot of things wrong with our country. We have zillions of complaints, for sure. But the United States has never looked at China benignly, despite claims that it wants to see a stable, peaceful China. People quite understandably feel that U.S. policy is not well-intended."

Both the Chinese government and ordinary urbanites frequently blame the Western media—and especially American journalists—for distorting the truth and for purposely reporting negatively about China. Many of my Chinese friends have asked me: "Why do foreign journalists only want to write about the dark sides of Chinese society?" Despite my attempts to explain the fundamental concept of objective and balanced reporting, they remain hurt by what they conceive as the Western media's goal to mortify China. They have had so little exposure to media used as anything other than a tool to propagate the "correct line" that they cannot grasp what it means to write a story from several different, even conflicting, points of view. Western journalism undoubtedly concentrates on the contradictions and failings in *every* society. I can empathize with my Chinese friends, whose lives have changed so very much for the better, who feel that the many Western media do not sufficiently credit China with the increased personal freedoms and higher standards of living.

Do articles about arbitrary arrests, torture, forced abortions, corruption, smuggling, and alarming rates of pollution tell the whole truth about China? Of course not. Nor do the audacious sermons and sharply worded briefings that Chinese officials present to foreign journalists about the "correct way" to report on the Taiwan issue or conditions in Tibet. A few officials in the Foreign Ministry's Information Department merely succeeded to make my blood boil in their attempts, in one-on-one meetings, to impress upon me the "responsible approach to writing about China." Jingoistic lectures hardly promote objective reporting.

Complicated by growing feelings of self-confidence and nationalism, Taiwan is key to understanding the escalation of resentment among ordinary Chinese toward the United States. President Bill Clinton's decision to allow Taiwanese president Lee Teng-hui to visit his alma mater, Cornell University, in June 1995 still fuels resentment even in informal conversation about Sino-American ties. Washington is accused of meddling in a matter that has "nothing to do with the United States."

Lee Teng-hui's private visit incensed the Beijing leadership. They interpreted it as a sign that the United States intends, step by step, to help Taiwan gain international recognition. China's leaders steadfastly and unanimously believe that Taiwan is a part of China—period. There is no reason to doubt their warnings that they will resort to force if Taiwan openly seeks independence. They have put the principle of "One China"* above even the economic well-being and prosperity of the country. The vast majority of mainland Chinese agree with their leaders on this point. They would approve of an invasion of Taiwan if the Taiwanese declared independence, regardless if such a move led to war with the United States.

Even a few of my younger Beijing friends who, unlike many others, speak very positively about America, feel that Washington is interfering in China's internal affairs when it engages the Taiwan question.

Since 1949, Beijing and the ruling Guomindang Party on Taiwan have each considered themselves the sole official representatives of the whole of China. Both have insisted that there is only "One China." In other words, both have endorsed unification, albeit under very different terms. Beijing considers Taiwan a renegade province and opposes any gesture which could enhance Taiwan's independent role in the international community.

The ultimate status of Taiwan is the biggest source of potential instability in China's future. The scenario of the southern provinces breaking away from the People's Republic does not seem realistic. Nor can I imagine a popular uprising so mighty that the Chinese leadership could not quell it with the help of the army. It is highly probable that in the coming years we shall witness numerous protest movements and small-scale revolts, triggered by discontent over the effects of rapid economic transformation. But in the name of stability, the armed forces can be expected to remain loyal to the central government. On the other hand, Taiwan could well derail China. If Taiwan were to declare independence, the most drastic consequence would be Beijing's decision to attempt to take the island by force. Even the imposition of a prolonged blockade by Beijing, combined with continued psychological terror, is an alarming prospect. How Washington would react to such a scenario is an open question.

Before the Taiwanese presidential elections, at the height of the worst crisis of the 1990s in Sino-Taiwan relations, I had dinner with a Chinese official specializing in foreign affairs. As we talked, intimidating footage of China's missile tests in the Taiwan Straits ran on Chinese television. The American aircraft carrier "USS Independence" had already taken up position east of Taiwan, and another U.S. Navy battle group was on its way.

"China must acquire its own aircraft carrier," the Chinese official burst out passionately. "Now would be the perfect time for the government to collect donations for an aircraft carrier."

---

* According to the Shanghai communiqué of 1972, issued jointly by the U.S. and mainland China, "the government of the People's Republic of China is the sole legal government of China; Taiwan is a province of China."

Because I had witnessed the reluctance with which my friends had contributed money to the never-ending campaigns for various causes, I expressed my doubt that his idea would receive much support.

"Listen, every Chinese would gladly give money to such a project. Of that I am sure," my acquaintance replied. "We find those pictures of American aircraft carriers repellent."

During the next three weeks, I did some *ad hoc* polling on my own. In the small restaurant down my lane, at the post office, the bank, in taxis, and among my acquaintances and friends, I asked: "Would you give 10 yuan if the government collected money to build an aircraft carrier?"

It was my turn to be startled. Only one individual out of eighty or so did not say something like, "Of course! China needs an aircraft carrier of its own," or "Yes, I would donate money to such a project." Quite a few people assured me they would give more than 10 yuan. (Ten yuan is only $1.20, but it is perceived as roughly equivalent to ten dollars in America.)

The possibility of military conflict is not exaggerated. The Taiwan issue evokes fierce emotions on both sides of the Taiwan Straits. In addition, political liberalization on Taiwan has drastically complicated cross-straits relations. The Guomindang Party, the Communists' enemy during the civil war, is now—ironically—the Taiwanese force Beijing needs to ally with if it wants to realize its goal of unification.[19] The Taiwanese opposition party, the Democratic Progressive Party (DPP), favors independence. The ruling Guomindang still considers reunification its ultimate aim, but only when China has become more democratic and more prosperous.

When the Communists founded the People's Republic in 1949, the "Republic of China" under the leadership of Chiang Kai-shek fled to the island of Taiwan, about 100 miles off the southeast corner of mainland China. Of Taiwan's population of 21.5 million today, only about 15 percent are former Guomindang officials and soldiers, or their offspring. The overwhelming majority of the Taiwanese are descendants of Chinese migrants who arrived between the seventeenth and early twentieth centuries. About 85 percent have their roots in Fujian, the coastal province across the Taiwan Straits, and they speak Hokkien dialect. The others—two and a half million *hakkas* whose ancestors came from Guangdong hundreds of years ago—speak their own distinct dialect.

When I moved to China in 1987, any discussion about Taiwan was still taboo. I remember the brisk December day in Jinan as I was bicycling up the hill to our college when one of my students pedaled up beside me. In between our huffing and puffing, he asked me for a favor: Would I post a letter to his uncle in Taiwan the next time I went to Hong Kong? His family had heard, in a roundabout way, that his uncle was still alive. Though a recent news item had spelled out favorable new investment conditions on the mainland for Taiwanese businessmen, no one really yet dared to speak of Taiwanese relatives. People still vividly remembered that only a few years earlier the mere mention of a Guomindang uncle would have meant a black mark in one's personal dossier, to be used against him or her when he or she applied to study or was up for promotion.

Today my student's caution, a mere decade ago, seems incredible. A Taiwanese relative is no longer a liability, but rather an asset. Hordes of Taiwanese have flocked to the mainland during the 1990s, to visit relatives, to sightsee, and for business.[20] They are in a unique position to work on the mainland because they speak the language and share the same cultural traditions. Like the Hongkongese, they are bringing new ideas and a different outlook to far-flung corners of the People's Republic. Though the leaders in both Taipei and Beijing still rely on obscure ideological language in all official communications between them, at the grassroots level interaction is relaxed and carefree.

The explosive increase in contacts with Taiwanese has, however, also caused mental agony on the mainland. I have heard several acquaintances ask out loud: "Would China be as prosperous and free as Taiwan is today, if the Guomindang had won the civil war?"

When I visited Jinan in 1996, my former student told me his Taiwanese uncle had just been to see the family for the second time. And his Taiwanese cousin now runs a Chinese-Taiwanese joint-venture company in Fujian province, across the straits where many Taiwanese have concentrated their investments. Taiwan has been as important to the development of Fujian as Hong Kong has been to Guangdong.

By the beginning of 1998, more than 30,000 Taiwanese companies were conducting business with China. Taiwanese investments on the mainland were estimated at 30 billion dollars. By the end of the century, the Taiwanese are set to be China's largest trading partner, although exact and accurate figures are hard to come by because of complex trade regulations. Until 1997 goods, money, and people moving between the mainland and Taiwan had to travel via Hong Kong or a third country. Though the first direct shipping route opened with much fanfare in April 1997, Hong Kong is expected to remain the main trans-shipment center for the near future.

Having witnessed numerous family reunions of Taiwanese with mainland Chinese relatives in restaurants in Beijing, I can understand my friends who say: "We belong together; we are the same people." Despite my friends' insistence that Taiwanese independence will never be accepted by the mainland, it is very difficult to envision the two sides going to war against each other. When President Jiang Zemin greeted a Taiwanese delegation in Beijing in 1990, he suddenly recognized the group's deputy leader as an old schoolmate. "He sat in front of me in the third year of junior high school," Jiang recalled. "Even after fifty years I could call out his name." Jiang's conclusion from the experience: "The problem between China and Taiwan is not that complicated."[21]

But complicated it is. Today, Taiwan is one of Asia's wealthiest and most democratic societies. The first free presidential elections in Chinese history took place in Taiwan in March 1996. Claims by authoritarian leaders (like Singapore's Lee Kwan Yew) that the notion of Western democracy is incompatible with the Chinese cultural heritage were proven hollow.

The international debate about "Asian values" has, to a certain extent, brought about erroneous perceptions in the West. In all Asian societies there are groups demanding a more democratic style of government. It is true that Asians, on the whole, are horrified by the high crime rate in many Western cities and, for this reason, tend to shun too strong an emphasis on the rights of individuals. Individualism is not dominant in the Asian cultural tradition, nor is it stressed in the way Asian parents bring up their children. But the famous "Asian values"—a family-centered outlook, reverence for education, and a spirit of entrepreneurship—do not contradict the individual's desire to be a part of the political decision-making process.

Taiwan's democratically elected president, Lee Teng-hui, claims to be devoted to building a new Chinese culture, "free of repression and paternalism."[22] Though his increasingly autocratic style of leadership provokes criticism, no one denies that the political freedoms that Taiwanese enjoy today are considerably more than just a decade ago—vastly different from the political system on the other side of the Taiwan Straits.

Taiwan's industry is well developed economically and the population is well educated. A growing number of people on the island feel that they are, first and foremost, Taiwanese—their Chinese heritage is secondary. For decades, mainlanders controlled the ruling Guomindang Party. But today, as a result of political liberalization, native Taiwanese not only dominate the main opposition party, the DPP, but they are also an important force within the Guomindang. A "Taiwanese conciousness" and the distinct Taiwanese culture are important parts of public debate. The younger generation especially does not feel it belongs to mainland China and, understandably, the thought of obeying the

Communist government in Beijing is not an appealing alternative. The DPP, which favors Taiwan's independence, won 21 percent of the votes in the 1996 presidential elections. Their representatives hold nearly one-third of the seats in the legislature.

For the next five or ten years, it is highly probable that the majority of Taiwanese will support maintaining the status quo: In practice, Taiwan is an independent state, though it lacks international recognition. But it is impossible to foresee the volatility of the situation prior to the next presidential elections in the year 2000, or in 2004.

Though Taiwan has always been a source of tension in Sino-U.S. relations, mutual hostility to the Soviet Union motivated both Beijing and Washington to keep this point of contention in check. The question of China's future was also easier to deal with during the Cold War as decisions in Taiwan were made by a handful of military leaders in Taipei. But since the end of martial law in Taiwan in 1987, Taiwanese voters have claimed a crucial role in shaping the island's future through the democratic process.

Taiwanese are well aware that Jiang Zemin has embraced the concept of "one country, two systems," one of Deng Xiaoping's several famous catchphrases. First capitalist Hong Kong, then capitalist Taiwan will be reunited with the motherland. Taiwanese are naturally watching events in Hong Kong with keen interest.

Though the majority of Hongkongese, as well as many foreign analysts, have expressed faith in the Beijing leadership's intentions to safeguard Hong Kong's economy, few feel as confident about the vitality of the rule of law. Contrary to the Guangdongese business directors with whom I spoke, many Hongkongese envision "the rot from Guangdong seeping in, bit by bit." At the time of the handover on July 1, 1997, several Hongkongese I interviewed said that they were resigned to the fact that certain civil liberties would be curtailed under Beijing's rule.[23]

Hongkongese magnates are quick to declare their public support for the Beijing leaders. It is easy for them to do so. The overwhelming majority of well-to-do Hongkongese either have foreign passports or have obtained permanent residency abroad. And they have transferred part of their wealth away from Hong Kong. There are those in Beijing who feel that affluent Taiwanese will similarly accept Beijing's rule or else take their U.S. dollars and U.S. passports and run. "The others," to quote Columbia University Professor Andrew Nathan, "will come to terms with reality."[24]

Jeremy Chong is a Taiwanese businessman with whom I watched the results of the Taiwanese presidential elections on CNN in March 1996. "The only reason I do not support Taiwan's independence is because I am certain that Beijing would immediately attack us," he said as we sat in the lobby bar of the Taiwan Hotel in Beijing. The relaxed atmosphere offered a stark contrast to the hostile images of missile exercises that had aired regularly on television during the past weeks. The bar was full of Taiwanese and Beijing businessmen, chatting amiably, while their respective leaders were lambasting each other in public.

Jeremy Chong told me he would like to see Taiwan maintain its present status "for at least the next hundred years." He was born in 1950, shortly after his father, a Guomindang official, had fled to Taiwan. He repeatedly expressed the hope that younger Taiwanese will be realistic. "We cannot change our geographic location," he said with a pained smile.

He reminded me that Taiwan's economy depends entirely on foreign trade and relies heavily on imported oil. If Beijing were to sink even one ship in the Taiwan Straits, it would devastate the island's economy. "Beijing can have us on our knees without even a single mainland soldier setting foot on Taiwan," he said. "All they would have to do is to block our shipping routes."

Despite the agreement between Washington and Taipei regarding U.S. military aid to Taiwan in the event of a mainland attack, Jeremy Chong does not believe that the United States would be willing to sacrifice the lives of American soldiers to defend Taiwan. This projected weakness in the American position comes up regularly in discussions with mainland Chinese military strategists. They also tend to underestimate the military power of the United States. A report circulated in January 1998 by the Pentagon's Office of Net Assessment, which reviewed Chinese military literature, concluded: "China's leadership holds a number of dangerous misperceptions that may well cause serious political friction or even military conflict with the United States."[25]

Though the military technology the Taiwanese army has purchased from the United States and France is superior to that of the Chinese army, there is no doubt that the mainland could crush the Taiwanese with the sheer strength of its manpower, unless the Americans were to come to the defense of Taiwan. A senior officer in the Chinese air force, with whom I have had confidential discussions since the late 1980s, called my attention to General Zhang Wannian. Zhang was promoted by President Jiang Zemin to army chief-of-staff in 1992. Three years later, he became vice-chairman of China's Central Military Commission. He was a leading commander in the brief war between China and Vietnam in 1979, when Chinese casualties reached the tens of thousands. "That shows that China is willing to sacrifice its soldiers when it wants to, and here I quote Deng Xiaoping, 'teach a lesson,'" the air force officer reminded me in the spring of 1996.[26]

While Taiwanese businessman Jeremy Chong dares not vote for independence, he does not support reunification either. "I will never accept Taiwan joining together with the mainland under the same conditions as the Hongkongese. They had no choice, the British did the negotiating. Our democracy is much more advanced than that of Hong Kong under the British. Today, Taiwan and the mainland are already joined together through our economic relations. Why not build an economic federation? I am Taiwanese. In Beijing I am in a foreign country, just like an American when he visits Britain. Yes, my genes are from the mainland, but over time they have been transformed. Taiwan is a nation in itself. Best just to let things stay as they are."

But Beijing does not plan "just to let things stay as they are." From the mainland's view, there is no reason to postpone unification. Now that Hong Kong is a part of China, next is Taiwan's turn. Professor Andrew Nathan claims that much more than Chinese nationalism is at stake. Fundamental national security interests of China are involved, and both Taipei and Washington would be wise to take this into account. Beijing will never permit an island a hundred miles off its coast to engage in an independent foreign policy. A potential enemy—for example, Japan or the U.S.—could end up using Taiwan as a base to threaten China.

Nathan contends that China's offer of "one country, two systems" is sincere and "Beijing can be satisfied with something less than unification."[27] As long as Beijing will have the right to determine Taiwan's foreign policy, China will be flexible about what kind of a federation or union it builds with Taiwan. Party Secretary Jiang Zemin affirmed this position during the Fifteenth Party Congress in September 1997: "Under the prerequisite of one China, any issue can be discussed, and any comment and proposal, if it is helpful to the reunification of the motherland, can be put forward."

The air force officer with whom I keep in contact confesses to deep anxiety over Taiwan. He has, on several occasions, mentioned his fears of the immense damage a war with Taiwan would have on both China's economy and its international reputation. But, he has warned me, Chinese army commanders are becoming impatient. The generals know that the younger generation of Taiwanese does not look favorably upon reunification, and this trend will only become stronger over time. The generals feel that steps toward unification should be agreed upon before the next presidential elections in Taiwan, when pro-independence forces might win even more support.

The air force officer regards talk about the threat of Chinese expansionism as completely unfounded, though he does admit to the possibility of a Chinese military attack on Taiwan. In his opinion, "China poses no threat to anyone but those obstinate Taiwanese." The reason is simple enough: Chinese leaders have too many huge domestic problems on their hands. "If there is one country that really needs stability in Asia, it is China," he said. Nonetheless, after he had seen translations of the two articles in *Foreign Affairs* in spring 1997, he surprised me with the remark: "In a way I understand outsiders who claim that China is so critical of America, but, in reality, China just wants to be like the United States. Sometimes I myself doubt the sincerity of our leaders who vow that China will never use force outside its own territory. When our military capabilities are on par with those of our competitors—let's say in thirty to forty years' time—we might well become as bossy as the United States."

This is precisely what China's neighbors are afraid of. For this reason they regard the continued military presence of the United States in Asia as crucial—to counterbalance the rise of China. America is also needed to stabilize the tug-of-war between Japan and China, which will intensify as China's military strength grows. Even though Japan is an important trading partner and the number two investor in China after Hong Kong, resentment between the former enemies still simmers below the surface.

Japan has not yet come to terms with its past. Whereas Germany has repeatedly apologized for the horrors it committed during World War II, Japan seems to harbor the conviction that it was more a victim of the war, rather than a brutal aggressor. Japanese school children are not told of the atrocities of the Japanese army. Nor do official Japanese history texts make mention of events like the Nanjing massacre, when tens of thousands of Chinese, perhaps more than 300,000, were slaughtered mercilessly by the Japanese invaders during 1937–1938. Many groups in Japan, regardless of political persuasion, still do not approve of Prime Minister Morohiro Hosokawa's historic inauguration speech in August 1993 when he acknowledged that the Imperial Army of Japan, as the aggressor in World War II, had inflicted great suffering. In China and Korea alike, there have been sporadic anti-Japanese protests during the 1990s.

Though the majority of Chinese I know do not have personal memories of the war, many have told me that, in their hearts, they detest the Japanese. But, "it is necessary to tolerate them because China needs Japanese technology and money."

Another former enemy, the Soviet Union, does not evoke similar emotions in China. Though Beijingers look askance at the throngs of Russian tourists who have converged on the capital with their huge shopping bags since the early 1990s, the subject of Russia hardly ever comes up in everyday conversation. Naturally, the situation is different in northern China, where border trade has increased significantly during the open-door policy era.

Political relations have warmed considerably since 1992. In 1997, Beijing and Moscow agreed to reduce the number of troops along their border, and military cooperation has increased on many fronts. As a result, the Chinese have purchased Russian weapons, submarines, and aircraft. Chinese officers, like their predecessors in the 1950s, are once again being sent to train in Russian military academies. However, despite the declaration of a "strategic partnership," there are military experts in both capitals who maintain that over the long term Russian and Chinese hostility will reappear. Both the growing capabilities of the Chinese army and the large numbers of Chinese businessmen investing heavily in Siberia and Central Asia understandably provoke fears in Moscow: Is Russia doomed to be "eclipsed by China?"[28]

In previous decades, the Soviet "Big Brother" was known to regard its Chinese comrades a bit condescendingly. Thousands of older Chinese intellectuals, as well as many of China's present leaders, including President Jiang Zemin, have studied in Moscow. Now the roles are reversed. "Many Chinese feel a bit sorry for the Russians," political scientist Jia Qingguo said. "In our youth, the Soviet Union was the greatest and the mightiest; now their country is in a state of chaos. Their economy is in a bad way. No one wants China to follow down that road."

That is exactly what Chinese officials preach at every turn.

Police, on the lookout for any sign of political protest, were at first not quite sure how to react when this Beijinger appeared on Tiananmen Square with a large portrait of Deng Xiaoping on the day of Deng's memorial service (February 25, 1997). In the end, the policemen escorted the man off the Square. (Photo: John Lee)

十二

The Legacy of Deng Xiaoping

"The Government No Longer Meddles in People's Lives"

A book about my experiences in China during the past decade would be incomplete without Yang's story. In a country of 1.2 billion people, "typical" is an ill-advised term, but I feel safe in describing Yang as "not an average guy." Yang does not easily fit into any category. Despite his enormous success, he still has not found his place in society. He left China, but he returned. He is cosmopolitan, but deeply patriotic. Many people, Chinese and Western alike, think he has adopted a Western outlook on life, but he remains at heart a very traditional Chinese.

Nor is Yang's view of China without its contradictions. At some moments he despairs of the backwardness, the bureaucracy, and the corruption. But he is also immensely proud of the improvements which took place during his absence. Like many returnees, he is well-placed to contemplate his country's international standing and future development from a broader perspective than most of his countrymen. (Though a representative of the United States Embassy in Beijing believes that returnees are among the most critical of America.)

The majority of those who left to study in the West have chosen to remain abroad, but there has been a small flow back to China during the 1990s. These returnees have strong cultural ties to their homeland or they would not have come back. On the other hand, because of their long-term exposure to the outside world, they are more aware than most of China's need for thorough reform, as they put it. Or else they say, "The whole system has to be changed." They have tasted the freedom of the West, and they have seen for themselves how a society governed by the rule of law works in practice. But they are also impressed by the changes that occurred in their country while they were away, and are surprisingly optimistic about the future.

In 1987, I got to know three young men who, over the years, have become "my Chinese younger brothers"—Yang, engineer Song, and the father of my godchild, Xiao Ping. All three were penniless at the time, but over the course of the last decade each, in his own way, has done very well. Yang in particular represents a Chinese success story in the eyes of my friends and family in Finland. He had only about a hundred dollars to his name when he fled China in 1989. But he came up with a sound business idea, worked hard, and returned to China with a million yuan in his bank account.

It was not hard for me to envision the picture a friend conveyed when she phoned me in Beijing on her mobile phone from Finland in May 1994. "You'll never believe what just happened," she exclaimed excitedly. She was sitting on the terrace of one of Helsinki's most popular restaurants. "A taxi pulled up and out stepped this tall, slim Chinese who looked like he owned a Paris fashion boutique. He wore a peach-colored blazer with a matching scarf, and carried a slim leather briefcase that suited his outfit perfectly. He rushed into the restaurant with a mobile phone in one hand and a large bunch of roses in the other. I suddenly realized that man was Yang. He must be here on a visit from Tallinn, I thought, on his way to meet your parents. I saw them go inside just a moment ago. Who would have guessed that same young man first arrived in Finland with only a hundred bucks in his pocket?"

Undeniably Yang had traveled a long way from the time I first met him. I had been standing at the bus stop on the very day I arrived in Jinan (September 1, 1987), headed for the city center to have passport photos made for my work permit. I had declined my boss's offer of the university car or of a secretary's assistance, stubbornly insisting that I wanted to go into town on my own. At the bus stop, I reckoned that the distinctly urban-looking young man would not be startled if I asked him where I might find a photo studio. All the others waiting for the bus were peasants. Yang nodded when I explained what I was looking for, and he offered to accompany me to town. I was a bit surprised when he took me to a park. Only when I saw the photographer snapping shots of tourists, with Jinan's famous hot springs in the background, did I realize the misunderstanding. It was the first of many between us. But that's how our friendship began.

"You were the first foreigner I had ever met," Yang said, when we laughed together later at the quirks of fate.

Yang was no ordinary Jinanese back in 1987. I often point this out to Western friends who say that he must have changed a lot in my company. Of course, if I had not approached him at the bus stop that day, his life would not have taken all the turns it has. But he was already an exceptional individual then—the oddball of Jinan. Despite his six years abroad, Yang is less Western in his thinking than John Lee, for example, who feels quite at home in the Western enclaves of Beijing. When Yang meets Chinese outside his inner circle of friends, he behaves traditionally, adhering to the many complicated norms of "face," which other Chinese returning from the West have abandoned. Nor has Yang acquired the Western habit of discretion about discussing what things cost. "Doesn't this tie go well with my suit? It cost me 300 yuan!" he exclaimed loudly, laughing as always, when I complimented him on his outfit one evening in 1996. We were out with one of his childhood friends, a former cadre who is now a businessman in Spain. The man threw me a startled glance, raising his eyebrows in disapproval.

Yang was remarkably different from any other Chinese I knew. He used to pedal along the empty streets of Jinan in the evenings, singing *jingju*-verses or patriotic songs at the top of his lungs. He would write poems and send them to local newspapers to be published (many were). He would spontaneously strike up conversations with strangers. He often got his own way in the strangest situations simply because, in a society where conformity is a virtue, people were not used to his temperamental, unorthodox manner. He had a natural ability to win people over. In conservative Jinan he was conspicuous because of his slightly longer than normal hair. Even in those days he was very particular about his clothes, though he earned the same 100 yuan per month ($26) as everyone else. He worked as a lawyer, but hated his job. Though he had always dreamed of going to drama school, he had twice failed the entrance examinations. I still think a career as a theater director would have suited him perfectly.

When the subject of his stylistic originality comes up, Yang alludes to the strong influence of his mother. "My mother is just an ordinary factory worker. She never went to school, but she is a very tolerant and broad-minded person. She always encouraged me to use my own brains to think. She was just like her own mother."

Yang's parents both belonged to the Hui minority of the Islam faith. (His father died in 1996.) Neither Yang or his sister, *Jiejie*, know very much about their parents' religion, nor do they seem interested. "As a child I was teased because I'm a Hui, not a Han like all the other children on our street. But now it makes no difference at all," Yang said. Like other younger Hui people I know, he does not feel a common bond with the Muslims in Xinjiang. "I do not eat pork meat. That is the only thing that sets me apart from the Han. It's a habit I learned at home, and I have continued to abstain from pork out of respect for my parents."

My parents and I celebrated my father Max's seventieth birthday together with Yang's family in Beijing in 1993. The photos are of my mother, Marilyn, with Yang's father (above) and of Yang's sister (Jiejie) and her husband with my father (right). (Photos: the Jakobson family album)

Yang's background has virtually nothing in common with my own. Our cultural heritage, our religious heritage (I was born into a Jewish family), and our mother tongues are utterly different. I could not help thinking about this when our families spent a wonderful evening together in a Muslim restaurant in Beijing, celebrating my father's seventieth birthday. By chance, it was also the eve of the traditional autumn Moon Festival. Yang's entire family had come from Jinan to meet my parents. They had traveled eight hours by train, my parents eight hours by plane.

Of the many people I came to know in Jinan, not one approved of Yang. To this day, many of my close friends sometimes wonder out loud, "How do you put up with Yang's weird ideas?" Others are quite openly irritated by Yang. "Only a questionable person would give up his cadre's rights and look for a job on his own," engineer Song declared in 1987, when he heard that Yang had refused to take up the teaching job the state had assigned him in a small town, seventy miles from Jinan. In retrospect, Yang was merely one step ahead of the times. In the mid-1980s such independence was unheard of in Jinan, but ten years later it was typical (engineer Song in fact gave up his job in a state-run unit in 1993). Except for Yang, my friends in Jinan were all conventional citizens, solidly mainstream. No one wanted to be too different from the rest. Yang was lucky, as he has so often been, to find an employer who paid for his legal training for one and a half years. (Requirements for a law degree have increased during the reform policy period, to keep pace with the growing demands of the legal profession, but a lawyer's education is still not comparable to that in the West.)

From my point of view, Yang's individuality is his greatest asset. Yes, he tends to want to be the center of attention, and that kind of a friend is always a bit trying at times, but he is never dull company. My other friends in Jinan were not interested in Chinese culture, or, with the exception of Guo Hairong, in debating politics. Yang loves both. Every weekend he would take me to at least one theater performance or concert. When we went to see Shandong's own *luju*-theater or a *jingju*-performance, we were the only people under the age of sixty in the audience. Yang enjoyed himself as much as they did. Yang's sister, *Jiejie*, was a well-known pop singer in the province, her mother-in-law was a famous *jingju*-singer, and her husband played the traditional *piba*-lute in the Jinan music ensemble. I could not have had a better cultural guide than Yang.

In the beginning, our discussions about China were limited. Yang did not speak a word of English, and my Chinese language proficiency left much to be desired. But Yang was an excellent teacher. With no choice but to learn to express myself when we got into arguments, my vocabulary expanded by leaps and bounds. Our debates became more intense with every passing month, especially when we were joined by a British teacher, also working in Jinan. The Brit was much more impatient than I when he heard Yang discuss the situation in China. He used to tell Yang outright, "That sounds to me like propaganda of the Communist Party." In those days, Yang couldn't imagine—nor could 99 percent of China's population—any other political system in China than the monopoly rule of the Communist Party.

We had animated disagreements over terms like "freedom of speech," "press freedom," and "freedom of religion" because Yang insisted that all three of these liberties existed in China. "They are guaranteed in our constitution," he would argue. There was no doubt that we hurt Yang's strong patriotic feelings with our objections. Sometimes, when the two of us were alone, Yang would say, "It's insulting for a Chinese to hear a Brit say that our system of government is doomed to failure." (The British teacher, with whom I have since become a close friend, is a composed, thoughtful person. He never put forth his opinions in a disparaging way.)

I found Yang incredibly naive. He had no clear notion of what representative democracy entails. On the other hand, his ideas about how political reform should be carried out were daring, considering the situation in China in 1987. He was very critical about the unequal opportunities for Chinese young people pursuing careers. One's connections (*guanxi*) were far more important than one's talents or willingness to learn a trade.

Yang remembers that I used to try to calm him down by saying, "If you ever have a chance to visit me in Finland, you will see with your own eyes what we are talking about." In those days, a trip to Finland was a utopian dream. Yang's parents received a modest pension from the factory where they had worked. Yang's salary was not even enough to pay for a trip to Shanghai. Then, in the winter of 1988, Yang angered his superiors with his stubborn opinions about how to deal with certain problems in his work unit. When tensions rose to a boiling point, he was left with no choice but to resign. My memories of Yang during my last months in Jinan are of a restless soul: He had still not found his own place in Chinese society.

Before I left China in the spring of 1988, a new housing reform was launched. As a result, Yang's family was able to sell the house his grandmother had once owned. Yang's parents gave him the equivalent of a thousand dollars to "start a home," a small fortune in those days. When I heard about the gift, I invited him to spend a month in Finland. I could think of no better way to thank him and his family for all they had done for me when I lived in Jinan. Yang used the thousand dollars to buy a train ticket to Finland. To this day, he has yet to "start a home."

Upon arriving in Finland, Yang had the shock of his life. I will never forget the evening he spent in the garden at my parent's summer house five days into his visit. He said he wanted to write a letter home. We had first spent a few days together in Helsinki, then had driven to western Finland for a chamber music festival. For a devoted fan of classical music, Isaac Stern's concert in an old stone church was an unforgettable experience, as was meeting the maestro himself after the concert. On the surface, everything seemed fine. Yang had charmed my parents and other family members with his warm-hearted disposition. Yang appeared to be taking all the new experiences in his stride.

When it grew dark and Yang had still not come in, I went out to the garden. He was sitting by the picnic table, pen in hand, with his gaze fixed in the direction of the sea. Only after I sat beside him did I notice the tears flowing down his cheeks, dripping on the blank paper in front of him. "There is not a single Chinese who can even imagine a paradise country like this," he sobbed. "Not even Deng Xiaoping lives in conditions like these. Now I know how horribly backward my country is." We sat together in the garden into the wee hours of the morning, while Yang tried to sort out the chaotic state of his soul. "You always told me I could not fathom how different things are in the West," he said shaking his head as we finally headed back into the house.

After he recovered from his initial culture shock, Yang began to enjoy himself. He visibly reveled in "the freedom of choice," as he called his escapades around Helsinki. We have often since laughed about the events of that summer. Some of my girlfriends rebuked me for being such an irresponsible "big sister," because I encouraged Yang to explore the many facets of Western life to his heart's content. They often reminded me of the numerous dangers that an unknowing Chinese might encounter.

"Have you warned Yang about drunkards?" and "Have you told him not to accept a ride from strangers?" were common questions whenever Yang did not show up at precisely the prearranged time. Yang spent quite a lot of time on his own because I often worked the evening shift at the newspaper where I was employeded in those days. Yang was curious about everything, and was, by Western standards, a very childish twenty-five-year old, with an unwavering belief in the goodness of other people. But he coped admirably with all the newness, despite knowing only a few words of English. Members of the Pentecostal Church persuaded him to attend their prayers; he saw his first pornographic movie; he made friends with other foreigners in one of the popular bars downtown; he went flying with the husband of my colleague, astounded that one could have a private pilot's license. At that time, neither of us knew a single Chinese who owned a private car.

Returning to Jinan, Yang decided to study English in earnest and apply to study at Helsinki University. His hazy goal was someday to promote cultural exchanges between China and the West. Then the Tiananmen demonstrations in Beijing began. Along with millions of other young Chinese, Yang was swept up in the events. He spent May (1989) in the capital, debating China's future, day and night, with friends, acquaintances, and even strangers. At no point did Yang question the primacy of the Communist Party. Instead, like the majority of the movement's supporters, he believed the Party could be nudged, or pushed, to reform itself. Yang sparkled with optimism. He was furious when I voiced concern that the movement might be heading for a dreadful backlash. I never envisioned that the People's Army would open fire indiscriminately on civilians. But, after the students prevented Mikhail Gorbachev's official welcoming ceremonies from being held at Tiananmen Square on May 15, I worried that the Chinese government would avenge this immeasurable loss of face. I predicted a harsh crackdown in the form of a ferocious political campaign.

After martial law was declared on May 20, I became anxious about Yang's personal safety. As Marja Sarvimäki and I bicycled home from Tiananmen Square one afternoon, we saw Yang addressing a crowd at a street corner on the Boulevard of Eternal Peace. He was spelling out the basic rights of all citizens, as ensured by the Chinese Constitution. Yang loves to perform. He made a great speech.

On the night of the massacre, I naturally worried about my friends. I was immensely relieved that Yang was in Jinan. He had returned a few days earlier, dispirited that the democracy movement had stalled, nearly to a standstill. Of all the people I knew, he was the most passionate and fervent. I was certain that had he been in Beijing on June 4, he would have been among the daring civilians who tried to stop the onslaught of the tanks with their bare fists.

When news of the massacre reached Yang in Jinan, he and a few friends decided to organize a protest march. Similar demonstrations were held in dozens of cities throughout the country. Though the marchers numbered no more than a few thousand people, it was an extremely bold action in view of the tense political atmosphere. Four days later, Deng Xiaoping appeared on television, thanking the soldiers of the People's Liberation Army for quelling a "counter-revolutionary rebellion." When Deng said that a small minority of bad people had led the young students and their supporters astray, I knew that Yang was in danger. This expression, "a small minority of bad people," had been used before in the People's Republic, when the authorities needed scapegoats. Yang was no longer a student—much worse, he was unemployed. In the end, the government did not punish students for their involvement in the democracy movement as severely as workers. After my father called from Finland with word that the *International Herald Tribune* had reported that forty-five persons in Jinan had been imprisoned or sentenced to death, we all feared the worst.[1]

In the end, Yang was lucky once again. Because of his holiday visit to Finland the previous summer, he had a passport, unlike most Chinese, even today. He had already applied to study at Helsinki University and been informed that he had to take the entrance examination. He promptly obtained a Finnish visa, thanks to my parents, who had immediately sent off a letter of invitation.

After I explained the situation to an understanding professor at Helsinki University, Yang was accepted as a student, though he could not possibly have answered all the questions on the entrance examination. (His knowledge of English was still quite elementary.) Yang never fails to mention this professor when he reflects on his life: "It was a tremendous humanitarian gesture."

Yang's second trip to Finland signaled the beginning of a new life. An entire book could be written about all the mishaps, some of them hilarious, others less humorous, of his first few months when he stayed with my parents. "I had a much easier time adapting to a strange society than other Chinese, because your family took me under their wing," Yang often reminds me. "I know they were sometimes bewildered by my actions. Don't forget. I could hardly speak English, and you were in Beijing."

Word of any major problems never (thank goodness) reached me. The incident I heard about was my mother Marilyn's argument with Yang when he refused to wear a cap in sub-zero temperatures. Yang was too vain to accept any of the hats or caps Marilyn had offered him. I tried to persuade him, long-distance from Beijing, at Marilyn's prodding, but to no avail. Another thing that annoyed Marilyn, and others in Finland, was Yang's habit of bursting into laughter at the most inappropriate time. Over the years, scores of Westerners have asked me about this Chinese tendency. A Chinese does not necessarily laugh, or giggle, only to express delight or amusement, but also when he or she is embarrassed or at a loss for words.

My family, in turn, learned something of Chinese customs from Yang. It took them awhile to understand that a Chinese does not, as a rule, reply, "Yes, thank you, I'll have some more," at the dinner table when the hostess serves second helpings, even if the Chinese guest is still ravenous. One has to repeat the offer, three or even four times, before a Chinese feels it appropriate to accept. The expression, "Now is this a Chinese 'no' or a real 'no'?" became part of my family's vocabulary.

The reality of everyday life set in once Yang moved to a student dormitory. His first two years in Finland were mentally grueling. He studied English at Helsinki University and in courses arranged by the British Council, and worked as a cleaner at a hospital. He felt rootless and worried about his future. Besides being homesick, he was depressed by the manual labor he was obliged to do. "A Western student cleans or works at a gas station during summer vacations, and it is the most natural thing in the world. But for a Chinese intellectual, it is an utter disgrace. Every day I boarded the bus to go to the hospital and thought, if only I could just sit here forever and ever, and never get off," Yang later told me.

At the dormitory, Yang became friends with a young Estonian named Kale, who was finishing his medical degree in Helsinki. Together they decided to start a bed-and-breakfast service in Tallinn, Estonia. Yang had thought up this idea on holiday in Hungary, where he was impressed with how well the family home-stay system worked. Estonia was just opening up at that time, and there was an acute shortage of inexpensive or even mid-range hotel rooms in Tallinn.

Yang had saved $6,500 after two and a half years of cleaning at the hospital, an impressive feat considering that he sent his family $500 through me at least three times during that period. Nor did he live as frugally as so many other Chinese who hardly ever venture out of their dormitories. He bought cheap air tickets and took off on holidays to Budapest, London, Varna, and Istanbul. (Later he also visited the United States twice.) An elderly relative of mine recalled that Yang bought her a bunch of flowers from his first salary—a gesture typical of Yang. Since the rise in his own living standards, he has equipped the homes of his parents, his sister, and his brother with luxury goods and every imaginable electrical appliance. On his first visit back to Jinan, he also installed a phone, for $300, in the apartment of his favorite middle-school teacher. "Her husband had recently passed away. She seemed so lonely," Yang explained.

The popularity of his bed-and-breakfast in Tallinn surpassed all expectations during its first summer (1992). Emboldened, Yang concentrated on starting a Chinese restaurant. In true Chinese style, he enlisted the help of his sister and brother in Jinan. They bought him all the necessary utensils and bric-a-brac and tracked down two well-trained Shandongese cooks. Restaurant Aishaniya (meaning "Estonia" in Chinese) opened with great fanfare in 1993. It soon became Tallinn's most popular dining place for Estonia's nouveau riche and growing middle class. Yang, one of a handful of Chinese residing in Tallinn, became an overnight celebrity. He was regularly invited to appear on television talk shows and entertainment programs.

This tall Chinese, with his long bushy hair, impressed the Estonians, not only because of his authentic restaurant (no kitsch!) and tasty food, but also because of his various charity projects. One Christmas, he held an open house for the blind and the deaf. The next Christmas, he arranged a party for residents of an old-age home and solicited the prime minister of Estonia to hand out Christmas presents. After an Estonian ship disaster, he donated 20,000 Estonian crowns (about $5,000) to the victims' families. But success was not without its problems. He began to receive threats from envious competitors and had to hire a guard for his apartment. And he felt terribly lonely.

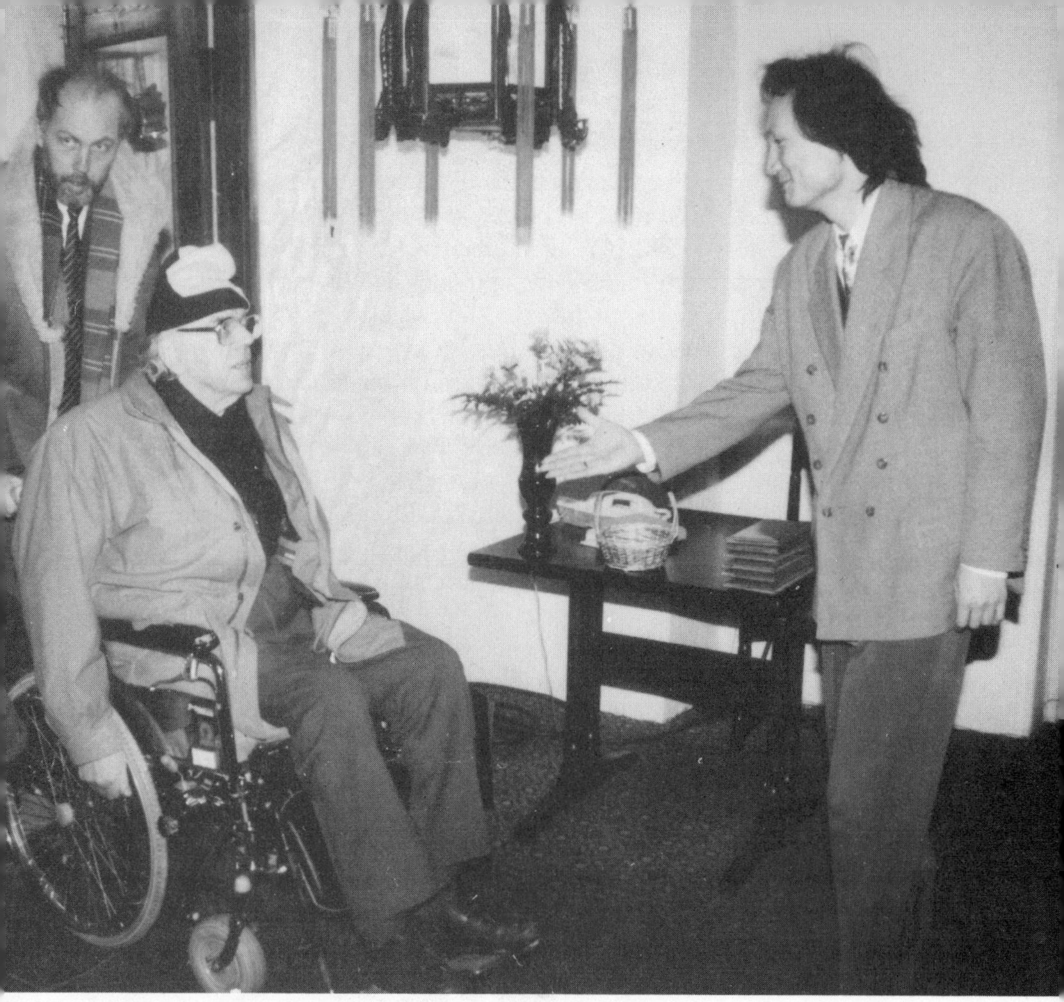

Yang welcoming Estonian author Enn Soosar to a Christmas party at his restaurant in 1994. (Photo: Yang's album)

After his third summer in Estonia, Yang started to talk about moving back to China. "I knew from the beginning I wouldn't remain in Tallinn for the rest of my life," he said. "It's just too small a place. Two years as a restaurant owner was enough. I was beginning to tire of the increasing problems with the Estonian authorities to obtain work permits for my Chinese employees. I've fulfilled my dream. I could have gone on earning more and more money, but it would have no longer been a challenge. I'm really not a businessman at heart."

By the early 1990s, the Chinese leadership, wanting to distance itself from the political fallout, had ceased its persecution of those involved in the 1989 events, thus removing any political obstacles for Yang's return.

"I know I can live a comfortable life in China for quite some time with my savings," he said. "I need to contemplate my next move."

The country to which Yang returned in May 1995 was not the one he had left in 1989. "We joke among friends that 'if you don't look for the authorities (*i.e.*, cause trouble), they don't look for you.' The government no longer meddles in people's lives," Yang mused, after living for two years in Beijing. "In big cities, an educated person can arrange his life as he wishes. If one is diligent and capable, one can do well. There are far more opportunities than ten years ago. One can rent an apartment on the free market. One can earn a living doing freelance work. This is the kind of freedom I dreamed about in the 1980s. It's certainly the biggest change that has occurred, besides the fact that so many people enjoy higher standards of living than before. I'm not even considered rich in China, just well-off."

But despite the positive changes he saw, Yang was aghast at the money-grabbing mentality that seemed to prevail wherever he turned. All my Chinese friends complain about this. "No one thinks about anything other than money anymore, " Yang said. "It has had a terrible effect on people's relations. I can no longer trust anybody except my family members and a few close friends. Ten years ago, I still felt that friends were sincerely willing to help one another. Now everyone thinks only of how to benefit from the relationship. It's dreadful."

Yang is also critical of the pressure on school children. "Families have become nearly neurotic about their only child's education. Parents are willing to invest all their savings and use all their spare time to ensure that their child goes to a good school. The whole family adapts to awkward and inconvenient arrangements, just so the pampered child can study in peace. Children have become unbearably self-centered. The Cultural Revolution is always referred to negatively, but at least teenagers learned to be independent in those days. That's the way it should be."

Though ability and a willingness to work figures more prominently than ever before in determining an individual's advancement, Yang experienced firsthand the continuing importance of *guanxi*. He had an idea to produce a television series about the everyday life of well-known Europeans, and he signed a contract with a company under the jurisdiction of China Central Television. For six months, he put all of his amazing energy into negotiating sponsor contracts and arranging interviews (Czech President Vaclav Havel and a dozen other prominent Europeans consented). But the project stalled when the film crew applied for passports. The television company Yang had signed with lacked connections with the right officials in the Department of Propaganda, whose signatures were needed on the passport applications.

"Yang has been away from China so long that he has forgotten how bureaucratic and arduous it is to realize even the most viable of new ideas," a mutual acquaintance commented. Yang himself said he failed because the amount promised by the sponsors was not large enough to allow for the television company's bosses to profit personally from the project. That's why they did not pursue the passports vigorously enough.

Though Yang was momentarily disheartened by the setback, he was soon churning out new ideas. "At least ability and initiative are just as important as *guanxi*. Before, you were totally helpless without connections," he said. He has not regretted returning to China, though he still has not found a suitable goal. To keep active, he writes articles as a freelancer for various publications. And, like millions of other Chinese, he has taken to studying the stock exchange. In the beginning of 1997, an estimated 25 million people speculated on China's two stock exchanges, double the number of investors only six months earlier.

"The stock exchange and the future of China have many traits in common," Yang said, relating a joke he had heard in May 1997. "It's impossible to predict either." When I asked his view of China's future, he turned serious and spoke optimistically. "Now that we are going in the right direction, the system will gradually change. I am not in a position to predict how it will happen, and I am not minimizing the enormous problems, starting with the gravest one of all, unemployment. But I feel confident we are moving forward all the time. So many things have improved since the days when you lived in Jinan."

Yang was amused when I responded that the picture he paints of China's future resembles the one I have of his own situation. Both China and Yang are at a crossroads. The next few years will be decisive. Circumstances are far more favorable now than they were ten years ago. Yang will succeed, of that I feel sure. I am not so certain about China.

When contemplating the future, many Chinese like to quote a saying from the Han dynasty, which implies that when your back is up against the wall you must succeed. "The Party has no other choice but to make sure the economy continues to prosper," they maintain. The Communist leadership is well aware that their popular legitimacy depends on their ability to guarantee a steady rise in living standards. People like Yang, who have already soared to the ranks of the well-to-do, or others who feel confident that goal is plausible, are understandably optimistic. They have every reason to anticipate a bright future.

When I interviewed China scholar Tony Saich in 1996, he said, "I am pretty sure the Chinese leaders themselves feel they've done a good job during the past eighteen years. In spite of the long list of flaws described by the Western press, the degree of personal freedom today is really inconceivable compared to what it was when I studied here in the 1970s. The loosening of social control has concretely affected the lives of over a billion people." Saich was working as the China representative for the Ford Foundation, overseeing numerous development and educational projects funded by the foundation.

"But this tremendous social transformation is difficult to keep under control. The present government is a reactive one," Saich continued. "It does not have its own agenda, so it is also very unpredictable. How the Party will be able to adapt to the increasingly diverse demands of the population is an open question. I do not think it is too late to evoke genuine enthusiasm for the Party, but it cannot be done by clinging to the past. If the Party wants long-term legitimacy, it needs to build a partnership with the new society which is evolving."

At the Fifteenth Party Congress in September 1997, the first without Deng Xiaoping since the beginning of reform, Party Secretary Jiang Zemin proclaimed the reform of state-run industry a top priority. This promise had been made before, but the fear of laying off too many workers always stalled implementation. Western analysts reckon that about one-third of all state enterprises should be allowed to go bankrupt. To keep unemployment in check, these factories are maintained through a continuous stream of subsidies, estimated to gobble up nearly 35 percent of the state budget. The debts of these money-losing units burden the entire economy.[2]

Though most Chinese economists or businessmen I have interviewed are skeptical about the leadership's ability truly to reform state industry, they do not see the situation as catastrophic. "We can no longer stop the market forces," said Liu, an old acquaintance, as we debated the miserable condition of state-run factories one evening in 1997. When I had first met Liu in 1987, he was working as a journalist. On the side, he was pursuing a career as a pop-singer. Now he is part of the top management at one of China's largest enterprises specializing in securities.

"The more the private sector grows, the easier it will be for it to absorb some of the debt-ridden state factories and to make them profitable," Liu predicted. He cited the latest statistics showing the increasing importance of the nonstate sector: Privately owned and collectively owned enterprises accounted for 57 percent of national industrial output. According to Liu, the state factories will have no choice but to change their management and employment structures, though it will mean firing large numbers of people. In Guangdong province, such measures have already been introduced.

"The process will have to inch forward slowly, so that the rate of unemployment does not get out of hand. Of course there will be setbacks. But we are moving in the right direction. The significance of the stock exchange is bound to grow. As a result, the government will have to loosen its control over the media because a functioning stock exchange requires reliable information." Liu paused a moment, then continued with a smirk. "Maybe I'll return to journalism. The post of economics editor will be one of the most challenging jobs around."

China's future looks completely different to those urbanites who still must struggle for basic subsistence, or to those who might be scraping by economically, but are increasingly incensed by the scale of social upheaval. Besides rampant corruption, they complain about the rise in crime, widespread prostitution, and the growing income gap—all consequences, they claim, of Deng Xiaoping's reform policies. A common complaint is that the rich are getting richer and the poor, poorer, though statistics do not bear this out. Nearly everyone has benefited economically from Deng's policies, though certain sectors of the population much more so than others. Ironically, because of Deng's policies, people are far more demanding than they were twenty years ago. The economic achievements of the Deng era are now taken for granted, and more and more people are focusing on the failings of his reforms.

Middle-aged and older salary-earners often exclaim, in reference to Mao's time when ideology was paramount: "There is no return to the old days. That's for sure." "Everyone knows so much more about the outside world nowadays," they say. But they predict that ordinary people will have to get used to life becoming more and more unjust. "We have no money to bribe anyone. All the people in power are corrupt." Many mention the sense of insecurity Deng's reforms have brought. They have two fears: Will their savings and their children's income be sufficient to see them through their old age? Might they be robbed in the dark of night or perhaps even in broad daylight? This latter worry is a relatively new phenomenon. For a city of over ten million inhabitants, Beijing is extremely safe compared to any Western metropolis. Of course one has to remember the point of reference for Beijingers: Fifteen years ago, my neighbors kept their front doors wide open on hot summer nights.

My own attitudes toward China have also changed over the years. It was easy to relate to Tony Saich's response when I asked whether he was optimistic or pessimistic about the future: "It depends which day you ask me." In the course of a single day, one's feelings can be tugged this way and that by China's countless contradictions. Sometimes situations fluctuate with mind-boggling intensity.

On one such day in August 1996, I was awakened before six in the morning by an acquaintance who phoned to say that residents of three blocks on the west side of Beijing were organizing a protest. Informed that their houses were about to be torn down, they claimed the eviction was illegal. They were in the process of taking to court both the local officials responsible for the eviction order and the building company that planned to construct a commercial shopping center in the place of their homes.

As I hopped on my bicycle, my annoyance at being yanked from bed at such an uncivilized hour disappeared. The sun had just risen. A group of elderly ladies and two or three sprightly grandfathers were practicing *taiji* in the tiny yard outside our building. I pedaled west, enjoying the beautiful August morning. Peasants were putting up their vegetable and fruit stalls; noodle shop employees were rolling out their dough; pie sellers were lighting their makeshift stoves. A few Beijingers were already impatiently awaiting their breakfast.

When I reached my destination, I sought out the lawyer employed by the residents to handle their case. A woman in her early fifties, in grey slacks and a white blouse, she appeared no different from the others crowded around me. But she had the air of a determined professional as she explained the details of the conflict. The police had been pressured (and, according to the residents, bribed) by the building company to evict the residents of the one-story buildings that very morning, by force if need be. The bulldozers were in position, ready to raze their dwellings. The most stubborn residents had chained themselves to the front doors of their homes. A group of retirees had even spread a red banner with the characters "Illegal Eviction!" over the nearby main street. It seemed that people of all ages and occupations had joined together. When two dozen policemen arrived and realized the extent of the opposition, they dispersed, followed by shouts of "Good for you!"

No one doubted that the residents would eventually have to move. But they wanted to be reimbursed properly for their inconvenience, and they demanded that the formalities be handled "in accordance with the law." Half the residents were factory workers employed by the state. The others were private shopkeepers or small-time businessmen. I marveled at the way they expressed themselves: "The law gives us the right. . . . " China is indeed changing, I thought. At least in the large cities, even rank-and-file citizens are increasingly aware of their rights.

That afternoon, I interviewed a thirty-seven-year-old woman named "Hopeful Cloud." She told me about the emerging world of antique and art auctions. Some of my artist friends had enthusiastically described these auctions, predicting that in coming years artists would no longer be as dependent on foreign galleries as they are now. Rich Chinese have begun to purchase art.

"Hopeful Cloud" had worked as a staff reporter for one of Beijing's most popular newspapers. She was fired after taking part in the journalists' demonstrations for a free press during the Tiananmen movement in 1989. "One day I will once again join the ranks of the daring, but now is not the right time. I prefer to concentrate on my own life and, at the same time, promote Chinese culture," she said. She is a gorgeous woman; charming, intelligent, open-minded.

My good spirits did not last long. After the interview I got into a taxi driven by a twenty-five-year old, who moaned about her difficulties learning English at night school. When she told me why it was imperative she learn English, I asked more about her life. She and her mother were about to depart for Australia to join her father, who had emigrated two years earlier, with financial help from his Taiwanese brother. The woman's father had spent thirteen years in prison in the 1950s and the 1960s as a result of various paranoid political campaigns, all on account of this Taiwanese uncle. In 1982, her father had been sent off for "re-education through labor" for an additional five years as punishment for a controversial article he had written.

"My mother is a very traditional woman. She wouldn't leave my father's mother alone in Beijing when my uncle succeeded in arranging for my father to go," the taxi driver explained. "A woman must care for her mother-in-law, no matter what the circumstances, my mother always says. You see, my grandmother only had two children, my father and my Taiwanese uncle. But now we can leave because my grandmother just died last spring." Finally she hissed: "And I will never return to this country."

"Never?" I asked. "You're only twenty-five. A lot can happen in your lifetime."

"Never," she answered. "China has no hope. Tens of thousands of people spend their lives in labor camps just for expressing their opinion in public at the wrong time."

In the evening, a friend from my student days phoned and asked me to call a number in Hangzhou, the capital of Zhejiang province. Chen Longde's sister answered. I had heard that thirty-nine-year-old Chen Longde had recently been sentenced to a three-year term of "re-education through labor" because he had appealed to the Chinese government to free all political prisoners. Chen's sister said her brother was in the hospital, with serious spine and knee injuries. "Prison guards tortured my brother with electric batons because he refused to write a self-criticism. When the pain became unbearable he charged past them and tried to flee by jumping out of a third-story window. The authorities claim he wanted to commit suicide, but my brother asked me to contact foreign reporters to tell them the truth."

A news report on the BBC World Service later that night described Chen's tragic fate. None of my Chinese acquaintances has ever heard of Chen Longde. When I mention these courageous souls, who obstinately defy the government against all odds, my friends answer laconically: "It's no use. A person is at the mercy of the authorities."

After 1989 a frequent refrain was, "I am no longer interested in politics." This signified the widespread skepticism that anyone could have a say about how the system needed to be changed. But by 1993, I noticed that Beijingers were once again ardently discussing current events. Whenever I visit the homes of close friends, I hear the latest political jokes or debates about recent directives. Like the residents who opposed their eviction bear witness, some people now do try to influence matters concerning their own lives. Theirs is but one of many examples of growing civil action.

In recent years, Western scholars have debated whether the signs of an emerging civil society signal the possibility of democracy taking root in China. Today, there are hundreds of grassroots organizations representing a wide variety of special interest groups. Many of them—in order to obtain official approval—are registered as research institutes or business associations. Some are unquestionably effective in defending the concerns of ordinary people at the local levels. The extensive legal reforms have been profound, especially considering the paltry state of China's legal system after the Cultural Revolution. But I doubt whether "the legal system will continue to grow as an institutional rival" to the Communist Party, as political scientist Pei Minxin of Princeton University asserts.[3] For his prediction to materialize, both the courts and the legislative bodies (the National People's Congress and its provincial and local counterparts) would have to be independent of Party control. The Communist leadership will not voluntarily abdicate this crucial power.

Those who see the growing private sector as a way for large numbers of citizens to develop a political agenda independent of the state overlook the nature of doing business in China. Private enterpreneurs find it as necessary to cultivate good connections within the bureaucracy as state-run enterprise directors.[4] Though they operate privately, they are still dependent on local officials, as Little Dictator Lin so explicitly spelled out.

Chinese dissident writer-in-exile Liu Binyan maintains that it is not the conservatives or the Maoists who are the main opponents of reform, but parts of the bureaucratic class, the ones who have benefited the most from the last two decades of reform. He contends that "they will fight to the death any further reform measures which will infringe upon their own interests."[5] I agree. In everyday urban life, it is the middle-level bureaucracy that obstructs genuine change. A credible rule of law would certainly cut into the privileges of these bureaucrats.

Besides the monumental task of restructuring the legal system in order to curb corruption and arbitrary abuses of power, the Chinese leaders face another equally important challenge to solidify their legitimacy: What to do about the crisis of faith?

"I no longer believe in anything," has become a standard colloquial expression in the 1990s, depicting the ideological vacuum left behind by an obsolete Marxism. Among the Chinese I know, Party Secretary Jiang Zemin's calls to promote "spiritual civilization" ring hollow. Over and over again I have been told, "I only believe in money."

Reading about the nostalgia for the Mao period before the 1993 centennial anniversary of Mao's birth, I came across the words of a Russian writer referring to a similar sort of Stalin-nostalgia: "The young neither fight against communism, argue against it, nor curse it; something much worse has happened to communism: they laugh at it."[6] So they do in China as well. At least in the cities, people poke fun at the Party and its attempts to justify its actions with ideology.

Jiang Zemin has not, despite numerous attempts, been able to define clearly what he means when he stresses *guoqing*, which can be roughly translated as "Chineseness." This catch-all term has been used to mean anything from Marxist or patriotic rhetoric to the importance of good manners. Only the appeals to patriotism have had any effect.

As the 1990s have progressed, discontent and, above all, cynicism, have percolated more openly in public discourse. Ten years ago the "searching for roots" movement swept through literary circles of urban China. The havoc of the previous Cultural Revolution decade prompted younger artists in particular to look for the source of their own cultural origins.

Today many writers, such as Liang Xiaosheng and Han Shaogong, both former "sent-down youth" in their forties, ask whether one must accept the evil in society for the sake of modernity. They charge that the worship of money has reached bizarre, morbid proportions. They challenge Party leaders who claim that the mistakes and negative byproducts of reforms are unavoidable while "crossing the river by feeling for the stones."* Millions of ordinary citizens are being raped by the reforms, Liang Xiaosheng insists.

Not only do the former rusticated youth, now middle-aged, mourn the lack of spiritual orientation and ridicule the Communist Party's pursuit of wealth. Among older intellectuals, like scientist Bao, I have heard embittered outpourings as they reminisce about the lost idealism of the 1940s and 1950s. Bao calls the present regime "even more spineless and corrupt than the Guomindang." To him and like-minded patriotic Chinese, regardless of political orientation, the May Fourth Movement of 1919 is still a source of inspiration. It was the first to "articulate, combine, and propagate the twin goals of science and democracy."[7]

Younger friends, born in the early 1970s, know China only as a country pursuing the open-door and reform policy. They vent their disillusion in their own way: "Nothing to my name," the signature song of China's best-known rock star, Cui Jian, has become a classic. "Why can't you stop criticizing me, why can't I stop loving you, please don't tell me that I'm destined to have nothing at all . . . ," Cui Jian hollers in his raspy voice.

One of the most popular and controversial cynics is the author Wang Shuo, whose twenty-odd novels depict the "hooligan" (*liumang*) culture of smooth-talking loafers, schemers, womanizers, small-time criminals, and ordinary alienated urban youth. Unlike their elder brothers and sisters, former Red Guards once driven by ideological mission, they reject any talk of ideals. Hypocrisy and cheekiness are Wang Shuo's hallmarks. His heroes want to enjoy life. Sex and easy money are foremost on their minds. But though they live on the edge of lawlessness, they are not driven by evil; Wang Shuo's antihero will give up his seat on the bus to a mother and child. Wang Shuo has tens of millions of avid fans who relish his coarse language and his masterful use of revolutionary slogans to depict the absurdities around him. In one of his books, a prostitute defends her profession by claiming that she is merely "serving the masses."

Wang Shuo is as critical of the intellectuals as he is of the authorities. "I hate people with a sense of mission," is one of his famous quotes. "How

* This is a widely used quotation reportedly by Deng Xiaoping, who is said to have encouraged experimentation in order to achieve economic growth.

can I write moral novels?" he quipped in an interview in 1996. "I didn't find heroic people around me. . . . How can I write beautiful things? I have no reference point. I want to write about reality."[8]

There are also those who believe in the salvation of China through chaos, including my writer friend Bei Ye. Many of his thoughts about the moral decay of society echo the trends in the "hooligan culture," but he backs up his views with theory. "Chinese civilization is doomed, so there's no point in pursuing high-brow culture of artistic quality because we are moving toward a Big Bang," he said in December 1996. He had just turned forty. "I have stopped writing seriously. I produce trashy novels and scripts for commercial television. They pay well. You have to know how to spend your last living days. Better to enjoy them. When people no longer have a faith, they become awful animals. That is what is happening in China."

Politically, neo-conservatism has dominated the 1990s. Scores of the bureaucrats, economists, and scholars who had been considered "reformists" in the 1980s have now concluded that the reform policy has gone too far and too fast. The idealism of the democracy movement of 1989 has been replaced with a "concoction of nationalism and authoritarianism with strong moralistic overtones."[9] These neo-conservatives condemn materialism and individualism as Western imports. They favor a strong, paternal form of governance, a more moderate pace of economic growth, and harsh measures to curb crime and corruption. Their return to "old-fashioned morals" is an eclectic mixture of the selflessness advocated by Mao and traditional Confucianist values.

In 1993, the neo-conservative book, *Viewing China Through A Third Eye*, created a minor sensation in political circles. It is a wide-ranging polemic about the negative social, political, and economic consequences of Deng Xiaoping's reforms. The forty-two-year-old author, Wang Shan, initially disguised as a "European sinologist," claims that China is caught in a trap of economic growth. He regards the 800 million peasants freed from the land by Deng's policies as "a great active volcano," an enormous hidden threat to the stability of the country.[10] After his stark, and occasionally compelling, portrayal of the contradictions spawned by the reform policy, Wang Shan concludes that China needs a strong leader. He favors moving "the realization of democratic politics" into the "fairly distant future." It was evidently because of this that Party Secretary Jiang Zemin first praised the book. He later had second thoughts, especially following the stir the book caused and after it became known that the author was Wang Shan, not a European. Subsequently, the book was banned.

Despite the obvious political restrictions, the widening range of public discussion in both cultural and political spheres is an encouraging sign. Since 1979, the very basis of Chinese society has been churned up, like the seabed during a torrential storm. The psychological and emotional turmoil, the soul-searching, are natural consequences. Cautious manifestations of free thought in official journals—for example, by Ji Hongzhen, who questions the rationale of only one "ism" and advocates diversification—are all indications that China is edging toward a more open and tolerant society.[11]

For the last hundred years, Chinese intellectuals have grappled with the question of how to modernize the country and, at the same time, maintain the special characteristics of their rich cultural heritage. A solution acceptable to one and all will probably never be found. Today China is undoubtedly in a state of confusion, but the current chaotic conditions do not necessarily portend anarchy. Disorder is natural in a society changing at a breakneck speed. Deng's revolution was preceded by centuries of isolation, then decades of colonialism, numerous wars, and, most recently, thirty years of experimentation with socialist central planning. The Chinese ability to adapt and persevere is now being tested as never before.

Will China stay the course to peaceful modernization? No profession has a worse record than China-watchers who try to predict the future. Even the revered historian John K. Fairbank wrote in 1967 that "the private automobile age, just dawning in Russia, will never reach China."[12] But it did. And Fairbank was still alive to witness it. A safer course would be to follow the parlance of a weatherman: "Mostly clear and sunny, with possible rain and thunderstorms." But because I am annoyed at long-time China residents who analyze the country's problems at length without stating their own opinions, I will take the plunge; though the odds are that my forecast will only be as accurate as those of Professor Fairbank about automobiles.

China will remain stable, provided the explosive Taiwan issue is not exacerbated by any of the parties involved. In practice, that means everyone accepting the status quo. I am pessimistic about Taiwan because I believe there is a real danger that the Beijing leadership will not continue to accept the current situation for too many more years. The United States has its own pivotal role to play in this process. Taiwan could well trip up the Chinese Communist Party.

If Taiwan does not derail China, I envision the country muddling through, for better or for worse, from one crisis to another. But the spectacular economic growth of recent years cannot continue. The country's

With the increase in the number of private cars, traffic jams have become commonplace in all the big cities in China. New roads, new bridges, and new pedestrian flyovers are constantly being built, but more are still needed. Photo from the center of Nanning in southern China in 1996. (Photo: John Lee)

infrastructure is simply too weak. A good example is the new Beijing Airport presently under construction. On the day that it begins operation (estimated to be sometime in 1999), it will already be too small to accommodate the number of passengers traveling through it (at least 15 million annually). China needs more roads, more power stations, more railway lines, more harbor containers, and more cranes—more of all basic services—than it can possibly produce to keep up with the demands of the present economic growth. Between 30 to 40 percent of the vegetables produced in China rot and end up in garbage dumps because of inadequate storage and distribution facilities.[13]

China cannot hope to attract the necessary foreign capital for even its most pressing infrastructure projects. Foreign investment—an impressive $361 billion during 1993–1996—is declining, partly as a result of the 1997 financial crisis elsewhere in Asia. Another reason is the increasing frustration and, in some cases, outright departure of foreigners in joint-venture operations. Expected profits are not materializing. With industrial overcapacity driving prices down, foreign investors' prospects are bound to deteriorate. In the past, foreigners tended to underestimate competition from local producers. According to the Ministry of Finance, 61 percent of the nearly 56,000 joint-venture companies in China lost money in 1996.[14] The general consensus among Western joint-venture partners is that it costs not only a lot more money to make money in China, but also a lot more time.

Besides its weak infrastructure and inadequate basic services, such as its dwindling energy capacity, China's export-fueled economic growth will decline because the rest of the world's ability to absorb Asian products is reaching its capacity. In the words of a Western economist, "There are just too many goods chasing too few consumers on a global basis."[15] The 1997 devaluation spiral in neighboring Asian countries dulled the competitiveness of Chinese goods internationally. For all these reasons, most estimates of the purchasing power and size of the Chinese economy in the year 2020 are overstated.

Part of my skepticism regarding China's economic growth relates to agriculture. *Who Will Feed China?* published by Worldwatch in 1994, is a provocative and, in parts, perhaps an exaggeratedly alarming evaluation of China's need to import grain in the future. But it was a timely reminder of the dramatic changes in Chinese eating habits and their effects on grain consumption. Between 1978 and 1993, grain consumption in China increased by 23 percent. The Chinese ate 2.5 times more pork and used four times more oil in 1993 than in 1978. As living standards rise, the Chinese will become more dependent on other countries' grain. Only 7 percent of the globe's arable land lies within the borders of the People's Republic, and even this area is diminishing as a result of industrialization and pollution. In 1994, China became a net importer of grain.

Japanese and Chinese agriculture experts also compiled a report on China's grain supply and demand, which was published in 1995.[16] It disproves some of the most pessimistic forecasts of the Worldwatch research, but its prognosis is still dismal. It estimates that China will have to purchase 136 million tons of foreign grain in 2010. The total volume of the entire world's grain exports in 1994 was 200 million tons, and China purchased a mere 20 million tons. It is possible that more effective farming methods, the conversion of wasteland to farmland, and gene technology will improve China's ability to produce more grain on its own. Even if this holds true, the government will have to divert substantially more funds to agriculture, thus decreasing its investments in industry. The prices of grain must also be freed, so as to motivate farmers to grow more rice and wheat. At present, they prefer to farm more profitable products such as vegetables and tobacco. This is a politically charged issue because freeing the price of grain will push up prices in the cities.

Prospects for the continuation of the Chinese economic miracle appear most grim considering the difficulty of transforming state-owned enterprises into sound business ventures. My friends are overly optimistic about the possibility of market forces taking control. Only part of the economy now relies on market-driven methods. The rest depends on the old system of central planning. In the early 1990s, the government budget began to limit payments to money-losing state factories. State banks took up the slack, providing subsidies to those factories. As a result, to quote *The Economist*, "China's banking system is insolvent: Its bad debts exceed its capital."[17]

Finally, the effects of environmental problems on economic growth and the well-being of the population will be detrimental. Even if the economy develops according to the best-case scenario, the quality of life will suffer. The pressures of population growth, industrial pollution, and abominable traffic will not disappear. Any vision of China must include the ever-burgeoning population, growing by at least 13 million people every year. In addition, the largest migration in history is under way. The tens of millions of new urbanites will inevitably cause new problems and aggravate the friction between the social classes.

Though my assessment of the economy may appear gloomy, I agree with friends like Yang and Liu that China is moving in the right direction. We differ in our appraisal of the speed with which the stupendous problems can be solved and of the difficulties that will arise if the government continues putting off authentic reform of the state sector. The private sector will indeed continue to grow. Millions of people will certainly be elevated from poverty. Millions more will join the ranks of the middle class. And the investments by the growing middle class in their children's education will yield results in the course of the coming decades.

I am most optimistic with regard to the flourishing of Chinese artistic talent. Mainland Chinese film directors, musicians, painters, sculptors, and writers have only just begun to leave their mark on world culture. The success of tens of thousands of Chinese students in American universities has shown what is possible, given the opportunities. Yang is right: China is a far more tolerant society than it was when I moved to Jinan ten years ago.

What about other clouds looming on the Chinese horizon? Former President Yang Shangkun reportedly sounded as if he were tiptoeing through a mine field when asked to assess China's future.[18] Certainly, potential pitfalls abound. The events of 1989 were only the beginning of an immensely long process that eventually will lead China toward greater pluralism. True parliamentary democracy will not be realized in China during my lifetime. At best I foresee urban residents voting for members of their city councils in open, democratic multi-candidate elections in twenty-five years or so. At worst, China could become a military dictatorship.

A stream of open letters and petitions in late 1997 and early 1998 to the government and Party, demanding a more tolerant and open system, are evidence of the roiling undercurrents of debate. In an essay, unpublished in China but aired in Mandarin by Voice of America and BBC, Beijing University professor Shang Dewen calls for a constitution that allows for elected leaders and a Western-style division of power between executive, legislative, and judicial branches. More importantly, in an article released by the official Xinhua News Agency, Liu Ji, vice-president of the Chinese Academy of Social Sciences, writes: "After people have enough food to eat and enough clothes to keep warm, as educational levels increase, they will want to express their opinions. If the Communist Party is really serving and standing at the forefront of the times . . . it must also push forward socialist democracy and political reforms."[19]

It is unlikely that students will command the center of attention the next time the urban population takes to the streets. Future protests will be led by the unemployed and by city residents fed up with injustices and inequalities. When I visited Shenyang in November 1996, I was surprised to see about 200 people demonstrating outside the city government headquarters. They had not been paid their pensions for many months. These types of protests are everyday occurrences, I was told. In one Sichuan city alone (Mianyang), the provincial paper, *Sichuan ribao*, reported that in 1997 the armed police had assisted public-security organs "in stopping 143 cases involving criminal riots." In mid-1997, workers, laid off by bankrupt state enterprises, staged large protests in Mianying.[20]

Even in Beijing, where security is tightest, the unofficial grapevine recounted the attempt by about a hundred bicyclists to arrange a demonstration in Tiananmen Square in June 1997. The police dispersed the crowd, but no one was arrested, said my girlfriend Dr. Feng, who happened to be in the Square at the time. Her comments reflect the times: "Those protesters were desperate unemployed people who demand nothing more than food to stay alive. If the police were to use brutal measures against them, the whole city would be in an uproar." It may well be that the outward calm is actually the lull before the storm.

The leadership's obsession with stability is understandable when one considers the overwhelming resentment in society over the widening gap between the haves and the have-nots. This friction will not decrease at any time in the near future. In the event that the badly needed reform measures are in fact taken, the situation will first deteriorate (as the ranks of the unemployed increase) until new jobs can be created. Social security benefits will remain minimal or nonexistent. The much-touted "Asian model" entails a harsh reality: The talented and industrious have a chance to succeed. The less fortunate have no safety net other than their families.[21]

When Deng Xiaoping died at ninety-two in February 1997, life went on as usual in China, just as he would have wished. He was a low-profile pragmatist who strongly opposed the personality cult of Mao. "No man should be looked upon as a demigod," Deng had constantly emphasized.[22] But at the behest of his children and the new leadership, the media began to sanctify Deng's image as a "Great Leader" during the 1990s. They had their own selfish reasons to promote the achievements of the patriarch. Though many Chinese today speak about Deng indifferently, even disapprovingly, I believe future generations will evaluate him more favorably. Deng changed China's course. He was a revolutionary reformer. It is due to him that China has become an integral part of the world community. Because of his policies, a larger portion of mankind has risen from poverty more rapidly than ever before in history. Younger Chinese tend to forget this when they now look at their country critically.

Deng's longevity gave Jiang Zemin time to solidify his power base and build his own constituency within the army. Jiang was a little-known Party Secretary of Shanghai when he was suddenly appointed to the highest position in the Party after the Beijing massacre in 1989. The transfer of power might not have been so smooth, if, for example, Deng had passed away at the age of eighty-five in 1990.

However, the picture of a unified Chinese leadership rallying behind Jiang Zemin is an illusion. All the top leaders want to continue the reform policy, but there are substantial differences of opinion about the pace and the way the reforms should be carried out. Despite Jiang Zemin's success in consolidating his position, Deng's death marked the start of a prolonged period of uncertainty. Many politically conscious Chinese admitted in private conversation that they are "a bit worried."

Haunted by the demise of the Soviet Union, the Chinese leaders are not likely to allow controversies over policy to jeopardize the stability of the country. Deng reportedly once quoted a famous British saying when trying to persuade his colleagues to form a united front: "If you don't hang together, you'll all hang separately." But differences of opinion could well lead to a state of indecision, weakening any clear-cut policy direction.

The new generation of leaders differs greatly from the revolutionary old guard to which Mao Zedong and Deng Xiaoping belonged. Today, 92 percent of the Party's Central Committee members have a university education.[23] On the other hand, as technocrats they lack the wide-ranging experiences of war and revolution that marked their predecessors. They certainly do not have a similar ideological calling. Consequently, it is far more difficult for them to justify their power.

Since his appointment in 1989, Jiang Zemin has been plagued by the designation "transitional leader." But, during the months after Deng's death, many observers, in both China and the West, changed their assessment. The Hong Kong handover was an acclaimed success; the Fifteenth Party Congress took place without a hitch; and the visit to the United

Deng Xiaoping was an avid bridge player. When the patriarch died on February 19, 1997, the only official title he held was that of honorary chairman of China's Bridge Association. (Photo: Xinhua Photo Agency)

States bolstered his image as an international statesman. At the time of Clinton's trip to China in June 1998, Jiang's position was stronger than at any point since his ascension. In the forever important world of symbolism, Jiang was seen as the leader firmly in control of the People's Republic. Not only does he hold the country's three most powerful titles, he has proved remarkably resilient at maneuvering among the various factions of the Party.

Despite the appearance of strength, Jiang is, and will remain, a compromise leader. Although he has no rival in sight, he is not the favorite of any one faction. Some see this as an asset, considering the nature of Chinese elite politics; others predict that it will ultimately lead to his downfall. China is ruled by men, not laws. Politics is highly personalized. Successful governance requires "skill in reading character, building and maintaining personal relationships and meticulously performing one's expected roles."[24] So far, Jiang has done just that. Yet he is said to lack the strong will, the sharp mind, and the ingenuity of Deng. In any case, Jiang does not enjoy the respect that Deng did. Jiang is well aware of the doubts about him: "At the moment it is impossible for China to produce another leader like Chairman Mao or Deng Xiaoping," he said in an interview in 1995.[25]

Whoever steers China into the twenty-first century faces a monumental challenge. The country's problems are enormous, the aspirations and demands of the populace daunting. China needs a visionary. The nation lacks a collective vision to balance the ups and downs which inevitably lie ahead, a cohesive sense of purpose to cushion the necessary hardships—a unifying thread to help them through the maze of contradictions.

The Chinese are as hard-pressed as outsiders to make sense of these innumerable contradictions. Then again, the word "contradiction" does not have the same negative connotation in Chinese as it does in English. "Contradiction" is made up of the characters for "sword" (*mao*) and "shield" (*dun*). According to legend, a man once boasted that he had acquired the world's sharpest sword. "There is no shield this sword cannot pierce," he declared. Then he found the world's most durable shield. "This shield can stop any sword," he bragged.

"But what happens when the world's mightiest sword strikes the world's most invincible shield?" the man was asked.

A Chinese contradiction.

NOTES

Ten Chinese Years

pp. 1–17

[1] John King Fairbank, *China: A New History*, p. xvi.

[2] When European traders started knocking on China's doors, they were met with suspicion and contempt. In 1759, Canton was the only port open to foreigners. The letter which a British lord was given by the Chinese Emperor to take back with him to the King of England is a remarkable attestation of the prevailing mood in the Imperial Court at Beijing. Lord George Macartney had been sent by King George II to negotiate with the Chinese about opening new Chinese ports for international trade and establishing a British diplomatic residence in Beijing, and he had with him two boatloads of expensive gifts representing the finest of British manufacturing technology. In his response to King George II, Emperor Qianlong wrote: "We have never valued ingenious articles, nor do we have the slightest need of your country's manufactures. Therefore, O king, as regards your request to send someone to remain at the capital, while it is not in harmony with the regulations of the Celestial Empire we also feel very much that it is of no advantage to your country" (Jonathan D. Spence, *The Search for Modern China*, pp. 122-123). According to Fairbank, the British requests for broader trade opportunities were "an invitation to China to join the modern world then being born." But the Emperor wasn't interested (*China: A New History*, p. 197).

[3] It was partly due to their superior disposition that the Chinese purchased far less from the Western traders than the Westerners bought from China; Chinese tea, porcelain, and silk were sought-after items in Europe. This resulted at first in a steady flow of silver into China, an alarming state of affairs from the point of view of the British, who then started to sell the Chinese opium from their plantations in India. Though the Chinese authorities tried their best to curtail the sale of opium, its use spread rapidly. In 1729, the British sold the Chinese a mere 200 chests of opium; by 1839, the number had increased to 40,000 chests. Already "by the 1820s enough opium was coming to China to sustain the habits of around 1 million addicts," historian Jonathan D. Spence concludes (*The Search for Modern China*, p. 129). A country that was already facing immense internal pressures degenerated further as a result of the opium, while parts of the educated class became even more critical of the cruel and greedy foreigners. In the words of Commissioner Lin, the specially appointed imperial commissioner in charge of ending the opium trade: "Poison has been allowed to creep in unchecked till at last barbarian smoke fills the market" (Spence, *The Search for Modern China*, p. 152).

When the Qing Emperor Daoguang forbade the opium trade altogether, the British responded with gunboats. The Opium Wars (1840–1842 and 1858–1860) thus signaled the end of an era. Humiliated in battle, China was forced to give up the right to decide over the comings and goings of foreigners on its own territory, and Britain, France, Germany, the United States, Russia, and Japan proceeded to carve out parts of the coast and the North. At the same time, population pressures led to famine and disease, while a series of rebellions seriously undermined the power of the Imperial Court. The monarchy fell in 1911 and a republic was declared the following year, but in practice the country then became a battleground divided among Chinese warlords and foreigners. More than a hundred years passed after the first Opium Wars before the Chinese were able once again to regain control of their own country.

4 Spence, *The Search for Modern China*, p. 517.

5 The Third Plenum of the Eleventh Party Congress in December 1978 inaugurated major economic reforms focusing on the "four modernizations." Though reforms had already been experimented with in various areas prior to the plenum, the reform policy is commonly referred to as having been launched in 1979.

6 The wife was released in late 1997 after five years in prison.

Returning to My Chinese Roots — pp. 19–37

1 Jinan, according to the precise transliteration rules, should be written as Ji'nan.

2 There are contradictory figures regarding the extent of poverty in China. *The Economist* estimates that 300 million (not 200 million) Chinese have been elevated above poverty level since 1979 ("China Survey" of Mar. 8, 1997, p.17).

According to a March 1997 State Council Information Office report, 58 million Chinese are still living below the official poverty line, which the Chinese determine to be $0.60 a day. In its September 1996 report "Poverty in China; What Do the Numbers Say?" the World Bank redefined the income level below which a Chinese is deemed poor, from $0.60 a day to $1.00 a day (the international standard for developing countries). As a result, the World Bank then revised its previous estimate of how many Chinese live in poverty, from fewer than 100 million to well over 300 million; in other words, close to one-third of the population (*The Economist*, Oct. 12, 1996, p. 67).

3 Officially, 37.7 percent of state enterprises were operating in the red at the end of 1996 (*Renmin ribao* [People's Daily] citing Zhang Sai, head of the State Statistical Bureau, Apr. 5, 1997). But according to Western economists, the figure is two times higher if one includes enterprises wavering around the zero line; *i.e.*, ones that do not make profits (*The Economist*, "China Survey," Mar. 8, 1997, p. 12).

Of state employees, 52.2 percent are working in loss-making units, reported *Gongren ribao* ([Workers' Daily], Aug. 13, 1996).

Officially, the rate of unemployment is 3.4 percent, but a more realistic figure, according to Western analysts, is closer to 20 percent. In February 1997, China scholar Tony Saich, who was living in Beijing as director of the Ford Foundation's China Office, estimated the level of unemployment in a city like Tianjin to be about 40 percent, in Shanghai 30 percent (from a talk at the Fairbank Center, Harvard University, Feb. 19, 1997).

4 My first book about China, by rough translation "The Crumbling Wall: One Year as a Chinese," was not published in English (*Mureneva muuri. Vuosi kiinalaisena.* Helsinki: Kirjayhtymä, 1988).

5 Zhongguo Xinwen She (China News Service), "Shandong Foreign Investment Tops $10 Billion," Oct 4, 1996 (translated in FBIS-CHI-96-195).

6 Fei Xiaotong, *From the Soil—The Foundations of Chinese Society: A Translation of Fei Xiaotong's* Xiangtu Zhongguo, p. 78.

The Closed World of a Work Unit pp. 39–57

1 *China Focus*, Vol. 1, No. 1 (Jan. 27, 1993), p. 10.

2 The April 1996 "Rules Governing Work of Chinese Communist Party Grass-roots Units in Institutes of Higher Education" state that Party Committees exercise leadership over educational units, Xinhua, Apr. 15, 1996 (in FBIS-CHI-96-074, Apr. 16, 1996).

3 "A Survey of China's Economy," *The Economist*, Aug. 1987.

4 The average per capita income of urban residents in Shandong was 375 yuan ($45) per month in 1996. In other words, even my former students, with salaries of 550 to 650 yuan ($66 to $78), were earning way above average, though some of them did have to support one or even two elderly parents (*Jinan dazhong ribao*, Feb. 27, 1997, p. 1).

Red Youth pp.59-79

1 An additional 460,489 "professional training students" began three-year university studies in 1996. State Statistical Bureau, *China Statistical Yearbook* 1997, pp. 640, 642.

2 World Bank, "China: Higher Education Reform," p. 9.

3 *South China Morning Post*, Sept. 28, 1996, p. 9, citing Vice-Minister of Education Liu Bin: "The proportion of spending relative to gross national product (GNP) is still rather low and on a per capita basis is among the lowest in the world" (FBIS-CHI-96-190, "PRC: Education Spending as Proportion of GNP Falling").

4 The figures for percentage of GNP spent on education are all from the *UNESCO Statistical Yearbook*, 1997.

5 Xinhua News Agency, Oct. 26, 1996 (FBIS-CHI-96-210, "PRC: NPC Vice Chairman Says Investment in Education Remains Low").

6 "On Coalition Government" (April 24, 1945), *Selected Works of Mao Tse-tung, Vol. 3* (Beijing: Foreign Languages Press), p. 257.

[7] Jung Chang, *Wild Swans*, p. 262. The second quote from *Wild Swans* is on p. 200.

[8] *Resolution on CPC History (1949–81)* (Beijing: Foreign Languages Press, 1981), p. 32.

[9] Roderick MacFarquhar, *The Origins of the Cultural Revolution III: The Coming of the Cataclysm, 1961–1966*, p. 4.

Spence writes in *The Search of Modern China*: "In the China of 1957, before the Great Leap began, the median age of those dying was 17.6 years; in 1963 it was down to 9.7. Half of those dying in China that year, in other words, were under ten years old. The Great Leap Forward, launched in the name of strengthening the nation by summoning all the people's energies, had turned back on itself and ended by devouring its young" (p. 583).

[10] The book by Chu Han, *Zhongguo 1959–1961: Sannian ziran huohai chengpian jishi* (A Documentary of the Three-Year Natural Disaster) was published by Sichuan renmin chubanshe in March 1996, but it was banned soon after its publication.

[11] Paul Johnson, *A History of the Modern World: From 1917 to the 1980s*, p. 556.

[12] Liu Binyan, "Unintended Earthquake," p. 22.

[13] When speaking English, many Chinese still refer to *Beijing Daxue* (Beijing University) as Peking University, using the former transliteration of Beijing (Peking). The university's stationery also has "Peking University" on its letterhead.

[14] In November 1996, nearly 37,000 documents, tape recordings, and exhibits from the Cultural Revolution were moved to a new Cultural Revolution archive in East Beijing, but the building was declared off-bounds for the public and academics (*China News Digest*, Nov. 26, 1996).

[15] Fairbank, *China: A New History*, p. 176.

[16] The official death count is 34,800 people, but *The Cambridge History of China* estimates that approximately half a million Chinese died as a direct result of the Cultural Revolution (Vol. 15, Part 2, p. 214).

[17] Roderick MacFarquhar, "The Party's Armageddon," p. 26.

[18] Fairbank, *China: A New History*, p. 385.

[19] Spence, *The Search for Modern China*, pp. 606–607.

[20] For example, the report describing Bo Yibo's interrogation and torture sessions in *China's Cultural Revolution, 1966–1969: Not a Dinner Party*, ed. Michael Schoenhals, pp. 122–135.

[21] Wang Ruoshui, "The Double Hundred Policy and Civil Rights," *Huasheng*, Aug. 8, 1986, p. 12, reprinted in *Zhengming* (Hong Kong), Sept. 1, 1986, and translated in *Summary of World Broadcasts*, FE8360, Sept. 10, 1986, p. BII/12. I dug out this article after reading about it in Merle Goldman's *Sowing the Seeds of Democracy in China.*

[22] Goldman, Link, and Wei describe the "discussion of alienation" that took place among Chinese intellectuals in the 1980s in detail in Lowell Dittmer and Samuel Kim, eds.,, *China's Quest for National Identity*, pp. 136–140. Earlier, Wang Ruoshui and many other Chinese Communists had accepted the orthodox interpretation that Marx's use of "alienation" applied only to the proletariat in a capitalist system. Wang Ruoshui changed his ideas about alienation after the Cultural Revolution and publicly argued that the model of

socialism developed in China after 1949 had in fact created alienation between the Party and the people. For his recent views, see Wang Ruoshui, "My Marxist Outlook."

[23] During the winter of 1991–1992, "The Red Sun: Singing the Praises of Chairman Mao," a rearrangement and recording of Cultural Revolution songs, was released on cassette tape and immediately became a nationwide bestseller. More than a million copies of the tape were sold within a few months. Geremie Barmé, *Shades of Mao: The Posthumous Cult of the Great Leader*, p. 192.

[24] There are differences of opinion as to how many young people actually were sent to the countryside, partly because of the various ways to define the term "youth." Thomas P. Bernstein refers to a figure of twelve million in his book, *Up to the Mountains and Down to the Villages*, p. 12. Matei Mihalca states that "from 1968 to 1978, 16.23 million high school students between the ages of sixteen and twenty-one were rusticated, many to backward regions on China's borders" ("Neo Conservatism: A New, Perhaps Disturbing Nationalism May Be Emerging," p. 54).

Tiananmen's Spark of Hope pp. 81–101

[1] This chapter relies heavily on research I did for my paper, "Lies in Ink, Truth in Blood: The Role and Impact of the Chinese Media During the Beijing Spring of '89." References for quotes from Chinese television broadcasts and newspaper articles, as well as interviews I conducted as a fellow at the Shorenstein Center on the Press, Politics, and Public Policy at the Kennedy School of Government are all listed with the endnotes for the above paper, pp. 21–22.

In addition, in the section dealing with the way the press developed in the 1980s, I have drawn from my discussion with Wang Ruoshui (December 1996) and Chap. 6 ("Radical Revisions of Ideology and Political Procedures," pp. 133–166) in Merle Goldman, *Sowing the Seeds of Democracy in China: Political Reform in the Deng Xiaoping Era.* Information concerning punishments dealt out to journalists after June 4, 1989, is from Allison Liu Jernow, *"Don't Force Us To Lie": The Struggle of Chinese Journalists in the Reform Era.*

[2] In my paper (p. 15), I state that "the protests spread to at least 81 cities." According to *Jingxin dongbo de 56 tian* [The Soul-Stirring 56 Days], published by Dadi chubanshe in Beijing in August 1989, "2.8 million people, 600 schools, and 84 cities from 29 provinces" were involved in the demonstrations in 1989.

[3] This is one of the many poems I was taught when I studied the Chinese language in Beijing. I have taken the translation from Wang Hui-ming, trans., *Ten Poems and Lyrics by Mao Tse-tung*, p. 63.

[4] Yi Mu and Mark V. Thompson, *Crisis at Tiananmen: Reform and Reality in Modern China*, p. 29.

[5] Harrison E. Salisbury, *The New Emperors: Mao and Deng*, pp. 320–321, based on Salisbury's interview with Deng Pufang, May 6, 1988.

[6] Jan Wong, *Red China Blues: My Long March from Mao to Now*, pp. 299–300.

[7] *China Daily*, Jan. 22, 1996, p. 4.

Notes

A Peasant Woman's Hard Lot pp. 103–125

1 Zhu Qingfang, "The Urban-Rural Gap and Social Problems in the Countryside," p. 82.

2 There are also great disparities among rural areas. Dissident journalist Liu Binyan notes that 80 percent of the money in rural savings accounts belongs to 20 percent of the population, while 50 percent of the peasants have no savings at all, and some are deeply in debt ("The Bankruptcy of a Fairy Tale," p. 1).

3 There is some debate whether it was the reform leadership under Deng Xiaoping or the farmers themselves who succeeded in dismantling Mao's collectives. Kate Xiao Zhou asserts that the farmers' own initiatives were instrumental in bringing about what has been called "Deng's revolution" (*How the Farmers Changed China: Power of the People*). Though many specialists agree that the farmers did begin decollectivization on their own and that they pushed the system further and faster than reform leaders had anticipated, they argue that the change in rural conditions still would not have occurred without the reform-minded central leadership. (See, for example David Zweig's review of Zhou's above-mentioned book in *The China Journal*, No. 38 [July 1997], pp. 153–168.)

4 Estimates regarding how many people remain in the countryside vary, as do predictions concerning the effects of the migration on society. This is because the Chinese government's method of defining a person's place of residence, based on whether a person belongs to the agricultural sector or the nonagricultural sector, is outdated in these times of great change. According to the State Statistical Bureau, even though 70.6 percent of the population (864 million people) officially resided in the countryside in 1996, only 26.7 percent of the population (326 million) made up the rural labor force. A new national survey is expected to be completed at the end of 1998.

The Chinese Academy of Social Sciences estimates that only 250 million people are actually farmers. If one adds their dependents to this figure, the peasantry now numbers between 480 and 530 million (Economist Intelligence Unit, *China: Country Profile, 1997–1998*, p.17).

Liu Futang, the deputy director of the Beijing Institute for Market Economy Studies, said in a phone interview (May 27, 1997) that the rural population is now only 230 million people. This is certainly the lowest of all the figures I have heard. Deputy Director Liu said his figures were based on a recent survey conducted by his institute.

5 Information Office, State Council of the People's Republic of China, "The Situation of Chinese Women," pp. 14, 18.

The Battle Against Despotism pp. 127–147

1 The National People's Congress promulgated the Organic Law of Villager Committees of the People's Republic of China (Experimental) in November 1987. Though the Ministry of Civil Affairs began to organize rural elections as of 1988, the political repression following the Tiananmen crackdown temporarily slowed the pace of implementation. According to Wang Zhenyao, deputy director of the Department of Basic-level

Government in the Ministry of Civil Affairs, grass-roots elections began to be held in earnest throughout the country in 1990.

2 In writing the first part of this chapter dealing with "village democracy reform," I have relied on interviews I conducted in Liaoning province in March 1995, interviews with Wang Zhenyao in March 1995 and January 1997, as well as, among others, the following Chinese-language articles: Wang Shihao, "Shiying shichang jingji xingshi gaohao xiangzhen he cunweihui jianshe" (Adapt to the Circumstances of a Market Economy and Build Village Committees That Have Good Relations with Townships and Towns), *Neibu wenzhai* [Internal Digest], No. 12 (1995); Yan Changzhao, "Zhege cun shi zenyang you luan dao zhide" (How This Village Proceeded from Chaos to Order), *Xiangzhen luntan* [Town & Township Forum], No. 7 (1991); Liu Jiang, "Jinyibu jiaqiang nongye de jichu diwei" (Further Strengthen Agriculture's Position as a Foundation), *Zhonggong zhongyang dangxiao baogao xuan* [Selected Reports from the Central Party School], No. 10 (1995); Zheng Quan, "Quanguo cun ji zuzhi zhuangkuang de diaocha" (National Survey of the State of Village-Level Organization), *Zhongguo minzheng* [China's Civil Administration], No. 9 (1989); Gao Jie, "Cunmin weiyuanhui zuzhi jianshe de beijing, xiangzhuang he zhengce daoxiang" (Background, Current Status, and Policy Direction of Establishing Village Committees), *Faxue yanjiu* [Legal Research], No. 2 (1994).

In addition, there is an abundance of English-language articles about "village democracy." As background I have found the following useful: Allen Choate, "Local Governance in China"; *The Economist*, "China's Grassroots Democracy," Nov. 2, 1996; Amy Epstein, "Village Elections in China: Experimenting with Democracy"; Daniel Kelliher, "The Chinese Debate over Village Self-Government"; Susan Lawrence, "Democracy, Chinese Style," *Australian Journal of Chinese Affairs*, No. 32 (July 1994); Jean C. Oi, "Economic Development, Stability and Democratic Village Self-Government"; Xu Wang, "Mutual Empowerment of State and Peasantry: Grassroots Democracy in Rural China," *World Development*, Vol. 25, No. 9 (Sept. 1997).

3 Xu Wang, "Mutual Empowerment of State and Peasantry," p. 1433.

4 While doing final research for this book, it was interesting to note that the mouthpiece of the Chinese Communist Party, *Renmin ribao*, published a lengthy article explaining the system of "self-rule by villagers" on November 20, 1997. Though this was not the first article on the subject in the official press, it is noteworthy for its positive tone and lavish praise of the self-rule system (translated in FBIS-CHI-97-358, "China: System of Self-Rule by Village Explained").

5 The *Far Eastern Economic Review* (Feb. 5, 1998, p. 5) reports that elections had taken place in 60 percent of China's one million villages, "according to China's own figures." However, it is not clear whether the figure refers to multicandidate elections.

6 In 1985 there were only 11.7 television sets per 100 rural households; by 1996 this number had increased to 88 televisions per 100 rural households (State Statistical Bureau, *China Statistical Yearbook 1997*, p. 291).

7 For an overview of how the Administrative Ligitation Law has been implemented and the law's effects, see Pei Minxin, "Citizens vs. Mandarins: Administrative Litigation in China." For statistics, see Pei's table on p. 836.

8 Pei, "Citizens vs. Mandarins," p. 835.

[9] After passage of the Administrative Ligitation Law, a number of subsequent laws were passed to refine the process by which a citizen can sue the government. Tang's parents used both the Administrative Ligitation Law and the State Compensation Law, effective as of January 1995, which is invoked in disputes with a government institution that result in monetary losses or losses of human life.

Optimists and Individualists

pp. 149–170

[1] John Naisbitt, *Megatrends Asia*, p. 246. The Chinese translation of this book was a best-seller on mainland China in the mid-1990s.

[2] World Bank, "China: Higher Education Reform," p. 9.

[3] Martin King Whyte, "The Fate of Filial Obligations in Urban China."

[4] Sex education manuals and telephone hotlines that advise callers about sexual problems became enormously popular in the cities during the early 1990s. The first major comprehensive survey of Chinese sexual habits and attitudes, *Sexual Behavior in Modern China*, which was published in 1992, was hailed as China's equivalent of the Kinsey Report (Liu Dalin, ed., *Zhongguo dangdai xing wenhua: Zhongguo liangwan lie "xing wenming" diaocha baogao*. Shanghai: Sanlian shudian, 1992). An English translation (by Man Lun Ng and Erwin J. Haeberle) was published by Continuum Press in New York in 1996.

[5] Zhao Tiantang, "*Zhongguo chuantong renge de xiaoji yinsu ji qi chengyin*" (The Negative Factors of the Traditional Personality and Their Causes), *Shehui* [Society], No. 2 (1991), p. 9.

[6] Despite this stark example of loyalty only toward one's own interest group, Chinese society is showing signs of change. A number of democracy activists have recounted random acts of kindness and help from strangers all over China in the aftermath of the Beijing massacre. Some were able to spend months in hiding before fleeing to the West.

[7] Bette Bao Lord, *Legacies: A Chinese Mosaic*, pp. 12–13.

[8] I have relied on Norwegian sociologist Børge Bakken's translation, "we-group" for the Chinese term *ziji ren*, which can also be translated as "one's own people." Børge Bakken, *The Exemplary Society: Human Improvement, Social Control, and the Dangers of Modernity in China*, Chap. 12.

[9] Susan W.L. Young, "The Ps and Cues of Chinese Inscrutability," in *Crosstalk and Culture in Sino-American Communication*, pp. 18–19.

[10] Ge Gao, Stella Ting-Toomey, and William B. Gudykunst, "Chinese Communication Processes," in *The Handbook of Chinese Psychology*, ed. Michael Harris Bond, p. 291 (quoting Bond, *Beyond the Chinese Face* [Hong Kong: Oxford University Press, 1991], p. 83).

[11] Perry Link, *Evening Chats in Beijing: Probing China's Predicament*, pp. 7–8.

[12] Bakken, *The Exemplary Society*, Chap. 12.

The South Is a World of Its Own pp. 173–197

1 The figure 164 million is from State Statistical Bureau, *China Statistical Yearbook 1997*, p. 77. However, the World Bank and numerous other sources (for example, the Economist Intelligence Unit) estimate the figure to be higher, about 205 million.

2 *Hubei Ribao*, Nov. 11, 1996, p. 1 (translated in FBIS-CHI-96-227).

3 In 1996, the average annual income in the whole of China was 4,377 yuan ($527) for urban residents, and 1,926 yuan ($232) for rural residents. The urban population in Beijing had an annual income of 6,885 yuan ($829). In contrast, urban residents of Guangdong had the highest income in the whole country—7,488 yuan ($902)—which is 1.7 times more than the average annual income of urban residents in China as a whole. Rural households in Guangdong earned an average income of 3,183 yuan, which is 1.6 times the national average income for rural households (1,926 yuan).

4 For example, in *When China Ruled the Seas*, Louise Levathes writes: "After the mid-fifteenth century the exodus of Chinese coupled with an official ban on private trading gave rise to piracy and an illegal trade in the China seas to an extent previously unknown" (p. 185).

5 Marja Sarvimäki expounds on this subject in her forthcoming doctoral dissertation thesis: "Structures, Symbols and Meanings: Chinese and Korean Influence on Japanese Architecture" (Helsinki: Helsinki University of Technology).

A Labyrinth of Ideas and Beliefs pp. 199–223

1 Diana Lary, "Regions and Nation: The Present Situation in China in Historical Context," p. 181.

2 Perry Link, *Evening Chats in Beijing: Probing China's Predicament*, p. 225.

3 Of the over 50 million Chinese residing outside mainland China, 21.5 million live in Taiwan; 6.5 million in Hong Kong; some 20 million throughout Southeast Asia; 1 million in California; about 0.5 million in Australia. See Constance Lever-Tracy, David Ip, and Noel Tracy, *The Chinese Diaspora and Mainland China: An Emerging Economic Synergy*, p. 14.

4 John K. Fairbank, *China: A New History*, p. 25.

5 James L. Watson, "Rites or Beliefs?" in *China's Quest for National Identity*, ed. Dittmer and Kim, pp. 93, 96.

6 Samuel S. Kim and Lowell Dittmer, "Whither China's Quest for National Identity," in *China's Quest for National Identity*, ed Dittmer and Kim, p. 256.

7 Benjamin Schwartz, one of the world's leading scholars of Chinese thought, reminds us that Confucius's *ren* is,"in its inner essence, beyond definition" (*The World of Thought in Ancient China*, p. 90). Many Western scholars prefer not to attempt to translate either *ren* or *li*.

[8] John K. Fairbank, Edwin O. Reischauer, and Albert M. Craig, *East Asia: Tradition and Transformation*, p. 68.

[9] *The Analects of Confucius*, tr. and notes by Simon Leys (the pseudonym of Pierre Ryckmans), p. xvi.

[10] Millions of Catholics remain "underground" because the government forbids recognition of the Pope as supreme spiritual leader. In recent years, the authorities have repeatedly cracked down on underground religious activities and persecuted dozens of religious leaders, claiming that religious gatherings are being used for political organization and opposition to Party rule. Statistics from Patrick E. Tyler, "Catholics in China: Back to the Underground," pp. 1, 8.

[11] Tauno-Olavi Huotari and Pertti Seppälä, *Kiinan kulttuuri*, p. 186.

[12] Fairbank, Reischauer, and Craig, *East Asia: Tradition and Transformation*, p. 49.

Jumbled Misunderstandings pp. 225–249

[1] So far, the number of reported AIDS cases has been modest. In 1996, Chinese health authorities reported that there were 4,305 persons with HIV, but they acknowledged the number of cases could be as high as 100,000. Patrick Tyler, "China Concedes Blood Product Contained AIDS Virus."

[2] Samuel S. Kim and Lowell Dittmer, "Whither China's Quest for National Identity?" *China's Quest for National Identity*, Dittmer and Kim, ed., p. 252.

[3] Immanuel C. Y. Hsü, *China's Entrance into the Family of Nations: The Diplomatic Phase 1858–1880*, p. 13.

[4] Kim and Dittmer, eds., *China's Quest for National Identity*, p. 259.

[5] Kim and Dittmer, eds., *China's Quest for National Identity*, pp. 258–259. This is taken from *Selected Works of Mao Tse-tung*, Vol. 4 (Beijing: Foreign Languages Press, 1961), p. 415.

[6] My friend, journalist and Harvard researcher Susan Lawrence, has delved deep into the lives of her grandparents for a forthcoming book about their extraordinary experiences, tracing through them the course of the West's tortured relationship with Communist China. She describes the home Michael Lindsay grew up in as "an intellectual hot house where Michael s parents and their eminent friends debated ethics, the imperative of involvement in public affairs, and the ideals of democracy." One of Michael's father's best-known works was a slim volume entitled *The Essentials of Democracy*.

[7] Perry Link, *Evening Chats in Beijing*, p. 12. In the note he adds: "Both these sayings are attributed to the scholar Fan Zhongyan (989–1052), although the textual source for the first is not known."

[8] Merle Goldman, Perry Link, and Su Wei, "China's Intellectuals in the Deng Era: Loss of Identity with the State," in Dittmer and Kim, ed., *China's Quest for National Identity*, p. 127.

[9] Link refers to reporter Zhang Shengyao's usage of "the sense of mission and responsibility" in Zhang's article "Baogao wenxue de juewu" (Awakening of Literary Reportage), published in *Wenyi bao*, Oct. 8, 1988, p.1. (*Evening Chats in Beijing*, pp. 249–250). The other quotes in this paragraph are also from Perry Link's *Evening Chats in Beijing*, pp. 292–293.

[10] In early 1998, Ding Zilin organized yet another petition to China's President Jiang Zemin and the National People's Congress asking that the outgoing prime minister, Li Peng, be disqualified from becoming the new chairman of the congress because of his leading role in the violent suppression of the Tiananmen democracy movement in 1989. The petition, signed by fifty-six people, had no effect. Li Peng, as expected, was appointed the new chairman in March 1998.

[11] John Pomfret: "Burying a Taboo, China Gives Figures on Death by Police Torture," *International Herald Tribune*, June 29, 1998, p. 4.

[12] In mid-1998, for the first time, China published statistics on the number of people who have been tortured to death by police. The unprecedented publication of case studies and the "fledgling attempts of elements within China's criminal justice system to rein in China's all-powerful police and other security services represent just one of many legal developments lending encouragement to American legal experts." John Pomfret: "Burying a Taboo, China Gives Figures on Death by Police Torture," *International Herald Tribune*, June 29, 1998, p. 4.

[13] Amnesty International, "Summary on the Human Rights Situation in the PRC," Sept. 8, 1996.

[14] There are a few exceptions. For example, in February 1994 China's most famous dissident, Wei Jingsheng, urged President Bill Clinton to take a tougher stand against the Chinese government on human rights. Some six months earlier, Wei had been released from prison after spending fifteen years behind bars for his role in the 1978–1979 "Democracy Wall" movement. Wei relayed his message to the American leadership in a meeting with U.S. assistant secretary of state for human rights, John Shattuck, who was visiting Beijing. "I said the U.S. government should be more firm in its position," Wei told foreign reporters after the meeting. "If the United States has great determination, there is hope for big results." (*International Herald Tribune*, "'Be Firm,' Dissident Tells U.S.," Mar. 1, 1994, p. 1.) In April, Wei was rearrested and, in December 1995, sentenced to an additional fourteen years in prison. However, after President Jiang Zemin's state visit to the United States in the autumn of 1997, Wei was released on medical parole and whisked off to the United States.

[15] Figure for 1995. "China Engaged" (Washington, D.C.: The World Bank, 1997), p. 22.

America Is No Longer Heaven on Earth pp. 251–273

[1] Charles R. Kitts, *The United States Odyssey in China, 1784–1990*, p. vii.

[2] Use of the Internet began to spread beyond China's academic and scientific circles in 1994. Many of my friends in Beijing, and even a few in Jinan, were "online" by 1997. According to the *China Daily*, by mid-1998 there were 1.06 million Internet users in

China. The government predicts that the number of Internet users will rise to 4 million by the year 2000, though the computer industry expects the figure to be far higher (Martyn Williams, "China Internet Users Reach One Million," Newsbytes, June 17, 1998).

[3] Wu Luping, "The United States in the Eyes of Young Chinese," *Zhongguo qingnian bao* (China Youth News), May 11, 1996, p. 4 (translated in FBIS-CHI-96-168, "PRC: Young People's Attitudes Toward U.S. Surveyed"). The respondents were also asked several questions about the U.S. One small detail at the end of the article caught my eye: "53.5 percent of the young people (taking part in the survey) believe that U.S. society practices not real but sham democracy."

[4] This detail was not mentioned when the survey results were published in *China Youth News.* It was reported by Susan Lawrence, who cites a private conversation with the agency that conducted the survey ("Beijing's Mixed Message").

[5] Data provided by the U.S. Information Center in Beijing, citing the U.S Bureau of the Census and the U.S. National Center for Health Statistics. It is important to bear in mind that the poverty line is not a universal measure. For example, in 1994 the poverty line in the U.S. was $21.20 per day, while in China it was $0.60 a day.

[6] "New Trade in Human Slaves," *Newsweek,* June 21, 1993, p. 8. In addition, there are an estimated 100,000 mainland Chinese students who have remained in the United States during the past two decades. The sharp class divisions that exist in the People's Republic also apply to Chinese residing in the U.S.—the world of a university lecturer and the world of a former peasant who slaves away in a Chinese take-out restaurant have little in common.

[7] The miserable state of higher education in China at the beginning of this century is reflected in the following figures: The sixteen Christian colleges had a total enrollment of about 3,500 students (which means there were only approximately 30,000 college students in the entire country). In 1925, there were also about 2,500 Chinese students studying in the U.S. Kitts, *The United States Odyssey in China, 1784–1990,* p. 62.

[8] Between 1979 and 1987, the U.S. issued about 62,000 visas for study or research to citizens of the People's Republic of China. This figure does not include recipients for other reasons—business, tourism, or immigration. Leo Orleans, *Chinese Students in America* (Washington, D.C.: National Academy Press, 1988), p. 110.

According to the Chinese-language journal *Liaowang* (Outlook), Apr. 8, 1996, pp. 10–13, between December 1978 and December 1995, nearly 250,000 Chinese students went abroad to study. Fewer than half (nearly 120,000) had returned by the end of 1995.

[9] Harry Harding, *A Fragile Relationship: The United States and China Since 1972,* p. 10.

[10] David Shambaugh, "The United States and China: Cooperation or Confrontation," p. 242.

[11] Richard Bernstein and Ross H. Munro, "The Coming Conflict with Amerca," p. 18.

[12] Perry Link, *Evening Chats in Beijing,* p. 302.

[13] Clinton further strengthened this image when, in March 1998, he decided that the United States would not sponsor an annual resolution condemning China's human rights abuses before the United Nations Human Rights Commission in Geneva. Commenting on the U.S. decision, Mike Jendrzejczyk, Washington director of Human Rights Watch in Asia, said: "They've caved in" ("Annual U.N. Ritual Condemning China Loses U.S. Support," *New York Times,* March 14, 1998, p. 1).

[14] Richard Bernstein and Ross H. Munro, "The Coming Conflict with America," p. 20. Though certain forces within the Chinese military advocate a surreptitious arms build-up to reach military capabilities on a par with the U.S., this particular passage from which Bernstein and Munro quote does not focus on Sino-U.S. relations. In the book *Megatrends China* (Beijing: Hualing chubanshe, May 1996) General Mi explains the key issues regarding development of China's high-technology weaponry, not ones regarding Sino-U.S. relations. Bernstein and Munro quote two proverbs with which General Mi ends his article, and they are open to interpretation.

Megatrends China, a portrayal of Chinese society and an assessment of the country's future, was widely talked about among educated urbanites in 1996. In Jinan, many of my former students had either already read it or were reading it. While traveling to the South in October 1996, I noticed at least seven people on the train immersed in the book.

[15] Robert S. Ross, "Beijing as a Conservative Power," p. 42.

[16] John M. Broder, "President Calls China's Course 'Morally Right,'" *International Herald Tribune*, July 2, 1998, pp. 1, 6.

[17] As with all statistics relating to China, there are great discrepancies. The United States and China calculate trade which goes through Hong Kong differently, thus the customs statistics from the two sides do not match. The figure for U.S. exports to China ($12 billion) is from the U.S. Department of Commerce; the corresponding Chinese figure for Chinese imports from the U.S. is $16 billion. The shares of each country's total exports are from "On Sino-U.S. Trade Balance," put out by the Information Office of China's State Council in March 1997.

[18] For example, from Jia's article about the Taiwan question in *The China Journal* (No. 36, July 1996), it is evident that the Chinese leaders, despite their staunch claims in public about "a united front," were not unanimous about how to react to the Taiwanese president's private visit to the United States in 1995.

[19] As a result of formal ties established between the People's Republic and the United States in 1979, Beijing announced that its intermittent shelling of the offshore islands (part of Taiwan) would cease. It then called for talks, as well as direct links, across the straits. On the other hand, Taiwan, until the death of President Chiang Ching-kuo in 1988, adhered to a policy of "three nos" in its relations with the mainland—no talks, no compromise, and no contact. After 1988, economic relations expanded greatly (Steven M. Goldstein, "Taiwan Faces the Twenty-first Century: Continuing the Miracle," pp. 49–54).

[20] In 1997, 1.8 million Taiwanese visited the mainland, according to the Hong Kong *Wen Wei Po* (Feb. 1, 1998, p. A8). Of the 57,000 mainland residents allowed by the Taiwanese authorities to visit Taiwan in 1997, 47,000 visited relatives or attended funerals of family members, and some 8,400 had been invited for various cross-straits exchanges (Xinhua News Agency, Jan. 26, 1998, FBIS-CHI-98-026).

[21] Susan Lawrence, "A Political Test When Guns Matter," p. 48.

[22] Tony Emerson, et al., "Making of a Democrat," *Newsweek*, May 20, 1996, p. 13.

[23] *Far Eastern Economic Review* reported in its February 5, 1998, issue that most Hong Kong people "continue to feel that they are losing their basic rights and are in danger of being overrun by a Leninist political culture imported from the mainland" ("China Eclipse," p. 23).

[24] Andrew Nathan, "China's Goals in the Taiwan Strait," p. 90.

[25] John Pomfret, "China's Officers Gape at America," p. 1.

[26] Susan Lawrence has pointed out that the month-long war with Vietnam also revealed China's willingess to risk confrontation with a superpower, as at that time Vietnam was backed by the Soviet Union. See her "China Practices Pulling the Trigger," *U.S. News and World REport*, March 18, 1996, p. 54.

[27] Andrew Nathan, "China's Goals in the Taiwan Strait," p. 88.

[28] Peter Ferdinand, "China and Russia: A Strategic Partnership?" p. 21.

The Legacy of Deng Xiaoping pp. 275–303

[1] "China Executes Three Students: 45 Sentenced as Sweep Goes On," *International Herald Tribune*, June 22, 1989, p. 1.

[2] State enterprises owed the banks a total of 405 billion dollars at the end of 1995, according to the *China Daily Business Weekly*, Oct. 6–12, 1996. To keep this figure in perspective, the article pointed out that the total personal savings in bank accounts amounted to only 358 billion dollars.

[3] Minxin Pei, "Is China Democratizing?" p. 77.

[4] This is a point put forth by Rachel Murphy in "A Dependent Private Sector: No Prospects for Civil Society in China" and Kristen Parris in "Private Interest and the Public Good: The Rise of Private Business Interests."

[5] Liu Binyan, "The Bankruptcy of a Fairy Tale," p. 6.

[6] Geremie R. Barmé, ed., "Shades of Mao: The Posthumous Cult of the Great Leader," p. 8. Barmé quotes Victor Zaslavsky, *The Neo-Stalinist State: Class, Ethnicity, and Consensus in Soviet Society* (Armonk, NY: M.E. Sharpe, 1982), pp. 15–16.

[7] Vera Schwarcz, "No Solace from Lethe," inWei-ming Tu, ed., *The Living Tree: The Changing Meaning of Being Chinese Today*, p. 68.

[8] Steven Mufson, "The Immoral of the Story: In China, a Popular Novelist Is in Official Disfavor," p. C6.

In 1992, Wang Shuo changed from writing novels to writing television series and film scripts. His popularity continued despite increasing problems with the film censors.

[9] Matei Mihalca, "Neo Conservatism," p. 52.

[10] "Viewing China Through A Third Eye" was translated in FBIS-CHI-075-S, Apr. 19, 1995, from Luo yi neng ge er, *Di san zhi yanjing kan Zhongguo* (Taiyuan: Shanxi renmin chubanshe, 1994), originally published under the name of a fictitious author, Dr. Leninger, "currently Europe's most influential Sinologist." Wang Shan, a novelist, was listed only as the translator. Wang Shan later acknowledged his authorship in an interview with the Hong Kong newspaper *Eastern Express* (Jan. 7, 1995, p. 7). In the interview, Wang said that besides the fear that mainland Chinese publishing houses would not accept such a polit-

ically sensitive book written by a Chinese, there was a creative reason for using a foreign name: "In China we have a tradition of praising the present and criticizing the past. As a foreigner, you can criticize the present and the future as well," he explained. Book quotes are from pp. 31 and 63 of the FBIS translation.

11 Ji Hongzhen, "With Ideology Waning, Intellectuals Search for New Role."

12 John K. Fairbank, *China: The People's Middle Kingdom and the U.S.A.*, p. 66.

13 Xinhua, Nov. 13, 1996 (FBIS-CHI-96-220, "PRC: Improper Storage, Shipping Cause Substantial Vegetable Losses").

14 Pamela Yatsko, "Rethinking China," p. 53. The figure of $361 billion for foreign investment in 1993–1996 is for *pledged* foreign investment, taken from State Statistical Bureau, *China Statistical Yearbook 1997*, p. 605.

15 Ed Yardeni, chief economist with Deutsche Morgan Grenfell. Quoted in Brian Caplen, "What Will Go Wrong Next," p. 38.

16 Overseas Economic Cooperation Fund, "Prospects for Grain Supply-Demand Balance and Agricultural Development Policy in China."

17 "The Long March to Capitalism," *The Economist*, Sept. 13, 1997, p. 26.

18 Harrison E. Salisbury, *The New Emperors*, p. 461.

19 Richard McGregor, "New Rumbles of Democracy: A Resonating Call for Reform," *The Australian*, Sept. 6–7, 1997 (as reported in *World Press Review*, Nov. 1997, p. 8).

20 "China in Transition," *Far Eastern Economic Review*, Feb. 5, 1998, p. 26.

21 Massive lay-offs were announced in early 1998; for example, the textile industry said that it planned to lay off 1.2 million workers, and the railroad system 1.2 million workers over the next three years ("Lay-offs by the Millions Are Sweeping China," *International Herald Tribune*, Jan. 21, 1998, p. 2).

22 Deng Xiaoping, "Uphold the Four Cardinal Principles," Mar. 30, 1979, *Selected Works of Deng Xiaoping* (1975–1982) (Beijing: Foreign Languages Press, 1984), p. 180.

23 Minxin Pei, "Is China Democratizing?" p. 71.

24 Lucian W. Pye, "Factions and the Politics of *Guanxi*: Paradoxes in Chinese Administrative and Political Behaviour," p. 39.

25 Susan Lawrence, "'The Problem is Political Will,'" *U.S. News and World Report*, Oct. 23, 1995, p. 72.

BIBLIOGRAPHY

Books

Allinson, Robert E., ed. *Understanding the Chinese Mind: The Philosophical Roots.* Oxford: Oxford University Press, 1989.

Asia Watch. *Detained in China and Tibet: A Directory of Political and Religious Prisoners.* New York: Human Rights Watch, 1994.

Bakken, Børge. *The Exemplary Society: Human Improvement, Social Control, and the Dangers of Modernity in China.* Oxford: Oxford University Press, forthcoming.

Barmé, Geremie. *Shades of Mao: The Posthumous Mao Cult of the Great Leader.* Armonk, NY: M.E. Sharpe, 1996.

Barmé, Geremie, and John Milford, eds. *Seeds of Fire: Chinese Voices of Conscience.* New York: Hill & Wang, 1988.

Baum, Richard. *Burying Mao: Chinese Politics in the Age of Deng Xiaoping.* Princeton, NJ: Princeton University Press, 1994.

Becker, Jasper. *Hungry Ghosts: China's Secret Famine.* London: John Murray, 1996.

Bernstein, Thomas B. *Up to the Mountains and Down to the Villages.* New Haven: Yale University Press, 1977.

Bishop, Robert L. *Qi Lai!: Mobilizing One Billion Chinese: The Chinese Communication System.* Ames: Iowa State University Press, 1989.

Bloomfield, Frena. *The Book of Chinese Beliefs.* London: Arrow Books, 1983.

Bond, Michael Harris, ed. *The Handbook of Chinese Psychology.* Hong Kong: Oxford University Press, 1996.

Brewitt-Taylor, C. H., trans. *Romance of the Three Kingdoms.* Rutland, Vt.: Charles Tuttle Company, 1959.

Brown, Lester. *Who Will Feed China? Wake-up Call for a Small Planet.* New York: W. W. Norton, 1995.

Cambridge History of China, The: Vol. 7. *The Ming Dynasty 1384–1644*, Part 1, eds. Frederick W. Mote and Denis Twitchett (1988). Vol. 11. *Late Ch'ing 1800–1911*, Part 1, eds. John K. Fairbank and Kwang Ching Liu (1980). Vol. 13. *Republican China 1912–1949*, Part 2, eds. Fairbank and Albert Feuerwerker (1986). Vol. 14. *The People's Republic: The*

Emergence of Revolutionary China, Part 1, eds. Roderick MacFarquhar and Fairbank (1987). Vol. 15. *Revolutions within the Chinese Revolution, 1966–1982,* Part 2, eds. MacFarquhar and Fairbank (1991). Cambridge: Cambridge University Press.

Chan, Kam Wing. *Cities with Invisible Walls: Reinterpreting Urbanization in Post-1949 China.* Hong Kong: Oxford University Press, 1994.

Chang, Jung. *Wild Swans.* London: Simon and Schuster, 1991.

Cheng, Nien. *Life and Death in Shanghai.* London: Grafton Books, 1986.

Ching, Julia. *Probing China's Soul: Religion, Politics and Protest in the People's Republic.* San Fransisco: Harper & Row, 1990.

Croll, Elisabeth. *Changing Identities of Chinese Women: Rhetoric, Experience and Self-Perception in Twentieth-Century China.* London: Zed Books, 1995.

Dittmer, Lowell, and Samuel S. Kim, eds. *China's Quest for National Identity.* Ithaca: Cornell University Press, 1993.

Evans, Richard. *Deng Xiaoping and the Making of Modern China.* London: Penguin Books, 1995.

Fairbank, John K. *China: A New History.* Cambridge, MA: Belknap Press of Harvard University Press, 1992.

Fairbank, John K. *China: The People's Middle Kingdom and the USA.* Cambridge, Mass: Belknap Press of Harvard University Press, 1967.

Fairbank, John K., ed. *The Chinese World Order: Traditional China's Foreign Relations.* Cambridge, MA: Harvard University Press, 1968.

Fairbank, John K. *The Great Chinese Revolution 1800–1985.* New York: Harper & Row, 1986.

Fairbank, John K., Edwin O. Reischauer, and Albert M. Craig. *East Asia: Tradition and Transformation.* Boston: Houghton Mifflin, 1973.

Fang, Qi, and Jiran Qi, eds. *Old Peking—The City and Its People.* Hong Kong: Hai Feng Publishing House, 1993.

Fei, Xiaotong. *From the Soil—The Foundations of Chinese Society: A Translation of Fei Xiaotong's* Xiangtu Zhongguo. Berkeley: University of California Press, 1992.

Feng, Jicai. *Ten Years of Madness: Oral Histories of China's Cultural Revolution.* San Francisco: China Books & Periodicals, 1996.

FitzGerald, C. P. *The Southern Expansion of the Chinese People.* Bangkok: White Lotus, 1993.

Forman, Harrison. *Report from Red China.* New York: Henry Holt & Co, 1945.

Franz, Uli. *Deng Xiaoping.* Boston: Harcourt Brace Jovanovich, 1988.

Fu, Zhengyuan. *China's Legalists: The Earliest Totalitarians and Their Art of Ruling.* Armonk, N.Y.: M. E. Sharpe, 1996.

Gao, Yuan. *Born Red: A Chronicle of the Cultural Revolution.* Stanford: Stanford University Press, 1987.

Garnaut, Ross, Shutian Guo, and Guonan Ma, eds. *The Third Revolution in the Chinese Countryside.* Cambridge, Mass.: Cambridge University Press, 1996.

Bibliography

Gittings, John. *Real China: From Cannibalism to Karaoke.* London: Simon & Schuster, 1996.

Goldman, Merle. *Sowing the Seeds of Democracy in China: Political Reform in the Deng Xiaoping Era.* Cambridge: Harvard University Press, 1994.

Goldstein, Alice, and Wang Feng, eds. *China. The Many Facets of Demographic Change.* Boulder, Colo.: Westview Press, 1996.

Gong, Ting. *The Politics of Corruption in Contemporary China: An Analysis of Policy Outcomes.* Westport, Conn.: Praeger, 1994.

Harding, Harry. *A Fragile Relationship: The United States and China Since 1972.* Washington, D.C.: Brookings Institution, 1992.

Harris, Stuart, and Gary Klintworth, eds. *China as a Great Power: Myths, Realities, and Challenges in the Asia-Pacific Region.* New York: St. Martin's Press, 1995.

Hsü, Immanuel C. Y. *China's Entrance into the Family of Nations: The Diplomatic Phase, 1858–1880.* Cambridge, Mass.: Harvard University Press, 1960.

Huotari, Tauno-Olavi, and Pertti Seppälä. *Kiinan kulttuuri* (The Culture of China). Helsinki: Otava, 1990.

Jakobson, Linda. *Mureneva muuri. Vuosi kiinalaisena* (The Crumbling Wall: One Year as a Chinese). Helsinki: Kirjayhtymä, 1988.

Jakobson, Linda, and Marja Sarvimäki. *Uusi Kiina-opas* (China: A New Guide). Helsinki: Kirjayhtymä, 1995.

Jenner, W. J. F. *The Tyranny of History: The Roots of China's Crisis.* London: Penguin Books, 1992.

Jernow, Allison Liu. *"Don't Force Us To Lie": The Struggle of Chinese Journalists in the Reform Era.* New York: Committee to Protect Journalists, 1993.

Johnson, Paul. *A History of the Modern World: From 1917 to the 1980s.* London: Weidenfield & Nicolson, 1983.

Karnow, Stanley. *Mao and China: A Legacy of Turmoil.* London: Penguin Books, 1990.

Kitts, Charles R. *The United States Odyssey in China, 1784–1990.* Lanham, Md.: University Press of America, 1991.

Kleinman, Arthur, et al., eds. *Culture and Healing in Asian Studies: Anthropological, Psychiatric and Public Health Studies.* Cambridge, Mass.: Schenkman Publishing Company, 1978.

Kristof, Nicholas, and Sheryl WuDunn. *China Wakes: The Struggle for the Soul of a Rising Power.* New York: Times Books, 1994.

Lam, Willy Wo-lap. *China After Deng Xiaoping: The Power Struggle in Beijing Since Tiananmen.* Hong Kong: PA Professional Consultants, 1995.

Lau, D. C., trans. *Lao Tzu: Tao Te Ching.* London: Penguin Books, 1963.

Levathes, Louise. *When China Ruled the Seas.* New York: Simon and Schuster, 1994.

Lever-Tracy, Constance, David Ip, and Noel Tracy. *The Chinese Diaspora and Mainland China: An Emerging Economic Synergy.* New York: St. Martin's Press, 1996.

Leys, Simon. *Chinese Shadows.* New York: Viking Press, 1977.

Leys, Simon, trans., *The Analects of Confucius.* New York: W. W. Norton, 1997.

Li, Lincoln. *Student Nationalism in China, 1924–1949.* New York: SUNY Press, 1994.

Li, Lu. *Moving the Mountain: My Life in China from the Cultural Revolution to Tiananmen Square.* London: Pan Books, 1990.

Liang, Heng. *Son of the Revolution.* New York: Knopf, 1983.

Lindsay, Michael. *The Unknown War: North China 1937–1945.* London: Bergström & Boyle Books, 1975.

Link, Perry. *Evening Chats in Beijing: Probing China's Predicament.* New York: W. W. Norton, 1992.

Liu, Binyan. *A Higher Kind of Loyalty: A Memoir of China's Foremost Journalist.* New York: Pantheon Books, 1990.

Liu, Zongren. *Hard Time: Thirty Months in a Chinese Labor Camp.* San Fransisco: China Books & Periodicals, 1995.

Lo, Ruth Earnshaw, and Katherine S. Kinderman. *In the Eye of the Typhoon: An American Woman in China during the Cultural Revolution.* New York: Harcourt Brace Jovanovich, 1980.

Lord, Bette Bao. *Legacies: A Chinese Mosaic.* New York: Knopf, 1990.

MacFarquhar, Roderick. *The Origins of the Cultural Revolution.* I. *Contradictions among the People, 1956–1957.* II. *The Great Leap Forward, 1958–1960.* III. *The Coming of the Cataclysm, 1961–1966.* London: Oxford University Press, 1974, 1983, 1997.

MacFarquhar, Roderick, ed. *The Politics of China: The Eras of Mao and Deng.* New York: Cambridge University Press, 1997.

Meisner, Maurice. *The Deng Xiaoping Era: An Inquiry into the Fate of Chinese Socialism, 1978–1994.* New York: Hill & Wang, 1996.

Metzger, Thomas A. *Escape from Predicament: Neo-Confucianism and China's Evolving Political Culture.* New York: Columbia University Press, 1977.

Miles, James. *The Legacy of Tiananmen: China in Disarray.* Ann Arbor: University of Michigan Press, 1996.

Mo, Yan. *Red Sorghum.* North Sydney: Minerva, 1994.

Mosher, Steven W. *A Mother's Ordeal: One Woman's Fight Against China's One-Child Policy.* London: Warner Books, 1995.

Munro, Robin. *Death by Default: A Policy of Fatal Neglect in China's State Orphanages.* New York: Human Rights Watch, 1996.

Naisbitt, John. *Megatrends Asia.* New York: Simon and Schuster, 1996.

Ng, Man Lun, and Erwin J. Haeberle. *Sexual Behavior in Modern China.* New York: Continuum Press, 1996.

Nygren, Christina. *Frukter från Päränträdgården. Teater i Kina* (Fruit from the Pear Tree Garden: Theater in China). Stockholm: Liber, 1986.

Pruitt, Ida. *A Daughter of Han: The Autobiography of a Chinese Working Woman.* Stanford: Stanford University Press, 1967.

Ross, James R. *Escape to Shanghai: A Jewish Community in China.* New York: The Free Press, 1994.

Ruan, Fang Fu. *Sex in China: Studies in Sexology in Chinese Culture.* New York: Plenum Press, 1991.

Salisbury, Harrison E. *The New Emperors—China in the Era of Mao and Deng: A Dual Biography.* London: HarperCollins, 1993.

Schell, Orville. *Mandate of Heaven.* London: Warner Books, 1996.

Schoenhals, Michael, ed. *China's Cultural Revolution, 1966–1969: Not a Dinner Party.* Armonk, N.Y.: M. E. Sharpe, 1996.

Schuman, Julian. *China: An Uncensored Look.* Sagaponack, N.Y.: Second Chance Press, 1979.

Schwartz, Benjamin I. *The World of Thought in Ancient China.* Cambridge, Mass.: Belknap Press of Harvard University Press, 1985.

Seagrave, Sterling. *Lords of the Rim: The Invisible Empire of the Overseas Chinese.* New York: G. P. Putnam and Sons, 1995.

Shen, Tong. *Almost a Revolution.* Boston: Houghton Mifflin Co, 1990.

Simmie, Scott, and Bob Nixon. *Tiananmen Square.* Seattle: University of Washington Press, 1989.

Snow, Edgar. *Red Star over China.* New York: Random House, 1938.

Song Qiang, Zhang Zangzang, Qiao Bian, et al. *Zhongguo keyi shuo bu: lengzhan hou shidai de zhengzhi yu qinggan juece* (China Can Say No: Political and Emotional Choices in the Post Cold War Era). Beijing: Zhonghua gongshang lianhe chubanshe, 1996.

Spence, Jonathan D. *Chinese Roundabout.* New York: W. W. Norton, 1992.

Spence, Jonathan D. *The Death of Woman Wang.* London: Penguin Books, 1978.

Spence, Jonathan D. *The Search for Modern China.* New York: W. W. Norton, 1990.

Spence, Jonathan D. *To Change China: Western Advisers in China, 1620–1960.* London: Penguin Books, 1980.

Starr, John Bryan. *Continuing the Revolution: The Political Thought of Mao.* Princeton, N.J.: Princeton University Press, 1979.

State Statistical Bureau. *China Statistical Yearbook 1997.* Beijing: Zhongguo tongji chubanshe, 1997.

Sullivan, Lawrence R., with Nancy Hearst. *Historical Dictionary of the People's Republic of China: 1949–1997.* Lanham, Md.: Scarecrow Press, 1997.

Terrill, Ross. *Mao: A Biography.* New York: Harper Colophon Books, 1980.

Terrill, Ross. *The White-Boned Demon: A Biography of Madame Mao Zedong.* New York: William Morrow, 1984.

Tu, Wei-ming, ed. *The Living Tree: The Changing Meaning of Being Chinese Today*. Stanford: Stanford University Press, 1994.

Tyson, James, and Ann Tyson. *Chinese Awakenings: Life Stories from the Unofficial China.* Boulder, Colo.: Westview Press, 1995.

Unger, Jonathan, ed. *Chinese Nationalism.* Armonk, N.Y.: M. E. Sharpe, 1997.

Wang, Hui-ming, trans. *Ten Poems and Lyrics by Mao Tse-tung.* Amherst, Mass.: University of Massachusetts Press, 1975.

Wen, Chihua. *The Red Mirror: Children of China's Cultural Revolution.* Boulder, Colo.: Westview Press, 1995.

Wong, Jan. *Red China Blues: My Long March from Mao to Now.* Toronto: Doubleday, 1996.

Wu, Harry, and Carolyn Wakeman. *Bitter Winds: A Memoir of My Years in China's Gulag.* New York: John Wiley & Sons, 1994.

Yang, Bo. *The Ugly Chinaman and the Crisis of Chinese Culture.* North Sydney: Allen & Unwin, 1992.

Yang, Jiang. *Six Chapters from My Life "Downunder."* Seattle: University of Washington Press, 1984.

Yi, Mu, and Mark V. Thompson. *Crisis at Tiananmen: Reform and Reality in Modern China.* San Francisco: China Books & Periodicals, 1989.

Young, Susan W. L. *Crosstalk and Culture in Sino-American Communication.* New York: Cambridge University Press, 1994.

Yue, Daiyun, and Carolyn Wakeman. *To The Storm: The Odyssey of a Revolutionary Chinese Woman.* Berkeley: University of California Press, 1985.

Zha, Jianying. *China Pop: How Soap Operas, Tabloids, and Bestsellers Are Transforming a Culture.* New York: New Press, 1995.

Zhang, Xianliang. *Half of Man is Woman.* London: Penguin Books, 1986.

Zheng, Yi,. *Scarlet Memorial: Tales of Cannibalism in Modern China.* Boulder, Colo.: Westview Press, 1996.

Zhou, Kate Xiao. *How the Farmers Changed China: Power if the People.* Boulder, Colo.: Westview Press, 1996.

Zhu, Hong, trans. *The Serenity of Whiteness: Stories by and about Women in Contemporary China.* New York: Ballantine Books, 1991.

Bibliography

Articles, Research Papers, Reports, Lectures, etc.

Barmé, Geremie R. "To Screw Foreigners is Patriotic: China's Avant-Garde Nationalists." *The China Journal*, No. 34 (July 1995): pp. 209–234.

Barmé, Geremie R., ed., "Shades of Mao: The Posthumous Cult of the Great Leader." *Chinese Sociology and Anthropology* 28 (Fall 1995).

Barmé, Geremie R. "Wang Shuo and *Liumang* ('Hooligan') Culture." *The Australian Journal of Chinese Affairs*, No. 28 (July 1992): pp. 23–64.

Bernstein, Richard and Ross H. Munro. "The Coming Conflict with America." *Foreign Affairs* 76 (Mar./Apr. 1997): pp. 18–32.

Bruun, Ole. "The *Fengshui* Resurgence in China." *The China Journal*, No. 36 (July 1996): pp. 47–65.

Cabestan, Jean-Pierre. "Towards a Food Crisis in China and the Whole World?" *China Perspectives*, No. 13 (Sept./Oct. 1997): pp. 11–19.

Caplen, Brian. "What Will Go Wrong Next?" *Euromoney* (Dec. 1997): pp. 38–42.

Chan, Anita. "Boot Camp at the Shoe Factory. Where Taiwanese Bosses Drill Chinese Workers to Make Sneakers for American Joggers." *Wall Street Journal*, Nov. 3, 1996: pp. C1, C4.

Chen, Chunlei. "Recent Developments in Foreign Direct Investment in China." Adelaide: Chinese Economy Research Unit, University of Adelaide, 1996.

China Academy of Social Sciences, Institute of Sociology and Kitakyushu Forum on Asian Women. "A Study of Life and Consciousness of Contemporary Urban Family in China." 1994.

Choate, Allen. "Local Governance in China." Working paper for the seminar on Asian Perspectives: Focus on China, organized by the Asia Foundation, Mar. 20, 1997, Washington, D.C.

Chung, Jae Ho. "Shandong: The Political Economy of Development and Inequality." In *China's Provinces in Reform*, edited by David S. G. Goodman, pp. 123–157. London: Routledge, 1997.

Davin, Delia. "Migration, Women and Gender Issues in Contemporary China." In *Floating Population and Migration in China*, edited by Thomas Scharping, pp. 297–314. Hamburg: Institut für Asienkunde, 1997.

Economist, The. "China Plays the Europe Card." May 11, 1996, pp. 23–24.

Economist Intelligence Unit. *China, Mongolia: Country Report 1997–98*. London, 1998.

Economist Intelligence Unit. *Taiwan: Country Report 1997–98*. London, 1997.

Epstein, Amy. "Village Elections in China: Experimenting with Democracy." In *China's*

Economic Future: Challenges to U.S. Policy, edited by Joint Economic Committee, U.S. Congress, pp. 403–422. Armonk, N.Y.: M. E. Sharpe, 1997.

Ferdinand, Peter. "China and Russia: A Strategic Partnership?" *China Review*, No. 8 (Autumn/Winter 1997): pp. 16–21.

Funabashi, Yoichi, Michel Oksenberg, and Heinrich Weiss. "An Emerging China in a World of Interdependence: A Report to the Trilateral Commission." Mar. 1994.

Garnaut, Ross and Guonan Ma. "How Rich is China? Evidence from the Food Economy." *The Australian Journal of Chinese Affairs*, No. 30 (July 1993): pp. 121–146.

Gipouloux, Francois. "Expansion or Normalisation? Guangdong's Position in Asian Trade." *China Perspectives*. No. 4 (Mar./Apr. 1996): pp. 14–19.

Goldman, Merle. "Politically-Engaged Intellectuals in the Deng-Jiang Era: A Changing Relationship with the Party-State." *The China Quarterly*, No. 145 (Mar. 1996): pp. 35–52.

Goldstein, Steven M. "Taiwan Faces the Twenty-first Century: Continuing the Miracle." New York: The Foreign Policy Association, 1997.

Guldin, Gregory Eliyu and Daming Zhou, eds. "China's Rural Urbanization." *Chinese Sociology and Anthropology* 28 (Winter 1995–96).

Guo, Xiaolin, ed. and trans. "Chinese Research on Matrilineal/Matriarchal Systems in Minority Societies." *Chinese Sociology and Anthropology* 25 (Summer 1993).

Harris, Peter. "Chinese Nationalism: The State of the Nation." *The China Journal*, No. 38 (July 1997): pp. 121–137.

Hershkovitz, Linda. "China's 80 Million: Dimensions of Poverty." Toronto: Centre of Asia Pacific Studies, University of Toronto-York University, 1994.

Honig, Emily. "The Gender of Violence: Reassessing the Red Guards." Paper presented at the conference "The Cultural Revolution, 1966–1971: A Retrospective View." Hong Kong: The Hong Kong University of Science and Technology, July 4–6, 1996.

Honkavaara, Topi. "Dengin vallankumous jatkuu. Kiinan avautuminen on tosiasia—onko edessä vuorovaikutuksen aika?" (Deng's Revolution Continues. So Does the Open-Door Policy—Does Genuine Interaction Lie Ahead?) Lecture presented at EVA Seminar, Helsinki, June 2, 1995.

Huang, Shumin. "Folk Reproductive Medicine in Northern China: The Cultural Constraints of Pregnancy, Delivery and Post-Natal Care." *Bulletin of the Institute of Ethnology* (Academia Sinica), No. 70. (Autumn 1990): pp. 14–36.

Huang, Yasheng. "Why China Will Not Collapse." *Foreign Policy*, No. 99 (Summer 1995): pp. 54–68.

Information Office, State Council of the People's Republic of China. "The Grain Issue in China." Oct. 1996.

Information Office, State Council of the People's Republic of China. "Progress in China's Human Rights Cause in 1996." Mar. 1997.

Information Office, State Council of the People's Republic of China. "The Situation of Chinese Women." June 1994.

Information Office, State Council of the People's Republic of China. "On Sino-U.S. Trade Balance." Mar. 1996.

Jacques, Martin. "Western Culture Defies the Rising Eastern Sun." *The Sunday Times*, Nov. 13, 1994.

Jakobson, Linda. "America through a Chinese Lens: Idol Turned Bully?" *Harvard Journal of Press/Politics*, No. 2 (Summer 1997).

Jakobson, Linda. "China's Rural Democracy Brings in New Chiefs." *The Guardian*, Apr. 17, 1995, p. 8.

Jakobson, Linda. "Lies in Ink, Truth in Blood: The Role and Impact of the Chinese Media During the Beijing Spring of '89." Cambridge, Mass.: Joan Shorenstein Barone Center, John F. Kennedy School of Government, Harvard University, 1990.

Ji, Hongzhen. "With Ideology Waning, Intellectuals Search for New Role." *Dushu* (Reading), No. 7 (July 1996): pp. 20–25. (Translated in FBIS-CHI-96-212, "PRC: Intellectuals as Instigators, Victims of Political Turmoil.")

Jia, Qingguo. "The Dilemma of Power: The Choice of the People's Republic." In *The United States Constitution: Its Birth, Growth, and Influence in Asia*, edited by J. Barton Starr. Hong Kong: Chinese University Press, 1988.

Jia, Qingguo. "Reflection on the Recent Tension in the Taiwan Strait." *The China Journal*, No. 36 (July 1996): pp. 93–97.

Kelliher, Daniel. "The Chinese Debate over Village Self-Government." *The China Journal*, No. 37 (Jan. 1997): pp. 63–86.

Lary, Diana. "Regions and Nation: The Present Situation in China in Historical Context." *Pacific Affairs* 70 (Summer 1997): pp.173–194.

Lawrence, Susan. "Beijing's Mixed Message." *U.S. News & World Report*, Feb. 20, 1995, pp. 58–59.

Lawrence, Susan. "Beijing's Nightmare Across the Strait." *U.S. News & World Report*, Mar. 25, 1996, pp. 47–48.

Lawrence, Susan. "Family Planning at a Price." *U.S. News & World Report*, Sept 19, 1994, pp. 56–57.

Lawrence, Susan and Richard J. Newman. "A Delicate Pas de Deux in the Pacific." *U.S. News & World Report*, Apr. 1, 1996, p. 41.

Lawrence, Susan and Tim Zimmermann. "A Political Test When Guns Matter." *U.S. News & World Report*, Oct. 30, 1995, pp. 47–48.

Li, Cheng. "University Networks and the Rise of Qinghua Graduates in China's Leadership." *The Australian Journal of Chinese Affairs*, No. 32 (July 1994): pp. 1–30.

Link, Perry. "The Old Man's New China." *New York Review of Books*, June 6, 1994, pp. 31–35.

Liu, Binyan. "The Bankruptcy of a Fairy Tale." *China Focus* 6 (Jan. 1998): pp. 1, 6.

Liu, Binyan. "Unintended Earthquake." *Newsweek*, May 6, 1996, p. 22.

Lu, Feng, ed. "The Origins and Formation of the Unit (*Danwei*) System." *Chinese Sociology and Anthropology* 25 (Spring 1993).

MacFarquhar, Roderick. "The Anatomy of Collapse." *New York Review of Books*, Sept. 26, 1991, pp. 5–8.

MacFarquhar, Roderick. "Demolition Man." *New York Review of Books*, Mar. 27, 1997, pp. 14–17.

MacFarquhar, Roderick. "The Party's Armageddon." *Time*, May 13, 1996, p. 26.

Martin, Howard J. "The Hakka Ethnic Movement in Taiwan, 1986–1991." In *Guest People: Hakka Identity in China and Abroad*, edited by Nicole Constable, pp. 176–195. Seattle: University of Washington Press, 1996.

McCormick, Barrett L. "Democracy or Dictatorship?: A Response to Gordon White." *The Australian Journal of Chinese Affairs*, No. 31 (Jan. 1994): pp. 95–110.

Mihalca, Matei. "Neo Conservatism: A New, Perhaps Disturbing Nationalism May Be Emerging." *Harvard Asia Pacific Review* (Winter 1996–97): pp. 52–53.

Mufson, Steven. "The Immoral of the Story: In China, a Popular Novelist Is in Official Disfavor." *Washington Post*, Nov. 26, 1996, pp. C1, C6.

Murphy, Rachel. "A Dependent Private Sector: No Prospects for Civil Society in China." Murdoch: Asia Research Center, Murdoch University, 1996.

Nathan, Andrew. "China's Goals in the Taiwan Strait." *The China Journal*, No. 36 (July 1996): pp. 87–93.

Oi, Jean C. "Economic Development, Stability and Democratic Village Self-governance." *China Review 1996*, edited by Maurice Brosseau, Suzanne Pepper, and Shu-ki Tsang, pp. 125–144 (Hong Kong: Chinese University Press, 1996).

Overseas Economic Cooperation Fund. "Prospects for Grain Supply-Demand Balance and Agricultural Development Policy in China." Tokyo: OECF Discussion Paper, 1995.

Parris, Kristen. "Private Interest and the Public Good: The Rise of Private Business Interests." Paper presented at the conference "The Non-Economic Impact of China's Economic Reforms." Cambridge, Mass.: Fairbank Center, Harvard University, Sept. 20–22, 1996.

Pei, Minxin. "Citizens v. Mandarins: Administrative Litigation in China." *The China Quarterly*, No. 152 (Dec. 1997): pp. 832–862.

Pei, Minxin. "Is China Democratizing?" *Foreign Affairs* 77 (Jan./Feb. 1998): pp. 68–82.

Pomfret, John. "China's Officers Gape at America." *International Herald Tribune*, Feb. 17, 1998, p. 1.

Pye, Lucian W. "Chinese Politics in the Late Deng Era." *The China Quarterly*, No. 142 (June 1995): pp. 573–583.

Pye, Lucian W. "Factions and the Politics of *Guanxi*: Paradoxes in Chinese Administrative and Political Behaviour." *The China Journal*, No. 34 (July 1995): pp. 35–53.

Pye, Lucian W. "How China's Nationalism was Shanghaied." *The Australian Journal of Chinese Affairs*, No. 29 (Jan. 1993): pp. 107–133.

Ren, Hai. "Taiwan and the Impossibility of the Chinese." In *Negotiating Ethnicities in China and Taiwan*, edited by Melissa J. Brown, pp. 75–97. Berkeley, CA: Center for Chinese Studies, Institute of East Asian Studies, University of California, 1995.

Riley, Nancy. "Gender Equality in China: Two Steps Forward, One Step Back." In *China Briefing 1995–96: The Contradictions of Change*, edited by William A. Joseph, pp. 79–108. Armonk, N.Y.: M. E. Sharpe, 1997.

Rosen, Stanley. "Women and Politics in China (I)." *Chinese Law and Government* 26 (Sept.–Oct. 1993).

Ross, Robert S. "Beijing as a Conservative Power." *Foreign Affairs* 76 (March/April 1997): pp. 33–34.

Saich, Tony. "Changing Party/State-Society Relations." Talk at Fairbank Center for East Asian Research, Harvard University, Feb. 19, 1997.

Saich, Tony. "Most Chinese Enjoy More Personal Freedom Than Ever Before." *International Herald Tribune*, Feb. 1–2, 1997, p. 6.

Sarvimäki, Marja. "Nousevan auringon maat" (The Countries of the Rising Sun). In *Maailmalle, maailmalta. Kulttuurisia katsauksia* (From the World, to the World: Cultural Reviews), edited by Anna-Liisa Syrjänen and Irmeli Westermarch, pp. 178–202. Helsinki: WSOY, 1997.

Scalapino, Robert A. "China—Achievements and Challenges." Lecture at Bilderberg Conference, Helsinki, June 2–5, 1994.

Seckington, Ian. "Recent Political Developments." *China Review*, No. 7 (Summer 1997): pp. 11–14.

Seymour, James D. and Eugen Wehrli, eds. "Religion in China." *Chinese Sociology and Anthropology* 36 (Spring 1994).

Shambaugh, David. *China and Europe 1949–1995*. London: Contemporary China Institute, University of London, 1996.

Shambaugh, David. "Exploring the Complexities of Contemporary Taiwan." *The China Quarterly*, No. 148 (Dec. 1996): pp. 1045–1053.

Shambaugh, David. "The United States and China: Cooperation or Confrontation." *Current History*, 96, No. 611 (Sept. 1997): pp. 241–245.

Smil, Vaclav. "Who Will Feed China?" *The China Quarterly*, No. 143 (Sept. 1995): pp. 801–813.

Solinger, Doris. "China's Floating Population: Implications for State and Society." Paper presented at the conference "The Non-Economic Impact of China's Economic Reforms." Cambridge, MA: Fairbank Center for East Asian Research, Harvard University, Sept. 20–22, 1996.

Stone, Brewer. "Governmental Corruption in China and India." Ph.D. dissertation, Harvard University, 1995.

Thurston, Anne. "In a Chinese Orphanage." *The Atlantic Monthly*, Apr. 1997, pp. 28, 30, 38, 40, 41.

Tyler, Patrick E. "Catholics in China: Back to the Underground." *New York Times*, Jan. 26, 1997, pp. 1, 8.

Tyler, Patrick E. "China Concedes Blood Product Contained AIDS Virus." *New York Times*, Oct. 25, 1996, pp. A1, A8.

Unger, Jonathan. "The Cultural Revolution in the Villages." Paper presented at the conference "The Cultural Revolution, 1966–1971: A Retrospective View." Hong Kong: The Hong Kong University of Science and Technology, July 4–6, 1996.

Unger, Jonathan and Anita Chan. "China, Corporatism, and the East Asian Model." *The Australian Journal of Chinese Affairs*, No. 33 (Jan. 1995): pp. 29–53.

Van Ness, Peter. "The Impasse in U.S. Policy Toward China." *The China Journal*, No. 38 (July 1997): pp. 139–150.

Wakeman, Carolyn. "Personal Politics: The Struggle at Beijing's Foreign Language Institute." Paper presented at the conference "The Cultural Revolution, 1966–1971: A Retrospective View." Hong Kong: The Hong Kong University of Science and Technology, July 4–6, 1996.

Wang, Ruoshui. "My Marxist Outlook." *Contemporary Chinese Thought* 29 (Fall 1997): pp. 35–96.

Wang, Xu. "Mutual Empowerment of State and Peasantry: Grassroots Democracy in Rural China." *World Development* 25, No. 9 (Sept. 1997): pp. 1431–1442.

Wang, Youqin. "Student Attacks Against Teachers." Paper presented at the conference "The Cultural Revolution, 1966–1971: A Retrospective View." Hong Kong: The Hong Kong University of Science and Technology, July 4–6, 1996.

White, Gordon. "Democratisation and Economic Reform in China." *The Australian Journal of Chinese Affairs*, No. 31 (Jan. 1994): pp. 73-92.

Whyte, Martin King. "The Fate of Filial Obligations in Urban China." *The China Journal*, No. 38 (July 1997): pp. 1–31.

Wilson, Scott. "The Cash Nexus and Social Networks: Mutual Aid and Gifts in Contemporary Shanghai Villages." *The China Journal*, No. 37 (Jan. 1997): pp. 91–112.

Wong, Yu. "Wang's World." *Far Eastern Economic Review*. Aug. 8, 1996, pp. 46–48.

World Bank. "China: Higher Education Reform." Washington, D.C., 1997.

Yan, Yunxiang. "The Culture of *Guanxi* in a North China Village." *The China Journal*, No. 35 (Jan. 1996): pp. 1–25.

Yatsko, Pamela. "Rethinking China." *Far Eastern Economic Review*, Dec. 18, 1997, pp. 52–57.

Zhang, Geng. "Kiinan uudistukset ja avautuminen, ja oikeusvaltion luominen" (China's Reforms and Open-Door Policy, and the Making of a Civil Society). Lecture by China's Deputy Minister of Justice at the Sino-Finnish Seminar in Beijing, Sept. 1994.

Zhu, Qingfang. "The Urban-Rural Gap and Social Problems in the Countryside." *Chinese Law and Government* 28 (Jan.–Feb. 1995).

Zweig, David. "Rural People, the Politicians, and Power." *The China Journal*, No. 38 (July 1997): pp. 153–168.

INDEX

Index

Index

About the Author

Linda Jakobson, 39, won the 1998 Finnish National Award for Non-Fiction for the Finnish edition of her book *A Million Truths: Ten Years in China.* It was critically acclaimed for its sensitive description of everyday life in China. In particular, her skillful portrayal of how the rapidly changing Chinese society of the last ten years has influenced the personal lives of her many Chinese friends has been highly praised.

Linda Jakobson, a journalist by profession, first moved to China in 1987. She taught English at the Shandong College of Economics in Jinan, while at the same time continuing her Chinese language studies. From 1989 to 1991, she did research in Beijing on Chinese society and the economy and in 1992 became the China correspondent for the leading Finnish newsmagazine, *Suomen Kuvalehti.*

Several of her articles have appeared in *The Guardian* in London. In 1990, Harvard University published her paper "Lies in Ink, Truth in Blood: The Role and Impact of the Chinese Media During the Beijing Spring of '89" which she wrote while a Fellow at the Shorenstein Center on Press, Politics, and Public Policy at Harvard University. She is a Mandarin speaker and has previously published three books on China.